PRAISE FOR JEFF LIKER
AND *THE TOYOTA WAY*, 2ND EDITION

New technology is disrupting the automotive industry dramatically and on a massive scale. Toyota is responding by seeking to strengthen its core values and develop new capabilities in software and mobility services. Jeff Liker has brought together both objective data and expert analysis, and has delivered a thought-provoking, insightful narrative on the Toyota Way to navigating challenges.

— James Kuffner, PhD, CEO of Toyota Research Institute–Advanced Development and Toyota Director

An update adding value by providing more guidance for successful implementation of a company excellence system. The additional material on lean deployment characteristics, developing habits, work group structure and leader development, lean in a digital age, and value stream mapping provide a useful insight for all companies in the ever-changing, unpredictable digital world.

— Nicholas Day, Head of Airbus Operating System in France, Central Function, Airbus SAS

In the second edition of *The Toyota Way*, Dr. Liker brings his valuable insights on execution, the importance of people, and the behaviors of each and every employee that eventually shape an organization's culture. It dawns on the reader that it's not just the tools and methods that make the Toyota Production System what it is, but the relentless focus on incremental improvement using meaningful gemba walks, structured toolsets or "scientific thinking," and the role management plays in promoting the desired behaviors that over time get ingrained in the way work is performed.

— Vic Ganesan, Director Operations Excellence, thyssenkrupp Materials NA

THE
TOYOTA
WAY

THE TOYOTA WAY 2ND EDITION

14 MANAGEMENT PRINCIPLES
FROM THE WORLD'S GREATEST MANUFACTURER

JEFFREY K. LIKER

New York   Chicago   San Francisco   Athens   London
Madrid   Mexico City   Milan   New Delhi
Singapore   Sydney   Toronto

1 2 3 4 5 6 7 8 9   LCR   25 24 23 22 21 20

ISBN   978-1-260-46851-9
MHID   1-260-46851-8

e-ISBN   978-1-260-46852-6
e-MHID   1-260-46852-6

This publication is designed to provide accurate and authoritative information in regard to the subject matter covered. It is sold with the understanding that neither the author nor the publisher is engaged in rendering legal, accounting, securities trading, or other professional services. If legal advice or other expert assistance is required, the services of a competent professional person should be sought.

—From a Declaration of Principles Jointly Adopted by a Committee of the American Bar Association and a Committee of Publishers and Associations

Library of Congress Cataloging-in-Publication Data
Names: Liker, Jeffrey K., author.
Title: The Toyota way : 14 management principles from the world's greatest manufacturer / Jeffrey K. Liker.
Description: Second edition. | New York : McGraw Hill Education, [2020] | Includes bibliographical references and index.
Identifiers: LCCN 2020029822 (print) | LCCN 2020029823 (ebook) | ISBN 9781260468519 | ISBN 9781260468526 (ebook)
Subjects: LCSH: Toyota Jidōsha Kōgyō Kabushiki Kaisha. | Production management—Case studies. | Industrial productivity. | Corporate culture—History. | Industrial management. | Lean manufacturing.
Classification: LCC TL278 .L54 2020 (print) | LCC TL278 (ebook) | DDC 658—dc23
LC record available at https://lccn.loc.gov/2020029822
LC ebook record available at https://lccn.loc.gov/2020029823

*To Deb, Emma, and Jesse
and Our Amazing Life Journey*

Contents

Contents

Foreword (to the First Edition)

When I joined Toyota after 18 years in the US automobile business, I didn't know exactly what to expect. But I was hopeful. I knew that I wasn't comfortable with the direction that American automobile manufacturing was taking, and I felt Toyota might be different. In no time at all I noticed a fundamental difference between Toyota and my previous employers. At a Toyota/GM joint venture plant in Fremont, California, called NUMMI (New United Motor Manufacturing Inc.), I witnessed the transformation of a workforce from one of the worst in the General Motors system to one of the best in any manufacturing facility in the United States. The difference was the "Toyota Way." In this book, Dr. Liker explains the management systems, thinking, and philosophy that form the foundation of Toyota's success, providing the reader with valuable insights that can be applied to any business or situation. While there are many books that provide insight into the tools and methods of Toyota's Production System (TPS), Professor Liker's book is unique in its explanation of the broader principles at work in the Toyota culture.

The Toyota Way is not the Japanese Way or the American Way or even the Gary Convis Way of managing. It is the fundamental way that Toyota views its world and does business. The Toyota Way, along with the Toyota Production System, makes up Toyota's "DNA." This DNA was born with the founders of our company and continues to be developed and nurtured in our current and future leaders.

The Toyota Way can be briefly summarized through the two pillars that support it: "Continuous Improvement" and "Respect for People." Continuous improvement, often called *kaizen*, defines Toyota's basic approach to doing business. Challenge everything. More important than the actual improvements that individuals contribute, the true value of continuous improvement is in creating an atmosphere of continuous *learning* and an environment that not only accepts, but actually *embraces* change. Such an environment can only be created where there is respect for people—hence the second pillar of the Toyota Way. Toyota demonstrates this respect by providing employment security and seeking to engage team members through active participation in improving their jobs. As managers, we must take the responsibility for developing and nurturing mutual trust and understanding among all team members. I believe management has no more critical role than to motivate and engage large numbers of people to work together toward a common goal. Defining and explaining the goal, sharing a path to achieving it, motivating people to take the journey with you, and assisting them by removing obstacles—those are management's reasons for being. We must engage the minds of people to support and contribute their ideas to the organization. In my experience, the Toyota Way is the best method for fulfilling this role.

However, readers of this book should understand that each organization must develop its own way of doing business. The Toyota Way is the special product of the people who created Toyota and its unique history. Toyota is one of the most successful companies in the world. I hope this book will give you an understanding of what has made Toyota successful, and some practical ideas that you can use to develop your own approach to business.

—*Gary Convis*
   Former Managing Officer of Toyota and Chairman,
   Toyota Motor Manufacturing, Kentucky

Acknowledgments

The original version of *The Toyota Way* book was the product of 20 years of study of Toyota. Much of that work was done under the auspices of the Japan Technology Management Program at the University of Michigan, Ann Arbor, where I was co-director, then director. This program was started in 1991 with generous funding through the US Air Force Office of Scientific Research. I learned a ton under the mentorship of Japan-expert Dr. John Campbell who was co-director with me. In the more than 15 years since the original version, I continued to write books about different aspects of the Toyota Way, continued to teach and consult, and, most importantly, continued to learn. Enough had changed and I learned enough more, that I decided to do a major rewrite for this second edition.

Toyota has been remarkably open in sharing a main source of competitive advantage with the rest of the world. A milestone occurred in 1982 when Toyota chairman Eiji Toyoda and Toyota president Shoichiro Toyoda approved the agreement with GM to create NUMMI, a joint auto manufacturing venture specifically intended to teach the Toyota Production System to GM, a major global competitor. Another milestone in opening up TPS to the world was the decision to create what is now called the Toyota Production System Support Center (TSSC) in 1992 to teach the Toyota Production System to US companies by setting up working models across industries. TSSC has been spun off as a nonprofit and does free work for other nonprofits and charitable organizations and paid work for private companies.

Toyota has been unbelievably open to me, asking only in return to check documents for factual errors, but never trying to alter the content of my work. Unfortunately, I cannot acknowledge all the individuals at Toyota who graciously agreed to lengthy interviews and reviewed parts of this book for accuracy, both for the original version and for this revised version. Several of these people were particularly helpful in increasing my understanding of the Toyota Way, including (job titles are from the time of the interviews) the following:

Toyota
In no particular order.

- Akio Toyoda, President: For playing his Elvis guitar made of a muffler from Tupelo, Mississippi. How can a guy be so powerful and so much fun?

- Eiji Toyoda, former President and Chairman: A privilege to meet this great man, and flattering that he read the first edition of *The Toyota Way* in both English and Japanese (he preferred the English).
- Nampachi Hayashi, former Director and Senior Technical Officer, TPS: It was an honor to meet the most senior living student of Taiichi Ohno and hear his great stories.
- Kenji Miura, former General Manager, OMCD, and later President of supplier Toka Rika: One of the deepest students of TPS.
- Bruce Brownlee, General Manager, Corporate Planning and External Affairs of the Toyota Technical Center: My key liaison for the book.
- Jim Olson, Senior Vice President, Toyota Motor Manufacturing North America: Carefully considered *The Toyota Way* book and then supported Toyota's full participation to ensure I got it right.
- Jim Wiseman, Vice President, Toyota Motor Manufacturing, North America: Opened the doors to the Toyota Production System in manufacturing.
- Irv Miller, Group Vice President, Toyota Motor Sales: Opened the door to the world of sales and distribution at Toyota.
- Fujio Cho, President of Toyota Motor Company: Shared his passion for the Toyota Way.
- Gary Convis, President of Toyota Motor Manufacturing, Kentucky: Helped me to understand the process of an American penetrating the depths and learning the intricacies of the Toyota Way.
- Toshiaki (Tag) Taguchi, President and CEO of Toyota Motor North America: Provided insights into the Toyota Way in sales.
- Jim Press, Executive Vice President and Chief Operating Officer of Toyota Motor Sales, USA: Gave me a deeper understanding of the philosophy of the Toyota Way.
- Al Cabito, Group Vice President, Sales Administration, Toyota Motor Sales, USA: Thoroughly explained Toyota's emerging build-to-order strategy.
- Tadashi (George) Yamashina, President, Toyota Technical Center, USA: Introduced me to hourensou and imparted a deeper appreciation of genchi genbutsu. (See the Glossary for the definitions of these terms.)
- Kunihiko (Mike) Masaki, former President, Toyota Technical Center: Took every opportunity to get me in the door at Toyota to study the Toyota Way.
- Dave Baxter, Vice President, Toyota Technical Center: Shared more hours than I had a right to expect, to explain Toyota's product development system and its underlying philosophy.
- Ed Mantey, Vice President, Toyota Technical Center: Ed is a real engineer who is living proof Toyota can train American engineers to deeply understand the Toyota Way.

- Dennis Cuneo, Senior Vice President, Toyota Motor North America: Drew on his wealth of experience at NUMMI and beyond and helped me to understand Toyota's commitment to social responsibility.
- Dick Mallery, Partner, Snell and Wilmer: Passionately described how as a lawyer for Toyota he was transformed by the Toyota Way.
- Don Jackson, Vice President, Manufacturing, Toyota Motor Manufacturing, Kentucky: Explained and demonstrated what it means to respect and involve workers on the shop floor.
- Glenn Uminger, Assistant General Manager, Business Management & Logistics Production Control, Toyota Motor Manufacturing, North America: Explained how an accountant at Toyota developed a TPS support office and then led logistics for North America—and had fun at every step along the way.
- Teruyuki Minoura, former President, Toyota Motor Manufacturing, North America: Enthralled me with real-life stories of learning TPS at the feet of the master Taiichi Ohno.
- Steve Hesselbrock, Vice President Operations, Trim Masters: Shared generously of his years of learning and trial by fire as Trim Masters became one of the best Toyota seat suppliers in the world.
- Kiyoshi Imaizumi, President Trim Masters: Gave me the real story on what it took to be a Toyota supplier in Japan.
- Ichiro Suzuki, former Chief Engineer, Lexus, and Executive Advisory Engineer: Showed me what a real-life, super engineer can be.
- Takeshi Uchiyamada, Senior Managing Director and former Chief Engineer, Prius: Taught me what it means to lead a revolutionary project (Prius) by collaborating with people.
- Jane Beseda, General Manager and Vice President, North American Parts Operations: Articulated the Toyota Way view of information technology and automation in a way that made the lightbulbs come on for me.
- Ken Elliott, Service Parts Center National Manager: Shared his story of building the Toyota Way culture in a new parts distribution center.
- Andy Lund, Program Manager, Sienna, Toyota Technical Center: Shared insights into the translation of Toyota's culture in Japan into US operations from the perspective of an American who grew up in Japan.
- Jim Griffith, Vice President, Toyota Technical Center: Always with dry wit, corrected my misconceptions and challenged my understanding of the Toyota Way.
- Chuck Gulash, Vice President, Toyota Technical Center: On a test-track drive, taught me "attention to detail" in vehicle evaluation.
- Ray Tanguay, President, Toyota Motor Manufacturing, Canada: Taught me that technological innovation and TPS can go hand in hand.

- Dr. Gill Pratt, CEO of Toyota Research Institute and Toyota Chief Scientist: Delightful to speak with Gill and James (see below), both of whom grew up in the fast-paced software innovation world and quickly learned and adapted the Toyota Way.
- Dr. James Kuffner, CEO of Toyota Research Institute–Advanced Development and Toyota Director: I was glad to hear he was put on the board of directors to help the diversity of thinking at Toyota's highest leadership level.
- Brian Lyon, Senior Manager Advanced Technical Communications, Toyota Motor North America: An invaluable resource. I worked closely with Brian on another book, *Toyota Under Fire*.

Toyota Motor United Kingdom (TMUK)

I hosted dozens of full-day tours of this plant and learned a great deal.

- Marvin Cooke, Senior Vice President Manufacturing, Toyota Motor Europe: When he was Managing Director of TMUK, he taught me a great deal about the Toyota Way and how to model leadership behavior.
- Jim Crosbie, Managing Director: Humble and knowledgeable, Jim— and other leaders at the UK facility—always inspired me.
- Alan Weir, General Manager, Quality: Shared the group's quality philosophy.
- Dave Richards, General Manager, Human Resources: Helped me to understand the HR systems.
- Rob Gorton, Corporate Planning & External Affairs: Explained the hoshin kanri system. (See the Glossary for the definition.)
- Andrew Heaphy, General Manager Body Engineering: Gave a lengthy tour focused on hoshin kanri.
- Stuart Brown, Section Manager, Manufacturing Skills Development, HR: Taught me about Toyota's Floor Management Development System (FMDS) and how the system develops people.
- Simon Green, Group Leader, Senior Manufacturing Skills Development: The person behind the detailed work of developing the new FMDS.

SigmaPoint Technologies

All in on learning and improving.

- Dan Bergeron, President
- Stephane Dubreuil, Vice President of Supply and Operations
- Robert Joffre, Director of Lean Transformation

Herman Miller

Exemplifies the thinking of the Toyota Production System Support Center.

- Matt Long, Vice President of Continuous Improvement
- Jill Miller, Continuous Improvement Manager, Learning and Development

Zingerman's Mail Order

The most fun company I ever worked with.

- Tom Root, Managing Partner
- Betty Graptopp, Partner

Other Prominent Case Study Companies

- Rajaram Shembekar, Vice President, North American Production Innovation Center, IOT, Denso USA
- Dr. Prasad Akella, founder and CEO of Drishti Technologies
- Einar Gudmundsson, CEO, Rejmes Bil Volvo Dealership
- James Morgan, former student and former Chief Operating Officer, Rivian
- Dr. Jeri Ford, former Vice President of Business Operations and New Model Introduction, Rivian
- Scott Heydon, former Vice President of Global Strategy at Starbucks Coffee Company
- Edward Blackman, President, Kelda Consulting
- Richard Sheridan, Chief Story Teller, Menlo Innovations
- Charlie Baker, former Vice President, Product Development, Honda Motor

I owe a special debt to John Shook, the former Toyota manager who helped start NUMMI, the Toyota Technical Center, and the Toyota Supplier Support Center and then became president of the Lean Enterprise Institute. John has dedicated his career to understanding the Toyota Way. He brought this passion to the University of Michigan, where he joined us for several years as Director of our Japan Technology Management Program. John was my mentor on the Toyota Production System, teaching me first the basics and then, as I developed my understanding, the ever more sophisticated lessons in the philosophy of the Toyota Way. He read and provided key comments through both versions of the book.

For this second edition, I also owe special thanks to my former student and colleague at the University of Michigan, Mike Rother. Mike continued to research the TPS and diligently applied it at the gemba (the place where value is created) throughout the world. He emerged one day with a book, *Toyota Kata*, which he enthusiastically shared with me. I not so enthusiastically tried to understand the book. As I dug deeper, and after an endless series of coffee shop discussions with Mike, I came to question some of my assumptions about the Toyota Way and to consider more deeply what it means to think scientifically about overcoming seemingly impossible challenges. It led me to develop a more fluid and dynamic view of lean transformation and to reframe the section on problem solving: "Think and Act Scientifically to Improve Toward a Desired Future" (Principles 12 to 14 in this edition). Thank you, Mike.

My coauthor and coworker James Franz unearthed revealing statistics on Toyota's profitability and quality that I discuss in the Introduction. I also appreciate the assistance of my former doctoral student Eduardo Lander, who reviewed chapters drawing on his Toyota experience. Many of the non-Toyota case examples described in this book were clients of Liker Lean Advisors that I worked on with partner Dr. John Drogosz. I also learned a great deal about hoshin kanri from my German partner, Dr. Daniela Kudernatsch.

Most of the original book was written in 2003 when I was privileged to spend a very cold East Coast winter in sunny and warm Phoenix visiting my former student and now Professor Tom Choi of Arizona State University. With mornings in a nice, private office without windows and afternoons of golf, it was the perfect climate for writing. The four-month adventure with my loving wife, Deborah, and my children Jesse and Emma is a once-in-a-lifetime memory.

This book looks beyond the four walls of Toyota manufacturing to the broader value chain. My understanding of "lean logistics" was greatly enhanced by research funded by the Sloan Foundation's Trucking Industry Program, which is led by my close friend and colleague Chelsea (Chip) White at Georgia Institute of Technology.

Finally, I had a lot of editing and writing help. In the original version, when informed by my publisher that my book was twice as long as allowable, in a panic, I called my former developmental editor, Gary Peurasaari, to bail me out. He worked his magic on every page, reorganizing content where necessary, but more importantly, and in the true Toyota Way fashion, he eliminated wasted words, bringing value-added words to life. He was more of a partner in writing than an editor. Then Richard Narramore, the editor at McGraw-Hill who originally asked me to write the book, led me through a second major rewrite, which brought the book to a new level. For this edition, I had the expert help of developmental editor and writer Kevin Commins to help clarify my message and the detailed and loving copy editing and typesetting by Patricia Wallenburg of TypeWriting.

And of course, I am always inspired and supported by (and put up with) by my loving family, Deb, Em, and Jesse.

Preface

The Wonderful
Wacky World of Lean

We want organizations to be adaptive, flexible, self-renewing, resilient, learning, intelligent—attributes found only in living systems. The tension of our times is that we want our organizations to behave as living systems, but we only know how to treat them as machines.

—Margaret J. Wheatley, author of
Finding Our Way: Leadership for an Uncertain Time

THE PROBLEM: MISUNDERSTANDING OF LEAN AND "HOW IT APPLIES HERE"

Nobody can reasonably question the global impact of Toyota's system of management and manufacturing on the world today. The Toyota Production System (TPS) is the framework for what is often call "lean" management and has been embraced in mining, retail, defense, healthcare, construction, government, finance, or name your sector. While we might assume that senior TPS experts, called "sensei," or teachers, are delighted to see the system they are passionate about used in so many different industries, the reality is they are often disappointed and frustrated by how lean programs have turned a beautiful living system into a lifeless tool kit.

The problem is that so many have the view described by Margaret J. Wheatley in the opening quote and think that their organization is like a machine. Too many business executives are driven by the desire for certainty and control, and by the assumption that decisions made at the top of the organization will be carried out in a planned and orderly way. Anyone who has been on the shop floor guiding a "lean conversion" knows this is far from the truth. What happens is disorderly and surprising. A good consultant understands how to take positive advantage of unintended consequences for learning.

I have consulted to and taught leaders of companies all over the world who have the mistaken belief that lean transformation can be planned and controlled, just like updating your computer software (and even that may not go as planned). I consulted with a nuclear energy company whose vice president of continuous improvement believed his lean program was going gangbusters for the last three years. He proudly described a lengthy "lean assessment" that was tied to plant managers' bonuses and his attempts to quickly deploy lean tools across the enterprise.

The VP was a bit concerned when his CEO requested Toyota's help and Toyota loaned the organization one of its most senior TPS sensei, a student of the famed Taichii Ohno, father of the Toyota Production System. In Japan "sensei" suggests *honored* teacher, and it's expected that students listen respectfully and follow the sensei's lead. After the VP described the company's lean program to the TPS master, he expected praise and congratulations. Instead, the sensei said, "Please stop doing that"—meaning stop doing assessments, stop value stream mapping all the processes, stop connecting implementation to bonuses, and stop trying to rapidly deploy the company's version of lean across all manufacturing and service departments. Instead, the sensei said to start a "model line" example of TPS in a single department on a nuclear fuel production line and stop everything else. This would be a pilot led by the sensei to demonstrate TPS as a system and learn from it.

I spent two hours with the frustrated and confused vice president, who bemoaned: "Why did he want us to stop our good progress? Why did he want us to go slow like a snail when we have hundreds of thousands of people to train? How does he think he is going to get managers on board without any financial incentive?"

I tried to explain the thinking of the Japanese sensei. In a nutshell, I said, the Toyota Production System is a total "living system." The goal is to produce a continual flow of value to the customer, without interruptions known as wastes. Toyota often uses the analogy of a free-flowing river, without stagnant pools and without big rocks or other obstacles slowing the flow. To accomplish this type of free flow in a business setting requires a system of people, equipment, and processes that operate at peak performance. And since the world is constantly changing, variability has to be addressed through continuous improvement by the people closest to the "gemba" (or properly spelled "genba"),* which means where the work is performed.

I went on, "The Toyota master trainer looks at your operations and sees assorted tools of TPS mechanistically scattered around. But nowhere is lean oper-

---

* There is no *m* sound in Japanese, and "genba" is the correct English version, though "gemba" has become common usage. Jim Womack explains this and other similar terms well in http://artoflean.com/index.php/2016/03/25/is-it-genba-or-gemba/.

ating as an organic system of people using tools for continuous improvement. He wants you to see and experience real TPS and the results that are possible, at least once in one part of your company, before you start broadly trying to spread something nobody really understands. Trying to do it right one time in one area does not seem to him like a lot to ask."

I could see the lightbulbs going on for the vice president as he listened and asked more questions. It seemed he was getting it. He lamented that the Toyota sensei had not explained TPS in this way before. He also explained that when he told the Toyota advisor that he was bringing me in to teach people about lean product development, the sensei responded that it would be a "waste of time." I explained that the sensei was saying you are not ready to move beyond manufacturing since you had not a single example of a lean system. It is like asking beginning piano students to learn a Bach sonata before they can even put their fingers on the right keys and play a scale. As I was feeling proud of myself for enlightening this struggling soul, I saw the lightbulbs go dark again.

Finally, the VP confessed that he had not stopped anything—not the lean assessments tied to plant manager bonuses and not the rapid deployment of lean tools across the enterprise. In fact, he had brought me in to help "deploy" lean product development despite the sensei's warning. He said the Toyota sensei did not understand that the nuclear energy company was very large and it was vital to spread lean as rapidly as possible. Such are my triumphs . . . and failures . . . as a consultant trying to persuade people. The sensei was right—even my best attempts to try to teach lean product development to this organization were a "waste of time."

Lean, along with variations such as six sigma, theory of constraints, lean startup, lean six sigma, and agile development, is a global movement. As in any management movement, there are true believers, resisters, and those who get on the bandwagon but do not care a lot one way or the other. There is a plethora of service providers through universities, consulting firms of various sizes, not-for-profit organizations, and a book industry promoting the movement. For zealots like me, this is in a sense a good thing—they are building consumers of my message. But there is also a downside. As the message spreads and is passed through many people, companies, and cultures, it changes from the original, like the game of telephone in which the message whispered to the first person bears little resemblance to the message the tenth person hears.

Meanwhile, well-meaning organizations that want to solve their problems are searching for answers. What is lean and how does it relate to six sigma and agile? How do we get started? How do these tools that were developed in Toyota for making cars apply to our organization that has a completely different product or service? Can lean work in our culture, which is very different from Japanese culture? Can we upgrade lean methods using the latest digital technology? Do the tools have to be used exactly as they are in Toyota, or can they be adapted to our circumstances? And how does Toyota reward people for using these tools to improve?

These are all reasonable questions, and there are lines of people ready to answer them, often in very different ways. But the starting point should be the questions themselves. Are these the right questions? As reasonable as they seem, I believe they are the wrong questions. The underlying assumption in each case is that lean is a mechanistic tool-based process to be implemented as you would install a hardware or software upgrade. Specifically, the assumptions can be summarized as:

1. There is one clear and simple approach to lean that is very different from alternative methodologies.
2. There is one clear and best way to get started.
3. Toyota is a simple organization that does one thing—builds cars—and uses a core set of the same tools in the same way everyplace.
4. The tools are the essence of lean and therefore must be adapted to specific types of processes.
5. There may be something peculiar about lean, as it was developed in Japan, that has to be modified to fit cultures outside Japan.
6. Toyota has a precise method of applying the tools in the same way everyplace that others need to copy.
7. The formal reward system is the reason why people in Toyota are engaged in continuous improvement and motivated to support the company.

In fact, none of these assumptions are true, and that is the problem—there is a huge gap between common views of lean and the reality of how Toyota evolved this powerful management system for over one century and how it can help your organization accomplish its goals.

My goal in this book is to give you a very clear understanding of what "lean," or "lean six sigma," or whatever you want to call it, really is: a philosophy and a system of interconnected processes and people who are working to continuously improve how they work and deliver value to customers. We will start by dismissing the common and simplistic notion that it is a program of using tools to remove waste from processes. If this is your organization's view, you are doomed to mediocre results, and you likely will embrace the next management fad with similar mediocre results. I have seen this happen time and time again.

To help break through this cycle, I will demonstrate the real meaning of what Toyota discovered through discussions of the origin of the Toyota Way, the 14 principles I have distilled (summarized in the Appendix), and actual examples of organizations in manufacturing and services that have made progress on the challenging road to becoming a lean enterprise.

THE REAL TOYOTA PRODUCTION SYSTEM

Until recently, Toyota never used the term "lean" to refer to its production system. At first it had no name at all. It was simply the way the fledgling auto company learned to manufacture cars and trucks in the 1940s in order to deal with very real problems the company faced when first formed. The problems were clear— the company did not have money, it had limited factory space, and parts suppliers had to take a risk and invest in factories and equipment along with Toyota. Demand for automobiles in Japan after the devastation of World War II was low. The company struggled to get funding and had no choice but to eliminate waste. In response, it made low volumes of multiple models of vehicles on the same production line. It kept inventories low, because it lacked storage space and could not afford to tie up cash in parts or finished vehicles. And it kept lead times short both in the procurement and utilization of parts and in the production and sale of vehicles. All of this lowered production costs and enabled Toyota to get cash fast and, in turn, to pay suppliers (which were also struggling financially) quickly. (See a further discussion of Toyota's history in "A Storied History: How Toyota Became the World's Best Manufacturer" in the Introduction.)

A cornerstone of the Toyota Way is "challenge," and there was no shortage of challenges. When Toyota was struggling to survive in its early years, with few resources and very low demand, Taiichi Ohno was asked to find a way to match Ford Motor Company's productivity, which, owing to its size and economies of scale, was about nine times greater than that of Toyota. Faced with a seemingly impossible task, Ohno did what every Toyota leader has done before and after— go to the gemba, experiment, and learn. And like other great Toyota leaders he succeeded. He built on the core philosophies and methods of founders Sakichi Toyoda and his son Kiichiro Toyoda to develop the framework now called the Toyota Production System.

Ohno originally did not want TPS drawn as a picture, because he said TPS was something live on the shop floor, not something dead in a drawing. He said, "If we write it down, we kill it." Nonetheless, it was eventually drawn as a house with two pillars and a foundation (see Figure P.1), a structure that is only as strong as all the parts working together.

The in-station quality pillar is attributed to Sakichi Toyoda, who invented the first fully automated loom for making cloth. One of his many inventions along the way was a device that automatically stopped the loom when a single thread broke, which called attention to the problem so humans could fix it as quickly as possible. He called this "jidoka," a machine with human intelligence. These days it is often referred to as in-station quality—which means, don't let a defect escape your station. The second pillar is just-in-time, attributed to Kiichiro Toyoda, who founded the automotive company. He declared Toyota would "remove slack

Figure P.1   The Toyota Production System.

from all work processes" and follow the principles of JIT—a move that was necessary at the time just to avoid bankruptcy. He designed detailed processes for doing this. The foundation of the house in the figure, or the company by extension, is operational stability, which means a level, stable workflow. A smooth and steady flow of work is necessary to have any chance of achieving just-in-time flow (Principles 2, 3, and 4) and fixing problems as they occur (Principle 6). And at the center of these processes are flexible, capable, motivated people who are devoted to continually improving (Principles 9, 10, and 11).

If we step back from the model, we see a brilliant logic. It is a living, organic system. The missing safety net—lots of inventory (or time or information buffers)—means problems show themselves very quickly and must be solved quickly. Built-in quality comes about as abnormalities are identified by every team member and addressed before they can bleed out to later processes or to the customer. As the problems are solved, the foundation of stability becomes stronger, allowing for less inventory, better flow, and a smaller number of problems, most of which can be effectively controlled as they occur.

At the center of surfacing and solving problems are developed people (Principle 12). They are the brains doing the problem solving. Take away their brains and motivation to improve, and what you have left is a system that hopelessly runs itself into the ground. Continuous improvement means getting better every day and is the driver for building a sustainable enterprise. Only those at the gemba can understand the problems fast enough to react quickly. Continuous improvement depends on a different paradigm of the role of the human—all humans are problem detectors and problem correctors—thinking scientifically.

James Womack, Dan Jones, and Dan Roos called "lean production" the next paradigm beyond craft production and mass production in their classic 1991 book *The Machine That Changed the World:*[1]

> *The lean producer . . . combines the advantages of craft and mass production, while avoiding the high cost of the former and the rigidity of the latter. . . . Lean production is "lean" because it uses less of everything compared with mass production—half the human effort in the factory, half the manufacturing space, half the investment in tools, half the engineering hours to develop a new product in half the time. Also, it requires keeping far less than half the needed inventory on site, results in many fewer defects, and produces a greater and ever-growing variety of products.*

One of the greatest insights in this simple explanation is the idea of combining the "advantages of craft and mass production." Lean production was not entirely new, and it did not toss away concepts from craft or mass production; rather, it built on the strengths of each, with a few twists. Even in today's digital age Toyota reveres the craftsworker. I emphasize throughout this book how much Toyota places people at the center of its systems and expects that they spend a lifetime working to perfect their craft. "Use all your senses" is a common Toyota refrain to fully understand what you are working on and how to improve it.

THE TOYOTA PRODUCTION SYSTEM AS A MIX OF ORGANIC AND MECHANISTIC

In contrast to mechanistic organizations, "organic organizations are living systems, evolving, adapting, and innovating to keep pace with our complex, rapidly changing world." According to BusinessDictionary.com, an organic organization is an:

> *organizational structure characterized by (1) Flatness: communications and interactions are horizontal, (2) Low specialization: knowledge resides wherever it is most useful, and (3) Decentralization: great deal of formal and informal participation in decision making. Organic organizations are comparatively more complex and harder to form, but are highly adaptable, flexible, and more suitable where external environment is rapidly changing and is unpredictable.*

My fascination with production systems began when I was an undergraduate industrial engineering student at Northeastern University and was first exposed to organic organization structure. In 1972, I began a cooperative-education assignment at General Foods Corporation (since merged and acquired several times). Little did I know at the time that General Foods was a pioneer in sociotechnical systems, which were intended to "jointly optimize the social and technical systems." General Foods had applied the approach in dog food plants where "self-directed work teams" were at the center of processes. It worked. Performance improved over traditional top-down command and control organizations.

In 1982, after taking a job as an assistant professor of industrial and operations engineering at the University of Michigan, I was exposed to Japanese manufacturing. What I discovered was that Toyota, in particular, stood out to me as an example of an organization with a systems perspective, but its focus was different from the autonomous work groups I first saw at General Foods. It contained some elements that were mechanistic and others that were organic.

The source of my confusion started to come into focus when I read the work of then Stanford assistant professor Paul Adler. Adler was excited to study the new Toyota–General Motors joint venture, NUMMI, in Fremont, California. He had read about the incredible quality and productivity of the plant and how Toyota was bringing organic forms of organization to the most rigid of bureaucracies—the assembly plant. How in the world was Toyota making such a regimented process as a moving assembly line organic? When he toured the plant, what he saw was baffling. In many ways it was one of the most bureaucratic organizations he had ever seen. Rules and procedures were visible everywhere. All these artifacts suggested a highly regimented organization in which workers were tightly controlled.

Yet on further study he found workers were organized in work groups with team leaders and group leaders and everyone was deeply engaged in improvement (Principle 10), what the Japanese called "kaizen." Morale was high, absenteeism and turnover were low, and the general climate was one of openness and learning. Toyota had hired back over 80 percent of the workers from when the plant was owned and managed by General Motors. Back then, the employees were reported to be angry and rebellious—and were represented by a militant union. Absenteeism, wildcat strikes, drugs, alcohol, prostitution, and every other societal ill imaginable ran rampant in the GM plant. Everyone wanted to know, how did Toyota turn around this plant in its first year of production and create an organization that combined mechanistic and organic organizations?

Adler came up with a bold new distinction. He concluded that bureaucracy was not a single and monolithic organizational form, but rather had different flavors. Most bureaucracies at the time were "coercive" and focused on control of people. Workers were expected to keep their heads down, do what they were told, and avoid thinking. At NUMMI, Adler observed what he called an "enabling bureaucracy," which served to empower the workforce to generate creative ideas and continuously improve. He described Toyota as turning classical industrial engineering on its head. As Adler, in his article "Time and Motion Regained,"[2] observed:

> *Formal work standards developed by industrial engineers and imposed on workers are alienating. But procedures that are designed by the workers themselves in a continuous and successful effort to improve productivity, quality, skills, and understanding can humanize even the most disciplined forms of bureaucracy. Moreover, NUMMI shows that hierarchy can provide support and expertise instead of a mere command structure.*

John Krafcik, who originally came up with the term "lean production" as a student at MIT, tells a great story in his seminal article on lean production.[3] As an undergraduate student, he had the opportunity to work at NUMMI. He recounts:

> *One GM industrial-engineering manager, intent on discovering the real secret of the plant's superb productivity and quality record, asked a high-ranking NUMMI executive (actually a Toyota executive from Japan on loan to the joint venture) how many industrial engineers worked at NUMMI. The executive thought for a while and replied, "We have 2100 team members working on the factory floor; therefore, we have 2100 industrial engineers."*

MECHANISTIC, ORGANIC, MIXED, AND LEAN MANAGEMENT

Given all the distinctions among mechanistic organization, organic organization, and innovative combinations in enabling bureaucracy, how do most organizations deploy lean systems? I teach a three-day master class on lean leadership and pose this question to my "students," who are mostly executives. With only a broad definition of the distinction between organic versus mechanistic deployment of lean, I ask them to call out characteristics of each. They typically do so enthusiastically. Figure P.2 is an example of some of the items generated in classes in England in 2019. The participants delineated a clear difference between the mechanistic approach—project based, expert driven, top down, tools—and the organic approach—purpose driven, a journey, engaging people, coaching.

When I ask the students which they prefer and believe is most effective, they overwhelmingly vote for the organic approach. They usually say the mechanistic approach is faster and more efficient, but the organic approach is more robust and sustainable. Someone will inevitably point out that maybe it is not either-or, but there may be a role for both. I then describe enabling bureaucracy, and the lightbulbs go on. Heads nod, and they all agree that is what they are aiming for.

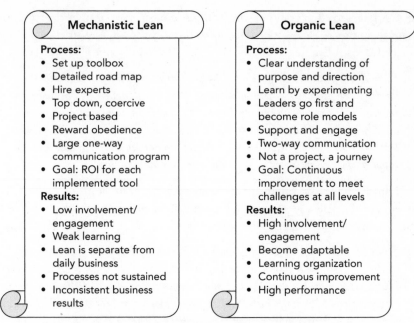

Mechanistic Lean

Process:
- Set up toolbox
- Detailed road map
- Hire experts
- Top down, coercive
- Project based
- Reward obedience
- Large one-way communication program
- Goal: ROI for each implemented tool

Results:
- Low involvement/ engagement
- Weak learning
- Lean is separate from daily business
- Processes not sustained
- Inconsistent business results

Organic Lean

Process:
- Clear understanding of purpose and direction
- Learn by experimenting
- Leaders go first and become role models
- Support and engage
- Two-way communication
- Not a project, a journey
- Goal: Continuous improvement to meet challenges at all levels

Results:
- High involvement/ engagement
- Become adaptable
- Learning organization
- Continuous improvement
- High performance

Figure P.2   Master class delegate input—characteristics of mechanistic and organic lean deployment.

Most report that they are using a mechanistic approach and wonder if they should abandon that and move toward an organic approach. I answer that there may be some sense in starting with a broad mechanistic deployment led by lean specialists, as we saw at the beginning of the chapter, and then build on that base more organic approaches. The mechanistic approach often leads to measurable results and captures the interest of senior executives. There is an ROI. And the mechanistic approach can begin to establish a flow in the process and educate people about basic lean concepts. But if the rollout of lean is limited only to mechanistic deployment, the new systems are likely to devolve toward the original mass production systems when the lean specialists move on to other projects. In contrast, Toyota prefers to start organically with the model line process—learn deeply by starting with developing the system in one place—which takes more time and does not provide the quick results across the enterprise that many senior executives impatiently expect. On the other hand, the model line approach leads to deep learning and ownership by the managers and workforce, which is critical to building sustainability and continuous improvement in the new systems. We will discuss deployment approaches in the "Conclusion" chapter.

LEARNING FROM TOYOTA WAY PRINCIPLES VERSUS COPYING TOYOTA PRACTICES

Like any other author, I have my pet peeves about the way readers and reviewers interpret my books compared with my intentions. I'm sometimes accused of being a biased Toyota lover and not believing Toyota can do anything wrong. They believe I am portraying Toyota as organizational nirvana and that I am advocating that every company should try to be like Toyota. Yes, I greatly admire Toyota, and my battery is recharged every time I visit one of the company's sites. But Toyota is far from perfect, and copying it is a bad idea.

I have spent enough time in Toyota to hear many complaints from Toyota managers and team members about the company and to learn of many chinks in the armor. For example, I once visited a plant and later got an email from an employee who informed me that the managers avoided showing me all the cars being repaired that day for defects. A veteran manager in that plant lamented to me that in the old days when there were Japanese trainers, metrics were used as a guide for improvement, and now "making the numbers" had become the main goal. Toyota is made up of people with all our human imperfections. Even when I lead tours of Toyota plants, employees openly share short periods where they went backward on key principles, such as failure to regularly update standardized work as improvements were made, difficulties in developing managers who deeply understand the Toyota Way, defects not being caught in process, and more.

Takahiro Fujimoto, a student of the Toyota Production System, explains that Toyota's system can be best understood as developing in an evolutionary way, not in a brilliantly planned, prescient way:

> *Although Toyota's manufacturing system looks as if it were deliberately designed as a competitive weapon, it was created gradually through a complex historical process that can never be reduced to managers' rational foresight alone.*[4]

Even Toyota factories do not blindly copy the "best practices" of other Toyota factories. Sure, all the plants have similar processes to stamp, mold, weld, paint, and assemble; that being the case, why not simply identify the best practices and require that they be replicated everywhere? But Toyota sensei will tell you that TPS should really stand for "Thinking Production System." They want people to think. Copying is not thinking or learning. Toyota could try to enforce best practices from headquarters so everyone does things the same way, but then continuous improvement would die. The company would get compliance, not thinking.

The journey of learning from Toyota for more than 35 years has been life changing for me, and after all that time, I continue to admire Toyota as a great company. Toyota's approach to scientific thinking and improving is a model to learn from. How can Toyota as a model help you develop a vision for your organization? What can you learn from the principles? What specific, high-priority challenges are you working on, and how can ideas from Toyota possibly help? There are no "solutions" from Toyota, but there is great wisdom that can help in crafting your vision for the future. It is also now clear to me that even great manufacturing processes that yield quality, low cost, and high-speed delivery are not enough. You need products and services customers want to buy and an appealing business proposition. You need strategy, and that will be unique to your company (Principle 14).

WHAT IS NEW IN THE SECOND EDITION?

In the original *The Toyota Way*, I introduced 14 principles of lean management organized around 4 Ps—philosophy, process, people, and problem solving. I have learned a lot since 2004 when the book was published. I wrote 11 more books about specific aspects of Toyota and consulted to many organizations. I learned so much from these experiences that I decided to update the original book. Here is a high-level summary of what is new:

1. **Distinction between mechanistic and organic approaches.** I started using this as a framework in my courses to give students a clearer picture of what is different about the Toyota philosophy. It also helps bring the systems perspective to life.

2. **Lean deployment as developing the mindset of scientific thinking.** My former student Mike Rother gave me his book *Toyota Kata*, and I found it corresponded with my observations at Toyota and filled in some gaps in my thinking. He noticed that despite the initial success of lean interventions, managers tended to resort to their previous habits and sustainment was difficult. He took to heart that Toyota worked to create a new way of thinking based on facts and experimenting in a scientific way. Rother researched how people learn new behaviors and skills and was inspired by the martial arts, where students learn to develop extraordinary physical capabilities. In karate, the term "kata" refers to small skills that are taught as habits through repeated practice with corrective feedback from the black belt. He applied this to developing in people the habit of thinking scientifically through repeated practice and corrective feedback. I discuss his approach under Principle 12 and often draw on the insights I gained from Mike throughout the book.

3. **Revision of the 4P model.** The four Ps are the same, but I put in the center scientific thinking, which Taiichi Ohno referred to as the core of TPS and Mike Rother teaches through kata. There are still 14 principles, but I updated some of the wording, combined some, and added others. In particular, I almost completely revamped the "problem-solving" principles to focus on scientific thinking, policy deployment to align goals, and the connection between strategy and execution.

4. **New examples.** I included descriptions of how lean has been applied in services and knowledge work, which drew on my research and writing for *The Toyota Way to Service Excellence*[5] and *Designing the Future*.[6]

5. **A detailed explanation of Toyota's work group structure.** I find there is a great deal of interest in the way Toyota develops leaders and organizes work groups, and it is quite different from the typical organization. Among other things, Toyota's organizational structure encourages coaching and learning. I provide examples of this in Principle 10.

6. **Streamlined parts of the book.** In the original, it took 6 chapters and 68 pages to reach the first principle, including chapters on developing the first Prius and first Lexus. In this new edition, I moved examples of how Toyota designs cars and its long-term product strategy into Principle 14. I also tightened up the discussions of Toyota's history and lean concepts.

7. **Discussion of lean in the digital age.** In Principle 8 the discussion is about technology, including the internet of things, and in Principle 14 it is about how lean thinking can help more effectively develop and use new technology as part of a business strategy.

8. **Glossary.** There are quite a few words that have specific meanings in the lean lexicon, so I included a short Glossary.[7]

The Toyota Way—the philosophy, not the book—is centered on learning by doing under the watchful eyes of a knowledgeable coach. You learn it at the gemba, not sitting in a comfortable chair reading a book. Nonetheless, I hope this book helps to stretch your vision about what is possible in your own organization. The people I know who have been part of a serious lean journey describe how much they learned and how they changed as individuals. It is about personal growth, clarifying your values, and developing confidence that you can make a difference. Please read, but then please do!

KEY POINTS

- *The Machine That Changed the World* was based on studies of the Toyota Production System and popularized concepts of "lean production" across most sectors of society.
- The Toyota Production System is represented by a house with the twin pillars of just-in-time and jidoka resting on a foundation of stable, leveled processes. In the center are people continuously improving.
- In many ways, TPS methods resemble classical industrial engineering methods, but Toyota turned traditional IE on its head by empowering frontline team members to use the tools to improve their own processes.
- When an organization is looked at as a machine, mechanistic lean becomes a tool kit that is used to eliminate waste, as prescribed in classical industrial engineering.
- When an organization is viewed as a living system, organic lean focuses on people at all levels challenging the system and continually improving.
- The term "enabling bureaucracy" was introduced by Paul Adler to refer to a mix of mechanistic and organic elements, where structure, policies, and management support empower people to improve their processes.
- Toyota practices are not effective if benchmarked and copied, because they were developed as solutions to Toyota's problems at a point in time. It is much better to learn from the principles and use them as ideas or inspiration in pursuit of your vision of excellence.
- The digital age has advanced to the point that there is a whole new level of lean systems possible that appropriately use these technologies to support people and processes.

Notes

1. James P. Womack, Daniel T. Jones, and Daniel Roos, *The Machine That Changed the World: The Story of Lean Production* (New York: Harper Perennial, November 1991).
2. Paul S. Adler, "Time and Motion Regained," *Harvard Business Review*, January–February 1993, pp. 97–108.
3. J. F. Krafcik, "Triumph of the Lean Production System," *Sloan Management Review*, 30, 1988, 41–52.
4. Takahiro Fujimoto, *The Evolution of a Manufacturing System at Toyota* (New York: Oxford University Press, 1999), pp. 5–6.

5. Jeffrey Liker and Karyn Ross, *The Toyota Way to Service Excellence* (New York: McGraw-Hill, 2016).
6. James Morgan and Jeffrey Liker, *Designing the Future: How Ford, Toyota, and Other World-Class Organizations Use Lean Product Development to Drive Innovation and Transform Their Business* (New York: McGraw-Hill, 2018).
7. Chet Marchwinski, et. al., *Lean Lexicon: A Graphical Glossary for Lean Thinkers*, Brighton, Mass.: Lean Enterprise Institute, 2006.

Introduction

The Toyota Way: Using Operational Excellence as a Strategic Weapon

We place the highest value on actual implementation and taking action. There are many things one doesn't understand and therefore, we ask them why don't you just go ahead and take action; try to do something? You realize how little you know and you face your own failures and you simply can correct those failures and redo it again and at the second trial you realize another mistake or another thing you didn't like so you can redo it once again. So by constant improvement, or, should I say, the improvement based upon action, one can rise to the higher level of practice and knowledge.
—Fujio Cho, President, Toyota Motor Corporation, 2002

Toyota first broadly caught the world's attention in the 1970s, when it became clear that there was something special about Japanese quality and efficiency. Japanese cars were lasting longer than American and European cars and required much less repair. And by the 1980s, it became apparent that there was something even more special about Toyota compared with other automakers in Japan.[1] It was not eye-popping car designs or performance—though the rides were smooth and the designs pleasant. It was the way Toyota went about engineering and manufacturing autos that led to unbelievable consistency in the process and product. The result of the culture, methods, processes led to designing and making autos more quickly, cheaper, and better than their competitors. Equally impressive, every time Toyota showed an apparent weakness and seemed vulnerable, the company miraculously fixed the problem and came back even stronger—as was illustrated in the dramatic recall crisis of 2009–2010 that at the time seemed like it could bury the company.[2] Toyota remained profitable through that difficult period, and after it addressed the problems, its quality ratings again surged.

There are many metrics that can be used to judge an auto company. We will focus on two indicators for illustrative purposes: profits and quality experienced by the customer. Toyota's success cannot be appreciated by selecting a single year; rather, one must look at its remarkable consistency of high performance over long periods of time. For profits, I used annual net income/loss in US dollars over a 15-year period, starting in 2004, when the original *Toyota Way* was published, through 2018 (see Figure I.1). For comparison, I used several large automakers with full vehicle lineups—Toyota, Ford, Volkswagen, and General Motors, although the same pattern would apply if we added in other automakers.

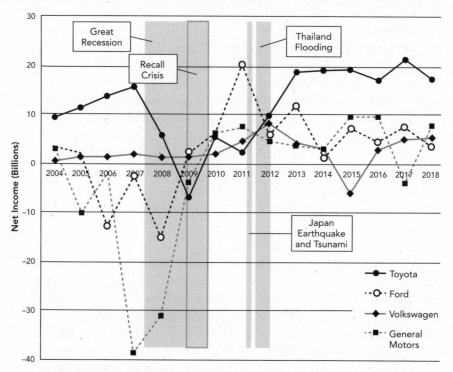

Figure I.1   Annual net income/loss across automakers, 2004–2018.
The data were compiled by James Franz. Toyota data were converted from yen based on the exchange rate quarter by quarter, and the fiscal year data were converted to calendar years. Note that Ford's profit in 2011 was inflated by over $11 billion by an accounting change for "deferred tax assets."

In most years, Toyota is the clear winner. In the year of the Great Recession of 2008, after 50 straight years of profits, Toyota lost just over $5 billion, worse than Ford and Volkswagen. Otherwise, Toyota was profitable in each of the other 14 years despite the recall crisis, the Japan earthquake and tsunami that shut down parts supplies, and the worst recorded flood ever in Thailand that shut down parts supply and vehicle production. Take out those bad years due to crises and natural disasters, and the pattern tilts strongly upward. In 2007, just before the recession, Toyota earned almost $14 billion, an auto industry record. By 2013, it again earned record industry profits of almost $19 billion and then surpassed that record with $21 billion in 2017. Only Ford earned near a similar amount, over $20 billion in 2011, but most of that was due to an accounting change.*

If we look at the cumulative profits minus losses of auto companies over the 15-year period, Toyota really stands out (see Figure I.2). On net, Toyota earned $179.7 billion. Honda, which we added in this comparison, was next at $75.4 billion, less than half of what Toyota earned. Ford, which ranked third, managed $46.9 billion, and even that was a bit overstated due to the accounting change

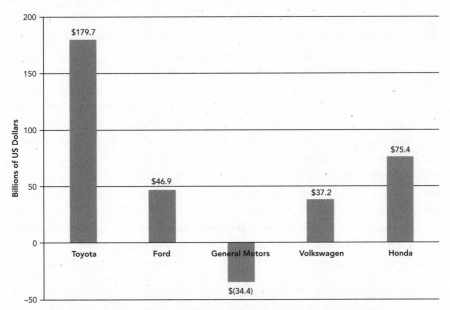

Figure I.2   Total net income for automakers, 2004–2018.

---

* Of Ford's $20 billion in profits in 2011. According to autoblog.com, $11.5 billion was "the result of a valuation allowance held against deferred tax assets, which the company needed as it saw profits disappear. As profitability returned, the valuation was no longer necessary."

in 2011. Volkswagen, which was the world's largest automaker when I wrote this book, came in at $37.2 billion, about 20 percent of Toyota's net profits. It is interesting that the cumulative earnings of Ford, GM, Volkswagen, and Honda of $125.1 billion over this period are still far less than Toyota's earnings. Even taking out the negative contribution of General Motors in this period, the other three companies' total of $159.5 billion still fell short of Toyota's profits.

As a result of its industry-leading profitability, Toyota always has a strong credit rating (Aa3 by Moody's as I write this) and plenty of cash available to invest in this tumultuous transformation of the industry toward connected, autonomous, shared, electrified vehicles. For example, in 2019 it had a record $57.5 billion in cash on hand.[3]

To some stock market analysts, having this much cash on hand is criminal. Why isn't it using the money to reward shareholders through acquisitions, stock repurchases, or larger dividends? Toyota violates conventional business practice and follows your grandparents' advice: save for a rainy day. Toyota's purpose is to contribute to society, contribute to its customers, contribute to the well-being of the communities where it does business, and to contribute to the well-being of its team members and business partners. A key to achieving these goals is to smooth out the natural ups and downs in the market through a large buffer of cash. The wisdom of this philosophy was never more apparent than in 2020 when the Covid-19 pandemic swept the world and threatened the future viability of many companies.

Toyota and Lexus are consistently near or at the top of quality measures that different organizations use to compare automakers. One of the most respected rating organizations in the United States is J.D. Power, which is frequently quoted on its initial quality ratings that cover the first three months of ownership. I prefer the three-year dependability ratings, which reflect the natural wear and tear on the vehicle and measure the problems experienced in the final year of the three. The biggest honor is winning the best dependability award within a vehicle segment (e.g., small car, midsize car, compact SUV, midsize pickup, etc.). Figure I.3 shows how many segment awards Toyota and its brand received from 2004 to 2019. The graph is up and down, but we can see that out of all the automakers selling in the United States, Toyota brands won between 20 percent and almost 60 percent of the first-place awards depending on the year. In 2019, Lexus was the number one brand in three-year vehicle dependability, and the Toyota brand was number three.[4]

Toyota vehicles do even better over longer periods. Consider vehicles that people keep for over 200,000 miles in the United States:[5] Number one was the Toyota Sequoia (nine times more likely to be kept over 200,000 miles versus average); number five was the Toyota 4Runner; number seven, the Toyota Highlander; tenth, the Toyota Tacoma; eleventh, the Toyota Tundra; and twelfth, the Toyota Avalon. In short, six of the top fourteen vehicles that Americans keep for over 200,000 miles were made by Toyota.

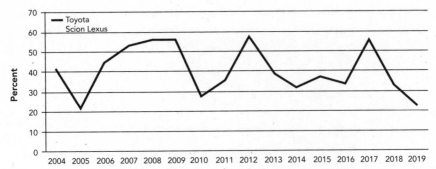

Figure I.3   Percent of first-place segment award winners for
J.D. Power three-year dependability, 2004–2019.
The data for the graph were compiled by James Franz
adding up the segment award winners by year.

Evaluations by other firms reach similar conclusions. Autobytel, which looks at vehicle history and the judgment of mechanics, forecasted the 2019 models that are likely to last the longest. Not a surprise—Camry, Corolla, Prius, and Lexus ES were all in the top 10.[6] Another firm, Dashboard Light, considers vehicles toward their end of life. It focuses on the powertrain, since historically failure of the conventional gas engine or transmission is the costliest repair, as well as focusing on the age when the failure occurs and the time when the vehicle is first turned in to a dealer at wholesale price. Dashboard ranked Lexus number one, Toyota number two, and the canceled brand Scion number five for long-term reliability (see Figure I.4).

I am not arguing that all that matters in mobility is absence of defects. As I discuss under Principle 14, excitement about the vehicle may be more important, particularly as we move forward into the future of mobility, and Toyota is working hard at this. Tesla has become a model of how exciting customers with the features of the cars can override nagging quality issues. But to this point the distinguishing features that propelled Toyota have been extreme reliability, affordable price, and functionality.

THE TOYOTA WAY MODEL

What is the secret of Toyota's success? Toyota gets credit for developing the Toyota Production System (TPS) and leading the way in the "lean manufacturing" revolution. But tools and techniques are no secret weapon for transforming a business. Toyota's continued success stems from a deeper business philosophy rooted in its understanding of people and human motivation. Ultimately, its success derives from its ability to cultivate leadership, teams, and culture; to devise

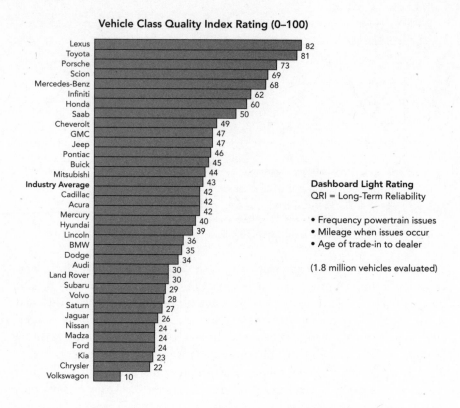

Figure I.4   Long-term reliability according to Dashboard Light.

strategy; to build relationships across the value chain; and to maintain a learning organization.

This book describes 14 principles that, based on over 35 years of studying the company, constitute my perspective on the Toyota Way. I divided the principles into four categories, all starting with "P"—philosophy, process, people, and problem solving (see Figure I.5). I revised the model for the new edition. Instead of using a pyramid as I did in the first edition, I show the principles as pieces of a puzzle that represent a system of interconnected parts. I also added a new construct at the center, "scientific thinking," which brings the four Ps to life, as described later in the chapter. Practical scientific thinking in this context means taking a fact-based, iterative learning approach to working toward a difficult challenge. It starts with recognizing that the world is far more complex and unpredictable than we often think . . . by a lot.

Scientific Thinking and The Toyota Way as a System

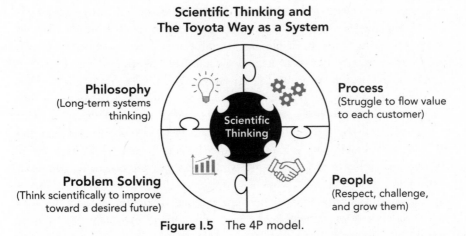

Figure I.5   The 4P model.

The 14 principles associated with the 4P model are summarized in Figure I.6. For an executive summary of the 14 principles of the Toyota Way, along with a table for assessing where you are and where you want to be, see the Appendix. Those familiar with the first edition of this book will notice that there are still 14 principles, but some have been reworded and the sequence changed a bit, with the section on problem solving changed the most. I now place far greater empha-

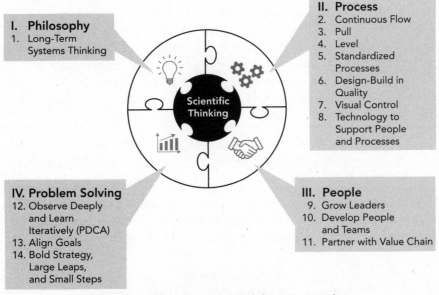

Figure I.6   The 4P model and the 14 principles.

sis on "scientific thinking" by observing deeply and learning iteratively (Principle 12), by aligning plans and goals through policy deployment (Principle 13), and by incorporating a new principle on the connection between strategy and execution by large leaps and small steps (Principle 14). Following the next chapter, which focuses on the history and philosophy of the Toyota Production System, each of the 14 subsequent chapters will discuss one principle with examples from manufacturing and service.

The Toyota Way and the Toyota Production System (Toyota's manufacturing philosophy and methodology) are the double helix of Toyota's DNA; they define Toyota's management style and what is unique about the company. I hope to explain and show how the Toyota Way principles can help any organization in any industry to improve any business process, including sales, product development, software development, marketing, logistics, and management. To assist you in this journey, I offer numerous examples of how Toyota maintains a high level of achievement, as well as highlighting companies from a variety of manufacturing and service operations that have effectively applied Toyota's principles.

SCIENTIFIC THINKING IS THE HUB . . . AND WE ARE NOT GREAT AT IT

The biggest change in the Toyota Way model in this second edition is placing scientific thinking in the center. This is not a new idea for Toyota. The first TPS manual, published by Toyota's Education and Training Department in 1973, taught Ohno's view of the "scientific mindset": "On the shop floor it is important to start with the actual phenomenon and search for the root cause in order to solve the problem. In other words, we must emphasize 'getting the facts,' . . ."*

This was reiterated years later by an Ohno student, Mr. Ohba, who started the Toyota Production System Support Center (TSSC) in the United States. In a public presentation, he explained:†

> TPS is built on the scientific way of thinking. . . . How do I respond to this problem? Not a toolbox. [You have to be] willing to start small, learn through trial and error.

The image of scientific thinking may bring to mind professional scientists rigorously using a defined method to formulate and test their hypotheses, perhaps in a lab, so they can publish a paper and advance a body of knowledge. The

---

* As conveyed by Art Smalley, former Toyota manager.
† I received a PowerPoint file of this presentation in 2011, and I am not sure where or when it was presented.

goal of pure science is identifying general principles that get peer-reviewed evaluating the rigor of the research process. The normal pattern is to identify a gap in our knowledge and explain why it is important (problem definition), advance a notion about the way things might work (hypothesis), explain the study design (methods), present the findings (results), discuss the implications of the study, and suggest further research (discussion/reflection). The process should be done objectively and without bias. By contrast, Ohno was not trying to prove generic hypotheses about the nature of the world, but rather he was, as Ohba said, trying to address "this" problem. He was dealing with messy real-world circumstances and wanted team members to think scientifically about problems they identified, which meant gathering data and facts, taking time to test their ideas, examining results, and reflecting on what they learned. One can even say that the core of Toyota culture is a practical approach to scientific thinking.

If, in fact, improvement based on scientific thinking is what brings TPS to life, how do we develop people who think this way? Toyota's answer is the coach-learner relationship and daily practice. Toyota has developed each of its executives, managers, and supervisors as coaches over many decades, something few other organizations have done.

Mike Rother's book *Toyota Kata*[7] offers a simple step-by-step process, along with starter kata (practice routines) to develop scientific thinking skills—which might help organizations interested in adapting Toyota's approach. I discuss this in some detail under Principle 12: "Observe deeply and learn iteratively (PDCA) toward a desired future state."

In the abstract, science is hard to define, and there are endless philosophical debates over what it means. Rother is not focused as much on defining science per se, but rather on developing a practical approach to teaching people to think scientifically in everyday life. He describes it as:[8]

a mindset, or way of looking at the world/responding to goals and problems, that's characterized by . . .

■ *Acknowledging that our comprehension is always incomplete and possibly wrong.*
■ *Assuming that answers will be found by test rather than just deliberation. (You make predictions and test them with experiments.)*
■ *Appreciating that differences between what we predict will happen and what actually happens can be a useful source of learning and corrective adjustment.*

By contrast, when we respond to goals and problems by assuming we already understand the current reality and solution, by neglecting to test our assumptions, and by viewing failed predictions as personal failures that have no learning value, we are not using a scientific mindset, and we are not learning to think more scientifically in the future.

Of course, we encounter problems where we have some level of experience and knowledge to guide our decision-making, and we do not need to pretend we know nothing. Rother calls this a "threshold of knowledge." What is within our threshold of knowledge, and what are assumptions to be tested? In the physical sciences, for example, there is a huge body of knowledge, and it would be wasteful to pretend we know nothing about rich topics like physics, chemistry, and biology when we design a manufacturing process. There is also a huge body of knowledge on how to engineer software. We can apply that knowledge, though generally tailoring it to the specific situation and even generating new ideas. Unfortunately, our general human tendency is to assume with great certainty that we know far more than we really do. Our primitive brain hates uncertainty and drives us to assume we know the right answer or there is a known best way.

I discussed in the Preface the fallacy in thinking about lean as a mechanistic process of applying off-the-shelf solutions to an organization's problems. This is decidedly unscientific. As an example, when I teach short courses or give public presentations, I am usually bombarded with questions from people asking me to solve their problems on the spot: How can we level our schedule if our customers are not level? How does TPS apply in a highly regulated environment like ours? Do we need to hang paper documents on the wall, or can we put all our information on a computer? Do we need to use pull systems for everything, or can we schedule our thousands of end items? Have you seen lean applied to oil exploration in deep ocean waters? How do I convince our CEO to come to the gemba? What these people are really asking is, "Can you give me the correct solution to my problem?"

I used to struggle to give a general, but hopefully sensible answer to prove my credibility. But what could these people do with my answers? I now realize that throwing out solutions in a public forum is totally contrary to scientific thinking and is no help to the people posing the questions. I am not sure exactly what their goals are. I have not studied their current condition. And I certainly have not experimented at their gemba. In other words, generic "solutions" are simply uninformed guesses, even coming from a so-called expert like me. We are used to how-to books, road maps, and IT and consulting companies boldly advertising they are "solution providers." Plug in these solutions and play. It would be nice, but it rarely works.

Spoiler alert for our discussion of Principle 12—scientific thinking is not our default. We are not naturally good at it. Nobel Prize winner Daniel Kahneman provides an exhaustive and science-based explanation of the many biases that interfere with scientific thinking.[9] He boils it down to "fast thinking," which is fast, automatic, and emotional and feels really good. Jumping to conclusions based on something we thought worked in the past is fast thinking. Scientific thinking is based on "slow thinking," which is slow, deliberate, and systematic, and generally speaking we find it arduous, boring, and even painful. He presents the "law of least mental effort," which is how our brains prefer us to live, because thousands of years ago survival required jumping to conclusions, acting fast, and conserving energy. Global conditions have changed, and we now need more humans who can think scientifically, but our hardware is quite old and does not naturally function that way.

SCIENTIFIC THINKING UNDERLIES EACH OF THE FOUR Ps

Philosophy

Toyota's philosophy is based on long-term systems thinking and a clear sense of purpose. What is our vision and what are we trying to accomplish? Thinking long term and thinking in terms of systems require complex reasoning. It is easy to implement X to immediately get Y. But what if you introduce X (such as developing employees) as part of a system that indirectly over some years, in combination with other parts of the system (such as one-piece flow), is likely to improve business outcomes? Toyota works hard at planning and setting challenging goals (see Principle 13), but then expects to pursue those goals through continuous improvement. The direction is clear, but the pathway to get there is fuzzy at best. Solving complex system problems requires leadership to oversee the entire process, but also to work toward the vision by dividing and conquering, breaking down the desired future system into pieces, and putting people close to each process in charge of learning through continual experimentation. As Mr. Cho queries in the opening quote: "Why don't you just go ahead and take action; try to do something?"

Process

Processes are not static things, but rather dynamic approaches to work that can be improved through experiments and learning. We often see in the lean community so-called experts implementing their pet lean methods that have worked for them in the past—build cells, make it neat and tidy, and put up a board for daily huddles. The Toyota Way does not assume you can implement solutions to repair or build a high-performing system. In fact, for Toyota a major reason for creating lean, or what Krafcik called "fragile" systems, is to surface problems so people can scientifically solve the problems one by one and learn.

People

As mentioned, our evolutionary past did not reward slow and deliberate thinking, and we are still products of that evolution. We have many nasty habits such as letting our faulty impressions of past experience cloud our judgment of future possibilities and seeing the current situation through cloudy and biased lenses. At Toyota, every leader is a coach who teaches new ways of thinking at the gemba (where the work is done), often with relatively little classroom or online training. After a great deal of repetition, neural pathways are created, and those new ways of thinking scientifically begin to feel comfortable.

Problem Solving

In many organizations, problem solving often amounts to putting Band-Aids on processes; typically, the problems reoccur, and the organization never gets to a higher level of performance. While Toyota does a lot of reactive problem solving when there is a deviation from standard, it tries to get to the root cause. More fundamentally, Toyota's heavy investment in proactive improvement to meet challenges tends to anticipate and reduce future problems.

THE TOYOTA PRODUCTION SYSTEM AND LEAN PRODUCTION

The Toyota Production System is Toyota's unique approach to manufacturing and the basis for much of the "lean production" movement that has dominated manufacturing trends for the last 30 years or more. I discuss the history of TPS in more detail in the next chapter. Despite the huge influence of the lean movement, I hope to show that most attempts to implement lean have been superficial. Most companies have focused too heavily on tools such as 5S (cleaning and organizing the place) and work cells, without understanding lean as an entire system that must permeate an organization's culture. In most companies where lean is implemented, senior management is not involved in the day-to-day operations and continuous improvement efforts that are at the center of lean.

Toyota developed TPS to address pressing problems—not as a way to implement known solutions. Toyota was fighting for survival after World War II and faced very different business conditions than Ford and GM faced. While Ford and GM used mass production, economies of scale, and big equipment to produce large volumes of parts as cheaply as possible, Toyota's market in postwar Japan was small. Toyota had to make a variety of vehicles on the same assembly line to satisfy its customers. Thus, the key to its operations was flexibility. As it confronted this challenge, Toyota made a critical discovery: when you make lead times short and focus on keeping production lines flexible, you actually achieve higher quality, better customer responsiveness, better productivity, and better utilization of equipment and space. This discovery became the foundation for Toyota's success globally in the twenty-first century.

In some ways, the TPS improvement tools look a lot like classical industrial engineering methods that seek to eliminate waste, but in fact the TPS philosophy in other ways almost the opposite of traditional industrial engineering. Consider the following counterintuitive truths about non-value-added waste within the philosophy of TPS:

- **Often, the best thing you can do is to idle a machine and stop producing parts.** You do this to avoid overproduction, which is considered the fundamental waste in TPS.
- **Often, it is best to build up an inventory of finished goods in order to level out the production schedule, rather than produce according to the fluctuating demand of customer orders.**
- **Often, it is best to selectively add and substitute overhead for direct labor.** When waste is stripped away from your value-adding workers, you need to provide high-quality support for them as you would support a surgeon performing a critical operation. Toyota has an additional level called "Team Leaders," who are offline ready to jump in when any team member pulls the andon cord asking for help.
- **It may not be a top priority to keep your workers busy making parts as fast as possible.** You should produce parts at the rate of customer demand. Working faster just for the sake of getting the most out of your workers is another form of overproduction and actually can lead to employing more labor overall.
- **It is best to selectively use automation and information technology and sometimes better to use manual processes even when automation is available and would seem to justify its cost in reducing your headcount.** People are the most flexible resource you have. Automation is a fixed investment. And people, not computers, can continually improve processes.
- **Often, planning slowly and carefully, then experimenting, then deploying efficiently, is faster than rushing to judgment and implementing immediately.** Toyota plans in great detail and will pilot anything new before spreading the new practice throughout the organization. Further deployment is then fast and efficient.

In other words, Toyota's solutions to particular problems often seem to add waste rather than eliminate it. The reason for these seemingly paradoxical approaches is derived from Ohno's experiences walking the shop floor. He discovered that non-valued-added waste had little to do with running labor and equipment as hard as possible, and had everything to do with the manner in which raw material is transformed into a salable commodity. He learned to observe the *value stream* of the raw material moving to a finished product that the customer was willing to pay for, and he learned to identify "stagnation" where value was not flowing. This was a radically different approach from the mass production thinking that focused on identifying, enumerating, and eliminating the wasted time and effort in separate production processes.

As you make Ohno's journey for yourself and examine your organization's processes, you will see materials, information, service calls, and prototype parts in R&D (you fill in the blank for your business process) being transformed into something the customer wants. But on closer inspection, they are often diverted into a pile of material or a virtual information file where they sit and wait for long periods of time, until they can be moved to the next process. Certainly, people do not like to be diverted from their journeys and to wait on long lines. Ohno viewed material and information as having the same degree of impatience. Why? If any large batches of material are produced and then sit and wait to be processed, if service calls are backed up, if R&D is receiving prototype parts before it has time to test them, then this sitting and waiting to move to the next operation becomes waste. It is overproduction and often means quality problems are hidden and we do not have the right stuff that our customers want. This results in both your internal and external customers becoming impatient and frustrated.

This is why TPS starts with the customer. Always ask, "What value are we adding from the customer's perspective?" *Because the only thing that adds value in any type of process—be it a manufacturing, service, or development process—is the physical or information transformation of that product, service, or activity into something the customer wants.*

WHY COMPANIES OFTEN THINK THEY ARE LEAN—BUT AREN'T

When I first began learning about TPS, I was enamored of the power of one-piece flow. I learned that all the supporting tools of lean, such as quick equipment changeovers, standardized work, pull systems, and error proofing, were essential to creating flow. But along the way, experienced leaders within Toyota kept telling me that these tools and techniques were not the key to TPS. Rather the power behind TPS is a company's management commitment to continuously invest in its people and promote a culture of continuous improvement. I nodded like

I knew what they were talking about and continued to study how to calculate kanban quantities and set up one-piece flow cells.

Let's say you bought a book on creating one-piece flow cells or perhaps went to a training class or maybe even hired a lean consultant. You pick a process and do a lean improvement project. A review of the process reveals lots of "muda," or waste, muda being Toyota's term for anything that takes time but does not add value for your customer. The process is disorganized, and the place is a mess. So you clean it up and straighten out the flow in the process. Everything starts to flow faster. You get better control over the process. Quality even goes up. This is exciting stuff, so you apply it to other parts of the operation. What's so hard about this?

The world has been exposed to TPS for decades. The basic concepts and tools are not new. TPS has been operating in some form in Toyota since shortly after World War II. Yet, organizations that to some degree embrace lean tools often do not understand what makes them work together as a system. Typically, management adopts a few of these technical tools and struggles to go beyond a basic application in an effort to get immediate results. The problem is that the people in charge do not understand the power behind true TPS: the development of a continuous improvement culture that brings to life the principles of the Toyota Way. Within the 4P model, most companies are dabbling at only one level—"process." Without adopting the other three Ps, and missing the scientific thinking mindset, they will do little more than dabble, because the improvements they make will not have the heart and intelligence behind them to make them sustainable throughout the company. Their performance will continue to lag behind that of companies that adopt a true culture of continuous improvement.

I heard a great story of a retired lean sensei from Toyota who was invited by the CEO of a large manufacturing company in Europe to visit and tell him whether the company was "world class." After the expensive sensei spent most of the day visiting plants and observing carefully, he finally was ready for his report. At the end of the day, the CEO asked, "So are we world class?"

The sensei replied, "I do not know. I was not here yesterday." The sensei was making the profound point that he could only judge by whether he saw improvement from day to day, not the state at a point in time.

The quote at the beginning of this chapter from Mr. Fujio Cho, former president of Toyota, is not just rhetoric. From the executives to the shop floor workers performing the value-added work, Toyota challenges people to use their initiative and creativity to experiment and learn. Toyota is a true learning organization that has been evolving and learning for most of a century. This investment in its employees should frighten those traditional mass production companies that merely focus on making parts and counting quarterly dollars and adopting new "cultures" with every change in CEO.

IF THE TOYOTA WAY DOES NOT OFFER SOLUTIONS, WHAT IS ITS VALUE?

Critics often describe Toyota as a "boring legacy auto company." If boring means high levels of performance consistently over decades, I will take it any day. Top quality year in and year out. Steadily growing sales. Consistent profitability. Huge cash reserves to fund innovation for the future. Long-term contributions to society and local communities.

Toyota remains a model for careful and efficient delivery of on-time products that customers pay a premium for based on high quality, reliability, and high value. The Toyota Way provides a model for fast, efficient, and effective execution of long-term strategy based on:

- Carefully studying the market and planning in detail future products and services
- Putting safety first for team members and customers
- Eliminating wasted time and resources in execution of those plans
- Building quality into every step of design, manufacturing, and service delivery
- Using new technology effectively to work in harmony with people, not simply replace people
- Building a culture of people who learn and think scientifically to achieve aligned, challenging goals

I've included in this new edition of *The Toyota Way* case examples from a diverse group of organizations that have had success in using Toyota's principles to improve quality, efficiency, and speed. While many people feel it is difficult to apply Toyota's way of thinking outside Japan, Toyota is in fact doing just that—building learning organizations in overseas operations throughout the world and even teaching TPS to other companies.

This book is not intended as a blueprint on how to copy Toyota; there is no such blueprint, and blindly copying is a bad idea. Nor am I attempting to describe Toyota as the perfect company that does everything superior in every way; in fact, Toyota people will tell you they are far from perfect and make mistakes every day. I will not try to detail those mistakes made by self-confessed imperfect humans. *The Toyota Way* is not an evaluation of Toyota as a company, but rather a set of principles and ideas derived from Toyota and other sources that might help your vision and inspire you to become better at adapting and succeeding in a complex, unpredictable environment.

KEY POINTS

- Toyota's success can only be appreciated over long time periods. For example, its cumulative profits from 2004 to 2018 were greater than the sum of earnings for Ford, General Motors, Volkswagen, and Honda.
- Toyota repeatedly scores at or near the top for quality and especially stands out for long-term reliability.
- My version of the Toyota Way is based on four Ps: philosophy, process, people, and problem solving. In this new edition, I represent the four Ps as interconnected pieces of a puzzle with scientific thinking at the center.
- Practical scientific thinking in this context means taking a fact-based, iterative learning approach to working toward a difficult challenge. Test assumptions!
- This second edition builds on the 14 principles of the original with some wording changes and some major revisions. For example, I now emphasize under the philosophy category the importance of system thinking in the Toyota Way. The biggest changes focus the problem-solving principles on developing a scientific thinking mindset and applying that to strategy, planning, and execution.
- There is no blueprint to mimic Toyota's way, but the principles can help inform your vision and act as guidelines while you work on finding your way.

Notes

1. Womack, Jones, and Roos, *The Machine That Changed the World*, 1991.
2. Jeffrey Liker and Timothy Ogden, *Toyota Under Fire: Lessons for Turning Crisis into Opportunity* (New York: McGraw-Hill, 2011).
3. https://www.macrotrends.net/stocks/charts/TM/toyota/cash-on-hand.
4. https://www.jdpower.com/business/press-releases/2019-us-vehicle-dependability-studyvds.
5. "The 14 Cars Americans Drive Past 200 Thousand Miles," Business Insider, https://www.businessinsider.com/cars-americans-drive-the-most-are-suvs-2019-11.
6. https://www.autobytel.com/car-buying-guides/features/10-of-the-longest-lasting-cars-on-the-road-128961/#.
7. Mike Rother, *Toyota Kata* (New York: McGraw-Hill, 2009).
8. http://www.katatogrow.com (click on "scientific thinkers").
9. Daniel Kahneman, *Thinking Fast and Slow* (New York: Farrar, Straus and Giroux, 2011).

A Storied History: How Toyota Became the World's Best Manufacturer

I plan to cut down on the slack time within work processes and in the shipping of parts and materials as much as possible. As the basic principle in realizing this plan, I will uphold the "just in time" approach. The guiding rule is not to have goods shipped too early or too late.

—Kiichiro Toyoda, founder of Toyota Motor Company, 1938

The most visible product of Toyota's quest for excellence is its manufacturing philosophy, called the Toyota Production System (TPS). The importance of TPS in revolutionizing manufacturing cannot be overstated. The mass production system often associated with Henry Ford was a smashing success at the time. The focus was on large-volume production with little variety in a growing market. Toyota developed TPS in a time of low demand and high need for variety in Japan. The result is now called "lean production," which has transformed and improved countless organizations throughout the world, helping them to become more efficient and more profitable and to better serve their customers and employees.

In order to understand TPS and the Toyota Way, and how the company became the world's best manufacturer, it is helpful to appreciate the history and the personalities of the founding family members who left an indelible mark on the Toyota culture. What is most important about this is not that the family had an enduring influence (Ford is similar in this respect), but that there was remarkable consistency of leadership and philosophy throughout the history of Toyota. The roots of the Toyota Way principles can be traced back to the very beginnings of the company. And the "DNA" of the Toyota Way is encoded in every Toyota leader whether a Toyoda family member or not.

SAKICHI TOYODA AND HIS LOOMS

The story begins with Sakichi Toyoda, a tinkerer and inventor, who grew up in the late 1800s in a remote farming community in Yamaguchi, about a 1½-hour drive southeast of Toyota City. At that time, weaving was a major industry. Wishing to promote the development of small businesses, the Japanese government encouraged the creation of cottage industries across the country. Small shops and mills employing a handful of people were the norm. Housewives made a little spending money by working in these shops or in their homes. As a boy, Toyoda learned carpentry from his father and eventually applied that skill to designing and building wooden spinning machines. In 1894, he began to make manual looms that were cheaper but worked better than existing looms.

Toyoda was pleased with his looms, but he was disturbed that his mother, grandmother, and their friends still had to work so hard spinning and weaving. He wanted to find a way to relieve them of this punishing labor, so he set out to develop power-driven wooden looms.

This was an age when inventors had to do everything themselves. There were no large R&D departments to delegate work to. When Toyoda first developed the power loom, there was no power available to run the loom, so he turned his attention to the problem of generating power. Steam engines were the most common source of power, so he bought a used steam engine and experimented with using it to run the looms. He figured out how to make this work going through trial and error and getting his hands dirty—an approach that would become part of the foundation of the Toyota Way, "genchi genbutsu." In 1926, he started Toyoda Automatic Loom Works, the parent firm of the Toyota Group and still a central player in the Toyota conglomerate today.

Through endless tinkering and inventing, Toyoda eventually developed sophisticated automatic power looms that became "as famous as Mikimoto pearls and Suzuki violins" (Toyoda, 1987). His process was continuous improvement. Every experiment had a purpose—to address a specific need—a process we now call plan-do-check-act (PDCA).

At one point the looms were sufficiently automated that they could almost operate alone, with a human loading and unloading and watching to respond when a problem occurred. A frequent problem was that when a single thread broke, the loom would make defective cloth until the person shut the loom down. Toyoda observed that the person watching for this was wasting a large part of his human capacity. In response, Toyoda developed a mechanism to automatically stop a loom whenever a thread broke—freeing the person to take responsibility for multiple machines and to utilize a larger range of problem-solving skills. This simple invention evolved into a broader system that became one of the two pillars of the Toyota Production System: jidoka (automation with a human touch). Today, jidoka is often thought of as building in quality as you perform your work. The most visible symbol is the "andon," which is a light that goes on when a machine senses and abnormality or a human identifies an out-of-standard condition and pushes a button or pulls a cord (Principle 6).

Throughout his life, Sakichi Toyoda was a great engineer and later was referred to as Japan's "King of Inventors." But while his inventions and engineering skills were essential to Toyota's early success, his broader contribution to Toyota's development was his philosophy and his zeal for continuous improvement in all things. Interestingly, this philosophy, and ultimately the Toyota Way, was significantly influenced by his reading of a book, *Self-Help* by Samuel Smiles, first published in England in 1859.[1] It preaches the virtues of industry, thrift, and self-improvement, and was illustrated with stories of great inventors like James Watt, who helped develop the steam engine. The book so inspired Sakichi Toyoda that a copy of it is on display under glass in a museum at his birth site.

As I read Samuel Smiles's book, I could see how it influenced Toyoda. First, Smiles's inspiration for writing the book was philanthropic, not to make money. Smiles hoped the book would help young men in difficult economic circumstances who wanted to improve themselves. Second, the book chronicles inventors whose natural drive and inquisitiveness led to great inventions that changed the course of humanity. For example, Smiles concludes that the success and impact of James Watt did not originate from his natural abilities—but rather through hard work, perseverance, and discipline. These are exactly the traits displayed by Sakichi Toyoda in making his power looms work with steam engines. There are many examples throughout Smiles's book of "management by facts" and the importance of getting people to pay attention actively—a hallmark of Toyota's approach to problem solving—which is based on going to the gemba to observe the actual situation firsthand.

Sakichi Toyoda's personal and professional philosophy continues to influence Toyota today through what the company has distilled as his "five main principles":

1. Always be faithful to your duties, thereby contributing to the company and to the overall good.
2. Always be studious and creative, striving to stay ahead of the times.
3. Always be practical and avoid frivolousness.
4. Always strive to build a homelike atmosphere at work that is warm and friendly.
5. Always have respect for spiritual matters and remember to be grateful at all times.

KIICHIRO TOYODA AND
THE FOUNDATION OF TPS

Sakichi Toyoda's "mistake-proof" loom became Toyoda's most popular model.
In 1929, he sent his son, Kiichiro, to England to negotiate the sale of the
patent rights to Platt Brothers, the premier maker of spinning and weaving
equipment. His son negotiated a price of 100,000 English pounds, and in
1930, he used that capital to start building the Toyota Motor Corporation.[2]

It is perhaps ironic that the founder of Toyota Motor Company, Kiichiro Toyoda, was frail and sickly as a boy, who many felt did not have the physical capacity to become a leader. But his father disagreed, and Kiichiro Toyoda persevered. When Sakichi Toyoda tasked his son with building a business of his own, it was not to increase the family fortune. He could just as well have handed over to him the family loom business. He expected his son to make his own mark on the world. He explained to Kiichiro:

Everyone should tackle some great project at least once in their life. I devoted
most of my life to inventing new kinds of looms. Now it is your turn. You
should make an effort to complete something that will benefit society.[3]

Kiichiro's father sent him to the prestigious Tokyo Imperial University to study mechanical engineering, where he focused on engine technology. Kiichiro worked in his father's company and helped him to complete the first fully automated loom. He also went overseas to study loom making for one year in the United States and then for two years working at the Platt Brothers loom company in England. The Platt Brothers were world renowned in loom making, and it was there that the seeds of Kiichiro's ideas for TPS developed. Kiichiro Toyoda was never a great student, so he compensated by taking excellent notes and making detailed sketches. When working for the Platt Brothers loom company in England, he sketched the walking patterns of workers—which enabled him to identify a great deal of waste. He timed both the workers' actions and every step of the loom-making process. He was unimpressed by what he observed: "The workmen act as if they're half playing around; it takes them a long time to do something. They're only working about 3 out of 8 hours."* He also noticed

---

* For a brief history of Kiichiro Toyoda, see Jeffrey Liker, "Toyota and Kiichiro Toyoda: Building a Company and Production System Based on Values," Chapter 16 in *Handbook of East Asian Entrepreneurship*, edited by Fu-Lai Tony Yu and Ho-Don Yan (New York: Routledge, 2015). A more detailed history is in K. Wada and T. Yui, *Courage and Change: The Life of Kiichiro Toyoda* (Tokyo: Toyota Motor Company, 2002).

that the poor layout of the plant floor led to additional waste. For example, the biggest part of the workman's job was rework to fit parts together that did not fit properly at assembly, which was in the center of the shop. But the fitting required a vise and other tools that were located around the walls of the assembly shop. Throughout the day, the workman had to walk over with the part to file it down and then go back and forth to assembly until it fit. Kiichro Toyoda's insights from seeing these wastes led him to make improvements in the Toyota Loom Works manufacturing process, and later provided seminal ideas in the development of the Toyota Production System in automotive manufacturing.

Kiichiro's belief in the power of learning by doing at the gemba mirrored that of his father. After World War II, Kiichiro wrote, "I would have grave reservations about our ability to rebuild Japan's industry if our engineers were the type who could sit down to take their meals without ever having to wash their hands."

Along the way to building a car company, World War II happened, and Japan lost. The American victors could have halted car production. Kiichiro Toyoda was very concerned that the postwar occupation forces would shut down his company. The opposite occurred. The Americans realized trucks were needed to rebuild Japan, and they even purchased Toyota trucks, which helped Toyoda to expand production and establish a new plant in Koroma (later named Toyota City).

Kiichiro incorporated three principles that he developed in the loom company to become the core of TPS: just-in-time, jidoka (from his father), and standardization of processes and labor harmony.

Just-in-Time

In 1938, in the industry magazine *Motor*, Kiichiro wrote the golden words that headline this section: just-in-time (JIT). Wada and Yui[4] argue that Kiichiro created JIT because missing trains in England made him realize that arriving one second early wasted time and arriving one second late meant he missed the train. In fact, he missed the train on his first day of work at the Platt Brothers.

Toyoda's vision for the Koromo plant was to eliminate the need for a warehouse. In preparation, he developed a four-inch-thick binder that described in meticulous detail how the system should operate—which later was the basis for the kanban system that was developed and refined by Ohno. At the outset, slips of paper were used. For example, managers, using the plan for building engines that day, called for the exact number of castings from inventory that would be needed. As the castings moved through different stages of machining, slips of paper authorized production and movement to the next stage. His cousin, Eiji Toyoda, who had the task of introducing the new system, explained:

What Kiichiro had in mind was to produce the needed quantity of the required parts each day. To make this a reality, every single step of the operation, like it or not, had to be converted over to his flow production system. Kiichiro referred to this as the Just-In-Time concept.[5]

Built-in Quality

Kiichiro embraced his father's andon concept and took it a step further. He realized that in order for JIT to work, he needed quality built into the product at every step. A quality defect either would stop production because there were no inventory buffers or would require rework at the end of the line like what he saw at the Platt Brothers. In fact, in the early stages of automotive production, Toyota was doing an enormous amount of rework after the vehicles were built. Eiji Toyoda (later president and then chairman) was responsible for putting Kiichiro's production system into practice in a machinery shop in the plant. In his biography, he explained:

Each shop had three managers, of which one was responsible for inspection. Kiichiro's intention here was to catch any defective product and correct whatever processes were at fault. The task of the inspection manager was not simply to differentiate between a good and bad product, but to find a way to fix whatever had to be fixed. After the war, we studied quality control and actively incorporated this concept into our operations. The basic idea behind QC of "creating product quality within the process" is essentially identical to Kiichiro's thinking.

Standardization of Processes and Labor Harmony

At Platt Brothers, Kiichiro noticed that the craft knowledge developed by individual workers who controlled processes often was not shared or codified across the shop floor—which created a variety of problems. Standardization was slow to come to the spinning industry. In 1912, one company, Kanebo, adopted a "scientific method" of documenting and standardizing operations. When Kiichiro learned about what Kanebo had done, he wanted to introduce that to the Toyoda spinning companies.

Workers intentionally kept their secrets from management to maintain some control—which was the situation at Toyoda Boshoku's spinning factory when Kiichiro first joined the company in 1921. Kiichiro observed that "the standard methods the spinning technicians were keeping to themselves were something akin to professional secrets."[6]

At first, Kiichiro had to learn these "secrets" on his own, and he spent a whole year studying the jobs. He also learned from Toyoda Boshoku's sister company, Kikui Boshoku, which had been started with the philosophy of labor-management harmony and gave shares of the company to employees.

As time went on, Kiichiro worked hard to improve poor labor-management relations; he saw it as critical in building the right culture. Standardized work in Toyota is considered essential for continuous improvement, and continuous improvement depends on all workers sharing what they learn—from both successes and failures.

CONTINUITY OF PHILOSOPHY

As the economy revitalized under the occupation, Toyota had little difficulty getting sales orders, but rampant inflation eroded the value of money, and getting paid by customers was very difficult. Cash flow became so horrendous that at one point in 1948, Toyota's debt was eight times its total capital value.[7] To avoid bankruptcy and in lieu of layoffs, Toyota adopted strict cost-cutting policies, including voluntary pay cuts by managers and a 10 percent salary reduction for all employees. Unfortunately, the pay cuts were not enough. Despite a policy against firing employees, Kiichiro Toyoda was forced to ask for 1,600 workers to "retire" voluntarily—an action that led to work stoppages and public demonstrations by workers, which at the time were becoming commonplace across Japan.

Companies go out of business every day. Often, we hear stories of CEOs of failing enterprises taking no responsibility for bad decisions and fighting for huge golden parachutes. Kiichiro Toyoda took a different approach. He accepted responsibility for the demise of the automobile company and resigned as president. His personal sacrifice helped to quell worker dissatisfaction. More workers voluntarily left the company, and labor peace was restored. However, his tremendous personal sacrifice had a more profound impact on the history of Toyota. Everyone in Toyota knew what he did and why. The philosophy of Toyota to this day is to think beyond individual concerns to the long-term good of the company, as well as to take responsibility for problems. Kiichiro Toyoda was leading by example in a way that is unfathomable to most contemporary business executives.

No matter how emotionally charged an event might be, Toyota will take time to reflect and learn. In this case, Kiichiro's resignation was largely driven by money lenders who insisted that Kiichiro lay off people, even though Kiichiro had earlier promised the union that he would not lay off more people. The money lenders then pressured Kiichiro to resign. The lesson learned by Toyota from this episode was to never again allow an outside agent to determine its fate. The principle became self-reliance. Hino describes Toyota documents that illustrate its perspective on borrowing money:[8]

Financial Rule 1

Know that all loans are fearsome enemies.

No enemy is more terrible than money, and no friend is more trustworthy. Other people's money—borrowed money—quickly turns into an enemy. Money is a trustworthy ally only when it is your own; only when you earn it yourself.

It is all too common today for new leaders to arrive and put their personal stamp on the company. Out with the old and in with their new. As Toyota developed a distinctive culture, Toyoda family members built on the past and the philosophies that served the company through its inception and growth, creating a company DNA that continues today under Akio Toyoda's leadership. They all learned to get their hands dirty, embraced challenges enthusiastically, learned the spirit of innovation, understood the values of the company in contributing to society, and committed to self-reliance. Moreover, they shared a vision of creating a special company that would endure through successive generations.

After Kiichiro Toyoda, one of the Toyoda family leaders who shaped the company was Eiji Toyoda, the nephew of Sakichi and younger cousin of Kiichiro. Eiji Toyoda also studied mechanical engineering, entering Tokyo Imperial University in 1933. When he graduated, his cousin Kiichiro assigned him the task of building, all by himself, a research lab in a "car hotel" in Shibaura.[9]

A car hotel is a large parking garage. At the time, Toyota and other firms jointly owned many of these facilities, because they felt the "hotels" were necessary to encourage car ownership among the small number of wealthy individuals who could afford cars. Eiji Toyoda started by cleaning a room in one corner of the building and obtaining basic furniture and drafting boards. He worked alone until he got his bearings and then built a group of 10 people by the end of year one. His first task was to research machine tools, which he knew nothing about. He was also charged with checking and servicing defective cars and developing Toyota's initial quality control process. In his spare time, he investigated companies that could make auto parts for Toyota. Toyota was mostly purchasing parts from the United States and wanted to localize its supply chain.

So Eiji Toyoda, like his cousin and uncle, grew up believing that the only way to get things done was to do it yourself and get your hands dirty. When a challenge arose, the answer was to try things—to learn by doing.

Eventually Eiji Toyoda became (as mentioned earlier) the president and then chairman of Toyota Motor Manufacturing. He helped lead and then presided over the company during its most vital years of growth after World War II and through its expansion into a global powerhouse. Eiji Toyoda played a key role in selecting and empowering the leaders who shaped sales, manufacturing, and product development—perhaps, most notably, Taiichi Ohno, who led the creation of the Toyota Production System. Taiichi Ohno was unusually strong willed and aggressive for Toyota culture, and arguably he survived and gained influence under the protective cover of Eiji Toyoda.

THE OHNO PRODUCTION SYSTEM

In the 1930s, Toyota's leaders visited Ford and GM to study their assembly lines. They carefully read Henry Ford's book *Today and Tomorrow*.[10] They tested the conveyor system, precision machine tools, and economies-of-scale ideas in their loom production. Even before World War II, Toyota realized that the Japanese market was too small and demand too fragmented to support the high production volumes of US companies. A Ford auto line might produce 9,000 units per month, while Toyota would produce only about 900 units per month, which made Ford about nine times more productive. Toyota managers knew that if they were to survive in the long run, they would have to adapt the mass production approach for the Japanese market. But how?

Taiichi Ohno, who at the time was managing a Toyota machining plant for engine parts, was given the challenge of matching the productivity of Ford. Based on the mass production paradigm of the day, and given that Ford was nine times as productive, the economies of scale alone should have made this an impossible feat for tiny Toyota. This was David trying to take on Goliath. And like David, Ohno succeeded. He built on the concepts of Kiichiro Toyota to develop lean manufacturing processes, which eventually led to TPS.

Ford's mass production system was designed to make huge quantities of a limited number of models. This is why all Model Ts were originally black. In contrast, Toyota needed to churn out low volumes of different models using the same assembly line, because consumer demand in Toyota's auto market was too low to support dedicated assembly lines for one vehicle. Ford had a great deal of cash and a large US and international market. Toyota had little cash and operated in a small country. With few resources and little capital, Toyota needed to turn cash around quickly (from receiving the order to getting paid), so it could pay suppliers. Toyota didn't have the luxury of taking cover under the high volume and economies of scale afforded by Ford's mass production system. It needed to adapt Ford's manufacturing system to simultaneously achieve high quality, low cost, short lead times, and flexibility. While Ohno and his team learned from other companies, especially Ford, they had to develop unique solutions given the nature of the challenges. Through the 1950s, Ohno evolved an approach that originally had no name and was referred to as Ohno's Production System, until it eventually was named the Toyota Production System.*

Henry Ford wrote great words about flow and the elimination of waste in his book *Today and Tomorrow*.[11] For example, in Chapter 8, entitled "Learning from Waste," he said:

> *Saving material because it is material, and saving material because it represents labor might seem to amount to the same thing. But the approach makes a deal of difference. We will use material more carefully if we think of it as labor. For instance, we will not so lightly waste material simply because we can reclaim it—for salvage involves labor. The ideal is to have nothing to salvage.*

While Henry Ford seemed to appreciate the value of flow, as his manufacturing system evolved with larger volumes spread across many departments, the assembly line seemed to be the only place where flow was visible. Most of Ford's system was based on pushing large batches of material into huge inventory piles and then on to the next process.

Like Kiichiro before him, Ohno knew he could not afford to tie up cash in inventory, and he wanted to extend one-piece flow beyond the final assembly line. He successfully experimented with a one-piece flow cell in machining (Principle 2), but he still had to deal with all the materials coming into the cell, particularly those from inherent batch processes like casting. To connect batch processes, or distant processes from suppliers, to assembly, he extended Kiichiro's JIT concept into a direct communication mechanism called "kanban." Kanban means a sign or signal. Physically at that time the kanban was a card that was used by the downstream process—the direct customer—to pull material from the upstream process when workers were ready for more (Principle 3).

Some say this pull system was inspired by American supermarkets. In any well-run supermarket, individual items are replenished as each item begins to run low on the shelf. That is, material replenishment is initiated by consumption. Applied to a shop floor, it means that Step 1 in a process shouldn't make (replenish) its parts until the next process (Step 2) utilizes its original supply of parts from Step 1 (down to a small amount of "safety stock"). In TPS, when Step 2 is down to a small amount of safety stock, it triggers a pull signal to Step 1 asking for more parts.

---

* A succinct and informative discussion of the history of the Toyota Production System is provided in Takahiro Fujimoto's book, *The Evolution of a Manufacturing System at Toyota* (New York: Oxford University Press, 1999).

When Ohno and his team emerged from the shop floor with a new manufacturing system, it wasn't simply a set of tools to solve a problem for one company in a particular market and culture. What they had created was a new paradigm in manufacturing and service delivery—a new way of seeing, understanding, and interpreting what is happening in a production process—that ultimately led to the demise of traditional mass production in many respects and the rise of lean production.

THE SEVEN WASTES: OBSTACLES TO VALUE-ADDED FLOW

I mentioned that Kiichiro was very disappointed with all the waste he saw at the Platt Brothers' plant. While he was impressed by the final quality, it came at the expense of a lot of waste, including a great deal of rework filing down parts to get them to fit together. Within TPS, one-piece flow is the ideal to strive toward: pure value added from the start to the delivery to the customer—without interruption and without rework. The blockages to flow are all waste. Toyota categorized seven major types of non-value-adding waste in manufacturing processes, which are described below. In addition to production lines, with some small modifications, you can apply these ideas to product development, software development, operations of hospitals, and any office process.

1. **Overproduction.** Producing ahead of or in anticipation of demand, which generates such wastes as overstaffing and unnecessary storage and transportation costs because of excess inventory.
2. **Waiting (time on hand).** Watching or waiting for a machine, waiting for key inputs, or having slack with no immediate deadlines.
3. **Unnecessary transport or conveyance.** Carrying work in process (WIP) long distances, creating inefficient transport, or moving materials or information into or out of storage or between processes.
4. **Overprocessing or incorrect processing.** Taking unneeded steps to process the parts. Inefficiently processing due to poor tool and product design, causing unnecessary motion and producing defects. Waste is also generated when providing higher-quality products or services than is necessary.
5. **Excess inventory.** Excess raw material, WIP, or finished goods causing longer lead times, obsolescence, damaged goods, transportation and storage costs, and delay. Also, extra inventory hides problems such as production imbalances, late deliveries from suppliers, defects, equipment downtime, and long setup times.

6. **Unnecessary movement.** Any wasted motion employees perform during their work, such as looking for, walking to, reaching for, or stacking parts, tools, etc.

7. **Defects.** Production of defects and correction. Repair or rework, scrap, replacement production, and inspection waste time, effort, and handling.

(In *The Toyota Way to Service Excellence*, we broaden this list of wastes for services.[12])

It may seem counterintuitive, but Ohno considered the fundamental waste to be overproduction, since it causes most of the other wastes. Producing more than the customer wants by any operation in the manufacturing process necessarily causes a buildup of inventory somewhere downstream—which means the material is just sitting around waiting to be processed in the next operation. Mass or larger-batch manufacturers might ask, "What's the problem with this, as long as people and equipment are producing parts?" The problem is that big buffers (inventory between processes) lead to other suboptimal behaviors, like reducing your motivation to continuously improve your operations. Why worry about preventive maintenance on equipment when shutdowns do not immediately affect final assembly anyway? Why get overly concerned about a few quality errors when you can just toss out defective parts? Because by the time a defective piece works its way to the later operation where an operator tries to assemble that piece, there may be weeks of bad parts in process and sitting in buffers.

Figure S.1 illustrates some of these wastes through a simple timeline for the process of casting, machining, and assembling. In most traditionally managed operations, much of the timeline is waste; yet the customary focus of improvement is limited to taking small amounts of time out of the value-added processes—for example, increasing the throughput of machines so they become more "efficient."

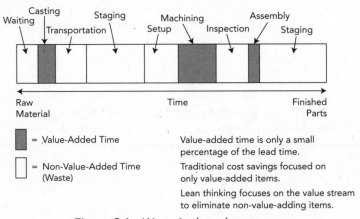

Figure S.1 Waste in the value stream.

I experienced an astonishing example of this while consulting for a manufacturer of steel nuts. The engineers and managers in my seminar assured me that their process could not benefit from lean manufacturing because it was so simple. Rolls of steel coil came in and were cut, tapped, heat-treated, and put into boxes. Material flew through the automated machines at the rate of hundreds of nuts a minute. When we followed the value (and non-value) stream, their claim became comical. We started at the receiving dock, and every time I thought the process must be finished, we walked across the factory one more time to another step or pile of inventory. At some point, the nuts left the factory for a few weeks to be heat-treated, because management had calculated that contracting out heat-treating was more economical. When all was said and done, the nut-making process that took seconds for most operations—except for heat-treating, which could take a few hours—typically took weeks and sometimes months for this manufacturer.

We calculated the percent value added for different product lines and got numbers ranging from 0.008 to 2 or 3 percent. Eyes opened! To make matters worse, equipment downtime was a common problem, idling machines and allowing for large buildups of material around them. Some clever manager had figured out that contracting outside maintenance was cheaper than hiring full-time people. So often there was nobody around to fix a machine when it went down, let alone do a good job on preventive maintenance. Local efficiencies were emphasized at the cost of slowing down the value stream by creating large amounts of in-process and finished-goods inventory and taking too much time to identify problems (defects) that reduced quality. As a result, costs were high, and the plant was not flexible to changes in customer demand.

In the original *Toyota Way*, I described an eighth waste, unused employee creativity, which I still think is perhaps the most fundamental waste. But it does not fit cleanly into this list. The seven wastes are obstacles to flow and are observable, while waste of employee creativity is a broader concept of what could have been. Throughout the book, I emphasize the centrality of continuous improvement at all levels to reduce waste in the process and how Toyota develops people to use their creativity.

STRIVING TOWARD A FUTURE STATE: THE ROLE OF VALUE STREAM MAPPING

The traditional approach to process improvement focuses on identifying local inefficiencies and making point improvements. For example, go to the equipment or value-added processes, and improve uptime, make it cycle faster, or replace the person with automated equipment. The result might be a significant percent improvement for that individual process, but it often has little impact on the overall value stream. In contrast, lean thinking focuses much of its attention on reducing the non-value-added.

Inside Toyota, the group tasked with teaching TPS to suppliers developed a way of visualizing at a high level the flow of material and information and identifying the big wastes. This technique was made available to the public through the bestselling book *Learning to See* by Mike Rother and former Toyota manager John Shook.[13] You pick a starting point in the value stream, often at the beginning of one large unit, such as the receiving docks in a manufacturing plant, and walk the value stream as the product is transformed—and draw a diagram of the journey. At first you are mostly documenting individual processes that push into inventory, represented by triangles, or time waiting in a queue. There is usually so much waste in the process, it can be humorous.

Figure S.2 is a generic example of a current-state map (I did not include data). Once you see all the inventory, which is one of the seven wastes, you may want to reduce inventory. A simple way to do this is to calculate minimum and maximum levels and create a visual with instructions to replenish when you reach the minimum. This is a simple type of pull system. Inventory will probably decrease. You now have eliminated waste—congratulations! But what is the purpose? This isolated action may not help much.

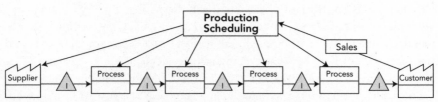

Figure S.2   Current-state value stream map.

Let's say that to be competitive your company needs to make a greater variety of products and shorten the order-to-delivery lead time so your customers can hold less inventory and still get what they want when they want it. You assemble a group of people with different specialties, including someone knowledgeable in lean concepts, and create a vision of a future state. What would the value stream need to look like to achieve your objectives?

The result might look something like the future-state map in Figure S.3. In this case, you designed a system of material flow that levels out the different products so you do not build batches of one product in the morning and batches of another product in the afternoon (Principle 4). You have eliminated scheduling of individual operations that tend to push lots of inventory and replaced the information flow with pull systems so each process only builds what the next process needs when it needs it (Principle 3). You probably would have to do other things to support the flow, like reduce the time to change over a machine between products and reduce equipment downtime. In value stream mapping, you show these other activities as point-kaizen bursts. The tendency is to go into the workplace and start to implement what is on the map, perhaps dividing into teams. Unfortunately, what you have in the future state is not a list of solutions to be implemented. Instead, what you have is a high-level picture of what you aspire to. You would be unlikely to get to this future-state vision if you simply chased wastes through point kaizen. And you probably will not achieve the overall vision the first time you try to implement lean tools. It is likely to take a set of experiments to try your ideas and learn your way to the future state.

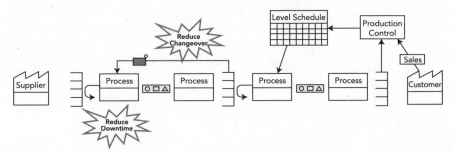

Figure S.3   Future-state value stream map.

Let's consider a service example. Thedacare emerged as one of the models for lean healthcare. In *On the Mend*,[14] its leaders describe examples of various parts of the system they improved. One example is inpatient care. Anyone like waiting a long time to get checked in? They mapped out the current state, in this case following the journey of a patient, rather than materials. They found large periods of wait time, such as waiting for a room, waiting for tests, and waiting for the doctor to arrive. Not only was this waiting annoying to patients, but it could be dangerous because it delayed providing healthcare. But instead of jumping in and eliminating waste in the current state, Thedacare spent months developing a vision for the future state:

> *In early 2007, a core team of nurses, pharmacists, administrators, social workers, and physicians was assigned to work for six months on redesigning the inpatient care process—addressing the facility design, the work duties, and the specialized skills of everyone involved. . . . The new unit, operational since late 2007, is essentially a large square, with all patient rooms facing an open meeting area where healthcare teams meet to confer on patient care. . . . Now, in the Collaborative Care unit, a nurse, physician, and pharma-*

cist gather with the patient and family within 90 minutes of admission to develop a care plan.[15]

The result was a dramatic reduction in wait times, better care plans, better-quality patient treatment, and lower costs. While huge amounts of waste were eliminated, that was not the focus of the effort. It was to improve overall patient care. It took a reimagining of the future state as a guide and then systematic improvement in the direction of that vision. This is the difference between cleaning up what exists and striving to achieve a bold new vision.

As Rother and Shook point out,[16] always develop a future state to strive for. Don't stop at mapping the current state and chasing waste. In *Toyota Kata Culture*, Rother and Aulinger challenge us to view the future-state value stream map as a set of nested challenges so each level of the organization understands what it needs to achieve to support the next level up from individual processes to the high-level value stream.[17] These challenges are beyond what we know today and need to be achieved through relentless PDCA. Each PDCA cycle is another experiment—hypothesize, test, reflect, and learn.

CONCLUSION

To understand the Toyota Way, we must start with the Toyoda family. They were innovators, they were pragmatic idealists, they learned by doing, and they always believed in the mission of contributing to society. They were relentless in achieving their goals. Most importantly, they were leaders who led by example.

TPS evolved to meet the particular challenges Toyota faced as it grew as a company. It evolved as Taiichi Ohno and his contemporaries put these principles to work on the shop floor through years of trial and error. When we take a snapshot of this at a point in time, we can describe the technical features and accomplishments of TPS. But the way that Toyota developed TPS, the challenges it faced, and the approach it took to solving these problems are really a reflection of the Toyota Way. Toyota's own internal *Toyota Way* document talks about the "spirit of challenge" and the acceptance of responsibility to meet that challenge. The document states:

> *We accept challenges with a creative spirit and the courage to realize our own dreams without losing drive or energy. We approach our work vigorously, with optimism and a sincere belief in the value of our contribution.*

And further:

> *We strive to decide our own fate. We act with self-reliance, trusting in our own abilities. We accept responsibility for our conduct and for maintaining and improving the skills that enable us to produce added value.*

These powerful words describe well what Ohno and the team accomplished. Out of the rubble of World War II, they accepted a seemingly impossible challenge—match Ford's productivity. Ohno accepted the challenge, and "with a creative spirit and courage," he solved problem after problem and evolved a new production system. This same process has been played out time and time again throughout the history of Toyota.

KEY POINTS

- The Toyota Way and the Toyota Production System evolved out of decades of practice and of learning to address the specific problems Toyota faced.
- The Toyota Production System is a system of people, equipment, and work methods aligned to achieve the objectives of the business. At a general level, these are quality, cost, delivery, safety, and morale.
- The goal of TPS is often defined as eliminating waste, but simply chasing waste will not create a high-performing system.
- A better approach is to develop a vision of a system that will achieve the organization's goals and then systematically strive to achieve that vision through kaizen. Always make the purpose clear.
- Value stream mapping is one tool that helps to understand the current state and to develop a high-level vision of how material and information needs to flow to achieve business objectives. This vision provides you a direction to strive toward through relentless PDCA.

Notes

1. Samuel Smiles, *Self Help* (Canton, OH: Pinnacle Press, 2017).
2. Fujimoto, 1999.
3. Edwin Reingold, *Toyota: A Corporate History* (London: Penguin Business, 1999).
4. Kazuo Wada and Tsunehiko Yui, *Courage and Change: The Life of Kiichiro Toyoda*, Toyota Motor Company, 2002.
5. Eiji Toyoda, *Toyota: Fifty Years in Motion* (New York: Kodansha International, 1985), p. 58.

6. Wada and Yui, 2002, p. 116.

7. Reingold, 1999.

8. Satoshi Hino, *Inside the Mind of Toyota: Management Principles for Enduring Growth* (New York: Productivity Press, 2002).

9. Toyoda, 1987.

10. Henry Ford, *Today and Tomorrow* (London, UL. CRC Press, Taylor & Francis Group, 1926/1988).

11. Henry Ford, 1926/1988.

12. Jeffrey Liker and Katherine Ross, *The Toyota Way to Service Excellence* (New York: McGraw-Hill, 2016).

13. Mike Rother and John Shook, *Learning to See* (Boston, MA: Lean Enterprise Institute, 1999).

14. John Toussaint and Roger Gerard, with Emily Adams, *On the Mend: Revolutionizing Healthcare to Save Lives and Transform the Industry* (Cambridge, MA: Lean Enterprise Institute, 2010).

15. Touissant and Gerard, 2010, pp. 22–23.

16. Rother and Shook.

17. Mike Rother and Gerd Aulinger, *Toyota Kata Culture* (New York: McGraw-Hill, 2017).

PART ONE

PHILOSOPHY

Long-Term Systems Thinking

Principle 1

Base Your Management Decisions on Long-Term Systems Thinking, Even at the Expense of Short-Term Financial Goals

The most important factors for success are patience, a focus on long-term rather than short-term results, reinvestment in people, product, and plant, and an unforgiving commitment to quality.
—Robert B. McCurry, former Executive VP, Toyota Motor Sales

Over the last century, the world has moved in the direction of capitalism as the dominant socioeconomic system. The prevailing belief is that as individuals and companies pursue their self-interests, the invisible hand of supply and demand will lead to innovation, economic growth, and the overall economic well-being of humanity. The evidence is clear that money motivates business activity and innovation, but it is also clear that it motivates mostly short-term results. While it is comforting to think we can each simply do what is best for our pocketbooks in the short term and all will be well in the world, there is a dark side to the pursuit of self-interest as the engine for economic growth. We saw it as Enron and other scandals left in their wake an extreme distrust of large corporations and the morality of corporate executives. We saw it in the Great Recession when the moneymaking scheme of subprime mortgages led to millions of people losing their jobs and homes. We see it in the huge economic inequality throughout the world. And we are seeing it as nations struggle to focus resources on fighting the existential threat of human-induced global warming, with many interested parties denying it is even real.

In a fascinating article in the *Atlantic*, Yale professor Daniel Markovits attributes this profit focus, and the shrinking of the middle class, to large consulting firms.[1] He goes back to post–World War II when business was booming and the idea of a job for life was common.

The mid-century corporation's workplace training and many-layered hierarchy built a pipeline through which the top jobs might be filled. The saying "from the mail room to the corner office" captured something real, and even the most menial jobs opened pathways to promotion.

Much of this pathway to the top ended as professional executives were hired from outside and worked with large consulting firms to cut labor costs and "rationalize" the enterprise:

When management consulting untethered executives from particular industries or firms and tied them instead to management in general, it also led them to embrace the one thing common to all corporations: making money for shareholders. Executives raised on the new, untethered model of management aimed exclusively and directly at profit: their education, their career arc, and their professional role conspire to isolate them from other workers and train them single-mindedly on the bottom line.

Toyota apparently did not get the memo. The primary company mission is still to add value to society. It invests in its team members, value chain members, and local communities. It begins by providing employees with a stable income. Profits will come, but they are an input to Toyota's broader purpose—and definitely are not the ultimate goal. Outdated thinking? Yesterday's news? Need a consulting firm to rationalize them? When we understand how interconnected and uncertain the world is, we can begin to see the business case for a more people-centered way of thinking and acting for the long term.

Toyota, for a variety of reasons, traces its roots to leaders who were natural systems thinkers. For example, any knowledgeable Toyota leader today will emphasize that the Toyota Production System is a system. The parts are all interconnected. Just-in-time exposes problems, but it is only useful if people are trained and motivated to solve problems. Daily problem solving leads to stable operations, a requirement for effective just-in-time. Remove one part, and the house will degrade and eventually collapse. To run a successful business, Toyota believes it needs every piece of the system to function at a high level, which means having the best people and processes in place, and everyone working to continuously improve in a common direction and toward a shared goal. As David Hanna asserts in his seminal book, *Designing Organizations for High Performance*, one of the key tenets of systems thinking is design for purpose.[2] It requires companies to ask: "Why does our organization exist? What is our long-term vision?"

In a meeting of Toyota investors on May 12, 2020, after it was revealed that because of the Covid-19 crisis, forecasted profits would be 80 percent below those of 2019, Akio Toyoda explained his priorities for the company:

As for the immediate crisis, the priorities are the same we always have at Toyota: first safety, second quality, third volume, and fourth profit-making. As times change, these priorities may need to be revisited. But, in the midst of this crisis, our traditional prioritization has continued to be very important. And based upon these priorities, we will try to develop the Toyota people, and this is also very important.[3]

His chief risk officer then elaborated:

We cannot stop investment in the future. This is one of the things that you have to continue forever, and it has to be supported with proper funding. At the time of the Great Recession, we had JPY3 trillion cash on hand. Today, we have JPY8 trillion cash on hand. This is still smaller than we'd like: Apple, for example, has JPY20 trillion. All companies experience ups and downs, of course, but expenditures in the future will be necessary to fund continued growth while ensuring we also continue to contribute to society. . . . However, I am keeping a keen eye on spending. If I see any wasteful spending, I will cut it.

A reason Toyota could continue investing in the future was because it had the highest amount of cash on hand in its history, which by late 2019 had grown to over $50 billion. I have referred to this as saving for a rainy day, though it should be noted that it is not simply hoarding, but investing in human resources and strategically in the future of the company . . . for the long term. This seems like such an obvious virtue. I was reminded how unusual it is when corporate financial advisor Stephen Givens, in an opinion piece in the *Nikkei Asian Review*, reprimanded this very practice: "Japanese companies must stop gloating about cash-hoarding. They should be returning money to shareholders instead of letting it pile up for a rainy day."[4]

His rationale was that successful modern corporations prove their worth through the investments shareholders are willing to make in purchasing stock:

In a healthy and dynamic economy, a CEO must constantly return to the equity markets for fresh capital. The CEO's ability to raise fresh capital depends on being able to show investors that prior rounds resulted in attractive returns. . . . Instead, Japanese CEOs have been liberated to appeal to fuzzy performance metrics—sustainable development goals, creating social value, fulfilling obligations to our (non-shareholder) stakeholders.

There you have it. The purpose of a corporation is to enrich shareholders, not fuzzy goals like "creating social value." The only scorecard that matters is stock price. Given this purpose, Toyota is mediocre or worse. Its stock has rarely been a good short-term investment. Taking an opposing perspective, journalist Michael

Steinberger wrote of stock buybacks, a favored way of transferring earnings from the company to shareholders:

> *Whatever the reason, some estimates indicate that between buybacks and dividends, the largest U.S. companies returned roughly 90 percent of their earnings to shareholders in the last decade. That's money that could have been used to give employees a raise, or to increase spending on research and development, or to cushion a future downturn, but instead it went to investors.*[5]

Toyota's public relations policy is to avoid criticizing the philosophies of other companies, but its purpose is clear and unwavering: add value to customers and society for the long term, and in that it has been remarkably successful. This is not simply a do-good philosophy, but a sound business strategy. It is the right principle for building a sustainable company that lasts: *base your management decisions on long-term systems thinking, even at the expense of short-term financial goals.*

A SOCIETAL MISSION GREATER THAN EARNING A PAYCHECK

Can a modern corporation thrive in a capitalistic world and be profitable while doing the right thing for all its stakeholders and society, even if it means that short-term profits are not always the first goal? I believe that Toyota's biggest contribution to the corporate world is demonstrating this is indeed possible and, ultimately, is good for business.

Throughout my visits to Toyota in Japan and the United States, in every department—engineering, sales, purchasing, and manufacturing—one theme stands out. All the people I talked with have a sense of purpose greater than earning a paycheck. They feel a sense of mission for the company and can distinguish right from wrong with regard to that mission. They have learned the Toyota Way from more senior leaders and internalized the values: *Do the right thing for the company, its employees, the customer, and society as a whole.* Toyota's strong sense of mission and commitment to its customers, employees, and society *is the foundation for all the other principles* and the missing ingredient in most companies that try to emulate Toyota.

When I interviewed Toyota executives and managers for this book, I asked them why Toyota existed as a business. The responses were remarkably consistent. For example, Jim Press, former executive vice president and chief operating officer of Toyota Motor Sales in North America, explained:

The purpose of the money we make is not for us as a company to gain, and it's not for us as associates to see our stock portfolio grow or anything like that. The purpose is so we can reinvest in the future, so we can continue to do this. That's the purpose of our investment. And to help society and to help the community, and to contribute back to the community that we're fortunate enough to do business in. I've got a trillion examples of that.

This is not to say that Toyota does not care about cutting costs. As we discussed in the last chapter, Toyota's near bankruptcy after World War II and dismissal of workers led to the resignation of the company founder—Kiichiro Toyoda. After that experience, Toyota leaders pledged to become debt-free, and that requires aggressive cost-cutting. Cost reduction has been a passion since Taiichi Ohno began eliminating wasted motions on the shop floor. Often this led to removing a process from a line or cell, but that didn't and doesn't translate into removing employees. The person was and still today is placed in another job. As Toyota views it, that's one less worker that has to be hired and trained in the future.

Toyota has a rigorous Total Budget Control System, in which monthly data are used to monitor the budgets of all the divisions down to the tiniest expenditure. I asked many of the Toyota managers I interviewed if cost reduction is a priority, and they just laughed. Their answers amounted to "You haven't seen anything until you've experienced the cost-consciousness of Toyota—down to pennies."[6] Former Toyota manager Michael Hoseus tells the story of a trip to Japan when a Toyota manager opened his desk drawer and showed him a pencil. It was made up of several taped-together old pencils that had been used until they were too small to hold.

Yet cost reduction is not the underlying principle that drives Toyota. For example, Toyota would no sooner fire its employees because of a temporary downturn in sales than most of us would put our sons and daughters out on the street because we just lost money in a stock market downturn.

Professor Hirotaka Takeuchi and his students studied many such cases in Japan and concluded that a focus on the social good was a key asset in surviving crises. For example, the great earthquake of 2011 and accompanying tsunami devastated many businesses and manufacturing plants, and yet company after company kept its people employed to rebuild and provided goods and services free to the community. One such company, Yakult, manufactures probiotic drinks, and they are delivered directly to customers homes by "Yakult Ladies" (yes, gender bias is still alive in Japan). Despite losing 30 percent of sales, Yakult's CFO Hiromi Watanabe reassured employees that the company would do everything possible to retain jobs, deliver food and drink to victims, and contribute to the recovery of the community, even if it meant "using all cash and earning reserves of the company." Professor Takeuchi reports:[7]

> *He distributed $300 in cash to each Yakult Lady from the company's safe, since banks were closed; used the firm's delivery center as a temporary shelter for employees and their families; and guaranteed jobs to the Yakult Ladies forced to evacuate their homes. When the supply of the probiotic drinks dwindled due to the Yakult factory shutting down and the Yakult Ladies ran out of products to deliver, some decided on their own to deliver water and instant noodles to their customers, for free. When Watanabe found out, he urged the workers to deliver more items to victims at shelters.*

Putting the community and customers first is also in the DNA of Toyota. The company is like an organism nurturing itself, constantly protecting and growing its offspring, so that it can continue to contribute to customers, communities, and society. In this day and age of cynicism about the ethics of corporate officers and the place of large capitalistic corporations in civilized society, the Toyota Way provides an alternative model of the great things that happen when you align almost 400,000 people to a common purpose that is bigger than making money.

THE NUMMI STORY: RESEARCH TO UNDERSTAND HOW TO EXPORT TPS OVERSEAS

In the early 1980s, Toyota realized it needed to build cars where it would sell them if it wanted to become a viable global company, but it was deeply concerned about how to bring TPS overseas. Could it translate outside Japanese culture? In 1972, Toyota had set up a small operation in California to make truck beds, referred to as TABC, where it introduced TPS successfully. But an entire vehicle manufacturing and assembly plant was a different animal. It is natural for Toyota to learn by doing, and it is always willing to experiment. The company thought there was value in a partnership and in 1984 launched a 50-50 joint venture with General Motors that became New United Motor Manufacturing, Inc., or NUMMI. Toyota was to teach GM the principles of the Toyota Production System. Toyota agreed to take over a light truck factory in Fremont, California, which had been closed by GM in 1982, and run it according to TPS principles. They also agreed to accept the United Auto Worker's union. Toyota lawyer Dennis Cuneo, who later became senior VP of Toyota Motor Manufacturing North America, was an attorney for Toyota at the time. He explains some of the challenges:

The perception that everybody had at that time was that the Toyota Production System just worked people to death. It was just basically "Speed up!" In fact, I remember the first meeting we had in the union hall with union leadership and there was this gentleman by the name of Gus Billy. He was sitting at the end of the table and we were talking about the Toyota Production System and kaizen, etc. He said, "It sounds like a production speed-up to me. It's the whole concept of making all these suggestions, trying to suggest your way out of a job."

Gus Billy's hostile attitude was widely shared by other workers. When the plant was run by GM, the union local had the reputation of being militant and had even called for illegal wildcat strikes. Workers would intentionally sabotage vehicles. Drugs, alcohol, and prostitution ran rampant. One supervisor was pushed by a worker in front of a moving forklift truck and other workers pointed and laughed.[8] Nevertheless, when Toyota and GM formed NUMMI, the United Auto Workers came as part of the package deal. The agreement included a commitment to hire back up to 85 percent of the former GM workers. Against the advice of GM, Toyota decided to bring back the original UAW local leadership who were largely responsible for the militant attitude of the workforce. Cuneo says:

I think it surprised GM. Some of the labor relations staff advised us not to. We took a calculated risk. We knew that the former GM workforce needed leadership—and the Shop Committee comprised the natural leaders of that workforce. We had to change their attitudes and opinions. So we sent the shop committee to Japan for three weeks. They saw firsthand what the TPS was all about. And they came back "converted" and convinced a skeptical rank and file that this Toyota Production System wasn't so bad.

Toyota shocked the automotive world when the old factory reopened in 1984 and in its first year surpassed all of GM's plants in North America in productivity, cost, and quality.[9] It is often used as an example of how TPS can be successfully applied even in a unionized US plant with workers who had grown up in the adversarial labor-management culture of General Motors. Cuneo explained that the key was building trust with the workers:

We built trust early on with our team members. GM had problems selling the Nova in 1987 to '88, and they substantially cut the orders to our plant. We had to reduce production and were running at about 75 percent capacity, but we didn't lay anybody off. We put people on kaizen teams and found other useful tasks for them. Of all the things we did at NUMMI, that did the most to establish trust.

According to Cuneo, GM's initial motivation for entering the venture was to outsource production of a small car. As GM learned more about TPS, the company became more interested in using NUMMI as a learning laboratory. Hundreds of GM's executives, managers, and engineers visited NUMMI and were impressed by the teachings of TPS and brought back lessons to their jobs at GM. In the late 1990s through about 2003, I visited several GM plants in the United States and China and discovered that the bible for manufacturing they used was a version of the Toyota Production System, first written by Mike Brewer, an early "alum" of NUMMI, who was sent by GM to learn TPS. After several versions, GM's "Global Manufacturing System" was a direct copy of the Toyota Production System.

Unfortunately, it took about 15 years for GM to take the lessons of NUMMI seriously, beyond words and into action. When it finally made a concerted effort to embrace what it learned from Toyota, it took GM about five years before productivity and quality improved corporatewide (as seen in the auto industry's *Harbour Reports* and customer surveys by J. D. Powers and *Consumer Reports*).

You might ask, "Why would Toyota teach its coveted lean manufacturing system to a major competitor, GM?" At the time, Toyota's purpose was to learn how to bring TPS to life in American culture. Toyota leaders thought there was value in having an American partner with a supply base, administrative and legal systems, and an understanding of America. Toyota offered to teach TPS in exchange. Now Toyota teaches TPS to many organizations, including to not-for-profit companies and charitable organizations for free.

But why teach a competitor? Toyota believes competition is good for everyone and is willing to help other automakers when they are struggling. For example, Toyota shared hybrid technology with Ford and Nissan when each company was struggling, and more recently opened all its hybrid patents, based on its belief in the value of competition. Part of the spirit of "challenge," as described in *The Toyota Way 2001* (a document that lays out Toyota's philosophy), is valuing competition. Toyota will "learn from the challenge and become stronger because of it." When American auto companies were struggling in the 1980s, Toyota was concerned it might become too dominant. Executive Vice President Yale Gieszl, speaking as the American companies in the 1980s were discovering quality methods and strengthening sales, is quoted in *The Toyota Way 2001* as saying:

> *We at Toyota welcome Detroit's resurgence and this fierce competition. First, because it proves that auto makers can learn from one another. Second, because competition drives the continuous improvement that is the best guarantee of corporate survival. Third, because competition is the only way*

we can assure a strong growing economy. And finally, because competition benefits all of our customers by providing the improved products they have a right to expect.

THE TOYOTA WAY 2001 AS THE GUIDING PHILOSOPHY

For most of Toyota's existence, there was no talk about the "Toyota Way." It was simply the way things were. Toyota was a Japanese company that developed and produced vehicles in Japan, and employees of the company were hired, often as their first job, and stayed with the company until they retired. From their first day, employees were immersed in Toyota's way. They saw no reason to document the theory behind the culture. But all this changed as Toyota globalized. Fujio Cho, the first president of the Georgetown, Kentucky, plant and later president of Toyota Motor Company, saw the need to explain the Toyota Way to people overseas who did not grow up in the company. When he became president of Toyota in 1999, he led an effort to document and teach the Toyota Way and was instrumental in creating the first formal document on the subject in 2001.

The Toyota Way 2001, as it is still called, is defined as a house with two pillars—respect for people and continuous improvement (see Figure 1.1). Respect for people extends from the team members on the shop floor to every one of Toyota's vast network of partners, to its customers, and to the communities in which Toyota does business. Some versions of the model show respect for people as the foundation of continuous improvement, because only highly developed people who care passionately about their work and about the company will put in the effort needed for continuous improvement. Continuous improvement literally means continually improving products, processes, and people at all levels of the organization. Note that continuous improvement does not only refer to small, incremental change. In fact, senior executives take responsibility for large, transformative changes, such as transforming the company to face the new age of electrified, autonomous vehicles. Toyota recognizes that even large, transformative change is the result of solving thousands of smaller problems spread out over time. The twin pillars of respect for people and continuous improvement are further defined by a foundation of five core principles that we summarize here.

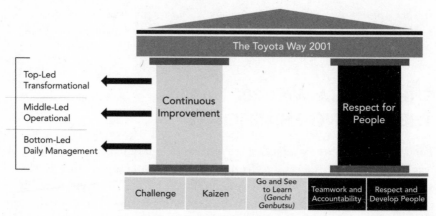

Figure 1.1   Toyota Way 2001 house.

Challenge

Toyota was founded on the willingness to tackle tough problems and work at them until they were solved. Every Toyota employee is expected not just to excel in his current role, but to work toward higher levels of performance with enthusiasm. Hoshin kanri, discussed under Principle 13, is a way of cascading challenging goals through all levels of the company. As *The Toyota Way 2001* puts it, "We accept challenges with a creative spirit and the courage to realize our own dreams without losing drive or energy."

Kaizen

Kaizen is a mandate to constantly improve performance for the better. Kaizen is now a fairly famous concept, and the term will be familiar to many readers. But the vast majority of people, we've found, misunderstand kaizen. Too often it has come to mean assembling a special team to tackle a discrete improvement project, or perhaps organizing a kaizen "event" for a week to make a burst of changes. At Toyota, kaizen isn't a set of projects or special events. It's the way people in the company work toward goals scientifically, harking back to Deming's never-ending PDCA (plan-do-check-act) cycles.

Genchi Genbutsu, or Go and See to Learn

It would seem that going to see something firsthand is simply a practical matter—although one that is infrequently practiced in most firms—rather than a value. The value of genchi genbutsu isn't necessarily the specific act of going and seeing, but the philosophy of deeply understanding the current condition before making a decision or trying to change something that you think will be an improvement. There are two main aspects of genchi genbutsu. First, decisions are made based on observed facts about the issue, rather than on hunches, assumptions, or perceptions. Second, decisions should be put into the hands of those closest to the problem and those who have gone to see it and have a deep understanding of its causes and the possible impact of proposed solutions.

In his Foreword to *The Toyota Way to Lean Leadership*, President Akio Toyoda explained his commitment to learning at the gemba:

> *In a speech I made shortly after becoming president in 2009 I vowed to be closest to the* gemba. *Whenever there are real objects there is a* gemba. *When customers drive our cars the* gemba *is how they are using our products and what works for them and what causes them difficulties. As the current leader of the company I must model the behavior I expect from others. Going to the* gemba *means observing firsthand how our products are being designed, built, used, and what problems we have. There are always problems because we are never perfect. The only way we can really understand the problems is at the* gemba.[10]

Teamwork and Accountability

Most companies say that teamwork is critical to success, but saying this is much easier than living it. At Toyota, the view is that individual success can happen only within the team and that strong teams require strong individuals. Critical to Toyota's success is single-point accountability. One person's name goes up next to each item in an action plan. But in order to succeed, the individual responsible must work with the team, draw on its collective talents, listen closely to all team members' opinions, work to build consensus, and ultimately give credit for success to the team.

Respect and Develop People

In many ways, this is the most fundamental of the core values. Respect for people starts with the desire to contribute to society through producing the best possible products and services. This extends to respect for the community, customers, employees, and all business partners.

For Toyota, respect does not mean encouraging a relaxing, work-at-your-own-pace environment. Toyota deliberately creates a steady flow of challenges for its people. The Toyota Production System, with its just-in-time system and andon to surface problems immediately, creates constant challenges on the shop floor. Toyota needs every employee to always be thinking about how to improve processes—continuous improvement—just to keep up with the demands of the highly competitive automobile business. That requires Toyota to invest in team members so that they can be problem solvers. It is these skills in deeply understanding the gemba, solving problems as they occur, and systematically improving through PDCA that make Toyota team members the company's most valuable asset. Thus, the scientific thinking skills of challenge, kaizen, and genchi genbutsu are integrally connected to respect and teamwork.

PUTTING THE TOYOTA WAY INTO PRACTICE IN THE GREAT RECESSION

Perhaps the most dramatic example of Toyota sticking to its core philosophy of respect for people and continuous improvement was during the Great Recession in 2008–2009. Even before the Lehman Brothers crisis, the auto industry was reeling from rapidly rising gasoline prices. By the summer of 2008, gasoline prices in the United States had almost doubled, topping the prices during the worst of the 1970s' oil crises on an inflation-adjusted basis. In most of the country, regular gasoline was going for more than $4 a gallon; in states such as California and New York, it was over $5. That meant that filling up the 20-gallon or larger tanks of large vehicles cost many people more than $100, a high enough threshold to make Americans question whether big was really better. Understandably, the sales of large vehicles all but came to a halt.

But then the bottom really fell out of the market in a way that Toyota did not anticipate. By the fall of 2008 there was no doubt that a major global recession was under way. Credit markets seized up, and suddenly no loans were available. That's truly a crisis for the automotive industry, since most vehicles are financed. Even consumers who still had access to credit or who could finance a car through other means stopped buying because they feared they might lose their jobs or decided it was a good time to reduce their debt burdens.

As each month passed, Toyota's North American year-over-year sales numbers plummeted further. By May 2009, sales were 40 percent below those of the previous year. To add insult to injury, the US dollar weakened in relation to the Japanese yen by 15 percent between July and December 2008. Every 1 percent reduction in the strength of the dollar translated to roughly a $36 million decline in operating income for Toyota in yen terms. As a result of the combined impact of plummeting sales and the currency adjustment, Toyota lost more than $4 billion in fiscal 2009 (April 2008 to April 2009), its first loss as a company since 1950. Vehicle sales plunged by 1.3 million units to 7.6 million units in 2009, the kind of drop in sales that would lead many companies to close plants and lay off workers.* Toyota had two plants in the United States that made large vehicles at the time, the Princeton, Indiana, plant made the Sequoia SUV and the Tundra, and in 2006 a new plant had been built near San Antonio, Texas, to also build the Tundra. Both saw sales drop by over 40 percent. Nonetheless, in the face of this calamity, Toyota kept both plants open and did not lay off regular workers. (A more detailed discussion of what happened is found in Chapter 2 of *Toyota Under Fire*.[11])

When the loss was announced, reporters began calling me daily to ask for a comment. "What will Toyota do now that it is in crisis?" "Whose decision was it to introduce the Tundra and build a new plant dedicated only to these large fuel guzzlers?" "Who is getting fired over the decision to build the new plant?" "Will the president be fired?"

Those are typical questions from the press when a company announces a $4 billion loss. We've become conditioned to the ways in which businesses react to losing money: executives lose their jobs; plants are closed down; people are laid off; projects are canceled; assets are sold. It's a fairly predictable recipe. In fact, it is the recipe that most of the automotive industry followed. Nissan, for instance, dumped 12 new models and laid off more than 20,000 people. A CNN article in July 2010 reported that the automobile industry in the United States alone laid off 300,000 workers because of plant closings.[12] The CEOs of Chrysler, GM, and Kia lost their jobs.

Early in the summer of 2008, when gas prices in the United States were skyrocketing, Toyota already had months of inventory of trucks and large SUVs. It decided to shut down the Indiana and Texas plants for three months from August through October (except Sienna minivan production in Indiana). Then the financial crisis hit . . .

In the winter of 2009, I decided to visit the Indiana and Texas plants to see for myself how Toyota was responding. Neither plant had laid off any regular "team members," though both had let go their "variable workforce." The variable workforce is employed by an outside agency that supplies temporary workers. For Toyota in the United States, these temporary workers can stay for up to two years and then must be either let go or made full-time. They provide a buffer that allows Toyota to offer what generally amounts to lifetime employment for the regular workforce. The temporary workers were let go during the downturn.

---

* We should note that in 2008, General Motors lost $30.9 billion, $9.6 billion in the fourth quarter alone. The firm's survival required that it be taken over by the US government and that it cut tens of thousands of jobs. Ford, meanwhile, lost almost $15 billion in 2008 and had already lost $30 billion in the three years since 2006.

Both plants had planned in advance how to deal with the three-month shutdown. They developed courses to be taught on the shop floor by group leaders and planned for intensive kaizen to achieve higher levels of performance for when the shutdown ended. When it only partly ended because of the recession, they operated at one shift instead of two. They pulled all the workers onto the day shift. While some worked production, others were training and working on kaizen. In Indiana the plant had an A team working production and a B team doing kaizen for half of each shift. In the middle of the shift, the teams reversed roles.

I learned that the managers had all given up their bonuses and took voluntary pay cuts months earlier, a development that was not even announced to the workforce by Toyota. When that was not enough, as part of a "shared pain" program, workers were required to take every other Friday off without pay.

What was striking during my visits was how busy everyone was, practically running from place to place. All the workers had a detailed schedule of things to do when they were not on production. One reason for the workload was that Toyota took this as an opportunity to move all Tundra production to Texas and bring the Highlander SUV from Japan to Indiana. There was a lot of work to do in both plants to prepare for the move, particularly in Texas because that plant would also be producing a brand-new Tundra model. To reduce costs, Indiana took a lot of the product launch work that would have been done by outside engineers and pulled it in-house. Workers were repurposing equipment where they could, saving Toyota much of the cost of carrying the extra team members. Team members learned to program robots so they could rebuild and reuse the old models they had instead of buying new ones.

One hourly employee, a team leader, explained it this way:

> *The difference between Toyota and the other companies is that instead of forcing us to go on unemployment, they are investing in us, allowing us to sharpen our minds. I don't think there's one person out there who doesn't realize what an incredible investment Toyota is making.*

As the new products were launched, the Indiana and Texas plants came back on stream, and eventually the company had to hire new workers. The experienced and committed employees that Toyota retained during the recession were now being asked to lead and train the new hires.

Not all was rosy, however. NUMMI became a casualty of the recession and General Motors' bankruptcy. In June 2009, the iconic plant was closed. After General Motors emerged from bankruptcy, it retained some assets, but it decided to let go of the NUMMI plant and its joint venture with Toyota. Toyota faced the choice to take over 100 percent of NUMMI or let it go. After agonizing discussions and attempts to find a new joint venture partner, Toyota shut it down, doing what it could like paying out severance to workers beyond the legal agreements.

SYSTEMS THINKING SEEMS TO COME NATURALLY IN TOYOTA

There are many possible reasons why Toyota's early leaders were systems thinkers. Sakichi Toyoda was a practicing Buddhist, a philosophy that tends to take a holistic perspective. The company was formed in a rice-growing region, and rice farming is complex, interacting with the environment, and requires cooperation among farmers. Japan is a small island nation that is tossed and turned by tsunamis and earthquakes; the impact of the environment is always visible. Whatever the reasons, Toyota leaders think long term and think in systems.

By "systems," I mean the parts interact in complex ways that make prediction and control difficult, if not impossible. This is why Toyota sees TPS as a system, and at its heart are people solving problems. If the world were simple, linear, and predictable, as the mechanistic world view suggests (see the Preface), we could forecast, schedule, develop elaborate rules and procedures, and expect the organization to behave according to our plans. Toyota never expects that to happen. Toyota recognizes that living systems are dynamic and unpredictable. People have to continually make adjustments as life happens. People trained in disciplined problem solving will make informed adjustments based on the facts of the situation.

Since Toyota leaders are natural systems thinkers, it allows them to make investments without always expecting a simple cause-and-effect relationship between the action and a bottom-line result. For example, Principle 4 is about leveling the schedule as the foundation of the Toyota Production System. Toyota works exceptionally hard at this, even when there is not a clear and direct effect on profits. Yet it is part of a system that over the long term consistently yields impressive profits.

Toyota's Global Vision 2020 focused on becoming a leader in "mobility," exceeding customer expectations, and, of course, engaging the talent and passion of its people.[13] While earlier visions focused on automobiles, the company broadened this vision to become the leader in many forms of mobility, including robots for assisting the disabled and people in hospitals, moon vehicles, and vehicles for single individuals. The document stated:

> ■ *Toyota will lead the future mobility society, enriching lives around the world with the safest and most responsible ways of moving people.*

- *Through our commitment to quality, ceaseless innovation, and respect for the planet, we strive to exceed expectations and be rewarded with a smile.*
- *We will meet challenging goals by engaging the talent and passion of people who believe there is always a better way.*

Systems thinking begins with a clear picture of the organization's purpose. Toyota's Global Vision and Guiding Principles (see Figures 1.2 and 1.3) make clear that the company must serve its customer with ever-better cars, but it cannot operate in a vacuum. Toyota must also contribute to society through new technologies and "enrich the lives of communities" where it does business. This is yet another reason why Toyota works so hard at maintaining job security and keeping manufacturing plants open. Communities and all the ancillary businesses that support Toyota are dependent on these well-paying jobs. Toyota challenges its workers to contribute to Toyota and make a mark on its history. Toyota genuinely wants its associates to grow, learn, and create lasting customer satisfaction—while contributing to the shared goal of getting repeat customers for life.

Toyota Guiding Principles	
1.	Honor the language and spirit of law of every nation and undertake open and fair corporate activities to be a good corporate citizen of the world
2.	Respect the culture and customs of every nation and contribute to economic and social development through corporate activities in the communities
3.	Dedicate ourselves to providing clean and safe products and to enhancing the quality of life everywhere through all our activities
4.	Create and develop advanced technologies and provide outstanding products and services that fulfill the needs of customers worldwide
5.	Foster a corporate culture that enhances individual creativity and teamwork value, while honoring mutual trust and respect between labor and management
6.	Pursue growth in harmony with the global community through innovative management
7.	Work with business partners in research and creation to achieve stable, long-term growth and mutual benefits, while keeping ourselves open to new partnerships

Figure 1.2 Guiding Principles of the Toyota Motor Corporation.
These principles were established in 1992 and revised in 1997.
(Translation from the original Japanese.)

will not match the deeds. Toyota's consistency of philosophy extends back to the founding of the firm. The culture runs unusually deep and is the foundation for excellence.

KEY POINTS

- Toyota's mission goes far beyond short-term profitability, and Toyota is willing to invest for the long term.
- Toyota thinks of its organization as a living sociotechnical system rather than mechanical parts guided by simple and direct cause-and-effect relationships. Investing in developing people allows them to locally control complex system dynamics.
- Toyota is a model for the world in demonstrating how doing the right thing is a profitable business strategy.
- What drives Toyota forward is people who believe there is always a better way and trust the company to do right by them.
- The foundation of team member trust is job security, and Toyota goes to unusual lengths to protect the jobs of its employees.
- The five foundational elements of *The Toyota Way 2001* drive continuous improvement in pursuing challenging goals through kaizen and a daily focus on developing people and teams.
- Toyota has a deliberate culture that is consistent across locations, levels, and time. Toyota walks the talk.

Notes

1. Daniel Markovits, "How McKinsey Destroyed the Middle Class," *Atlantic*, February 3, 2020.
2. David P. Hanna, *Designing Organizations for High Performance* (Reading MA: Addison-Wesley, 1988).
3. https://planet-lean.com/akio-toyoda-crisis-management/.
4. https://asia.nikkei.com/Opinion/Japanese-companies-must-stop-gloating-about-cash-hoarding.
5. https://www.nytimes.com/interactive/2020/05/26/magazine/stock-market-coronavirus-pandemic.html?action=click&module=Top%20Stories&pgtype=Homepage.
6. Jeffrey Liker and Michael Hoseus, *Toyota Culture: The Heart and Soul of the Toyota Way* (New York: McGraw-Hill, 2008).
7. Hirotaka Takeuchi "Why Japanese Businesses Are So Good at Surviving Crises," *Harvard Business School Working Knowledge*, June 26, 2020.
8. The supervisor was Leroy Morrow who went on to management positions at NUMMI and later Toyota's Georgetown, Kentucky, plant and later worked for me as a consultant.

9. James Womack, Daniel Jones, and Daniel Roos, *The Machine That Changed the World: The Story of Lean Production* (New York: Harper Perennial, 1991).

10. Jeffrey Liker and Gary Convis, *The Toyota Way to Lean Leadership* (New York: McGraw-Hill, 2011).

11. Jeffrey Liker and Timothy Ogden, *Toyota Under Fire: How Toyota Faced the Challenges of the Recession and the Recall Crisis to Come out Stronger* (New York: McGraw-Hill, 2011).

12. Chris Isidore, "7.9 Million Jobs Lost—Many Forever," CNNMoney.com, July 2, 2010: http://money.cnn.com/2010/07/02/news/economy/jobs_gone_forever/index.htm.

13. http://www.toyota.com.cn/company/vision_philosophy/guiding_principles.html.

14. Personal interview with John Shook, 2002.

15. Liker and Hoseus, *Toyota Culture*.

PART TWO

PROCESS

Struggle to Flow Value to Each Customer

II. Process
2. Continuous Flow
3. Pull
4. Level
5. Standardized Processes
6. Design-Build in Quality
7. Visual Control
8. Technology to Support People and Processes

Principle 2

Connect People and Processes Through Continuous Process Flow to Bring Problems to the Surface

If some problem occurs in one-piece flow manufacturing then the whole production line stops. In this sense it is a very bad system of manufacturing. But when production stops everyone is forced to solve the problem immediately. So team members have to think, and through thinking team members grow and become better team members and people.

—Teruyuki Minoura, former President,
Toyota Motor Manufacturing, North America

In the early days of Ohno's journey toward TPS, he discovered a fundamental principle that became the backbone of the system. Flow value to each customer, ideally one by one, without stagnation! Waste gets in the way of flowing value. The ideal process, perfectly executed, is all value-added work with zero waste. The iconic symbol of this is the one-piece flow cell. Processes with their associated equipment and tools are lined up in sequence, and workers move through the processes doing value-added work with minimum waste.

It is comforting to believe that if we could only implement the right cells and other lean tools to eliminate waste in the process, we could let it rip and get great results forever . . . or at least for a long time. But processes do not work that way. In fact, when we define and set up a lean process, it is just the starting point for the real action. As Mr. Minoura explains in the opening quote, the whole production line will stop when a problem occurs in one-piece flow. So physically shifting from batch and queue operations (explained in greater detail later in the chapter) to one-piece flow without inventory almost guarantees you will encounter many more problems. So why do it? Precisely to allow the processes to break so we can discover the weak points and improve through kaizen. John Krafcik, who came up with the term "lean production,"[1] later described it as "fragile production," designed to break and expose problems.

In this chapter, we begin looking at the first of 7 of the 14 Toyota Way principles that are part of the second broad category, "Struggle to Flow Value to Each Customer." Within these 7 principles are the TPS methods for improving routine manufacturing processes and routine parts of service processes. While these tools are important and powerful, the point is not to implement them as if they were physical things, but rather to use them to reveal obstacles that can be solved one by one. It is indeed a struggle. A "lean process" is actually a vision to strive for and an outcome of repeated problem solving. Building on the foundation of Principle 1, these tools come to life when they are part of a companywide, long-term management philosophy of developing people.

ONE-PIECE FLOW IS NOT FOR THE FAINT OF HEART

In Toyota, the ideal of continuous flow has become a core belief. Flow is at the heart of the lean message that shortening the elapsed time from raw materials to finished goods (or services) will lead to the best quality, lowest cost, and shortest delivery time. But there is a reason for buffers. Inventory buffers and gaps in time between steps in the process protect downstream processes from upstream processes. If you have a buffer of inventory of a supplier's parts, you will not be affected by short-term downtime of your supplier or late shipments. You can even sort out quality defects in large shipments to avoid disrupting your production.

On the other hand, this comfort level leads to complacency. Connected processes force all team members to strive for perfection. Ohno taught that lowering the "water level" of inventory exposes problems (like rocks in the water), and you are forced to deal with the problems. Coupling steps in the process so that there is little material or time buffer lowers the water level and exposes inefficiencies that demand immediate solutions. Everyone concerned is motivated to fix the problems and inefficiencies because the process will shut down if they aren't fixed. As Ohno disciple Mr. Minoura explained:

> When they run one-piece production, they can't have the quantity that they want so everybody gets frustrated and doesn't know what to do. But then, within that, they have to find ways to think: what is the way to get the quantity? That is the true essence of TPS and, in that sense, we create confusion so we have to do something different in approaching this problem.

I should warn that one-piece flow is not for the faint of heart . . . or something to plunge into in one big step. A simple calculation illustrates the pressure you will face if you suddenly jump from batch processing to continuous flow. Let's say you have four sequential processes like the ones shown in Figure 2.1, and each operates properly 90 percent of the time on average. The company has been using a batch and queue approach as long as you can remember, and there is a good deal of inventory between each process and other wastes, but it works pretty well most of the time. Since everyone keeps busy working from inventory, even when upstream or downstream processes break down, you end up with an average of 90 percent output (see Figure 2.1). By maintaining some finished goods in inventory and utilizing overtime when needed, you do not miss any shipments.

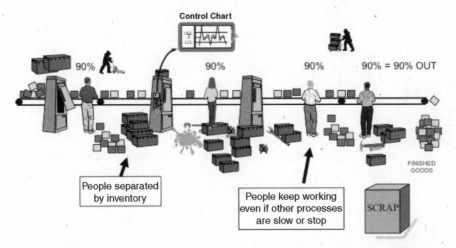

Figure 2.1   A batch and queue system with inventory buffers allows each process to work independently. As long as there is enough inventory, even if an upstream process stops, the downstream process can continue working from the inventory buffer.

All is well until you learn about this new lean stuff and decide to eliminate all excess inventory and enforce one-piece flow, so that when any process slows down, all other processes will be forced to stop and wait for that operation to catch up. Voilà! You have just bought a ticket to disaster and unhappy customers (see Figure 2.2). Now the average output at the end of the line is the product of all the inefficiencies of the four processes, or

$$90\% \times 90\% \times 90\% \times 90\% = 65.6\% \text{ overall output}$$

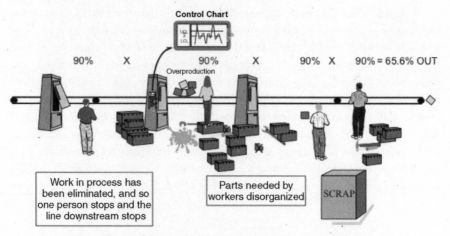

Figure 2.2   Disorganized "one-piece flow" filled with waste, so any process down shuts all processes down. In a sequential process without inventory, you multiply the uptime across processes to get the average output at the end of the line.

Toyota has high expectations for its factories. In a typical plant, Toyota expects about 97 percent of the scheduled vehicles to be built on time during planned operating hours (what's called OPR, or operational ratio). It has hundreds of processes lined up sequentially without inventory buffers in between, and so we might expect bottlenecks to occur almost continuously. And it even asks team members to pull a cord that may stop the line when they see a problem. Maybe "continuous line stop" is a more accurate term than "continuous flow." How can the company be so arrogant to expect a success rate of 97 percent?

At Toyota, it is not arrogance, but, in fact, the opposite. The company does not believe it can predict the future, and it expects to have many problems. It cannot guess at all the ways production will fail, so it connects operations with small amounts of inventory, and then as the inevitable failures occur, the employees solve the problems one by one. If no problems occur, there is too much inventory, and the company reduces it some more.

MOST OPERATIONS ARE FULL OF WASTE, EVEN IF WE DO NOT NOTICE

Traditional business processes have the capacity to hide vast inefficiencies without anyone noticing—people just assume that a typical process takes days or weeks to complete. They don't realize that a lean process might accomplish the same thing in a matter of hours or even minutes.

Let's say you have been promoted and you place an order for new office furniture with a genuine wood desk with drawers and compartments galore and a fancy ergonomic chair. You can't wait to get rid of that old scuffed and stained furniture from your predecessor. But don't turn in the old stuff just yet. For one thing, the promised delivery date is eight weeks out, and if you look at online comments of customers, the furniture is likely to be late. Why does it take so long? Your inconvenience is a result of a clumsy manufacturing process called "batch and queue." Your desk and office chair are mass-produced in stages. Large batches of material and parts sit in a queue at each stage of the production process and wait for long periods of (wasted) time until they are moved to the next stage of production.

Consider the custom-made office chair that is delivered two months after you order it. The value-added work (i.e., the work actually performed) in the assembly process consists of covering standard foam cushions and then bolting together the chair. This takes less than one hour. Actually, making the fabric and foam and frame and parts, which are done in parallel, takes another day at most. Everything else during the two months you are waiting is waste (muda). Why is there so much waste? The department making seat covers, the supplier making springs and frames, and the plant making foam are all producing big batches of these items and then shipping them to the final assembly operation—where they wait in piles of inventory. Then you, the customer, wait for someone to pull the components from inventory and build the chair. More wasted time. Add several weeks for the chair to get out of inventory at the plant and through the warehouse and distribution system to your office. Meanwhile, you have been waiting months sitting in that uncomfortable old chair. In a TPS/lean environment, the goal is to create one-piece flow by constantly eliminating wasted effort and time that is not adding value to your chair. Office furniture maker Herman Miller has spent more than two decades working with Toyota (discussed under Principle 10: "People") and has cut its process of making and shipping chairs to days. You can get the popular Aeron chair built and delivered to you in 10 days or less.

In the chapter "A Storied History: How Toyota Became the World's Best Manufacturer," we summarized the seven wastes that Toyota continually seeks to remove from its processes. That is fine for physical manufacturing processes like making chairs, but how do you distinguish the value-added work from waste in knowledge work? Consider an office where engineers are all very busy designing products, sitting in front of their computers, looking up technical specifications, and meeting with coworkers or suppliers. Are they doing value-added work? The truth is, you do not know. You cannot measure an engineer's value-added productivity by looking at what he or she is doing or thinking. You have to follow the progress of the actual product the engineer is working on as it is being transformed from concept into a final product (or service). Engineers transform information into a design, so you look at such things as (1) at what points do the engineers make decisions that directly affect the product? and (2) when do the engineers actually conduct important tests or do an analysis that impacts those decisions? Or on the other hand, (3) how much rework is there? Even more complex some of the "rework" is actually useful creative thinking ruling out some ideas that do not prove out. In any case you're likely to find that typical engineers (or any other white-collar professionals) are working like maniacs churning out all sorts of information. The problem is that very little of their work is truly "value added," i.e., work that ends up actually shaping the final product.

We worked with one supplier of automotive exhaust systems that needed to reduce its product development lead times to meet customer demands. In one piece of the value chain, the client was doing finite element analysis (FEA) to measure the impact of stress on the muffler to determine how likely it was to fail. Engineers submitted the design of the muffler, and the FEA analysts ran the computer program and provided data on the stresses and strains. Seemed simple enough.

My consultant worked with the FEA group in a three-day workshop. FEA is required by the client's customers for all muffler design projects, and the client had just received a big contract from General Motors. With the current capacity, the client company could not complete the work. Hiring analysts was difficult, as the work usually requires an advanced degree and analysts with the right credentials were in big demand. The objective of the company was to increase the capacity to handle the additional work with no new hires while reducing lead time.

After setting targets, the FEA group analyzed the current condition by examining a set of completed projects. There was a big difference between an iterative analysis of a partial change in the design and a full analysis of a completely new exhaust system, so the group members separated these out. They found that the average lead time was 18 days for the partial and 38 days for the full analysis. Only 8 percent of this lead time for the partial and 12 percent for the full were value added—about 90 percent was waste! In other words, engineers who needed the analysis results required by the customer were waiting weeks for no apparent reason.

The analysis further revealed that there was no obvious rationale for which projects were worked on and which were in a queue. Moreover, there was a great deal of rework, which seemed to be the result of incomplete or inaccurate data or poor assumptions. The group suggested a number of countermeasures:

- Improve upfront data collection to better understand customer requirements.
- Screen and reduce non-value-added FEA analyses.
- Create a cap on work in process (WIP).

■ Create a standard worksheet for the process.
■ Provide a visual status of FEA work orders and people loading, by recording the information on a whiteboard.

The WIP cap was on the number of FEA projects each analyst could work on at a time. The group calculated a reasonable maximum limit of six projects per analyst, split between partials and full. As new projects came in, they would be posted on a visual board and assigned to analysts in rows—set up for a maximum of six per analyst (see Figure 2.3). When an analyst's six slots were full, he or she would not start work on an additional project until after completing one of the six that were assigned—one comes out and another one is started, creating a flow.

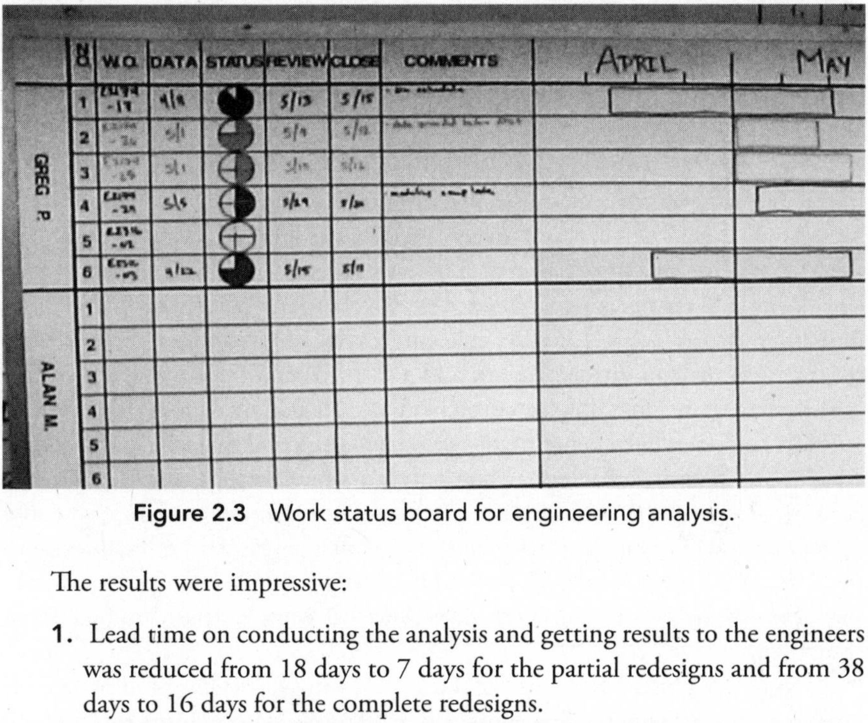

Figure 2.3 Work status board for engineering analysis.

The results were impressive:

1. Lead time on conducting the analysis and getting results to the engineers was reduced from 18 days to 7 days for the partial redesigns and from 38 days to 16 days for the complete redesigns.
2. A full 25 percent of capacity was freed up for new projects, enough to handle the forecasted demand and then some, with no additional people.
3. Quality went up, and rework became rare, satisfying the engineering customers.
4. The engineers could ask about the status of their projects and get an accurate answer for the first time—which was very important to their customers.
5. The analysts were no longer feeling stressed.

Note the paradox here. In order to increase throughput, the analysts had to work on *fewer* projects at a time. Toyota uses these kinds of methods routinely in its product development process, as documented in *Designing the Future*.[2]

MASS PRODUCTION THINKING VERSUS FLOW THINKING

The traditional way to schedule an operation that is organized into separate processes is to send individual schedules to each department. For example, if schedules are developed weekly, then each department head can decide independently what to make each day in order to optimize equipment and utilize people for that week. A weekly schedule also provides flexibility for people missing work. You just make less that day and make it up with more production another day in the week. As long as by Friday you meet the production target, everything is OK.

Lean thinking looks at this way of organizing production and predicts it will result in a lot of work-in-process inventory. The fastest equipment, such as stamping, will build up the most WIP. Material sitting in inventory is caused by the most fundamental waste, overproduction. Inventory sitting idle will cost money, take up valuable space, and, more importantly, hide problems.

Figure 2.4 illustrates a simplified view of a computer maker that is organized into three departments. One department makes computer bases, the second makes monitors and attaches them, and the third tests the computers. In this model, the material handling department decided it wants to move a batch size of 10 units at a time. Each department takes 1 minute per unit to do its work, so it takes 10 minutes for a batch of 10 computers to move through each department. Setting aside material handling time to move between departments, it would therefore take 30 minutes to make and test the first batch of 10 to be shipped to the customer. And it would take 21 minutes to get the first computer ready to ship, even though only 3 minutes of value-added work is needed to make that computer.

Figure 2.5 illustrates a view of the same computer-making process above, organized into a one-piece flow work cell. If Ohno were to manage this process, he would take the equipment needed to make one base from the base department, the equipment for making a monitor from the monitor department, and a test stand from the test department—and then put these three processes next to each other, organized by product family. That is, he would have created a cell to achieve one-piece flow. The differences are stark. The operators in the cell take 12 minutes to make 10 computers, while the batch flow process takes 30 minutes for 10 computers. Moreover, it takes the lean process just 3 minutes (all pure value-added time) instead of 21 minutes to make the first computer ready to ship.

Product requires three processes that take one minute each
(Batch size = 10)

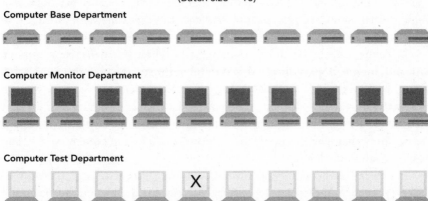

- Complete processing of first batch of 10 takes 30 minutes
- First computer out takes 21 minutes (plus transport time)
- There are at least 21 parts in process

Figure 2.4 Batch processing example.

Product requires three processes that take one minute each
(one-piece flow cell)

- 10 completed in 12 minutes
- First computer out in 3 minutes
- Only 2 subassemblies in process at a time

Figure 2.5 Continuous flow example.

WHY CONTINUOUS FLOW CAN BE FASTER AND BETTER

It seems logical that making equipment go faster will increase speed. We want to believe that changing A has a simple and direct effect on B. In this case, A is making a piece of equipment go faster, and B is the speed of the entire value stream.

With systems thinking we can see that there are more complex relationships. For example, replacing large batch-building equipment with smaller machines that might even be slower but can fit into flow cells can speed the value stream. And going fast but creating defects will slow the value stream even if machines are fast.

In Figure 2.4, the batch processing case, we show one defective computer, with an X on the monitor. It failed to turn on in the test stage. In this large-batch approach, by the time the problem is discovered, there are at least 21 parts in process that might also have that problem. And if the defect occurred in the base department, it could take as long as 21 minutes to discover it in the test department. Notice that speeding up the first process would lead to even more WIP and possibly even more defects.

In Figure 2.5, the one-piece flow cell, when we discover a defect, there can be only two other computers in process that also have the defect, and the maximum time it will take to discover the defect is two minutes from when it was made. The reality is that in a large-batch operation there are probably weeks of work in process between operations, and it can take weeks or even months from the time a defect was caused until it is discovered. By then the trail of cause and effect is cold, making it difficult to track down and identify why the defect occurred.

The same logic applies to a business or engineering process. Let individual departments do the work in batches and pass the batches to other departments, and you are almost certain to experience major delays in getting work done. Lots of excessive bureaucracy will creep in, governing the standards for each department, and lots of non-value-adding positions will be created to monitor the flow. Most of the time will be spent with projects waiting for decisions or action. The result will be chaos and poor quality. Take the right people who do the value-added work, line them up (physically or virtually), and flow the project through those people with appropriate meetings to work on integration, and you will get speed, productivity, and better quality. We have done this many times and it works.

TAKT TIME: THE HEARTBEAT OF ONE-PIECE FLOW

In competitive rowing, a key position is the coxswain—the little person in the back of the boat who is calling "row, row, row." He or she is coordinating the activities of all the rowers so they are rowing at the same speed. Get a maverick rower who outperforms everyone else and guess what!—the boat gets out of kilter and slows down. Extra power and speed can actually slow the boat down.

When you set up one-piece flow in a cell, how do you know how fast the cell should be designed to go? What should be the capacity of the equipment? How many people do you need? The starting point to answering these questions is to calculate the takt.

"Takt" is a German word for rhythm or meter. Takt is the rate of customer demand—the rate at which the customer is buying product. If we work 7 hours and 20 minutes per day (440 minutes) for 20 days a month and the customer is buying 17,600 units per month, then the customer demand requires us to make 880 units per day, or 1 unit every 30 seconds. In a true one-piece flow process, every step of the process should produce a part every 30 seconds. If the process goes faster, it will overproduce; if it goes slower, there will be a bottleneck. Takt can be used to set the pace of production and alert workers whenever they are getting ahead or behind.

Continuous flow and takt time are most easily applied in repetitive manufacturing and service operations. But with creativity, the concepts can be extended to any repeatable process in which the steps can be written out and non-value-added activities can be reduced or eliminated to create a better flow.

BENEFITS OF ONE-PIECE FLOW

When you try to attain one-piece flow, you are also setting in motion numerous activities to identify and reduce waste. Let's take a closer look at a few of the benefits of flow:

1. **Builds in quality.** It is much easier to build in quality in one-piece flow. Every operator is an inspector and works to fix any problems in his or her station before passing the product to the next station. But if defects do get missed and passed on, they can be detected very quickly, and the problem can be quickly diagnosed and corrected.
2. **Creates real flexibility.** If we dedicate equipment to a product line, it would seem we have less flexibility in scheduling it for other purposes. But if the lead time to make a product is very short, we have more flexibility to respond and make what the customer really wants. Instead of putting a new order into the system and waiting weeks to get that product out, if lead times are a matter of mere hours, we can fill a new order in a few hours. And changing over to a different product mix to accommodate changes in customer demand can be almost immediate.
3. **Creates higher productivity.** The reason it appears that productivity is highest when your operation is organized by department is because each department is measured by equipment utilization and people utilization. More pieces produced per machine and per person seems to indicate greater productivity. But in fact, it is hard to determine how many people

are needed to produce a certain number of units in a large-batch operation because productivity is not measured in terms of value-added work.
Who knows how much productivity is lost when people are "utilized" to
overproduce parts, which then have to be moved to storage? How much
time is lost tracking down defective parts and components and repairing
finished products? In a one-piece flow cell, there is very little non-value-
added activity such as moving materials around. You quickly see who is too
busy and who is idle. It is easy to calculate the value-added work and then
figure out how many people are needed to reach a certain production rate.
In every case of the Toyota Production System Support Center (TSSC),
set up by Toyota to teach TPS through a demonstration project, when
the company changed a mass-producing supplier to a TPS-style line, it
achieved a large productivity improvement, often exceeding 100 percent.

4. **Frees up floor space.** When equipment is organized by department, there
are a lot of bits of space between equipment that are wasted, but most of
the space is wasted by inventory—piles and piles of it. In a cell, everything is pushed close together, and there is very little space wasted by
inventory. By making greater use of the floor space, you can free up space
for new products or add new products without expanding the facility.
Often companies will use ropes to separate freed-up space with a sign
saying "reserved for new business."

5. **Improves safety.** Wiremold Corporation, one of the early adopters of
TPS in America, decided not to set up a separate safety program. Yet
when Wiremold worked to transform its large-batch-process company
to one-piece flow, its safety improved, and it even won a number of state
safety awards. Smaller batches of material were moved through the factory, which meant getting rid of forklift trucks, a major cause of accidents, and also meant lighter lifting of materials and reduced handling
of materials. Safety was getting better because of a focus on flow—even
without a formal safety program.*

6. **Improves morale.** Wiremold, in its lean transformation, also found its
morale improved in every year of the transformation. Before the transformation, only 60 percent of employees agreed that the company was
a good place to work. That went up each year, to over 70 percent by the
fourth year of transformation. In one-piece flow, people do much more
value-added work and can immediately see the results of that work, giving
them both a sense of accomplishment and job satisfaction.

---

* For a detailed analysis of Wiremold and its lean transformation, see Bob Emiliani, David
Stec, Lawrence Grasso, and James Stodder, *Better Thinking, Better Results* (Kensington, CT:
Center for Lean Business Management, 2002).

7. **Reduces cost of inventory.** Capital not tied up in inventory is cash flow that can be invested elsewhere. And companies do not have to pay the carrying costs of the capital they free up. On top of that, inventory obsolescence goes down. This was especially important at Dana Corporation, when under chapter 11 bankruptcy reorganization, the company freed up hundreds of millions of dollars of cash tied up in inventory to pay off high-interest-rate loans.[3]

8. **Unleashes creativity of people.** One of the greatest benefits of one-piece flow is that problems surface and challenge people to think and improve.

REAL FLOW VERSUS FAKE FLOW

Many companies change the physical layout of equipment and think that one-piece flow will automatically follow. But they often are creating fake flow. An example of fake flow would be moving equipment close together to create what looks like a one-piece flow cell, then batching product at each stage with no sense of customer takt. It looks like a cell, but it works like a batch process.

For example, the Will-Burt Company in Orrville, Ohio, makes many products based on steel parts. One of its larger-volume products is a family of telescoping steel masts that are used in vans for radar or for camera crews. Each mast is custom designed, depending on the application, so there is variation from unit to unit built. The company called its mast-making operation a cell and believed it was doing lean manufacturing. In fact, before I helped lead a lean consulting review of Will-Burt's processes, a production manager warned us that with the variety of custom products the company made, we would not have any luck improving the flow.

In a one-week kaizen workshop, we analyzed the situation and determined that this was a classic case of fake flow.* The work time (value added) it took to build one of these masts was 431 minutes. But the pieces of equipment for making each mast were physically separated, so forklifts were moving big pallets of masts from workstation to workstation. WIP built up at each station. With the WIP, the total lead time from raw material to finished goods was 37.8 days. Most of this was the storage of tube raw material and finished goods. If you just looked at the processing time in the plant, it still took almost 4 days from sawing to final welding to do 431 minutes of work. The travel distance of the mast within the plant was 1,792 feet.

---

* The kaizen workshop was led by Jeffrey Rivera, former senior lean consultant in my company, and Eduardo Lander, at that time my doctoral student at the University of Michigan.

The group came up with a new design and began moving the equipment closer together, moving one piece at a time through the system, eliminating the use of the forklift between the operations (a special dolly had to be created to move this large unit at workstation height between two of the operations that could not be placed next to each other), and creating a single shop order for one mast instead of batches of shop orders for a set of masts on one order. Figure 2.6 depicts the process flow before and after the one-week kaizen workshop. You can see that the "before" situation was really a case of fake flow. Pieces of equipment were sort of near each other, but there was not really anything like a one-piece flow. And the people working in the plant did not understand flow well enough to see that it was fake flow. The "after" situation was a marked improvement that surprised and delighted everyone in the company. People were shocked that such a transformation could be done in one week.

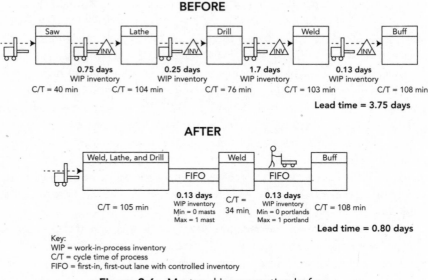

Figure 2.6   Mast-making operation before and after one-week lean transformation.

These changes led to significant improvements in lead time, reduced inventory, and reduced floor space (see Figure 2.7). One side benefit of the workshop was that the time to set up a shop order was investigated. The batching of shop orders created a lot of waste; and when the system was eliminated, time was reduced from 207 minutes to 13 minutes. This is not to say that the transformation was complete and after the workshop we could pack up and go home confident the patient would thrive. We advised the company that this was only the starting point to demonstrate the power of one-piece flow and warned that even more problems would become visible and the key to sustainability was continuous improvement.

	Before	After
Production lead time (dock to dock)	37.8 days	29.2 days
Production lead time (saw to weld)	3.8 days	0.8 days
Number of forklift moves	11	2
Travel distance (dock to dock per mast)	1,792 feet	1,032 feet
Shop order input time (mast)	207 min	13 min

Figure 2.7 Fake flow versus one-piece flow.

ONE-PIECE FLOW IS A VISION TO STRUGGLE TOWARD, NOT A TOOL TO IMPLEMENT

Toyota's vision for any process is true one-piece flow that is waste-free. Creating flow means linking together processes that otherwise are disjointed. When operations are linked together, there are opportunities for more effective teamwork, rapid feedback on problems, control over the process, and direct pressure for people to solve problems and think and grow. Ultimately, within the Toyota Way, the main benefit of one-piece flow is that it challenges people to think and improve. Toyota is willing to risk shutting down production in order to surface problems and challenge team members to solve them. The Toyota Way is to stop and address each problem as it is exposed. Principle 6 (on stopping to fix problems) explains this in more detail.

As the title of the "Process" set of principles suggests, flowing value to each customer without interruption is a vision, and a struggle. There is often confusion about one-piece flow, as in a work cell, being a solution versus a vision. For example, I hear things like "We can't implement one-piece flow because we have a lot of downtime on one finicky robot, and we would just shut down all production." Or "We are a job shop, and orders vary every hour and follow different routes, so there is no defined sequence of processes to put in a cell." In both these cases, a work cell is seen as a solution that people believe is a bad fit for their situation—and they are right that it probably is a bad solution for them. Their problem is that they think it is supposed to be a solution.

I recall one of the early examples of TSSC working with an automotive supplier, Grand Haven Stamped Products in Michigan, that made gear shift mechanisms. Mr. Ohba, who ran the center, walked the value stream, which included a robot that welded together steel parts and a series of assembly operations and asked then to make a one-piece flow cell with these processes grouped together.

The President and other key leaders described to me staying up all night to create the cell including pushing the robot across the shop floor. When they ran the cell, they could barely finish a single gear shift level. Some process always seemed to break down and stop production. Mr. Ohba came back and asked them to fix the problems. The cell was revealing many problems, and they had to either solve them or production would stop.

As Mr. Minoura pointed out, one-piece flow will, in fact, cause stoppage in production and is only a good idea if you use this as an opportunity to improve the process. Process flow and problem solving go hand in hand. In Figure 2.8, we flip the script. We often think of one-piece flow as an independent variable, something to technically manipulate to get the results (dependent variables) that we want. In this figure we view one-piece flow as a dependent variable (or at least intermediate to the outcomes we want).* We get closer and closer to one-piece flow as we think scientifically about why the chain is being broken and we improve the process. And in response, as we get closer to one-piece flow, the chain will tighten and expose new problems; one by one we solve them and get even closer to the ideal of one-piece flow. It is a repeated virtual cycle of continuous improvement.

Figure 2.8   One-piece flow and scientific thinking.

---

* Thanks to Mike Rother, who proposed the concept of thinking about many lean techniques, such as one-piece flow, as dependent variables and modified Figure 2.8 accordingly.

KEY POINTS

- The core concept in Toyota's just-in-time system is struggling toward the vision of one-piece flow of value to the customer, with zero waste.
- We often think of a process as if it were a physical thing, but it is actually an ideal to strive for, not a tool to implement.
- Mass production thinkers often have the mistaken impression that if they minimize the cycle time of individual processes, they will make the overall operation more efficient, but more often than not they simply create mountains of waste, slow the speed of materials and information to the customer, and create a lot of confusion.
- Not only does one-piece flow increase productivity, but it can lead to better quality, shorter lead time, enhanced customer responsiveness, higher morale, and better safety.
- While there are immediate benefits of shifting from process islands to a flow line, longer-term benefits come from surfacing problems so they can be addressed quickly, enhancing continuous improvement.
- The companion to one-piece flow is developing in people at the worksite a scientific mindset to solve problems as they surface.

Notes

1. J. F. Krafcik, "Triumph of the Lean Production System," *Sloan Management Review*, 1988, vol. 30, pp. 41–52.
2. James Morgan and Jeffrey Liker, *Designing the Future: How Ford, Toyota, and Other World-Class Organizations Use Lean Product Development to Drive Innovation and Transform Their Business* (New York: McGraw-Hill, 2018).
3. Jeffrey Liker and Gary Convis, *The Toyota Way to Lean Leadership* (New York: McGraw-Hill, 2011), chap. 6.

Principle 3

Use "Pull" Systems to Avoid Overproduction

The more inventory a company has, . . . the less likely they will have what they need.

—Taiichi Ohno

Imagine you discover a great internet service where you can get all your dairy products delivered directly to your house at a significant discount. The only hitch is that you must sign up and specify a weekly quantity of each item for the coming month. The company has to schedule weekly shipments of goods to its warehouse, so it wants advance orders locked in to make sure it sells all the inventory that it receives. If you're not home when your order arrives, the delivery person will leave it on your front porch in a thermo container to keep it cold. Since you are not sure how much you will use, you estimate the quantity of eggs, milk, and butter that you will need for a week and then add a little extra for a safety factor. The problem is that if you don't use everything you ordered in one week, it will accumulate in your refrigerator and possibly go bad. Week after week, your inventory grows, so you buy a second refrigerator and put it in the garage—a major expense. Another problem: if you go on vacation and happen to forget to cancel the order for that week, you will have a week's worth of bad dairy products on your front porch when you return.

This is an example of a scheduled *push* system. In business, goods and services are often pushed onto the retailer based on sophisticated scheduling systems. Some even use AI and big data. Perhaps they guess right more often than past systems, but it is still an educated guess about the future, and the goods are pushed onto the retailer, whether or not it can sell them right away. In response, the retailer tries to push them onto you, the consumer, through price discounts or other merchandising strategies. If you respond to the promotions, you very well may end up with an inventory of stuff that you do not need immediately; and most likely, the retailer is still left with a boatload of inventory.

Now imagine that the internet service we talked about earlier gets a lot of complaints and decides to benchmark Toyota's pull system and make major changes in its logistics system. The service sends you a wireless device that attaches to your refrigerator and has buttons for each of your frequently used dairy goods. When you open your next-to-last container of milk or begin to use your next-to-last carton of eggs, you push the button for that item. The next day, the company will deliver one unit to replenish the item you just started using. This means you will have the partially used unit, if you did not finish it, plus one more. Some inventory, but not a lot. If you anticipate you'll use a lot of a product in the near future, like milk, then you can send your order via the internet or an app, and the company will immediately deliver what you need. On its end, the internet retailer renegotiated agreements with its dairy suppliers so that when customers order more product, it triggers a signal to dairy companies to send the retailer that amount. These are examples of *pull* systems, aka just-in-time (JIT). You receive items only when you demand them, and the retailer receives product based on actual customer demand. To avoid having items pushed on you, you might even be willing to pay a little more for this "on-demand" service.

Many companies and service organizations within companies work to their own internal schedule. They do what is convenient for them within that schedule. So they produce parts, goods, and services according to their planned schedule and push products onto their customers, who must stockpile those products in inventory (see Figure 3.1).

Figure 3.1   From forecast to push systems.

I was impressed by an article about the fast-growing Sweetgreen chain of healthy food restaurants.[1] The founders are not cooks and did not know much about food when they started up. They were techies and developed a mobile app for advanced ordering and delivery—a pull system. Many companies seem to think if they have an app, all the logistics will take care of themselves. The founders could have viewed their new business as a tech company that happens to serve food—but they did not. The article described the challenges one of the company founders faced:

> *Mr. Neman said he was acutely aware that Sweetgreen is not a tech company. It is very much a restaurant company, beholden to the laws of gravity that define food service expansion: its employees chop every vegetable, roast every chicken thigh and make hummus and prepare nearly 60 other ingredients from scratch every day, at each and every restaurant. The company is in the business of atoms, not bits. . . . "Sometimes I complain that it's so hard, for all those operational reasons," Mr. Neman said. "Then I remind myself that maybe that's good, because it's hard for everyone else, too."*

Toyota has always been clear that it is at its core a manufacturing company. And unlike an internet company, supply chain logistics have to do with "atoms, not bits." Amazon is as much a warehousing and delivery company as an internet company. As you already know, the Toyota Way is not about managing inventory; it is about satisfying customers through lean value streams. Very early on, Ohno started thinking about pulling inventory based on immediate customer demand, rather than using a push system that tries to anticipate customer demand through forecasts. In the Toyota Way, "pull" means the ideal state of just-in-time manufacturing: giving the customers (which may be the next step in an internal process) what they want, when they want it, and in the amount they want. The purest form of pull is one-piece flow, discussed under Principle 2. If you can take a customer order and make a single product just for that order—using a one-piece flow production cell—that would be the leanest imaginable system. It is 100 percent on-demand, and you have zero inventory. But because there are natural breaks in flow in the process of transforming raw materials into finished products delivered to customers, some inventory is usually necessary.

The internet example we used above is not a zero-inventory system, even in its improved and leaner state. There is inventory, which can be thought of and referred to as a buffer. The (improved) internet service is asking you to simply indicate when you begin to use an item so the service can replenish what you have started to use while you still have some inventory in your refrigerator. It is replenishing what you are removing. This is how most supermarkets work. In fact, supermarkets are simply warehouses that operate in a particular way. There is a specific amount of inventory kept on the store shelves, based on past purchase patterns and expected future demand. Customers pull items they want off the shelves, and the supermarket clerks periodically look at what has been removed from the shelves and replenish it from the backroom inventory. The clerks are not simply pushing inventory onto shelves, nor are they directly ordering goods from the manufacturer to put on the shelf. The clerks draw from the supermarket's small and measured inventory through a replenishment system.

THE PRINCIPLE—USE PULL SYSTEMS TO AVOID OVERPRODUCTION

Taiichi Ohno and his associates were fascinated by the importance of the supermarket in daily life in America in the 1950s. Ohno recognized from the start that in many cases inventory was necessary to allow for smooth flow. He also recognized that individual departments building products to a schedule using a push system would naturally overproduce and create large banks of inventory, and as we learned, "overproduction" is the fundamental waste.

Ohno needed a compromise between the ideal of one-piece flow and push. Building on the earlier work of Kiichiro Toyoda on JIT systems, Ohno (and his associates) came up with the idea of creating small amounts of "shop stock" between operations to control the inventory. The idea was simple: When the customer begins to use a container of parts, the customer sends a signal and material handling brings to the customer the next container of parts, which triggers producing another container of parts. When the customer does not need the parts, the container sits in the customer's buffer and nothing needs to be produced. There is little overproduction, and at least indirectly, there is a clear and simple connection between what customers want and what the company produces—the customer simply signals in some way that "I am ready for some more of this product."

Since factories are often large and spread out and parts suppliers may be some distance away, Ohno needed a way to signal that the assembly line was getting low on parts and needed more. He used simple signals—cards, empty bins, empty carts. Collectively, these signals are called "kanban," which means signs, posters, billboards, cards—although the word is taken more broadly to indicate a signal of some kind. Send back an empty bin—a kanban—and it is a signal to refill it with a specific number of parts. Or instead of an empty bin, send back a card that specifies the item and number of parts in a batch.

In today's world of high-speed electronic communications, Toyota uses electronic kanban, but it also utilizes paper kanban on bins that have bar codes for scanning. This redundant system allows for the possibility that there will be errors in the electronic system and lets people still see the visual—for example, noticing if a container is traveling without any kanban attached. It is a remarkable, simple, effective, and highly visual communication system. This is not to say Toyota does no production scheduling. As we will see in the next chapter, production control uses a complex algorithm that takes customer orders and creates a leveled schedule. In Toyota, the ideal is to establish a production schedule in one place—which is the pacemaker of the operation—and let that operation pull parts to it based on kanban.

We have emphasized that the Toyota Way is based on systems thinking. One might think that planning for a complex system requires equally complex scheduling systems that have a macro view of the whole and also that planning optimizes what should be happening at each point in the process. Unfortunately, the world is too complex for even the most sophisticated scheduling systems, particularly when they are based on predicting the future. So Toyota's version of systems thinking is to break processes down into smaller parts and distribute local control to local customers—which creates small feedback loops based on the most recent information. Kanban gives the scheduling power to each customer in the value chain and allows each to flexibly place orders based on actual need. The faster the response time, the less inventory is needed, so Toyota is constantly taking waste out of the system to flow faster.

One of Spear and Bowen's four rules in their DNA of TPS article speaks to this approach of distributed control:

Rule 2

Every customer-supplier connection must be direct, and there must be an unambiguous yes-or-no way to send requests and receive responses.[2]

The kanban is one such yes-or-no communication device. In effect, by posting the kanban the customer is saying, "Based on my actual situation now, I am ready for what is on this card—yes."

PULL-REPLENISHMENT SYSTEMS IN EVERYDAY LIFE

One way to demystify the concept of kanban is by thinking of simple examples of pull-replenishment systems in everyday life. How do you decide when to buy standard grocery items you keep at home? You notice when inventory is running low on an item and say, "Yep, I better go and buy this amount of that." Similarly, for filling your auto with gas or replenishing your windshield wiper fluid, you look at the level and decide when to replenish.

On the other hand, not everything can be replenished based on a pull system; some things must be scheduled. Take the example of high-end products, like a Rolex watch, a sports car, or those killer high-tech golf clubs advertised by Tiger Woods. Whenever you are buying a special or single-use item, you have to think about what you want, consider the costs and benefits, perhaps save money in advance, and plan when to get it. In a sense, you create a schedule to purchase, since there is no immediate need for it.

Personal services are another type of scheduled purchase. They usually aren't needed immediately and generally have to be scheduled in advance. For example, we make appointments for our routine dental cleaning, medical exam, or haircut. If our medical needs are urgent and require a pull system, we go to urgent care or the emergency room.

TOYOTA'S KANBAN SYSTEM—PULL WHERE YOU MUST

The ideal one-piece flow system would be a zero-inventory system where everything in the value chain appears when needed. Toyota sees one-piece flow as a vision, a true north to provide a direction, not something you can perfectly achieve. Sometimes, one-piece flow is not possible because processes are too far apart, cycle times to perform the operations vary a great deal, or there is change-over time. In those situations, the next best choice is often Toyota's kanban system, utilizing small inventory buffers that you should try to shrink over time.

Rother and Shook, in their *Training to See Kit*, explain how to teach value stream mapping and provide guidance for developing the future-state map.[3] They suggest answering the question, "Where will you flow, where do you need to pull?" Rother began to use the catchier saying, "Flow where you can, pull where you must." You can go far with this simple slogan. The point is to aim for one-piece flow when you can, but if that is not possible, the next best thing is often a pull system with some type of material or information buffer.

Consider a pull system in a Toyota assembly plant. Orders accumulate from car dealerships. Production control creates a leveled schedule (discussed in Principle 4). That schedule is sent to the body shop, where stamped steel panels (from a "supermarket" of prestamped panels) are welded together into a body, which flows through small buffers to assembly, maintaining the sequence. On the other hand, stamping the panels (taking a few seconds each) is a much faster operation than the speed of the body shop. If you were to put a stamping press in a cell with welding that is doing 60 seconds of work to the takt, the stamping press would do work for a few seconds than stop and wait for the rest of the 60 seconds, so putting stamping into a one-piece flow is not practical. Instead stamping builds in batches to an inventory buffer based on kanban. At a certain trigger point when a certain number of steel panels have been used by the welding shop, a kanban goes back to a stamping press, ordering it to make another batch to replenish the store.

Similarly, when assembly-line workers begin to use parts from small batches in bins (hinges, door handles, windshield wipers), they take out a kanban and put it in a mailbox. A material handler on a timed route will pick it up, along with the empty container, and go back to a store to replenish what was used on the assembly line. Another material handler will replenish the store based on parts from a supermarket of supplier parts, which, in turn, will trigger an order back to parts suppliers. And so on.

Figure 3.2 illustrates a system like this, where parts in the assembly plant are replenished by a supplier. The process starts at the assembly factory (on the right side of the diagram); then "withdrawal kanban" and empty containers are sent back by truck to the supplier to be refilled (or electronic pull signals can be used). The supplier keeps a small store of finished parts in a "parts store," but may not want to build new parts in the exact sequence the kanban arrive. Rather, the supplier looks at the kanban and levels its own schedule, as we discuss in Principle 4 next. Figure 3.3 illustrates what this might look like internally from the perspective of the supplier plant.

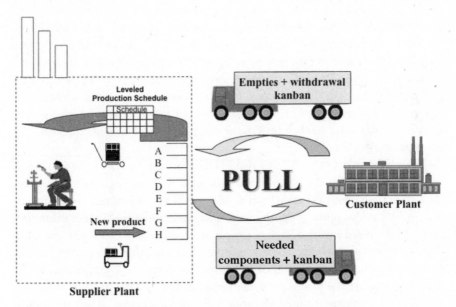

Figure 3.2 External pull system with suppliers.

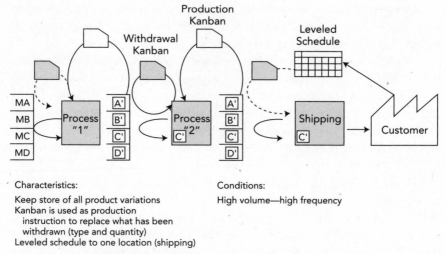

Figure 3.3 Example of internal pull systems.

USING PULL IN A GENERAL MOTORS TRAINING OFFICE

You can effectively use pull-replenishment systems in the office to save money and help avoid shortages of supplies. Most offices use some form of pull system already. Nobody knows exactly how many pencils, erasers, or reams of paper will be used in an office. If there were a standing, scheduled order for all these things, you would guess right in some cases, have too much in other cases, and run out of some critical items at other times. So in a well-run office, somebody's job is to keep the supply store stocked by looking and seeing what is used. You replenish when needed.

General Motors at one point had a Technical Liaison Office in California when the NUMMI plant was still open and used the office as a training ground for TPS coupled with NUMMI tours. Many GM employees had their first lesson on TPS at this office. Appropriately, GM made this a model lean office. For example, it created a formal kanban system for supplies, and as a result, the office rarely ran out of anything. There was a place for everything and everything in its place—in the storeroom, on desks, or by the computer. For example, in the supply storage area, it placed little, laminated kanban (cards) by every item that indicated when the item should be triggered. So, for instance, when the aspirin bottle reached one-quarter full, the aspirin kanban was put into a coffee can for reordering. And another example: The office originally had a conventional refrigerator that held soft drinks, and some drinks were always overstocked while others ran out. Since you could not see through the door, it was easy to hide the mess inside. So the office purchased a big soda machine with a glass front that allowed people to easily see the state of soft drink supplies. The soda machine was stocked with a variety of juices and soft drinks on marked shelves. When a certain soft drink reached a certain level, the user took out the kanban for that soft drink and put it in a box to get the drink reordered.

You might think a pull system in a small office is not appropriate—it would be too elaborate and bothersome to maintain when measured against the promised cost savings. You might even conduct a cost-benefit analysis to decide if it is a good use of time. But understand this: in conducting the analysis, you would be displaying traditional mass production thinking. The point is—and this gets closer to the heart of TPS—the benefits may go beyond the pennies saved. The power of the Toyota Production System is that it unleashes creativity and continuous improvement. So putting in place these kanban systems is likely to intrigue your office workers, get them interested in improving the process of ordering supplies, and ultimately lead them to find ways to create flow in their core work. Waste in offices is generally far greater than in factories. A little creative effort to improve the process will have huge multiplier effects.

Pull systems can also be used to regulate information flow. Under Principle 2, we saw how a simple visual board regulated how many projects the finite element analyst worked on. This was also a type of pull system. There was a defined amount of work-in-process inventory, and then when one project was complete, a replacement project could be pulled into the process.

SETTING UP PULL SYSTEMS IS ONLY THE BEGINNING

It is fascinating to watch a pull system work. A huge number of parts and materials move through the facility in a a kind of rhythmic dance. In a large assembly plant, like the Toyota plant in Georgetown, Kentucky, thousands of parts are constantly moving about. Alongside the assembly line, small high-frequency parts in small bins arrive from neatly organized stores while empty bins go back. It is hard to imagine how a central scheduling system could do such a good job of orchestrating an intricate movement of parts given the inherent uncertainty in complex systems.

At the same time, TPS experts get very impatient and even irritated when they hear people rave about kanban and declare that it is the be-all and end-all of the Toyota Production System. Kanban is a fascinating tool, and it is fun to watch. I have led many tours of lean plants, and you can spend hours talking about the technical details of many different types of kanban systems and fielding a variety of questions: "How is the kanban triggered?" "Should you replenish just what has been used or trigger the next order in a predetermined sequence?" "How are the quantities calculated?" "What do you do if a kanban gets lost?" But that is not the point. You do have to know those things when you set up your system, but they are pretty straightforward technically. The real purpose of kanban is to eliminate the kanban.

The challenge is to develop a learning organization that will find ways to reduce the number of kanban and thereby reduce and finally eliminate the inventory buffer. Remember, the kanban is an organized system of inventory buffers, and according to Ohno, inventory is waste, whether it is in a push system or a pull system. So kanban is something you strive to get rid of, not to be proud of. In fact, one of the major benefits of kanban is that it forces improvement in your production system. Let's say that you have printed up four kanban. Each one corresponds to a bin of parts. The rule is that a bin cannot move unless a kanban is traveling with it. Take one kanban and throw it away. What happens? There will now be only three bins of parts circulating in the system. So if a machine goes down, the next process will run out of parts 25 percent faster. It may stress the system and cause some shutdowns, but it will force teams to come up with process improvements.

Kanban is a simple visual system that sends a signal from a customer to a supplier. It is binary communication: "I see I reached the trigger point; please send more." Try it—it's fun and works!

KEY POINTS

- Most companies assume that they can use demand forecasts and complex scheduling algorithms to give instructions to each individual process.
- The traditional way of production scheduling often leads to push systems where even small changes in demand or conditions can throw off the process, leading to inventory banks, parts shortages, and missed shipments.
- Toyota uses scheduled systems, often to create leveled schedules, but prefers to schedule only at one point in the factory—the pacemaker.
- Ideally, Toyota would only use one-piece flow operations without work-in-process inventory, but for many situations this is not practical.

- When one-piece flow is not practical, Toyota pulls parts from small inventory buffers and then replenishes the buffers much like the modern supermarket does.
- Kanban (a physical or electronic signal) is often used so the upstream process (customer) can inform the downstream supplier process when it is ready for more of a particular part.
- The biggest value of the kanban system is to help visualize the flow, study it, and find ways to reduce inventory in order to get closer to one-piece flow.
- Pull systems are frequently used in service environments, like hospitals and offices, to regulate the internal flow of materials and are also powerful to regulate information flow.

Notes

1. Elizabeth G. Dun, "In a Burger World, Can Sweetgreen Scale Up?," *New York Times*, January 4, 2020.
2. Steven Spear and Kent Bowen, "Decoding the DNA of the Toyota Production System," *Harvard Business Review*, September–October 1999, p. 98.
3. Mike Rother and John Shook, *Training to See Kit* (Cambridge, MA: Lean Enterprise Institute, October 2002).

Principle 4

Level Out the Workload, Like the Tortoise, Not the Hare (Heijunka)

In general, when you try to apply the TPS, the first thing you have to do is to even out or level the production. And that is the responsibility primarily of production control or production management people. Leveling the production schedule may require some front-loading of shipments or postponing of shipments and you may have to ask some customers to wait for a short period of time.
—Fujio Cho, President, Toyota Motor Corporation

Following the early lead of Dell Computer and other successful companies, many businesses in America rushed to a build-to-order model of production. In the on-demand world we live in, they seek to make exactly what the customers want when they want it—the ultimate lean solution? Unfortunately, customers are not predictable, and orders vary significantly from day to day and week to week. If you build customized products as they are ordered, you may build huge quantities one week, paying overtime and stressing your people and equipment, but then if orders are light the next week, your people will have little to do and your equipment will be underutilized. You won't know how much to order from your suppliers, so you will have to stockpile the maximum possible amount of each item the customers might possibly order, or pressure your suppliers to hold stockpiles, perhaps at a warehouse near your plant (as Dell did). It is impossible to run a lean operation this way. A strict build-to-order model creates piles of inventory, hidden problems, and possibly poorer quality. Ironically, lead times are likely to grow because the factory will become disorganized and chaotic.

Often "build to order" turns into "pick to order" from a large warehouse of finished goods. Toyota has found it can create the leanest operation, and ultimately give customers better service and better quality, by leveling out the production schedule and not always building in the sequence of customer orders.

Some of the businesses I have worked with that try to build to order are in actuality asking customers to wait six to eight weeks for their "built-to-order" product. A few "special" customers may cut in line and get their orders expedited at the expense of the large majority of customers. In between the factory and the customers are distribution centers, local warehouses, and inventory in stores. Yet the manufacturing plants are under severe stress to build exactly what the customer has ordered day by day. This seems rather absurd. Why torture your manufacturing managers and create a huge amount of waste in the process to build an order received today when the customer will not get the product for weeks? Instead, why not accumulate some orders and level the schedule? Following that approach, you may be able to reduce production lead times, cut your parts inventories, and quote much shorter standard lead times to all your customers—resulting in greater overall customer satisfaction than you'll get from a "hurry up, then slow down" build-to-order method. To many companies, the concept of going slow to go fast seems absurd—that is, until someone can get them to try it.

Toyota managers and employees use the Japanese term "muda" when they talk about waste—and eliminating muda and the seven forms of muda are often the main focus of lean efforts because they are the most obvious. But two other Ms are just as important in making lean work, and all three Ms fit together as a system. In fact, focusing exclusively on the seven wastes of muda can actually hurt labor productivity and the production system. The *Toyota Way 2001* document refers to the "elimination of *Muda, Muri, Mura*" (see Figure 4.1). The three Ms are:

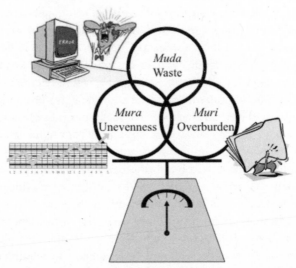

Figure 4.1   The three Ms: muda (waste), mura (unevenness), and muri (overburden). Eliminate all three to get to true flow.

- **Muda—non-value added.** The most familiar M, muda includes the seven wastes mentioned in earlier chapters. These wasteful activities lengthen lead times, cause extra movement to get parts or tools, create excess inventory, require rework time because of errors, or result in any type of waiting.
- **Mura—unevenness.** In normal production systems, at times there is more work than the people or machines can handle, and at other times there is a lack of work. Unevenness results from an irregular production schedule or fluctuating production volumes due to internal problems, such as downtime, missing parts, or defects. Mura will also cause muda. Unevenness in production levels makes it necessary to have on hand the equipment, materials, and people for the highest level of production—even if the average requirements are far less. And *unevenness leads to too little work sometimes and overburden at other times—leading directly to Muri.*
- **Muri—overburdening people or equipment.** In some respects, muri is on the opposite end of the spectrum from muda. Muda is underperforming, while Muri is pushing a machine or person beyond natural limits. Overburdening people results in safety and quality problems. Overburdening equipment causes breakdowns and defects. In other words, muri can cause muda. And even worse, overburdening people can cause health and safety problems.

Let's say you have a production schedule that swings wildly and a production process that is not well balanced or reliable. You've decided to start applying lean thinking and focus only on "eliminating muda" from your production system. You start to reduce inventory in your system. Next you look at the work balance and reduce the number of people from the system. Then you organize the workplace better to eliminate wasted motion. Finally you step back and let the system run. What you'll sadly witness is a system that will run itself into the ground. When work first begins to flow one piece at a time across work centers, without inventory, the only thing you will get is erratic one-piece flow. Workers will at times have little to do and at other times be overburdened. Equipment will break down even more than before. You will run out of parts. Then you'll conclude, "Lean manufacturing doesn't work here" and increase the inventory.

Interestingly, focusing on muda is the most common approach to implementing lean tools, because it is easy to spot the seven wastes. But many companies fail to pursue the more difficult process of stabilizing the system and creating "evenness"—which is essential to creating a true, balanced, lean flow of work. Toyota calls this concept of leveling out the work schedule "heijunka," and it is the foundation of TPS and perhaps the Toyota Way's most counterintuitive principle. Achieving heijunka is fundamental to eliminating mura, which is fundamental to eliminating muri and muda. As explained by Taiichi Ohno:

The slower but consistent tortoise causes less waste and is much more desirable than the speedy hare that races ahead and then stops occasionally to doze. The Toyota Production System can be realized only when all the workers become tortoises.[1]

I have heard this repeated from other Toyota leaders: "We would rather be slow and steady like the tortoise than fast and jerky like the rabbit." US production systems force workers to be like rabbits. They tend to work really hard, wear themselves down, and then take a siesta. In many US factories, workers will sometimes double up on the assembly line, one doing two jobs while the other has free time, and though the workers make production quotas for the day, they overburden themselves. At Toyota, muda is viewed as something that can be worked on by the frontline work group, but overburden and unevenness are the responsibility of management. Since I find that leveling is confusing to many businesspeople, and often seems impossible given the unpredictable fluctuations in customer orders, I will give examples in a number of different types of businesses.

HEIJUNKA—LEVELING SCHEDULES FOR LOW-VARIETY PRODUCTION

In manufacturing, heijunka is the leveling of production by both volume and product mix. It does not build products according to the actual flow of customer orders, which can swing up and down wildly, but takes the total volume of orders in a period and levels them out so approximately the same amount and mix are made each day for a period of time. The approach of TPS from the beginning was to keep batch sizes small and build what the customer (external or internal) wants. In a true build to order, you build products A and B in the actual production sequence of customer orders (e.g., A, A, B, A, B, B, B, A, B, B . . .).

The problem with building to an actual production sequence is that it causes you to build parts irregularly. If orders on Monday are twice those on Tuesday, you must pay your employees overtime on Monday and then send them home early on Tuesday. To smooth this out, you take the actual customer demand, determine the pattern of volume and mix, and build a level schedule every day. For example, you know you are making five As for every five Bs. Now you can create a level production sequence of ABABAB. . . . This is called leveled, mixed-model production, because you are leveling the customer demand for different models to a predictable sequence, which spreads out the different product types and leveling volume.

Figure 4.2 gives an example of an unleveled schedule from an engine plant that makes engines for lawn care equipment (based on an actual case).

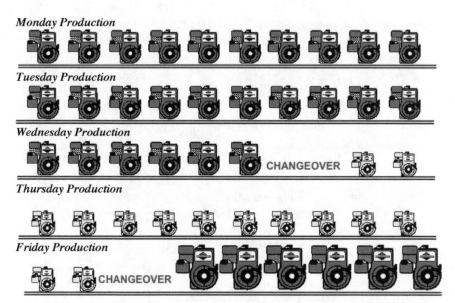

Figure 4.2   Traditional production (unleveled).

In this case, a production line makes three sizes of engines—small, medium, and large. The medium engines are the big sellers, so these are made early in the week—Monday through part of Wednesday. After a several-hour changeover of the line, small engines are made the rest of Wednesday through Friday morning. Finally, the large engines—in smallest demand—are made Friday afternoon. There are at least four things wrong with this unleveled schedule:

1. **Customers usually do not buy products predictably.** The customer is buying medium and large engines throughout the week. If the customer unexpectedly decides to buy an unusually large number of large engines early in the week, the plant is in trouble. You can get around this by holding a lot of finished-goods inventory of all engines, but this leads to an unnecessary high cost of inventory.
2. **There is a risk of unsold goods.** If the plant does not sell all its medium engines built Monday to Wednesday, it must keep them in inventory. If there is a design change, they can become obsolete.
3. **The use of resources is unbalanced.** Most likely, there are different labor requirements for these different-size engines, with the largest engines taking the most labor time. The plant needs a medium amount of labor early in the week, then less labor in the middle of the week, and then a lot of labor at the end of the week. The unbalance creates the potential for lots of muda and muri.

4. **There is an uneven demand placed on upstream processes.** This is perhaps the most serious problem. Because the plant purchases different parts for the three types of engines, it asks its suppliers to send certain parts Monday through Wednesday and different parts the rest of the week. Experience tells us that customer demand always changes and the engine plant will be unable to stick to the schedule anyway. Most likely, there will be some big shifts in the model mix, e.g., an unexpected rush order of large engines and the need to focus on making those for a whole week. The supplier will need to be prepared for the worst-possible scenario and will need to keep at least one week's worth of all parts for all three engine types. And something called the "bullwhip effect" will multiply these erratic ordering patterns backward through the supply chain.[2] Think of the small force in your wrist creating a huge and destructive force at the end of the whip. Similarly, a small change in the schedule of the engine assembly plant will result in ever-increasing inventory banks at each stage of the supply chain as you move backward from the end customer.

In a batch-processing mode, the goal is to achieve economies of scale for each piece of equipment. Changing over tools to alternate between making product A and making product B appears to be wasteful because parts are not being produced during the changeover time. You are also paying the equipment operator while the machine is being changed over. The logical solution is to build large batches of product A before changing over to product B. But this approach leads to mura and muri.

Guided by a lean advisor, the engine plant did a careful analysis and discovered that the long time to change over the line was due to moving in and out parts and tools for the larger engine and then moving in and out parts and tools for the smaller engine. There were also different-size pallets for the different engines. The plant tackled the problem by placing a small amount of all the parts on flow racks located next to the operator and mounting the tools needed for all three engines within easy reach. The plant also created a flexible pallet that could hold any size engine. These changes eliminated the equipment changeover completely, allowing the plant to build the engines in any order it wanted on a mixed-model assembly line. They then moved to a repeating (level) sequence of all three engine sizes matching the mix of parts ordered by the customer (see Figure 4.3). There were four benefits of leveling the schedule:

1. **Flexibility to make what the customers want when they want it.** This reduced the plant's inventory and its associated problems.
2. **Reduced risk of unsold goods.** The plant built only what the customers ordered, reducing the costs of owning and storing obsolete inventory.

Figure 4.3   Heijunka production (leveled).

3. **Balanced use of labor and machines.** The plant could then create standardized work that took into account that some engines required less work and others required more work. Toyota calls this the weighted-average standardized work. As long as a big engine that takes extra work is not followed by another big engine, the workers can handle the big engine, taking a little extra time, and then make up for it on the small engine. Once the plant took this into account and kept the schedule level, it had a balanced and manageable workload over the day with more productive operators.

4. **Smoothed demand on upstream processes and the plant's suppliers.** If the plant uses a just-in-time system for upstream processes and the suppliers deliver multiple times in a day, the suppliers will get a stable and level set of orders. This will allow the suppliers to reduce inventory and then pass some savings on to the customer so that everyone gets the benefits of leveling.

None of this would have been possible if the plant hadn't found a way to reduce or, in this case, eliminate the setup time for changeover. Though dramatically reducing setup time in most plants may seem unrealistic at first, Toyota did exactly that in the 1960s. Shigeo Shingo, an industrial engineer who was not a Toyota employee but worked closely with Toyota, helped the company achieve an average changeover time reduction of over 97 percent. A meticulous industrial engineer who paid attention to every microscopic reach and grasp of the worker, Shingo, in true Toyota style, thoroughly analyzed the setup process for large stamping presses and discovered that most of the work fell into one of two categories: it was muda, or it was something that could be done while the press was still making parts. He called the second category "external setup," as opposed to "internal setup," which was work that had to be done while the press was shut down.[3]

In traditional mass production, the first thing the setup teams did when they performed the changeover of a production line from one model to another was to shut down the press. Shingo wondered how much of the changeover he could perform while the press was still running, so he organized an operator's workplace for that purpose and made other technical improvements until there was no more setup the operator could do while the press was running. He found that things like getting the next die and tools, preheating the die, and setting it in place beside the press were external and could be done while the press was making parts. When he finally shut down the press, all that was basically left to do was to disconnect some hoses, swap the dies, and reconnect the hoses and start it up again. Amazingly, these several-hundred-ton presses that previously took many hours to change over could, it turned out, be changed over in minutes—a process that Shingo called single-minute exchange of dies (SMED). Think of it like a racing pit crew that quickly services and gets the car back on the track, often in less than a minute. The pit crew developed and continually improved this method, because it was a competitive advantage.

Southwest Airlines figured out early on that quickly changing over aircraft was a competitive advantage and worked hard at it, even changing aircraft engines when necessary. There was more air time, versus time sitting at airports. Customers did not have to wait as long. And it reduced the number of planes needed for a given number of flights.

Over the years, changeover has become a kind of a sport in Japan, a manufacturing equivalent of an American rodeo. On one trip I took to Japan in the 1980s, I visited a Mazda supplier of stamped door panels whose team had recently won a prize in a national competition for changing over a several-hundred-ton press in 52 seconds.

Toyota may seem obsessive about leveling the schedule, but it is a necessity to make the Toyota Production System work. The thought process behind heijunka is summarized in the flowchart in Figure 4.4. Leveling enables takt (stable rate of demand), which is necessary for doing standardized work and balancing work on the line, which is a requirement for leveled pull from upstream processes and suppliers, which leads to minimum inventory, minimum cost, and best quality.

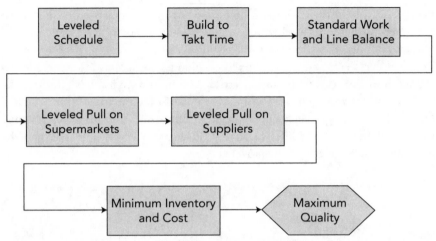

Figure 4.4   Why does Toyota level the schedule?

BUILDING SEMI-CUSTOM HOMES
IN A LEVELED FACTORY

Few people outside of Japan have ever heard of Toyota Housing Corporation. Surprise! Toyota has been designing and building homes in Japan since 1975. Toyota Housing Corporation is a viable business and expanded from private detached homes to condominiums and rental units. In fiscal 2017, the housing services business sold 10,321 units on a consolidated basis and generated net revenues of ¥300.8 billion (about $2.7 billion). Toyota builds most of the homes in factories on assembly lines. It looks more like an auto factory than a home construction site. The shortest time to build a home for a customer when I visited in 2013 was 15 days. We think of modular homes built in a factory as inexpensive and less desirable than homes built from scratch on-site, but Toyota homes are expensive and desirable, with the top-line 2,600-square-foot custom model selling for over $1 million. The homes are durable, resistant to earthquakes, and environmentally friendly. While profitable, the contribution to Toyota's overall bottom line is small, but they may have an equal, if not greater, benefit to Toyota as an experimental center for learning.

One research question addressed in the housing company is how to level the schedule when building such a complicated product with so many variants—heijunka in a high-mix, high-variety environment. One of Toyota's best TPS experts at the time, Kenji Miura, oversaw the effort. The process started with something that looked familiar in an auto plant—robots welding together the steel structures, only in this case the robots were outlining the various rooms of the house. From there, the steel structure moves to an assembly line, where rooms, not automobiles, flow through various stations (see Figure 4.5). Each room is a cubicle to be later assembled on-site, like building a Lego house. The room leaves the assembly line with plumbing, electrical, and most fixed features installed, like cabinets, and with the drywall and wiring piled inside the room to be installed on-site. Toyota is experienced in heijunka for mixed-model automotive assembly plants, but houses are a different animal. Each room is very different, and the level of customization is comparatively large.

Figure 4.5   Rooms for a Toyota home built on an assembly line
with the workload balanced to takt.

The first step to level the line is to define the tasks for each room and time each task. The tasks are then allocated to different workstations. Some rooms take a lot more time than others, and Toyota can help the cause by making sure high-task-time rooms are not built one after another, but rather spread out. Some individual tasks take longer than the rest of the tasks combined, and these are taken offline, for example, hand-built wooden stairs (see Figure 4.6). There is a very detailed schedule posted visually for the assembly line and a separate one for the offline stations.

Figure 4.6 Offline module (customized stairs take a lot of labor that varies with choices).

I visited Toyota's housing plant three times a few years apart, and each time there were major improvements. For example, on my first two visits, the team members built one house at a time—with all the rooms done one by one. This allowed them to level the workload across the rooms in that one house. On my third visit, managers had learned there was a big advantage to intermingling the rooms for two houses, which allowed for more rooms to level across. For example, one kitchen might be high end with more custom features than a smaller, standard kitchen that was just following it on the line. A group of team members could do tasks walking back and forth between the rooms, and the average of the two rooms could be completed within the takt. Intermingling rooms between two houses also allowed them to take some of the offline work online.

Lean construction has become a major global movement, but I have not seen this level of commitment to heijunka and attention to detail outside Toyota. It is easy to throw up your hands and say, "There is so much variation, heijunka is impossible." For Toyota, the impossible simply means the company needs to think harder and experiment more.

LEVELING THE SCHEDULE FOR SEASONAL ALUMINUM GUTTERS—SOMETIMES IT IS BETTER TO INTENTIONALLY BUILD EXTRA INVENTORY

These days seamless aluminum gutters for houses, at least in the United States, are mostly built to order, on-site at the house. Rolls of materials are brought to the jobsite, where they are cut to length, shaped, endcaps are added, and the gutters are installed. A plant in the Midwest makes much of the rolls of painted aluminum that installers use. While these rolls of aluminum are not complex, there is variation in the width of the gutters, the length, and the colors. They also are packaged in different boxes, for different businesses and stores.

This company originally adopted a build-to-order model. Deliveries were mostly made just in time, but the process of getting raw materials, scheduling operations, building the product, moving the finished goods to a warehouse, and then shipping those goods from the dozen or so shipping docks was chaotic, to say the least. There was inventory everywhere. Yet the plant regularly was short of critical materials needed to make the gutters ordered by customers. Costs of expediting shipments to large customers were getting higher and higher. People were added and laid off with regularity. A big problem was the seasonality of the business. Big-box warehouse stores like Home Depot bought large quantities of gutters in the spring and early summer, and then business dropped dramatically the rest of the year. A large number of temporary and inexperienced workers were added in the peak season and let go a few months later.

The Midwestern gutter plant decided to hire a consultant who used to work for the Toyota Production System Support Center. The consultant said the unthinkable—the overall operation would be leaner if the plant built select products to store away in inventory allowing for heijunka. Build more inventory to get leaner? Nuts! While it sounded unreasonable at first, the company followed the consultant's advice. Perhaps his Toyota credentials helped overcome the disbelief.

He made the proposition sound even more absurd because he wanted the company to keep four types of inventory in four different places. The first was real built-to-order product set in a staging lane so that it could be loaded on a truck immediately. The second was to build ahead seasonal product for high-volume items the plant knew it would later sell. It should be built steadily throughout the year, accumulated in a seasonal inventory buffer, and then drawn down in the busy spring-summer season. The third was safety stock, which is inventory used to buffer against unexpectedly high demand for products that are not in the seasonal buffer and that experience occasional spikes in demand. The fourth was buffer stock, which is held to cushion against downtime in the factory, so customers will continue to get their product even when machines are down for repair—essentially, inventory for plant-driven variation.

On the consultant's recommendation, each of these four types of inventory was stored in a separate area at the aluminum gutter plant with visual indicators, so that everyone would always be able to see at a glance the status of the inventory of each type (Principle 7).

The inventory was replenished by using a kanban system (cards instructing the production line to make a specific quantity of a particular product) as explained under Principle 5. For example, the largest amount of inventory is the seasonal inventory buffer. It is built up during the off-season and reaches a peak just before the spring, when sales are highest. There is a prespecified amount of seasonal buffer, and based on that forecasted amount, kanban is used by the production cell to make only that remaining number of packages needed. In front of the inventory stockpile is what looks like a clothesline labeled with months of the year. For example, the amount that should be completed by August, based on a constant level of production over the year, has a sign saying "August." In August, if the inventory pile is larger than should be built by that time, the pile of inventory will have moved beyond the August sign, alerting everyone that there is an excess inventory problem that needs to be addressed.

In kanban, the information flow begins with the customer order and works backward through the operation as a pull system. In this company, a final cutting and packaging (one-piece flow) cell gets real customer orders. But when those orders are low, the workers do not have to sit around with nothing to do. They can build to the seasonal inventory buffer or build to replace any safety stock or buffer stock that has been used. The seasonal inventory, safety stock, and buffer stock that need to be built are represented by kanban cards. The cards are sorted by a planner into a visual scheduling box called a "heijunka box," which levels the schedule (see Figure 4.7). For each product, the box says what to make at 8:00 a.m., 8:10 a.m., 8:20 a.m., etc. Cards are put in the slots and delivered to the production cell. These tell the cell what to make and at what pace. As the cell uses materials, like the painted aluminum product, a kanban is sent back to the prior operation asking it to make more. Leveled pull was established all the way back to suppliers, like the paint manufacturer.

At the suggestion of the TPS consultant, other improvements were made, such as standardizing work procedures, reducing changeover time, and putting in error-proofing devices. The result was a very smooth flow of product through the facility, so smooth that all outbound shipping could be handled through two docks, enabling the plant to close down the other ten shipping and receiving docks. In addition, the plant achieved incredible performance improvements. The overall lead time for making product was reduced by 40 percent, changeover time was reduced by 70 percent, WIP of painted product was reduced by 40

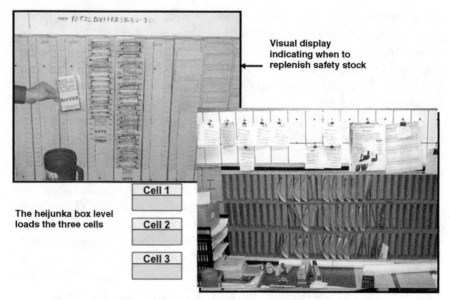

Figure 4.7 Scheduling the trim sheet cells for aluminum gutters.

percent, inventory obsolescence was reduced by 60 percent, and on-time delivery was close to 100 percent. A larger number of experienced workers could be kept on in the slow selling period and fewer temporary workers were needed in the busy period because the plant could ship high-volume items from the seasonal inventory buffer. Another lean paradox: hold more of the right inventory to have less overall inventory. This is systems thinking at its best!

LEVELING WORK IN AN UNPREDICTABLE CALL CENTER

Even with the digital age storming the business landscape, we are far from eliminating people who answer phones to talk to customers. Many companies seem to want to make it as difficult as possible to reach real people, with endless menus and terrible music playing while you are on hold. This is not true at Zingerman's Mail Order (ZMO) in Ann Arbor, Michigan, which ships high-end artisanal food all over the United States. When you call, it's likely a real person will answer immediately and will treat you like you are "the best part of their day."

ZMO has worked intensively on lean transformation in its warehouse since 2004, incorporating all the lean tools and developing an engaged workforce.[4] Along the way, the folks at ZMO turned their sights on improving the call center.

When they examined the data on call volumes, they found clear patterns, within the day, week, and year—so they could come up with reasonable estimates of staffing needs for forecasted peak volume in a day. Still, there was variation in call volume within the day, leading to idle time during slow periods, because they could not smooth out when customers called or how long the conversations lasted. Unevenness was the nature of the beast.

They decided to use a different concept of heijunka, not leveling the customer orders, but rather leveling the way people worked. How could they fill in time gaps of associates in a flexible way and create a smooth flow of work? They started by setting up call-in computer stations in work cells. The seats were numbered, with number one as the "hot seat." The hot seat gets the first call, and then as additional calls come in, service representatives fill the seats in sequence. In the busy Christmas holiday season when volumes explode, they have a hot cell and then staff additional cells as volumes grow. Those who are not on a call go to the visual board (shown in Figure 4.8) to pick the next card, which displays an off-cycle task such as processing credit card orders, organizing products on shelves, responding to voice mail, and processing gift cards. The cards on the board are organized at the beginning of the day in two-hour blocks and are placed red

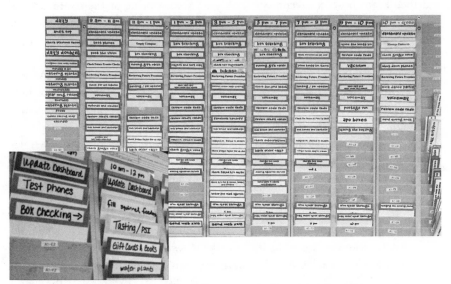

Figure 4.8 ZMO call center ancillary work board.
The board is organized in two-hour time blocks. Each card has a task on it
(e.g., "back-order calls," "check voice mail," "write out gift cards").
In the morning all the cards are loaded with their red side facing out,
and as the tasks are completed, the cards are turned over to the green side.

side facing out. As the tasks are completed, they are flipped to the green side so there is a visual indication of whether they were completed within the two-hour window—simple, but powerful. Without supervision, associates know what to do next, whether devoting all the attention needed to a customer or working on the various ancillary tasks that need to be completed.

PUTTING LEVELING AND FLOW TOGETHER—A TOUGH SELL

Every business would like to have a consistent volume over time so there is a consistent and predictable workload. But if you cannot control sales, are you stuck? The answer is that you are never stuck as long as you have your creative mind.

The TPS expert might suggest that a manufacturer hold some finished-goods inventory and build at a leveled pace to replenish what the customer takes away in a pull system, as in the aluminum gutter case. The manufacturer screams, "But we have 15,000 part numbers!"

The expert says, "Look for a smaller number of part numbers that are in big demand and perhaps even seasonal, build those when you have fewer real orders, and then keep those in inventory." This sounds reasonable to the manufacturer. But then comes the hard sell. The TPS expert asks the manufacturer to work hard to learn how to change over between product types more frequently to level the mix of products built every day. Many manufacturers balk. After all, it is so convenient to build in batches, making product A for a while, then retooling and making product B for a while, and so on. Quick retooling does not seem possible, until an expert shows the manufacturer how it can do a three-hour changeover in ten minutes. Even then, it is difficult for many manufacturers to maintain the discipline of quick changeover. And the real root cause of the problem may be sales promotion strategies that contribute to uneven customer demand, and heaven forbid sales people should be constrained. As organizations become more sophisticated in lean, they often begin to move to the enterprise level and change their policies in sales to maintain a more level customer demand. This requires a deep commitment at the very top of the company, but these organizations quickly find that the enormous benefits of heijunka make it a worthwhile investment.

It cannot be overstated. To achieve the lean benefits of continuous flow, you need Principle 4: "Level out the workload, like the tortoise, not the hare." Eliminating muda is only one-third of achieving flow. Eliminating muri and smoothing mura are equally important. Standardized work is far easier, cheaper, and faster to manage. It becomes increasingly easy to see the waste caused by missing parts or defects. Without leveling, wastes naturally increase, as people and equipment are driven to work like mad and then stop and wait, like the hare. Working according to a leveled schedule applies to all parts of Toyota, including sales. Everyone in the organization works together to achieve it.

KEY POINTS

- To get to lean flow requires seeking to eliminate the three Ms: muda (waste), mura (unevenness), and muri (overburden).
- The three Ms are all interrelated. Eliminating muda alone when there are high levels of unevenness and overburden can actually reduce productivity and value-added flow.
- In a Toyota mixed-model production plant, reducing mura and muri requires a leveled pattern of vehicles, for example Camry, Camry, Avalon, Camry, Camry, Avalon . . .
- Along with creating a leveled schedule, factories need to reduce setup time in order to quickly change over between products and build in small batches.
- Sometimes it is best to hold extra inventory of high-volume finished goods as a buffer against fluctuations in customer demand and allow building to order low-volume product types while replenishing the inventory for high-volume items.
- Heijunka may be different for service operations but still applies, as illustrated by the example of the Zingerman's call center.
- The challenge of heijunka is that it requires system thinking, instead of thinking about local optimization of individual operations.

Notes

1. Taichi Ohno, *Toyota Production System: Beyond Large-Scale Production* (New York: Productivity Press, 1988).
2. Hau L. Lee, V. Padmanabhan, and Seungjin Whang, "The Bullwhip Effect in Supply Chains," *Sloan Management Review*, April 15, 1997.
3. Shigeo Shingo, *A Revolution in Manufacturing: The SMED System* (New York: Productivity Press, 1985).
4. Eduardo Lander, Jeffrey Liker, and Tom Root, *Lean in a High-Variety Business: A Graphic Novel About Lean and People at Zingerman's Mail Order* (New York: Productivity Press, 2020).

Principle 5

Work to Establish Standardized Processes as the Foundation for Continuous Improvement

Standard work sheets and the information contained in them are important elements of the Toyota Production System. For a production person to be able to write a standard work sheet that other workers can understand, he or she must be convinced of its importance. . . . High production efficiency has been maintained by preventing the recurrence of defective products, operational mistakes, and accidents, and by incorporating workers' ideas. All of this is possible because of the inconspicuous standardized work sheet.

—Taiichi Ohno

Whether your employees are designing intricate new devices, styling new attractive products, processing accounts payable, developing new software, or working as nurses, they are likely to respond with skepticism to the idea of standardizing their work: "We are creative, thinking people, not robots." If you are not in manufacturing, you may be surprised to learn that even workers on the assembly line believe they have a knack for doing the job best their own way and that standardized work methods will simply set them back. But some level of standardization is possible and, as we will see, is the backbone of Toyota Way processes.

Standardizing tasks became a "science" when mass production replaced the craft form of production. Much of modern manufacturing is based on the principles of industrial engineering first set forth by Frederick Taylor, the "father of scientific management."[1] He preached that industrial engineers should scientifically design the work, supervisors should enforce compliance with the standards, and workers should do as told. He identified the fastest worker and used that as a model for the standardized work forced on others.

In the automotive world, plants had armies of industrial engineers who implemented Taylor's approach of time studies. Industrial engineers (IEs) were everywhere, timing every second of workers' tasks and trying to squeeze every extra bit of productivity out of the labor force. Open and honest workers who shared their work practices with the IEs would quickly find the job standards raised, and they would soon be working harder for no extra money. In response, workers withheld techniques and labor-saving devices they invented and hid them whenever the IEs were around. They deliberately worked slower when the IEs were doing a study, so expectations were set low. The IEs caught on to this and would at times sneak up on the operator or hide behind something to time them at work. Often companies changed the job descriptions and responsibilities based on efficiency and time studies, which sometimes led to union grievances and became a major source of conflict between management and workers. At American auto companies, unions negotiated prohibitions against IEs involving workers in changing work standards, and IEs were only allowed certain windows of time in the year when they could redefine standards.

Now companies use computers and cameras to monitor output and instantly report on the productivity of individual workers. As a result, people know they are being monitored, so they will work to make the numbers, often regardless of quality. Sadly, they become slaves to the numbers, rather than focus on a company's mission statement or philosophy. It doesn't have to be this way, as we will see with Toyota's approach to standardized work.

Ford Motor Company was one of the early mass production giants associated with rigid standardization on the moving assembly line, and Toyota's approach to standardized work* was partially shaped by Henry Ford's view. While the Ford Motor Company eventually became a rigid bureaucracy that followed the destructive practices of Taylor's scientific management, Henry Ford himself espoused a different view of standards:

> *Today's standardization . . . is the necessary foundation on which tomorrow's improvement will be based. If you think of "standardization" as the best you know today, but which is to be improved tomorrow—you get somewhere. But if you think of standards as confining, then progress stops.*[2]

Even more influential for Toyota than Henry Ford was the methodology and philosophy of the American military's Training Within Industry (TWI) service.[3] Established in 1940 during World War II to increase production to support the Allied forces and train civilians taking over factory jobs from men going

---

* The difference between "standardized work" and "standard work" is vague in the lean literature. I adopted the convention of "standardized work" because it is commonly used in Toyota. One Toyota explanation is that standard work implies a standard and standards are not regularly updated as improvements are made to the work. It can be argued either way, but I had to pick one.

to war, the program was based on the belief that the way to learn about industrial engineering methods was through application on the shop floor and that standardized work should be a cooperative effort between the foreman and the worker (Huntzinger, 2002). During the US occupation and rebuilding efforts of Japan after World War II, a former TWI trainer and his group, called the "Four Horsemen," taught Japanese businesses this approach. It included job methods (how to design efficient and safe workplaces), job instruction (how to train on standard methods), job relations (how supervisors should manage based on cooperation), and program development (how to spot, analyze, and resolve problems).

Toyota's training on standardized work was heavily influenced by TWI, and it became the backbone of Toyota's standardization philosophy. Toyota's job instruction training to this day has changed little since the 1950s and is almost exactly modeled after the TWI documents.

Standardized work in manufacturing at Toyota is much broader than writing out a list of steps the operator must follow. Former Toyota president Cho describes it this way:

> *Our standardized work consists of three elements—takt time (time required to complete one job at the pace of customer demand), the sequence of doing things or sequence of processes, and how much inventory or stock on hand the individual worker needs to have in order to accomplish that standardized work. Based upon these three elements, takt time, sequence, and standardized stock on hand, the standardized work is set.*

By "standardized work," we are referring to the most efficient and effective combination of people, material, and equipment to perform the work that is presently possible. "Presently possible" means it is today's best-known way, which can be improved.

There are many other types of standards, such as technical specifications for products, settings for equipment, rules for safety, inspection requirements for quality, minimum requirements for air quality, and on and on. I am often asked how Toyota can trust workers to make any changes they want to these standards. Quite the contrary, Team members do not have discretion to change professionally-defined standards without the approval of the highly regarded technical specialty groups who know the underlying science. These externally defined standards become inputs to standardized work. How can we perform the work to consistently achieve these specifications with minimum waste? What adjustments need to be made to the equipment to meet these standards?

In this chapter, we will see that, like so many organizational practices, the Toyota Way has turned the practice of standardized work on its head. What can be perceived as negative and stifling becomes positive and flexible within the Toyota Way and builds collaborative teams rather than conflict between workers and management. Standardized work was never intended by Toyota to be a management tool to be imposed coercively on the workforce. On the contrary, rather than enforcing rigid standards that can make jobs routine and degrading, standardized work is the basis for empowering workers, sharing ideas for improvement, and driving innovation in the workplace.

THE PRINCIPLE: WORK TO ESTABLISH STANDARDIZED PROCESSES AS THE FOUNDATION FOR CONTINUOUS IMPROVEMENT

Toyota's standards have a much broader role than making shop floor workers' tasks repeatable and efficient. Some degree of standardization is used throughout the company's white-collar work processes, even in engineering. For example, Toyota has standardized ways of training engineers, has macro-level standards for the stages and timing of product development, and extensively applies technical standards to the design of products and manufacturing equipment.

Managers have a misconception that standardization is all about finding the scientifically one best way to do a task and freezing it. As Imai explained so well in *Kaizen*,[4] it is impossible to improve any process until it is standardized. If the process is shifting from here to there, then any improvement will just be one more variation that will be altered by the next variation. One must standardize, and thus stabilize, the process before continuous improvements can be made. As an example, if you want to learn golf, the first thing an instructor will teach you is the basic golf swing. Then you need to practice, practice, and practice to stabilize your swing. Until you have the fundamental skills needed to swing the club with some consistency, there is little hope of learning the finer details of direction, fade, distance, and how the ball will land.

Standardized work is also a key facilitator of building in quality. Talk with any well-trained group leader at Toyota and ask how that leader believes zero defects are possible. The answer will be, "Through standardized work." Whenever a defect is discovered, the first question asked is, "Was standardized work followed?" As part of the problem-solving process, the leader will watch the worker and go through the standardized worksheet step-by-step to look for deviations. If the worker is following the standardized work and the defects still occur, then the standardized work may need to be modified.

In fact, traditionally in Toyota, the standardized worksheet is posted outward, away from the operator. The operator is trained using the standardized work but then must do the job without looking at the standardized worksheet.

The standardized worksheet is posted outward for the management to audit to see if it is being followed by the operator.

Any good quality manager at any company knows that you cannot guarantee quality without standard procedures for ensuring consistency in the process. Many quality departments make a good living turning out volumes of such procedures. Unfortunately, the role of the quality department is often to assign blame for failing to "follow the procedures" when there is a quality problem. The Toyota Way enables those doing the work to design and build in quality by writing the standardized task procedures themselves. For quality procedures to be effective, they must be simple and practical enough to be used every day by the people doing the work.

A sample standardized worksheet from Toyota for a job of welding a side support onto a steel vehicle body is shown in Figure 5.1. The actual welding is done by a robot, but the team member does the loading and unloading into a fixture. In this case, the takt is 76 seconds, and the cycle time of the manual

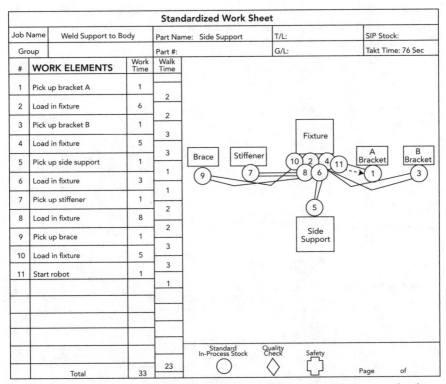

Figure 5.1 Standardized worksheet for welding a side support to a body.
Source: Jeffrey Liker and David Meier, *The Toyota Way Fieldbook*
(New York: McGraw-Hill, 2006).

steps of the person is 56 seconds. The figure does not show the robot time to do the welding; that would be displayed on a separate "standard work combination sheet" that shows the member's motions in relation to the robot's work.

The standardized worksheet is useful for analysis of the job. At a glance, where is there waste in this process? It is apparent from the walk pattern in the diagram that there is a great deal of movement waste. In total, about 40 percent of the job is walk time to and from the fixture. Clearly, that would be a prime target for reducing waste.

Once the standardized work is defined it provides a picture of what should be happening. To turn the desired behavior into actual behavior requires training through enough repetitions that the new way becomes a habit. To use job instruction training to develop the skills and habits of standardized work, we have to drill down to another level of detail—the Job Breakdown Sheet. Figure 5.2 shows a different Toyota job: removing a plastic-injection molded bumper from a mold. Demolding takes a fair amount of skill. On this sheet, each step that would go on a standardized worksheet with its associated time is broken down into further steps with key points that relate to safety, quality, technique, or cost. The reason for the key points is also provided, the why. In many cases, even

JOB BREAKDOWN SHEET DATE: 8/24/20		Steve Morgan	Pete Desoto
		Team Leader	Supervisor
AREA: Bumper molding	JOB: Rear bumper molding operator – de-mold	WRITTEN BY: D. Willard	
MAJOR STEPS	**KEYPOINTS** SAFETY: Injury avoidance, ergonomics, danger points QUALITY: Defect avoidance, check points, standards TECHNIQUE: Efficient movement, special method COST: Proper use of materials		**REASONS FOR KEYPOINTS**
Step #1 De-mold right side of bumper	1. Grasp at top and back 2. Pull out 2 to 5 inches 3. Pull down after pulling out		1. Easy to get hand hold 2. Less will fail, more will cause crease 3. Releases side from the mold
Step #2 De-mold center of bumper	1. Push down with left hand in the middle 2. Keep right arm extended		1. Release the center of bumper 2. Pulling right side to center can cause crease
Step #3 De-mold left side of bumper	1. Use left thumb to push along edge of bumper 2. Place pressure in the crease of thumb 3. Push towards left side away from mold 4. Grasp top edge when bumper is released		1. Peeling movement to release bumper 2. Pressure on tip will cause injury 3. Releases left side of bumper 4. To hold correctly preventing defects
Step #4 Place in trimming fixture	1. Keep arms spread 2. Make sure gate is not folded under 3. Trim nest must be free of debris		1. Arms together will crease bumper 2. Gate will distort causing scrap 3. Any debris will cause a dent and scrap

Figure 5.2   Job Breakdown Sheet for rear bumper demolding.
Source: Jeffrey Liker and David Meier, *Toyota Talent* (New York: McGraw-Hill, 2007).

for a 60-second job, each step on a standardized worksheet is broken down into about three to five substeps, each with key points. There are often photos that illustrate how to perform the steps. For example, each work element, as in Figure 5.1, would have an additional page breaking down the step.

You will not see these voluminous documents on a usual tour of a Toyota plant. They will be in notebooks hung by the process or stored in a cabinet where the group leader sits. They are pulled out for training purposes, then put away.* Standardized work, and some degree of stability, is necessary before you can train someone new to do the job. Job instruction training that comes from TWI is a very specific training method that consists of starting with a piece of the job; demonstrating that piece for the worker; letting the worker do it; then explaining key points while demonstrating a second time; letting the worker demonstrate and explain; then explaining key points and reasons while demonstrating a third time; and then having the worker imitate. This process is repeated as many times as necessary until the worker has mastered one piece; then the process begins again with the next piece. In a Toyota plant with one-minute-cycle jobs, it can take two weeks of this repeated teaching before the worker is left alone, more training than many people get in some professional roles.

But when you have developed standardized work and it is being reasonably followed, the magic really begins—at that point, standardized work becomes the basis for continuous improvement. One powerful tool for this is the work-balance chart (see Figure 5.3). With the work broken down into pieces, and some stability in the time it takes to do each piece, you can line up various jobs and compare them with the takt. In Figure 5.3, we show the "planned cycle time" (PCT), which is a bit faster than the takt and the current target. As long as there is variation in the process, for example, because of equipment downtime and quality issues, the team member needs to work faster than the takt in order to consistently stay within takt. The goal is for each job to match, but not exceed, the planned cycle time.

In the current state, process C is overburdened with work and cannot meet the PCT, while the other processes are light. After kaizen, the work has been balanced. In Toyota, you may see large versions of these charts with magnets for each work step so the work group can visualize the current state and then try moving some work elements around, and reducing the time for others, to balance the work. Eliminating waste from individual jobs that add to the PCT can lead the group to rebalancing and eliminating a process—a cause for celebration if you trust that none of the members of the team will lose their job. The key word here is "trust." Trust must be built up and maintained through consistently positive behavior.

---

* There are detailed discussions of training techniques in Jeffrey Liker and David Meier, *Toyota Talent* (New York: McGraw-Hill, 2007).

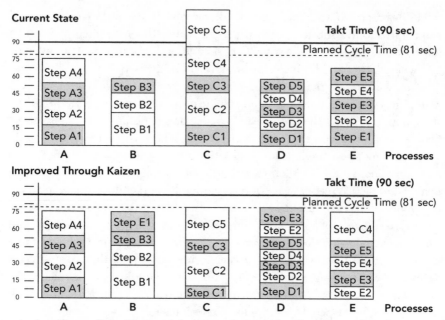

Figure 5.3 The work-balance chart to visualize the work and balance processes to planned cycle time.

STANDARDIZING WORK FOR A NEW PRODUCT LAUNCH

When a new vehicle is introduced, standardized work must be redesigned for all processes. The Toyota Way of handling the chaos of getting an army of people involved in creating and launching a new vehicle is to standardize the work in a balanced way that doesn't give complete control to any group of employees. Having only engineers devise the standards would be a form of Taylorism. On the other hand, having all the workers come to consensus on every step could be overly organic, resulting in a different type of waste.

Toyota's answer is to develop a "pilot team." When a new product is in the early planning stages, workers representing the major areas of the factory are brought together full-time to an office area where, as a team, they help with product design and vehicle launch. They begin by critiquing the design with an eye to making the vehicle easier to manufacture and assemble, which sometimes involves workers flying to Japan to join in the discussion. As the product is developed and the focus shifts to preparation of the plant, they work closely with production engineering to develop the initial standardized work for the launch. That work is then turned over to the production teams to improve. As Gary Convis, former president of Toyota's Kentucky manufacturing operations, explained:

> *Pilot teams are put together, especially when we launch a new model, like we just launched the Camry. Team member voices are heard by way of that link. Usually it's a three-year assignment. We have a four-year model change cycle, so we'll have an Avalon model change, then we'll have a Camry model change, and we'll have a Sienna model change. So there are enough big model changes to have these guys go through at least one or two before they rotate back out.*

Team members on the pilot team learn a great deal about the design and production of the new vehicle, and when they finish their rotation, they are often promoted to team leaders to contribute to and improve the standardized work. This is important, because launching a new vehicle is an exercise in coordinating thousands of parts, with thousands of people making detailed design decisions—and everything must fit together at the right time.

When my associates and I studied Toyota's product development system, we found that standardization promotes effective teamwork by teaching employees similar terminology, skills, and rules of play. From the time they are hired into the company, engineers are trained to learn the standards of product development. They all go through a similar training regimen of "learning by doing."[5, 6] Toyota engineers also make extensive use of design standards that have been developed and refined over decades. Within each part of the vehicle—plastic bumpers, steel body panels, seats, instrument panels—engineering checklists have evolved as the company learned about good and bad design practices. The engineers use these checklist books from their first days at Toyota and develop them further with each new vehicle program. Today these books are computerized in know-how databases, and finding the right balance between enough detail to be helpful, but not so much that checking becomes onerous and the standards confining is an ongoing process.

US companies have tried to imitate Toyota's engineering approach by utilizing computer technology at the start and creating large databases of engineering standards—often with limited success. The problem is, they have not trained their engineers to have the discipline to use and improve upon the standards. Organizing a bunch of standards into a computer database is not difficult. The hard part is getting knowledgeable people to selectively develop the most important standards and then use them in their engineering work. Toyota spends years working with its people to instill in them the importance of using and improving standards.

COERCIVE VERSUS ENABLING BUREAUCRACIES

Standardized work is like a drug to managers in a coercive bureaucracy—control the workers! Under Taylor's scientific management,[7] industrial engineers viewed workers as machines that needed to be made as efficient as possible. The process consisted of the following:

- Scientifically determine the one best way of doing the job.
- Scientifically develop the one best way to train someone to do the job.
- Scientifically select people who are capable of doing the job in that way.
- Train foremen to teach their "subordinates" and monitor them so they follow the one best way.
- Create financial incentives for workers to follow the one best way and exceed the performance standard scientifically set by the industrial engineer.

Taylor did achieve tremendous productivity gains at that time by applying these principles to very simple manual jobs like shoveling coal. But he also created very rigid bureaucracies in which industrial engineers were supposed to do the thinking, managers were to enforce the standards, and workers were to blindly execute the standardized procedures. After all, any change by the managers or workers to what the "experts" designed was assumed to be a step backward. The results were predictable:

- Red tape
- Top-down control
- Large staff groups
- Books and books of written rules and procedures
- Resistance to change
- Static and often poorly conceived rules and procedures

Most bureaucracies are static, internally focused on efficiency, controlling of employees, unresponsive to changes in the environment, and generally unpleasant to work in.[8] But bureaucracies can be efficient if the environment is very stable and if technology changes very little. However, as discussed in the Preface, most modern organizations need to be flexible, to focus on effectiveness, to be adaptable to change, and to do this by empowering their employees. Organic organizations are more effective when the environment and technology are changing rapidly. Given how the world around us is changing at the speed of thought, perhaps it's time to throw out slow-moving bureaucratic standards and policies and allow frontline teams to be flexible and creative. The Toyota Production System follows an interesting blend of the two approaches.

We discussed in the Preface how Paul Adler, an organizational theory expert, noticed at NUMMI that the team members followed very detailed and standardized procedures in performing highly repetitive work; and there was a place for everything and most everything was in its place. Waste was eliminated continually to increase productivity. Wasn't this exactly what Fredrick Taylor's scientific management tried to attain?

But NUMMI also had many of the characteristics associated with flexible organizations, that organization theorists call "organic": extensive employee involvement, good communication, innovation, flexibility, high morale, and a strong customer focus. This caused Adler to rethink some of the traditional theories about bureaucratic organizations.

He concluded that there are not two types of organizations—bureaucratic/mechanistic versus organic—but at least four, as shown in Figure 5.4. You can distinguish organizations with extensive bureaucratic rules and structures (mechanistic) from those unencumbered by bureaucracy (organic). The rules and procedures are all part of the technical structure of the organization. But there is also a social structure, which can be either "coercive" or "enabling." When you put together the two technical structures with the two social structures, you get the four types of organization and two types of bureaucracy. TPS at NUMMI was proving that technical standardization, when coupled with enabling social structures, could lead to something different—an "enabling bureaucracy."

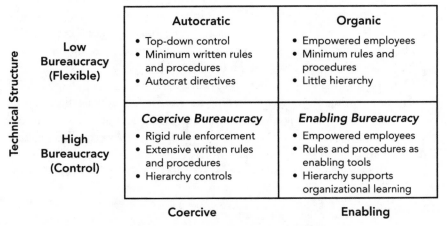

Figure 5.4   Coercive versus enabling bureaucracy.
Source: Adapted from P. S. Adler, "Building Better Bureaucracies," *Academy of Management Executive,* vol. 13, no. 4, November 1999, pp. 36–47.

The key difference between Taylorism and the Toyota Way is that the Toyota Way preaches that the worker is the most valuable resource—not just a pair of hands taking orders, but an analyst and problem solver. From this perspective, suddenly Toyota's bureaucratic, top-down system becomes the basis for flexibility and innovation. Adler called this behavior "democratic Taylorism" resulting in a "learning bureaucracy."

STANDARDIZATION TO BETTER SERVE CUSTOMERS AT STARBUCKS

As I write this Starbucks has over 30,000 stores globally and serves 87,000 different combinations of espresso beverages. Demand changes minute by minute. In any given store at any given time, no customers can come through the door, a few customers can come through the door, or a busload of customers can enter the store. How could standardized work possibly apply? After all, baristas are like artists, cleverly decorating each latte. Standardization and bureaucracy coming from headquarters makes more sense for a fast-food joint like McDonald's than for stores serving high-priced individualized espresso drinks. Would it surprise you to know Starbucks improved quality, reduced cost, provided better customer service, and even responded more effectively to a crisis through flexible standardization?

Starbucks learned from former Toyota managers and took lean principles seriously, including JIT, flow, 5S, problem solving, and standardized work. The book *Steady Work*,[9] written by former Starbucks regional director Karen Gaudet, chronicles the story of how this humongous company adapted and used standardized work with game-changing results.

Outside consultants helped develop coaches at the headquarters level, but the job of experimenting, learning, and leading was assigned to regional directors like Gaudet, who was responsible for district managers and 110 stores. When the lean program was first introduced in 2008, the regional directors were called together and taught to learn to see and measure work processes and waste. Suddenly, the daily routines of managers, shift supervisors, and partners, who worked in the stores and got shares of stock, came into focus. The picture was ugly:

- Cashiers put a bean in a cup each time they had to say no to a customer or "I am sorry we are out of that type of brewed coffee." Everyone was shocked to learn that 25–30 percent of customers warranted a bean. (Scott Heydon, vice president at the time, said he would never forget having to tell the CEO about this problem: "He was anxious to hear my solution.")

- The quality of espresso beverages was compromised when milk (per the standards from corporate) was steamed in large pitchers and then "held" for some period of time for use in future beverages. Over a short period of time, this steamed milk degraded in quality as it sat waiting for a beverage order. Sometimes, the milk "expired," resulting in unnecessary dairy waste.

- The corporate standard allowed for batch grinding of beans as part of the daily preopening process. This was mostly because of the way most stores were set up—where the grinder was far away from the brewing machine. It was a surprise to all leaders that there was a noticeable taste difference between freshly ground cups of coffee and cups created with coffee ground six to eight hours prior to brewing. Ultimately, as part of the Brewed Coffee Better Way standards, stores relocated their grinders near the brewers (as learned from one of the pilot lean sites).

- Coffee in urns that was supposed to be freshly made every 30 minutes was changed out late, resulting in lower-quality and thrown-out coffee.

When a target came down from corporate to save $25 million in a year by eliminating waste the goal seemed daunting, but after observation at the gemba, opportunities were abundant.

With the help of consultants, corporate developed "A Better Way" standards for common high-frequency activities in the stores (brewing coffee, making other beverages, preparing Frappuccino™, loading the pastry case, etc.). In formulating the system, corporate made a number of discoveries. For example, the lead time for espresso drinks was faster if two beverages were prepared in parallel, with the machine processing one while the barista prepared the other. Astonishingly, it was discovered that there was no standard system for making urns of brewed coffee.

Another big problem was running out of brewed coffee from large urns, leaving customers waiting. The existing process called for the four urns to be assigned to a particular coffee type: two for medium roast, one for bold, and one for decaf. An obnoxious buzzer went off every 30 minutes when a timer expired and it was time to make the next batch. It took 7 minutes to make the batch, and so there was a minimum of 7 minutes until that type of coffee would become available again (1 minute changeover and 6 minutes brewing). So roughly 25 percent of the time—by design of the recommended SOP—bold and decaf coffee weren't available for customers, and that's if everything went as planned. And there was no clear role responsible for making the coffee, and it often was delayed further, waiting for someone to get freed up. With the Better Way, the coffee in urns was now brewed in an 8-minute cadence. Just as a specific type of coffee (e.g., bold) was expiring, that same type of coffee was finishing the brewing process and thus becoming available (see Figure 5.5). A floater, who previously supported mainly

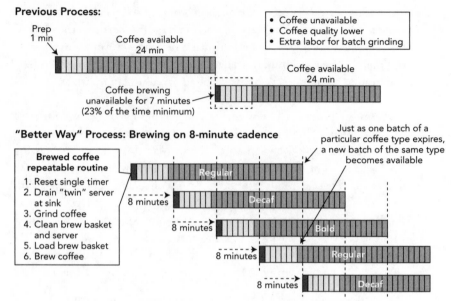

Figure 5.5 Better Way for brewed coffee—prior condition compared with new standardized work.
Source: Starbucks.

the barista and cashier, now was expected to prepare coffee every 8 minutes and fit in the other tasks in between. As it turned out, this also improved the quality of the coffee and reduced wasted labor.

As sensible as these ideas seemed, they did not always work as planned at the store level. For example, there was not always staffing for a floater, and what happened when the floater was busy with support work that he or she could not just drop? Fortunately, the corporate team had learned the value of flexibility and local adaptation. Scott Heydon, the VP who led the effort, explained:

> There was no way any corporate team can come up with one best way for all stores—or even one store. Instead each leader was asked to select and adopt a "seed store" and try out the Better Way for themselves. Then, with their store team, use the problem solving skills they were trained in to tailor the routine to that specific store's situation (layout of equipment and customer flow, beverage demand and mix, etc.).

This approach, which fit Adler's enabling bureaucracy, led to local adaptation. As Gaudet wrote:

> Every Better Way led us to the next problem and to thousands of solutions being created for those problems around the country. Over the next two years, we made small changes, adopted some practices, and rejected others.

Still it was difficult to make these Better Ways stick. We had learned a lot about how to observe and improve work, but we still did not know what we did not know: how to create an environment around the work that supported a standardized routine.

The Better Way led to dramatic improvements in product quality, availability, cost (exceeding the $25 million savings target), and rapid customer response, and it reduced team member burden like walking and bending and also reduced wasted product, but something was still missing. Under pressure of high customer demand, it was not enough for managers to shout "All hands on deck" and expect the Better Way to create a calm, smooth flow of work. Two years after the Better Way, "Playbook" was introduced as a comprehensive operating and management system that pulled all this thinking together. Starbucks needed managers to act like coaches who wrote out the "plays" and then called the plays throughout the shift based on circumstances on the field. How many baristas, cashiers, and store support roles did a store team need at different parts of the day, and what were their assignments? They taught this skill to managers, who controlled the standardized roles and acted like Toyota group leaders (see Principle 10). Creativity *and* adherence to the standards increased.

Standardization and empowerment at the local level is what allowed the baristas, shift supervisors, and the manager in Newtown, Connecticut, in 2012 to get through a horrible week following a mass shooting in a school. Grieving parents, teachers, and reporters came flooding into the store; for one week, demand went from 500 to 1,500 espresso drinks a day. Gaudet writes about how the manager called the plays, how she enlisted help from other regional stores, and how the team developed a steady work cadence and successfully served each customer exactly what the customer wanted:

Using techniques from the Playbook, we were able to ramp up operations and serve everyone who came into the store—from grieving families and townspeople to the international press—as well as carting out to-go urns of coffee to first responders and to memorials and other gatherings. With the help of standardization, we were able to provide the best comfort we could.

STANDARDIZED WORK IS A GOAL TO WORK TOWARD, NOT A TOOL TO IMPLEMENT

The critical task for standardized work is to find that balance between providing employees with rigid procedures to follow and providing the freedom to innovate and to be creative in consistently meeting challenging targets for cost, quality, and delivery. The key to achieving this balance lies in the way people write standards, as well as who contributes to them.

First, the standardized work must be specific enough to be a useful guide, yet general enough to allow for some flexibility. Repetitive manual work can be standardized to a high degree going into detail about sequences of steps and times. On the other hand, it would not make sense in engineering to specific a step-by-step way of performing the work. There are general plans with milestones, and then technical information about the product that appears in engineering checklists. For example, knowing how the curvature of the hood of a car will relate to the air/wind resistance of that body part is more useful than dictating a specific parameter for the curve of all hoods. In product development, this is often represented as trade-off curves.

Second, the people doing the work are in the best position to improve the standardized work. There is simply not enough time in a workweek for industrial engineers to be everywhere writing and rewriting standards. Nor do people like following someone's detailed rules and procedures when they are imposed on them. Imposed rules that are strictly policed are often viewed as coercive and become a source of friction and resistance between management and workers. However, people happily focused on doing a good job appreciate getting tips and best practices, particularly if they have some flexibility in adding their own ideas. In addition, it is very empowering to find that your team is going to use your improvement as a new standard. Using standardization at Toyota is the foundation for continuous improvement, innovation, and employee growth.

What Karen Guadet learned about standardized work at Starbucks gives a very different picture from the Tayloristic view of people as erratically functioning robots:

> *Humans just are not hardwired for repetition, it seems. And in service industries, quality human contact is central to the work. Human contact and standardization can seem like oil and water. But here is the truly important discovery from our observations: when task standardization is adopted and steady work cadences are achieved, people are freer to do the satisfying work of making human connections. When work tasks are both repeatable and rote, managers, executives, and frontline baristas all have more space in their lives to chat a little, to ask questions, and to listen to others.*

I think the problem with how standardization is used in many organizations is a result of our old nemesis, the mechanistic perspective. When the organization is viewed as a machine, then standardized work is a tool that is intended to make it a better machine. Figure 5.6 presents a common graphic in lean training that shows standards as backstops. You figure out the best known way to do the job, write out the worksheet, teach it, and then shove the standardized work in place to prevent the process from slipping back. This ignores the fact that it is the person who can slip back, not the process. People have a way of doing the work that they are comfortable with, and developing any new habit takes repetition—practice.

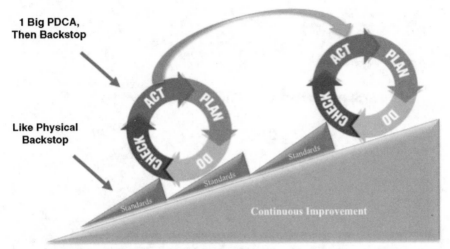

Figure 5.6   Mechanistic view of standards as a tool to implement.

Figure 5.7 presents a more dynamic, fluid view of standardized work that recognizes the time and effort required for humans to learn a new way of doing things. In this case, I used the model for improvement developed by Mike Rother that is part of Toyota kata and discussed under Principle 12. Kata are ways of doing things in the martial arts that you have to practice repeatedly with a coach to develop the skill and reduce variation. Kata also form the basis for job instruction training, practicing small pieces of the job repeatedly with a coach. The ideal state is to have standardized work that is practiced consistently by people coupled with step-by-step improvement through rapid PDCA cycles. The next level of performance can be thought of as a "target condition" that people need to strive for. You do this by experimenting with different methods for doing the work, and then when a performance threshold is achieved, you document the process and teach it as the best known way at that time. You turn the standardized work document into consistent behavior through job instruction training, which develops the new habits through repetition. Then the work group starts on the next lap with the next target condition (level of performance), experimenting and finding a better way. In this way standardized work and continuous improvement become two sides of the same coin.

Standardized work can be an ugly thing in the hands of control-oriented bureaucrats and a beautiful thing when it enables creativity and continuous improvement. Enabling bureaucracy takes more effort, but it is well worth it.

Some Key Points About Standards:
- Process standards are a desired state, and process variation is natural.
- What we call "standardized work" is also a desired state to work toward.
- There remains variation across team members even after improvement cycles.
- Achieving "standardized work" requires team members learning new habits and refining the process to continue to strive to reduce variation.

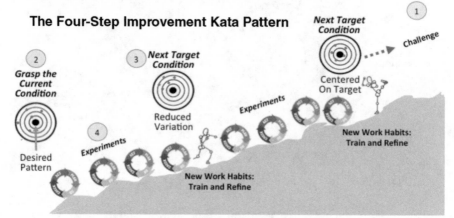

Figure 5.7 Fluid view of standards—reaching new levels of performance requires learning new habits and continued improvement.

KEY POINTS

- Classical industrial engineering focused on efficiency by designing the "one best way" to do a job.
- Under Taylor's scientific management, industrial engineers did the thinking, managers enforced their designs, and workers complied.
- Henry Ford had a different idea about standardized work, which he saw as only the best way until we could find a better way.
- Toyota turned scientific management on its head, giving the stopwatch to work groups who were responsible for designing and continuously improving their work.
- Job instruction training was taught to Toyota as part of Training Within Industry, and is the key to turning standardized work into a habitual way of working by focusing on key points for each tiny step.
- Even in a customer-facing service business like Starbucks, with a myriad of drink combinations and customer demand changing by the minute, it is possible to create a steady work cadence that reduces stress and enhances the customer experience.

- When standards become a tool owned by those who perform the work, bureaucracy turns from coercing to enabling.
- Standardized work is something to be achieved through continuous improvement and rigorous training based on practice until the new way becomes a habit.

Notes

1. Frederick Taylor, *The Principles of Scientific Management* (New York, Dover Publications, July, 1997).
2. Henry Ford, *Today and Tomorrow: Special Edition of Ford's 1929 Classic* (Boca Raton, FL: CRC Press, Taylor & Francis Group, 2003).
3. War Manpower Commission, Bureau of Training, Training Within Industry Service, *The Training Within Industry Report: 1940–1945* (Washington, DC: U.S. Government Printing Office, September 1945).
4. Masaaki Imai, *Kaizen: The Key to Japan's Competitive Success* (New York: McGraw-Hill, 1986).
5. Durward Sobek, Jeffrey Liker, and Alan Ward, "Another Look at How Toyota Integrates Product Development," *Harvard Business Review*, vol. 76, no. 4, July–August 1998, pp. 36–50.
6. James Morgan and Jeffrey Liker, *The Toyota Product Development System: Integrating People, Process, and Technology* (New York: Productivity Press, 2006).
7. Frederick Taylor, *The Principles of Scientific Management.*
8. Tom Burns and G. M. Stalker, *The Management of Innovation* (New York: Oxford University Press; revised edition, 1994).
9. Karen Gaudet with Emily Adams, *Steady Work* (Boston: Lean Enterprise Institute, 2019).

Principle 6

Build a Culture of Stopping to Identify Out-of-Standard Conditions and Build in Quality

Mr. Ohno used to say that no problem discovered when stopping the line should wait longer than tomorrow morning to be fixed. Because when making a car every minute we know we will have the same problem again tomorrow.
—Fujio Cho, President, Toyota Motor Corporation

Russ Scaffede was vice president of Powertrain for Toyota when it launched the first American powertrain plant to make engines in Georgetown, Kentucky, for the on-site assembly plant. He had worked decades for General Motors and had an excellent reputation as a manufacturing guy who could get things done and worked well with people. He was excited about the opportunity to work for Toyota and to help start up a brand-new plant following state-of-the-art TPS principles. He worked day and night to get the plant up to the demanding standards of Toyota and to please his Japanese mentors, including Fujio Cho, who was president of Toyota Motor Manufacturing in Kentucky.

Before joining Toyota, Scaffede had learned the golden rule of automotive engine production: do not shut down the assembly plant! At General Motors, managers were judged by their ability to deliver the numbers. Get the job done no matter what—and that meant getting the engines to the assembly plant to keep it running. Too many engines, that was fine. Too few, that could send you to the unemployment line.

So when Cho remarked to Scaffede that he noticed he had not shut down the assembly plant once in a whole month, Scaffede perked up: "Yes sir, we had a great month, sir. I think you will be pleased to see more months like this." Scaffede was shocked to hear from Cho:

Russ-san, you do not understand. If you are not shutting down the assembly plant, it means that you have no problems. All manufacturing plants have problems. So you must be hiding your problems. Please take out some inventory so the problems surface. You will shut down the assembly plant, but you will also continue to solve your problems and make even better-quality engines more efficiently.

When I interviewed Mr. Cho for this book, I asked him about differences in culture between what he experienced starting up the Georgetown plant and managing Toyota plants in Japan. He did not hesitate to note that his number one problem was getting group leaders and team members to stop the assembly line. They assumed that if they stopped the line, they would be blamed for doing a bad job. Cho explained that it took several months to "re-educate" them that it was a necessity to stop the line if they wanted to continually improve the process. He had to go down to the shop floor every day, meet with his managers, and, when he noticed a reason to stop the line, encourage the team leaders to stop it.

THE PRINCIPLE: BUILD A CULTURE OF STOPPING TO IDENTIFY OUT-OF-STANDARD CONDITIONS AND BUILD IN QUALITY (JIDOKA)

Jidoka, the second pillar of TPS, traces back to Sakichi Toyoda and his long string of inventions that revolutionized the automatic loom. We discussed in the history chapter his device that allowed looms to stop themselves when a single thread broke, a breakthrough invention that improved the quality of cloth and freed up operators to operate multiple looms and assume their rightful place as problem solvers. One of the leading American students of TPS, Alex Warren, former executive vice president, Toyota Motor Manufacturing, Kentucky, defined "jidoka" and how it relates to employee empowerment:[1]

In the case of machines, we build devices into them, which detect abnormalities and automatically stop the machine upon such an occurrence. In the case of humans, we give them the power to push buttons or pull cords— called "andon cords"—which can bring our entire assembly line to a halt. Every team member has the responsibility to stop the line every time they see something that is out of standard. That's how we put the responsibility for quality in the hands of our team members. They feel the responsibility—they feel the power. They know they count.

Jidoka is also referred to as "autonomation"—equipment endowed with human intelligence to stop itself when it has a problem. In-station quality (preventing problems from being passed down the line) is much more effective and less costly than inspecting and repairing quality problems after the fact.

Lean manufacturing dramatically increases the importance of building things right the first time. With very low levels of inventory, there is little buffer to fall back on in case there is a quality problem. Problems in operation A will quickly shut down operation B. When equipment shuts down, flags or lights, usually with accompanying music or an alarm, are used to signal that help is needed to solve a problem. This signaling system is referred to as "andon."

In addition to calling attention to quality problems, team members are instructed to pull the cord when they identify any out-of-standard conditions, which enables continuous improvement. As discussed later this does not immediately stop the line but rather alerts the team leader that this may be necessary. One of the more common reasons for pulling the cord is when team members get behind in the work cycle. There are marks on the conveyor that show the members what percentage of the standardized work should be complete so they can see if they are behind. The members are highly skilled and usually can catch up on their own if need be—but then that out-of-standard condition would not be identified and the problem would not be solved.

While it may seem obvious that you should catch and address problems immediately, the last thing management in traditional mass manufacturing permits is a halt in production. For example, bad parts, when they happen to be noticed, are simply labeled and set aside to be repaired at another time and by another department. The mass production mantra seems to be "Produce large quantities at all costs and fix problems later." As Gary Convis, former president of the Toyota factory in Georgetown, explained to me:

> When I was at Ford, if you didn't run production 100% of the shift, you had to explain it to Division. You never shut the line off. We don't run 100% of the scheduled time out here. Toyota's strength, I think, is that the upper management realizes what the andon system is all about . . . . They've lived through it and they support it. So in all the years I've been with Toyota, I've never really had any criticism over lost production and putting a priority on safety and quality over hitting production targets. All they want to know is how are you problem solving to get to the root cause? And can we help you? I tell our team members there are two ways you can get in trouble here: one is you don't come to work, and two is you don't pull the cord if you've got a problem. The sense of accountability to ensure quality at each station is really critical.

The built-in quality created by jidoka has never been more important to Toyota than with the Lexus because of the necessity of meeting the extremely high expectations of Lexus owners. When the brand was first introduced, Lexus vehicles were built only in Japan, where the culture and quality systems were undisputedly world class. But could Lexus be built in North America and still maintain the unbelievably meticulous levels of quality that customers have come to expect? The answer turned out to be yes. Toyota began manufacturing the Lexus in its Cambridge, Ontario, facility and later in its Kentucky plant.

Ray Tanguay, former president of Toyota Motor Corporation, Canada, knew that the bar was now higher as he moved from making the Toyota Corolla and Matrix models to the Lexus RX 330. There were a number of innovations designed into the processes, and technologies of the new Lexus line to ensure that Lexus buyers received Lexus quality. For example, production tools and robots on the line were designed with built-in sensors to detect any deviation from standard and used radio transmitters to send electronic signals to team leaders wearing headphone sets. Because not every problem can be caught in process, Lexus managers developed a highly detailed 170-point quality check for every finished RX 330. Tanguay wore a BlackBerry personal digital assistant on his belt wherever he went, and every time an error was found on a finished vehicle, a report was instantly sent to his BlackBerry, along with a digital photo of the problem. Tanguay had the ability to transfer the photo to a large electronic billboard in the plant that could be seen by all the workers if he felt that would increase awareness of the problem and prevent the same mistake from occurring again. While the technology was new, the execution still depended on alert, thinking people at the gemba and the principle remained the same: bring problems to the surface, make them visible, and go to work immediately on countermeasures.

"YOU MEAN THE LINE DOES NOT REALLY STOP?"

We seem to have a paradox. Toyota management says it is OK to run less than 100 percent of the time, even when the line is capable of running full-time, and yet Toyota is consistently ranked among the most productive plants in the auto industry. Why? Because Toyota learned long ago that solving problems at the source saves time and money downstream. By continually surfacing problems and fixing them as they occur, you eliminate waste, productivity soars, and competitors who are running assembly lines flat out and letting problems accumulate get left in the dust.

When Toyota's competitors finally did start using Toyota's andon system, they made the mistake of assuming that the line-stop system was hardwired to each and every workstation—push the button, and the entire assembly line comes to a screeching halt. I consulted to one of the large automakers in the United States to help its assembly plant engineering group understand TPS. The engineers became irate when I explained that most of the time the line does not really stop. "They are cheating," exclaimed one engineer. I explained that the line does stop, just not every time the cord is pulled. The purpose of most of the line stops is to call attention to problems so they can be first contained, then solved, not to shut everything down so the problem can be solved immediately while the line is down. Of course, in potentially dangerous situations that threaten safety and quality, the line will stop.

At Toyota, the andon is called a "fixed-position line-stop system." As shown in Figure 6.1, when an operator in Workstation 5 pulls the andon cord, Workstation 5 will light up in yellow, but the line will continue moving, allowing each team member to finish work on the current vehicle. The responsibility for deciding whether to stop the line falls on the team leader, a production team member who spends time in production and time offline responding to the andon. This is a unique role at Toyota and is critical to the functioning of the andon system (it is explained in detail in Principle 10). The team leader has until the vehicle moves into the next workstation zone to respond, before the andon turns red and the line segment automatically stops. On a normal assembly line that builds cars at a rate of one a minute, the team leader likely has 10–20 seconds to decide what to do. In that time, the team leader might immediately fix the problem or note it can be fixed while the car is moving into the next workstation. In that case, the team leader pulls the cord again, canceling the line stoppage. Or the team leader might conclude the line should stop. Team leaders are carefully trained in standardized procedures on how to respond to andon calls. Offline, team leaders examine andon pulls and pick the most common or serious ones to address through problem solving.

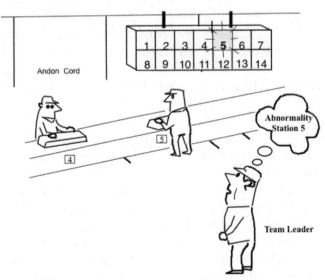

Figure 6.1   Andon and fixed-position line stop.

Even if the team leader allows the line to stop, the entire assembly line does not shut down. The assembly line is divided into segments with small buffers of cars in between (typically containing 7 to 10 cars). Because of the buffers, when a line segment stops, the next line segment can keep working for 7 to 10 minutes before it will shut down, and so forth. Rarely does the whole plant shut down. Toyota achieved the purpose of andon without taking needless risks of lost production. It took US auto companies years to understand how to apply this TPS tool, which perhaps explains why workers and supervisors were hesitant to stop the line—because it actually stopped the entire line! When they gained a better understanding of andon, the engineering group I consulted to that afternoon constructed a computer simulation of the assembly line to identify the number of buffers to put in and their size.

USING COUNTERMEASURES AND ERROR PROOFING TO FIX PROBLEMS

This point has been made earlier in the book, but it bears repeating: the closer you are to one-piece flow, the quicker problems will surface to be addressed. This hit home for me personally in the summer of 1999 when I was given a unique opportunity to learn more about TPS. General Motors had a program through its joint venture with Toyota, the NUMMI plant, in Fremont, California, to which GM sent employees for one week of training in TPS. The week included two days of working on the NUMMI assembly line—actually building cars. I was given the opportunity to participate.

I was assigned to a subassembly operation off the main assembly line that made axle assemblies for the Toyota Corolla and the equivalent GM model. In unibody cars, where there is no chassis, there is not a real axle, but four independent modules that include the wheel, brakes, and shock absorber. The axle assemblies were built in the same sequence as the cars on the assembly line, put on pallets, and delivered in the order of cars moving down the assembly line. It took about two hours from the time a module was built until it was attached to the car, so if there was a problem, you had a maximum of two hours to fix it before the main assembly line segment might be shut down.

The job I was assigned was an easy "freshman" job: attach a cotter pin to hold a ball joint in place. You put in the cotter pin and spread out the ends, and it locked the ball joint in place. This affected braking, so it was a very important safety item. At one point early in the afternoon, I saw people scrambling around and holding a number of impromptu meetings. I asked the team member working next to me what was going on, and he explained that a unit had gotten to the assembly line without a cotter pin. It was a big deal, he said. An assembly line worker who installed the subassembly on the car had caught it. The team knew it happened only a couple of hours earlier. I assumed it was my mistake and immediately felt terrible for having missed installing a cotter pin. The team member claimed that it happened while I was on break. Who knows? But his response to my guilt feelings was even more important. He said:

> *What is important is that the error went through eight people who did not see it. We are supposed to be inspecting the work when it comes to us. And the guy at the end of the line is supposed to check everything. This should never have gotten to the assembly line. Now we as a team are embarrassed because we did not do our jobs.*

Although this missing cotter pin went undetected through the entire system of inspection, there were a remarkable number of countermeasures that had already been put in place on the axle line to prevent things like this from occurring. In fact, at every workstation there were numerous poka-yoke devices. "Poka-yoke" refers to error proofing (aka mistake proofing or fool proofing). These are creative devices that make it nearly impossible for an operator to make an error . . . nearly. Obviously, there was not a poka-yoke to detect whether the cotter pin was in place. Nonetheless, the level of sophistication on the line was impressive—there were 27 poka-yoke devices on the front axle line alone. Each poka-yoke device also had its own standard form that summarized the problem addressed, the emergency alarm that will sound, the action to be taken in an emergency, the method and frequency of confirming the error-proof method is operating correctly, and the method for performing a quality check in the event the error-proof method breaks down. This is the level of detail that Toyota uses to build in quality.

As an example, though there was no poka-yoke to check if the cotter pin was in place, there was a light curtain over the tray of cotter pins. If the light curtain was not broken by the operator reaching to pick up a cotter pin, the moving assembly line would stop, an andon light would come on, and an alarm would sound. Another poka-yoke device required that I replace a tool (somewhat like a file, used to expand the cotter pin) back in its holder after I used it or the line would stop and an alarm would sound. It sounds a bit bizarre—and it might be perceived as one step removed from getting electric shocks for any misstep. But it is effective. Of course, there are ways around the system, and the workers on the line could find them all. But at Toyota, workers tend to be disciplined about following the standard tasks and adhering to quality processes.

Standardized work (Toyota Way Principle 6) is itself a countermeasure to quality problems. For example, the job I had was designed so it could be accomplished in 44.7 seconds of work and walk time. The takt time (line speed in this case) was 57 seconds per job, so there was plenty of slack time; hence it was a freshman job. Yet even for this simple job there were 28 steps shown on the "standardized work chart," right down to the number of footsteps to take to and from the conveyor. This standardized work chart was posted at my jobsite, where there were visuals that also explained potential quality problems. A more detailed version in a notebook had each of the 28 steps on its own sheet, described in greater detail, along with digital photos of each step being performed correctly. Very little was left to chance. Whenever there is a quality problem, the standardized work chart is reviewed to see if something is missing that allowed the error to occur, and if so, the chart is updated accordingly.

KEEP QUALITY CONTROL SIMPLE AND INVOLVE TEAM MEMBERS

If American and European companies learned anything from the arrival of competitive Japanese products into the US market in the 1980s, it was quality fever. The level of quality consciousness in Japanese companies made our heads spin. They crafted fine art while we were slapping parts together. But we woke up and worked hard to fix this. J.D. Power's recent surveys of the quality of new vehicles (during the first three months of ownership) show that the gap between Japanese auto companies and US and European competitors has shrunk to the point of being barely noticeable. But as discussed in the Introduction, longer-term data show that the quality differential has not been erased—it has just been hidden. It is relatively easy to inspect an assembled vehicle and fix all the obvious problems before the customer has a chance to see them. But inspected-in quality is often temporary quality; problems surface over the long term as there is wear and tear on the vehicle.

Unfortunately, for many companies, the essence of building in quality has gotten lost in bureaucratic and technical details. Things like ISO-9000, an industrial quality standard that calls for detailed, written standard operating procedures, for whatever good they have done, have made many companies believe that if they put together detailed rule books, the rules will be followed. Quality planning departments are armed with reams of data that they analyze using the most sophisticated statistical methods. Six sigma has brought us roving bands of black belts who attack major quality problems with a vengeance, armed with an arsenal of sophisticated technical methods.

In contrast, at Toyota, people tend to use simple visual charts and graphs to display quality problems and their causes, like Pareto charts and cause-and-effect diagrams. The main focus is on addressing problems as they occur, one by one.

Don Jackson, former VP of manufacturing for Toyota's Georgetown plant, was a quality manager for a US auto supplier before joining Toyota. He had been a stickler for detail and defended the complex quality manuals he had helped write. At Toyota, he learned the power of simplicity. As he described it, "Before joining Toyota I made a lot of policies and procedures too difficult to follow. They were doomed for failure." He still participated in quality audits of suppliers at Toyota, but his approach and philosophy were completely different from the more coercive-bureaucratic mindset he had before joining Toyota:

> *You can write a complex procedure that covers the operator, equipment main-tenance, and a quality audit—and theoretically, the process will run forever. But my philosophy is support the team members who are running the process. I want them to be able to know everything because they're the ones produc-ing the product. So those team members have to know that the preventative maintenance was done on schedule, and their equipment is in good shape by some visual control system. The quality check every hour . . . those team members should know that it was done and it was OK every hour or they stop the line. Then finally, they must know what their job requirements are and know that they're getting good built-in quality by some means. So those team members are in total control. I want team members to know that they have everything they need to build that product correctly . . . man, material, method, machine.*

Obviously, this audit is very different from the typical quality audit that follows detailed procedures from a manual, perhaps analyzes some statistical data, and maybe even checks to see if the procedures are being followed. Jackson is looking with a different set of eyes—the eyes of the operator controlling the process. He is looking at quality from the point of view of the shop floor—the actual situation (genchi genbutsu).

One of the most powerful tools in Toyota production besides the andon is the quality gate. The production line is laid out in sections, and at the end of each section is a place where quality is checked. Any defect is examined to determine the origin of the error, and that information is provided to the correct group leader who takes action to solve the problem. This goes on day in and day out. If the problem gets through to the final line, it is elevated to the attention of management. If it flows out to customers, it is a major crisis.

LONG-TERM LEARNING FROM A QUALITY CRISIS

On August 28, 2009, an off-duty California Highway Patrol officer was driving a Lexus ES 350 sedan with his family when the vehicle sped up out of control leading to a fiery crash. A passenger called 911 and desperately asked for help as the incident occurred. The call got on the internet and went viral. The *Los Angeles Times* speculated that electronic interference caused the car's computer to send the car accelerating out of control. The paper assigned two reporters to find the dirt and try to win a Pulitzer Prize. One year later, NASA, in an attempt to find an electronic cause for the accident, bombarded test vehicles with electromagnetic waves and analyzed hundreds of thousands of lines of computer code. It concluded there was no evidence of an electronic failure.

In the aftermath of the accident, a little-known police report was filed that showed convincingly that the cause of the sudden acceleration was the wrong size floor mat—it was a rubber all-weather mat and was intended for a larger SUV—that was placed in the vehicle by the Lexus dealer who loaned the car to the police officer while his car was being repaired. Millions of vehicles were recalled. Billions of dollars were paid out to settle disputes. Toyota cut down the accelerator pedal so it could not be impacted by floor mats that were piled one on another too high. A few unrelated problems with accelerators and brake pedals were discovered, but there were few instances reported and no reported serious accidents. Nonetheless, the media kept claiming Toyota had massive, sudden unintended acceleration problems and that its vehicles were not safe to drive. For Toyota, it was the worst blow to its reputation in the history of the company.

How do you deal with a crisis like this when the technical problems are greatly exaggerated by the media? Akio Toyoda was unexpectedly called to testify before Congress and was grilled on February 24, 2010. He apologized for the concern his company caused customers, he took responsibility, but he also claimed that Toyota cars were safe, an assertion supported by objective evidence.

Henry Ford said that "quality means doing it right when no one is looking." In 2020, no one is looking, and all the external quality studies put Toyota and Lexus at or near the top. Toyota's recall crisis is old news, but not within Toyota. Each year on February 24, the anniversary of Akio Toyoda's grilling by Congress, departments within Toyota across the globe do something to recognize the occasion and reaffirm the importance of quality. In each headquarters globally and every Toyota factory in the world, there is now a Quality Learning Center to raise quality awareness among all Toyota employees. Each location develops its own version that fits local circumstances.

At Toyota's assembly plant in the United Kingdom, every member went through the quality center in 2019. The center features a display of Akio Toyoda explaining that he requested each location to "gather and exhibit as unattractive matters as possible, such as sternly-worded articles in newspapers, customers' scolding voices, and the many issues from the market which have caused inconvenience to our customers." He asks everyone going through the center to "actively listen to what our customers are saying and to act quickly on what we learn."

The program begins with a video of the 911 call and images of the car crashing. It then moves on to a display of "unattractive matters." I was unpleasantly surprised to see a congresswoman waving my original *Toyota Way* around at the hearing admonishing Akio Toyoda to feel ashamed that MBA students were reading this book and thought Toyota was a model company. As you walk on you see an actual Toyota vehicle with an all-weather mat stacked on the carpet mat, which demonstrates how the accelerator pedal can get stuck. Then it moves on to quality problems that have been experienced at that plant and provides interactive exhibits to show how quality defects can be avoided, for example through standardized work. It ends with some good news—customers raving about the quality of their Toyota vehicles. Most of the world has forgotten the quality crisis, but Toyota continues to use it as motivation to always put the customer first.

DESIGNING IN QUALITY IN SOFTWARE DEVELOPMENT

Designing or building in quality is not just for manufacturing. It applies to every activity, including writing software code. Defective software can lead to critical data losses, and complex user interfaces can lead to losing customers. Ever happen to you? Ever not happen to you? In addition, defects lead to rework. Some software projects have almost as many hours dedicated to fixing the code as they did to writing the original code.

At Menlo Innovations, a small custom software development firm in Ann Arbor, Michigan, this almost never occurs. Customers use the software out of the box, without user manuals, and rave about it. The company credits its success to involving customers every step of the way, getting quality feedback to programmers, and designing in quality as the programmers create the code (see Figure 6.2).*

Once there is agreement on a vision for the software, Technical Anthropologists™ go to work to understand the customer by going to the gemba. What is the nature of the work the users do? How experienced are they with software? Where do they experience pain points in using current software? The Tech Anthropologists must develop the skills of deep observation and be empathetic, putting themselves in the place of the user.

The Tech Anthropologists develop a vision for the software and then develop "key personas," fictional stories of users in different roles, and work with customers to select the primary persona who will use the software. Next, the Tech

---

* See a detailed discussion of the process and culture in Richard Sheridan, *Joy, Inc.* (New York: Portfolio, 2013).

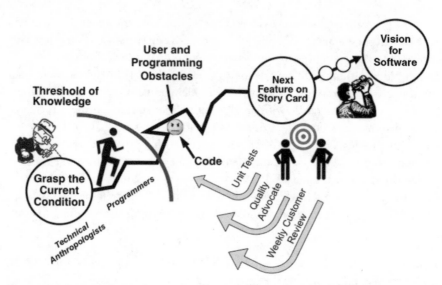

Figure 6.2   Menlo Innovations' system of designed-in quality in coding software.

Anthropologists draw the screens and show them to customers and users until they have agreement. The software features on the screen are converted to individual story cards that the program manager and customer post on a work authorization board for pairs of programmers to work on week by week. In essence, the Tech Anthropologists are creating the standard against which programmers' work will be judged.

Pairs of programmers take a story card and together do the coding. Two pairs of eyes keep the programmers focused; often, one person notices issues the other misses. They write unit tests for each small segment of code to test if it does what it is supposed to do. These are automated tests of the code that will repeatedly run as the code is further developed and compiled with new code—providing instant feedback on whether it works as intended. When programmers believe they have completed a story card, a quality advocate tests it, not to look at the technical details of the code, but to check if it does what the customer wants. This will generally happen during the same day shortly after the code is written. Then, on a set day every single week, the programmers meet with the customers who try to use the code, without instruction—which can lead to acceptance of the code as is or with some rework. Based on how this meeting goes, story cards are authorized for another week of work, and the process continues like this until the software is delivered—error free and with 100 percent customer satisfaction. All-nighters to fix problems just before release of the software are an alien concept at Menlo.

Menlo Innovations works obsessively to build a culture of stopping to identify out-of-standard conditions and build in quality. It has made designed-in quality and customer satisfaction a deliberate part of its culture, from employee selection to daily activities. "Menlonians" are selected for their propensity to think creatively, learn quickly, and work in pairs. I have talked to Menlo programmers who make it clear they would not want to go back to a traditional software organization where they would work in isolation with only guesses about what the customer really wants.

Continuous improvement of websites is becoming more common with the ability to quickly and cheaply run huge numbers of experiments.[2] In some companies, it has penetrated into the culture where employees are encouraged to propose any ideas, even outlandish ones, that they think will improve the web page. Online testing can be easily done by analyzing the responses of a random sample of users who see a new feature or function in the website compared with the people in a control group who do not see the change. The ideas that work, according to predetermined criteria like the number of hits on the site, are integrated into the site. Stefan Thomke, who has been studying this phenomenon, observes that success is achieved by conducting tests frequently and making experimentation and innovation a matter of culture and a normal expectation of daily work, even when budgets are tight. People at all levels must learn to value "surprises," even if they are disruptive in the short term. When things are going too smoothly, it probably means problems are being hidden.

BUILDING IN QUALITY IS A PRINCIPLE AND SYSTEM, NOT A TECHNOLOGY

A story I heard from a plant manager at Reiter Automotive (supplier of sound-dampening materials) helped put into perspective what it takes to build in quality. He ran a plant in Chicago and supplied Toyota. He had a Toyota mentor teaching him TPS. The Toyota mentor had suggested the plant needed an andon system to immediately alert people to quality problems. The plant manager energetically got his engineers to spec out an andon system similar to the kind Toyota uses, with light boards hung from the rafters and directly connected to buttons the operator pushed. While this was a relatively small plant compared with the Toyota plant, the plant manager wanted to use the very best technology to prove his sincerity to his mentor. The Toyota mentor said, "No, no, no. You do not understand. Come with me." He then drove the plant manager to a local hardware store. He picked out a red flag, a yellow flag, and a green flag. He handed them to the plant manager and said, "Andon."

His point was that a working andon system is not the same thing as buying fancy new technology. Andon works only when you teach your employees the importance of bringing problems to the surface so they can be quickly solved.

Unless you have people who quickly identify problems and a problem-solving process that they follow, there's no point in spending money on fancy technology. Americans tend to think that buying expensive new technology is a good way to solve problems. Toyota prefers to first use people and processes to solve problems, then supplement and support its people with technology later.

General Motors early on copied Toyota's NUMMI plant system of team leaders when it introduced andon. But the team leaders spent a good deal of their time in the back room smoking cigarettes or playing cards. What good is pushing the andon button if nobody is around to respond? In a later incarnation, GM got schooled on the philosophy of andon. In its Cadillac plant in Hamtramck, Michigan, it put in sophisticated fixed-position stop andon with all the technical bells and whistles. When the button was pushed, the line kept going until the car entered the next workstation and then the line automatically stopped at a "fixed position." Fortunately, Michael Brewer, one of the original GM managers sent to work at NUMMI to learn TPS, asked the plant to turn off the automatic stop system. He saw that the culture was not ready. Each work group had to pass a lean audit in order to earn the right to turn on the automatic system to stop the line. Were the operators following standardized work? Was the kanban system being used properly so all containers of parts were in the right place and in the proper quantity? Were quality key points built into standardized work and taught properly? Were the team leaders available near each process and responding to problems? As a result, each work team struggled to pass the audit and to gain the privilege of having the complete andon system turned on in the team's worksta-tions. There were celebrations each time a group succeeded.

In the Toyota Way of doing things, what matters when improving quality is enabling the process and the people. You can spend a great deal of money on the latest and greatest andon and have no impact whatsoever on quality. Instead, you need to constantly reinforce the principle that quality is everyone's respon-sibility throughout the organization. Quality for the customer drives your value proposition, so there is no compromising on quality, because adding value to your customer is what keeps you in business and allows you to make money so everyone can continue to be part of the company.

Designing and building in quality has become common across business sec-tors. Still, the number of companies like Menlo Innovations that have made quality an integral part of their culture, so it becomes the way work is done, is quite small. It should be clear to the reader by now that all aspects of the Toyota Way—philosophy, processes, people, and problem solving—support building in quality to satisfy customers.

KEY POINTS

- The customer is the final arbiter of how good a job the company is doing.
- The voice of the customer must be driven through every process from design to manufacturing.
- Toyota's famous andon system of stopping to fix problems is one of a number of ways to surface problems immediately so they can be solved quickly.
- One of the most dramatic examples of facing and addressing problems for Toyota has been its response to the sudden acceleration recall crisis. Over a decade later, Toyota is still using it to raise quality consciousness.
- Designing in quality also applies to digital companies. The best companies have built processes for getting rapid feedback as code is being written and to run experiments with customers to get continual feedback to improve the software.
- Quality is more than tools; it is a matter of creating a culture where even negative feedback is valued and used for continuous improvement from design through customer use.

Notes

1. *The Toyota Way 2001*, Toyota Motor Corporation, internal document, 2001.
2. Stefan Thomke, "Building a Culture of Experimentation," *Harvard Business Review*, March–April 2020.

When Americans were making pilgrimages to Japanese plants in the 1970s and 1980s, the first reaction was invariably, "The factories were so clean you could eat off the floor." For the Japanese, this was simply a matter of pride. Why would you want to live in a pigpen? But their efforts go beyond making the factory look clean and orderly. In Japan, there are "5S programs" that comprise a series of activities for eliminating wastes that contribute to errors, defects, and injuries in the workplace. Here are the five Ss (seiri, seiton, seiso, seiketsu, and shitsuke) translated into English:*

1. **Sort.** Sort through items and keep only what is needed while disposing of what is not.
2. **Straighten (orderliness).** "A place for everything and everything in its place."
3. **Shine (cleanliness).** The cleaning process often acts as a form of inspection that exposes abnormal and prefailure conditions that could hurt quality or cause machine failure.
4. **Standardize (create rules).** Develop systems and procedures to maintain and monitor the first three Ss.
5. **Sustain (self-discipline).** Maintaining a stabilized workplace is an ongoing process of continuous improvement as conditions change.

In mass production, without the five Ss, many wastes accumulate over the years, covering up problems and becoming an accepted dysfunctional way of doing business. The five Ss create a continuous process for improving the work environment, as illustrated in Figure 7.1.

Figure 7.1 The five Ss.

---

* Toyota only uses 4S. The company jokes that it is a little backward and has not caught up to 5S. Actually, Toyota drops the fifth S, sustain, because it says that is assumed. Without sustaining, why bother?

Here's how to incorporate the five Ss: Start by sorting through what is in the office or shop to separate what is needed every day to perform value-added work from what is seldom or never used. Mark the rarely used items with red tags and move them outside of the work area. Next create permanent locations for each part or tool you do use regularly. Store infrequently used items outside the workplace and dispose of the rest. Then shine, making sure everything stays clean every day. Visually standardize the quantities and locations to make clear where things belong and to make it clear when something is missing (such as a red square where the box should be).

The fifth S, sustain, is vital to realizing the benefits of 5S over time by making a habit of properly maintaining the correct procedures and creating new ones as conditions change. Sustain is a team-oriented continuous improvement process that is the responsibility of managers, group leaders, team leaders, and team members—in other words, clean up your own mess. It should be part of the core job role of everybody rather than a separate function by support staff.

Do 5S audits periodically, give scores to different groups, and hold them accountable for improving their scores. Toyota team leaders and group leaders audit their processes regularly, often with daily scores. The results of the audits, and the impetus they provide to make positive change, are part of continuous improvement. A deviation is a gap to improve through problem solving. What in the system allowed that to happen? Less mature plants rely on managers or specialists to do audits and tie specific rewards to keeping the place clean and orderly. One plant awarded the best team with a golden broom and rotated the award when another team scored better in a subsequent audit. In advanced lean plants, work teams take the responsibility to audit their own areas weekly or even daily, and managers inspect periodically to provide feedback.

STANDARD LOCATIONS NEED STABLE PROCESSES

Unfortunately, some companies seem to think 5S is lean production. More than one company I have visited related some version of the following story:

A few years back, management decided to try this lean stuff. They paid a million dollars to a training company who taught us 5S and did a lot of 5S workshops. The place got cleaned up and looked better than it ever had since I started working here. But we did not save any money, quality did not get better, and soon all the great 5S results started to degrade. Eventually management stopped the program. We ended up right back where we started.

The Toyota Production System is not about using 5S to neatly organize and label everything, including waste, to make the place appear tidy and shiny. It is not lipstick on a pig. Many companies with poorly organized mass production systems, little real flow, push systems, and an erratic schedule thought they could solve all their problems with 5S. But since processes and amounts of inventory fluctuated so much, 5S was like trying to hit a moving target. Just when you have places for everything neat and labeled a tsunami of inventory arrives and there is no place to put it.

Visual control of a well-planned lean system is different from making a mass production operation look neat and shiny. Lean systems use 5S to support a smooth flow to takt. 5S is also a tool to help make problems visible and, if used in a sophisticated way, can be part of the process of continuous improvement.[4] For example, in a well-organized inventory buffer there are clearly marked minimum and maximum levels, and if the process is stable the inventory should mostly stay within those boundaries. If there is too little or too much inventory it becomes apparent, and that should lead to problem-solving starting with: Why did this happen?

Consider, for example, a manual assembly process. Materials that will be assembled are brought to the operator. It is useful to think of the operator as a surgeon. Obviously, a surgeon needs to focus completely on the patient. The last thing you want is the surgeon to be distracted by having to go looking for an instrument or material. In a well-run operating room, every effort is made to predict what will be needed and make it available when required. Nurses place in the surgeon's hand exactly what is needed next, and the surgeon does not even turn around. That is the exact ideal for an operator in a plant—everything needed should be available within easy reach without turning away from the work.

Toyota plants traditionally used flow racks with boxes of each part as shown in Figure 7.2 (more frequently these days they use carts with exactly what is needed for each vehicle so team members need not search through different boxes of parts). Standard parts in bins on gravity-fed conveyors roll down to the assembler. There is room for a specific number of bins, and there are standard locations for the bins with easy-to-see labels. The bins are then replenished based on a pull system. In a pull system, a material handler will bring just enough to replenish what has been used. This works great, and 5S is very helpful. But in a push system, extra bins of the same part will come at the same time on occasion. Where will you put the extra bins of parts? Most likely they will be placed on the floor. Now the operator is bending down to get parts, and the great "standard organization" is all messed up. The lesson: TPS is a system, and changing only one part of the system rarely works. What we really want is visual control of a stable process, so when there are deviations, they will become immediately apparent.

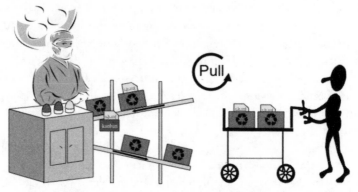

Figure 7.2 Operators as surgeons pull what is needed, when needed, in the amount needed, through visual signals.

VISUAL CONTROL AT THE WORKSITE

"Visual control" is any communication device used in the work environment that tells us at a glance how work should be done and whether it is deviating from the standard. It helps employees who want to do a good job see immediately how they are doing and in some cases what to do next. It might show where items belong, how many items belong there, what the standard procedure is for doing something, the status of work in process, and many other types of information critical to the flow of work activities. In the broadest sense, visual control refers to the design of just-in-time information of all types to ensure fast and proper execution of operations and processes. There are many excellent examples in everyday life, such as traffic signals. Because it is a matter of life and death, traffic signals tend to be well-designed visual controls. Look up—if the traffic light is red, then stop; if it's green, then go; if it's yellow, it will soon turn red. Good traffic signs don't require you to stop and study them: their meaning is immediately clear, or we may get into an accident.

Visual control goes beyond capturing deviations from a target or goal on charts and graphs and posting them publicly. Visual controls at Toyota are integrated into the process of the value-added work. The "visual" aspect means being able to look at a process, a piece of equipment, inventory, information, or a worker performing a job and immediately see the standard being used to perform the task and if there is a deviation from the standard. Ask this question: Can your manager walk through the shop floor, office, or any type of facility where work is being performed and recognize if standardized work or procedures are being followed? For example, if you have a clear standard for every tool to be hung in a certain place and it's made visual (perhaps through a shadow board), then the manager can see if anything is out of place. This practice can also help in the kitchen for preparing meals, or for organizing arts and crafts for your five-year old.

Zingerman's Mail Order (ZMO) uses a visual standard for the assembly of a standard gift box. ZMO ships artisanal foods, and its most frequent orders are gifts for others. Customers can customize a gift box or pick a standard set of items. Since the standard gift boxes such as the "weekender" tend to be high volume, and ZMO knows what items are needed, it has drawn outlines of the shape on a cardboard template (see Figure 7.3). The assembler places each item on the correct shape on the template and then puts those items in the gift box, and presto—it is difficult to miss items or pick the wrong items!

 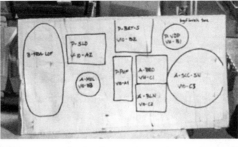

Figure 7.3   ZMO's mistake-proofing template for items in a standard gift box.

Selecting the right outer shipping box for gift boxes is more difficult. Picking one that's too large increases the shipping cost, and picking one that's too small requires extra labor to start over. About half the orders ZMO ships include a gift box or basket assembled in a standard container. On the wall, the company puts a sample of each standard container, color-coded to correspond to the outer box it goes into (see Figure 7.4). The box display covers about half the cases, so it is not complete, but it certainly helps.

Principle 7 of the Toyota Way is to use visual controls to support people. In fact, many of the tools associated with lean production are or have built in visual controls. Examples include kanban, the one-piece flow cell, andon, and standardized work. If there is no kanban card requesting that you refill a bin, then the bin should not be there. The filled bin without a kanban is a visual signal of overproduction. A well-designed cell will immediately reveal extra pieces of WIP

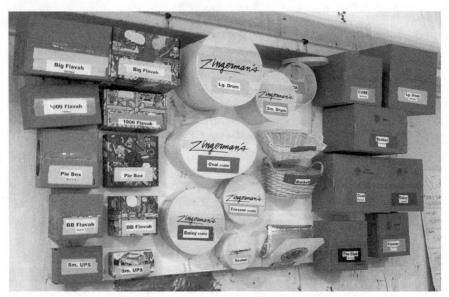

Figure 7.4   ZMO visual box size guide.

through clearly marked places for the standard WIP. The andon lights up and signals a deviation from standard operating conditions. Standardized work sheets are posted, so it is clear what the best-known method is for achieving flow at each operator's station. Observed deviations from the standard procedure indicate a problem. In essence, Toyota uses an integrated set of visual controls, or a visual control system, designed to create a transparent and waste-free environment.

CASE EXAMPLE: VISUAL CONTROL IN A SERVICE PARTS WAREHOUSE

Let's look at a most unlikely place where visual control enhances flow—a "lean" mega-warehouse.

Automakers in the United States, as well as in Japan, are required by law to keep service parts for vehicles for at least 10 years after they stop making the vehicles. This adds up to having millions of different parts available. Toyota's goal is to have them available just in time, as its manufacturing philosophy preaches.

Hebron, Kentucky, is home to one of the largest Toyota service parts facilities in the world. This facility ships parts all over North America to regional distribution centers, which ship them to Toyota dealers. Contrary to the tenets of JIT, it is a true warehouse, with 843,000 square feet of space and about 232 hourly and 86 salaried associates working there. In 2002 when I first visited the facility, the workers shipped an average of 51 truckloads of service parts a day, which constituted about 154,000 items every day. At the same time, parts were coming in from over 400 suppliers in the United States and Mexico, with most of the parts placed on the shelves until a Toyota dealer needed them. Being global and modern, the facility used sophisticated information technology, though the basic Toyota principles were apparent, and some pretty primitive tools were used for visual control. You might ask: Given the huge number of parts and the variability in demand, how could you possibly use the tools of TPS like takt, one-piece flow, and standardized work?

First, the warehouse is organized into cells called "home positions." The home positions have similar-size parts, e.g., small parts, stored in the same way. Teams of associates are dedicated to home positions. Second, Toyota uses a powerful custom-designed computer system. The volume of each part and the location of each part are meticulously entered into the computer. A batch of different small parts is packaged into a standard-size box to be shipped to a regional distribution center. A computer algorithm figures out what parts going to a particular location will just fill the box going to that destination, based on the part volume and location in the home position, and simultaneously develops a parts-picking route that can be completed in 15 minutes. Pickers have a handheld radio frequency–controlled device with a small screen; it tells them what to pick next, and they scan each item as they pick it. Third, even with this digital program, visual control is used extensively. Throughout the facility, you will see various types of whiteboards called "process control boards." These are the nerve centers of the operation. Figure 7.5 illustrates a process control board with actual data from the Hebron facility in 2002. The data were handwritten with dry-erase markers. This one was for picking parts in a home position to be put into a box for shipment. It captures an enormous amount of information, including the status of the operation every 15 minutes. It is worth describing how it operates to illustrate the power of visual control to pace an operation with highly variable demand and monitor progress versus takt time.

Each morning before the pickers arrive to work, the parts orders for the day come in by computer. The computer sorts them by home position. Then the algorithm described above assigns parts to 15-minute batches, and identifies picking routes. The supervisor of the team fills in the process control board by hand.

The supervisor starts with the data to the right. In this case, he wrote in the number of pieces that would be picked for the day—2,838—which the computer assigned to 82 (15-minute) batches. The total "time window" for picking those parts is 420 minutes in the shift, after breaks are taken out. Dividing 420 minutes by 82 batches gives a takt time of 5.1 minutes per batch—the rate at which boxes must be filled with parts to satisfy the customers. A 15-minute cycle

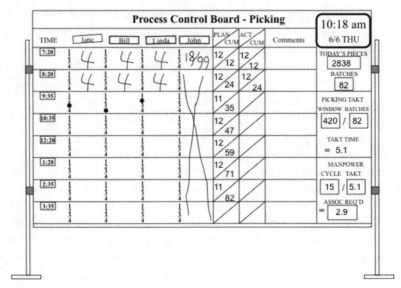

Figure 7.5 Process control board at the Kentucky parts distribution center.

time per batch divided by the takt time of 5.1 minutes means that 2.9 people will be needed to pick the orders for the day.

To the left, the team supervisor notes that three of his four team members will be needed to pick parts for that day, so he finds another assignment that day for John. He then writes in the planned number and cumulative number of batches to be picked, spread evenly throughout the shift. There are a few light periods during which there will be 11 boxes filled instead of 12 to allow for breaks. At the beginning of each 15-minute part-picking route, the associates will put a small round magnet on the batch they are picking—a green magnet if they are on time or a red magnet if they are running late. In this case, you can see that Jane is right where she should be, since it is 10:18 a.m., while Bill is ahead, and Linda is behind. But in this period the load is light—11 boxes—so they are taking breaks, and there is some flexibility. Everyone is OK. Immediately, the supervisor knows the status of the operation. Moreover, the board helps to enforce a continuous flow of work throughout the day. Associates will immediately know if they are getting behind and call for help to catch up. If they try to work ahead of the leveled schedule, it will be clear to the supervisor. A leveled workload, heijunka, is reinforced daily.

This system at Hebron is quite powerful and is a good example of the ingenuity of the Toyota TPS experts who figured out how to create continuous flow in a nontraditional, pick-to-order, high-variety environment—an environment in which many people would have thrown up their hands and said TPS tools "do not apply here." Although complex computer systems are utilized, the key tools that govern daily operations are visual management tools. One of the bigger stories at Hebron is how hard people have worked to build a culture of associate involvement to improve this world-class system (discussed under Principle 10).

But even before this huge distribution center was built, Toyota's smaller service parts facilities using these same TPS methods led the industry in productivity and facing fill rates and system fill rates—the key indicators that track and measure such facilities. (The facing fill rate is the percentage of time a part ordered is immediately available at the distribution center assigned to that dealer. The system fill rate is the percentage of time a part ordered is immediately available somewhere in a Toyota parts distribution center.) For example, from 1992 to 1998, Toyota's parts distribution center in Cincinnati, Ohio, had the highest fill rates in the industry: the facing fill rate was 95 percent, and the system fill rate was over 98 percent. Toyota's fill rates are routinely among the top three in the industry.

VISUAL CONTROL FOR PLANNING AND PROJECT MANAGEMENT—OBEYA

I have spent a lot of time at the Toyota Technical Center in Michigan, where employees engineer vehicles such as the Camry and Avalon. For much of this time, Kunihiko ("Mike") Masaki was the president there. Masaki had worked in many different engineering and manufacturing organizations during his career at Toyota, always using excellent visual management, so it seemed quite natural to him that the office environment at the Toyota Technical Center should follow the principles of 5S. Twice a year, Masaki would visit each person at his or her desk and ask to see a file cabinet (as part of Toyota's document retention program). He audited the file cabinets to see that they were organized properly and no documents were there that were not needed. There is a standard way to organize files at Toyota, and Masaki was looking for deviations from the standard. A report is then filed, and a grade is given. If an area is deficient, associates in the area must prepare a plan for countermeasures, and a follow-up review is scheduled to be sure any deficiencies are taken care of.

Though this may seem excessive or even intrusive for such mundane activities as filing, for the employee it clearly signals the importance of visual control, especially in light of the fact that this was the *president* following the Toyota principle of teaching by going directly to the source and seeing for himself (genchi genbutsu). Some years later, this responsibility shifted to a vice president and has been expanded to spot auditing of each employee's email organization system, to make sure messages are well organized in folders and old messages are discarded.

One of the biggest visual control innovations in Toyota's globally bench-marked product development system is the "obeya" (big room), which was used in the development of the first Prius model discussed in the next-to-last chapter (Principle 14). For the first Prius, the chief engineer resided in the obeya, along with the heads of the major engineering groups working on the project. It is a very large conference "war room" in which many visual management tools are displayed and maintained by representatives of the various functional specialties. These tools include the status of each area (and each key supplier) compared with the schedule, design graphics, competitor tear-down results, quality information, financial status, and other important performance indicators. Any deviation from schedule or performance targets is immediately visible in the obeya. The system has continued to evolve for Toyota product development projects and is a common part of lean transformation in other companies.[5]

The obeya is a high-security area, and Toyota team members and select suppliers are given access. Toyota has found that the obeya system enables fast and accurate decision-making, improves communication, maintains alignment, speeds information gathering, and creates an important sense of team integration.

I had the opportunity to interview Ichiro Suzuki, the chief engineer of the first Lexus. Suzuki was a legend and was sometimes referred to as the "Michael Jordan" of chief engineers. He returned to the Toyota Technical Center just before retirement to teach one final lesson. He chose to teach "the secret to excellent engineering." Not a shock, his focus on this trip was visual management. He emphasized the importance of using visual management charts and graphs (showing schedule, cost, etc., on one sheet of paper). He also pointed out that "using an electronic monitor does not work if only one person uses that information. Visual management charts must allow for communication and sharing."

KEEPING IT VISUAL THROUGH TECHNOLOGY AND HUMAN SYSTEMS

In today's world of computers, information technology, and automation, one of the goals is to make the office and factory paperless. You can now use computers, the internet, and the corporate intranet to access large storehouses of data, both written and visual, at lightning speed and share information via software and email. As we will discuss in the next chapter, Toyota has resisted this information technology–centric trend. As Suzuki pointed out, looking at a computer screen is typically done by one person in isolation. Working in a virtual world removes you from hands-on teamwork and, more importantly, usually (unless you do all your work on the computer) takes you away from where the "real" work is performed. There are certainly ways to make good use of visual computer systems, for example when people work in different locations, but it takes work and a well-designed visual display, and it depends on people using the information effectively.

The Toyota Way recognizes that visual management complements humans because we are visually, tactilely, and audibly oriented. And the best visual indicators are right at the worksite, where they can jump out at you and clearly indicate by sound, sight, and feel the standard and any deviation from the standard. A well-developed visual control system increases productivity, reduces defects and mistakes, helps meet deadlines, facilitates communication, improves safety, lowers costs, and generally gives the workers more control over their environment.

As digital technology continues to replace the work of people and as companies continue to move whole departments to countries like India that have a workforce steeped in technology, Toyota has been challenged to take advantage of these digital tools. It is not an either-or. The question is, how can Toyota continue to make the workplace visual and people oriented while utilizing the power and benefits of computer technology? The answer is to follow Toyota Way Principle 7: Use visual control to support people in decision-making and problem solving. The principle does not say to avoid information technology: it simply means to think creatively and use the best available means to create true visual control. Toyota has already replaced some physical prototype models with digital models on large screens, an effort that involved engineers and even production team members in critiquing the design. One thing is certain: Toyota will not readily compromise its principles and goals for something that is merely faster and cheaper. Simply putting everything on the corporate intranet and using information technology to cut costs can produce many unintended consequences that can profoundly change and even damage a company's culture.

The Toyota Way will seek a balance and take a conservative approach to using information technology to maintain its values. This may entail a compromise, such as maintaining a physical visual signal along with a computer in the background, like in the Toyota service parts warehouse in Hebron. Or it may mean using a wall-size screen to display a 3-D image of a complete vehicle. But the important principle will remain: support your employees through visual control so they have the best opportunity to do work efficiently and effectively.

KEY POINTS

- Humans are naturally visual creatures and are more likely to recall and use information if it is in a visual format, preferably pictures.
- 5S—sort, straighten, shine, standardize, sustain—is a powerful tool to help create a visual workplace, but it is most powerful as part of a lean system with stable operations, standardized work, and continuous improvement.
- Visual control at the worksite should make it clear at a glance what the standard is and if anything is out of standard.
- For project management, Toyota uses a big visual meeting room, the obeya, so each specialty group can present up-to-date information on project status and any problems the group needs help on.
- Many companies see physical visuals as a waste of paper and inefficient and view the use of digital tools as modern and admirable. Computers often distract a group rather than enable it, but when properly designed and used, computer systems can help provide visual control.

Notes

1. John Medina, *Brain Rules: 12 Principles for Surviving and Thriving at Work, Home, and School* (Seattle, WA: Pear Press, 2014).
2. http://www.brainrules.net/pdf/mediakit.pdf.
3. Jeffrey Liker (editor), Chapter 8 in *Becoming Lean: Inside Stories of U.S. Manufacturers* (Boca Raton, Florida: CRC Press, 1997).
4. Hiroyuki Hirano, *5 Pillars of the Visual Workplace* (New York: Productivity Press, 1995).
5. James Morgan and Jeffrey Liker, *Designing the Future* (New York: McGraw-Hill, 2018).

Principle 8

Adopt and Adapt Technology That Supports Your People and Processes

Society has reached the point where one can push a button and be immediately deluged with technical and managerial information. This is all very convenient, of course, but if one is not careful there is a danger of losing the ability to think. We must remember that in the end it is the individual human being who must solve the problems.

—Eiji Toyoda, *Creativity, Challenge and Courage*,
Toyota Motor Corporation, 1983

In 1991, toward the end of the Japanese bubble economy, Toyota launched the Lexus LS400 with the most advanced automation in the company at its plant in Tahara, Japan. As usual, almost all the paint and welding was automated with robots, but automation was also selectively introduced in the assembly for engine-transmission-suspension installation decking and installation of air conditioner units, batteries, instrument panels, and windshields. Toyota made the automation work and meticulously maintained it at high levels. Quality was among the best in the world. The problem was that when the investment bubble burst, vehicle sales declined, and "the plant was criticized for its high capital investment, which was a high fixed-cost burden for Toyota."[1]

Toyota prides itself on only building to actual demand, and when demand declines, the company wants the flexibility to reduce costs to remain profitable. Typically, in downturns, the company reduces labor costs by eliminating overtime, reducing the temporary labor pool, and redeploying people to work on kaizen. But fixed capital cannot be temporarily removed. After the Tahara experience, Toyota raised the hurdle on introducing new automation. Toyota's principles of production equipment became "simple, slim, and flexible."

This lesson was painfully learned once again during the Great Recession of 2008. The pickup truck and large-SUV market tanked, and Toyota lost money as a corporation for the first time in 50 years. Toyota's reflection: fixed costs were too high leading to high breakeven points. The countermeasure: review every aspect of design and manufacturing and lower the breakeven points of all plants from about 80 to 70 percent of planned capacity. If a plant is running at full capacity and sales drop quickly by 30 percent, the plant should at least break even.

One implication of this could be to go slow and be cautious in adopting new technology. In today's age of lightning-speed technological change, particularly in the digital world, I believe that would be a mistake. The real message is to *adopt and adapt technology that supports your people and processes.* The starting point is this: where are real needs that technology can address to help achieve your goals? It is a question of pulling the technology based on the opportunity, instead of pushing the technology because it is the latest fad. And streamline processes that can be improved with little investment, before introducing expensive technology. As Bill Gates wisely observed:

> *The first rule of any technology used in a business is that automation applied to an efficient operation will magnify the efficiency. The second is that automation applied to an inefficient operation will magnify the inefficiency.*

Over the years, Toyota has tended to lag behind its competitors in acquiring the latest technology. Notice that I said "acquiring," not "using." Toyota uses an amazing number of robots in painting and welding vehicle bodies. Toyota's engine and transmission plants are filled with automated machining and forging equipment. Toyota has supercomputers and very advanced computer-aided technology to support product development. The company is investing billions of dollars in artificial intelligence for autonomous vehicles and is building and selling "mobility" robots to help patients in hospitals and the sick or elderly at home. Toyota's philosophy of automation has remained consistent over time: "Regardless of expansion in research fields, we would keep 'automation with a human touch' which have been always cherished by our predecessors of Toyota as the most important elements in technologies, which means the system such as robotics or AI should not replace the human, but always cherish 'the sense of agency' of humans."[2]

Unfortunately, a great deal of technology acquired by so-called leading-edge companies does not get effectively used. The notion of plug and play may work for hooking up a printer to your laptop, but most computer systems are far more complicated, and there is plenty that can and does go wrong. One example is Tesla's dive into advanced automation for automotive assembly at the former NUMMI plant in California, which was touted by Elon Musk in a fourth-quarter 2017 investor call as the greatest breakthrough since Henry Ford's integrated River Rouge complex. The goal was to eliminate all human touching of the product and to produce vehicles at superfast speed.[3] Interestingly, even with the "advanced" automation, labor productivity was far worse than when the plant was run by Toyota. A few months later when Musk admitted that the company was in "production hell" and could not meet production goals for the Model 3, Tesla built a second, simpler assembly line under a tent. Musk learned a valuable lesson: "We had this crazy complicated network of conveyor belts. And it was not working. So, we got rid of the whole thing."[4] Musk then tweeted "humans are underrated," and perhaps had turned the corner in appreciating the value of people.[5]

This is not to say that technology in the digital age does not fit with lean thinking, or that Elon Musk will never fulfill some version of his advanced manufacturing dreams. To take that perspective would mean putting on blinders and ignoring some of the greatest technological advances of our time. I believe the issue is to avoid the temptation to buy and implement the latest gee-whiz digital tools, and instead to thoughtfully integrate technology with highly developed people and processes. Later in the chapter, we will consider an example from Toyota's largest supplier, Denso, which has made remarkable progress in adapting real-time data collection, the internet of things (IoT), and data analytics to support lean systems and amplify kaizen. At the center of Denso's approach are people, and their ability to sense reality and think creatively. Denso demonstrates that technology has the greatest potential with highly developed people who are continuously improving.

COMPUTERS PROCESS THE INFORMATION. PEOPLE DO THE THINKING

I have taught plenty of courses on TPS basics like kanban, which is mainly a manual visual process. Information technology specialists immediately want to eliminate the paper kanban and digitize the process. Toyota successfully used paper kanban for many years. It has the advantage that it is tactile and physically travels with the containers of parts so you can see at a glance whether it is present or absent. No kanban and the container should not be moved. On the other hand. Toyota switched some years ago to electronic kanban, though there is also a parallel system of paper kanban to be scanned and disposed of. The point of using various kinds of artifacts is for people to easily visualize whether the process is in or out of standard as they do the work.

The folly of pushing technology became clear to me on a consulting job with an American automotive seating supplier that had worked with Toyota for years and learned TPS. My client's CEO got hooked on the idea of increasing inventory turns as a major corporate "lean" goal. He gave every business unit an aggressive target for inventory turns, which on the surface seemed to support the TPS principles of eliminating waste. It became a corporate mania.

A large group of "supply chain engineers" within the company was tasked with reducing inventory. The background of the leader of the supply chain group was in information technology, and he wanted to use internet technology to provide "visibility into the supply chain." There are many supply chain software "solutions" that promise to radically cut inventory and provide control over the process. They supposedly do this by showing anyone who logs into the website how much inventory there is in real time at every stage of the supply chain and to alert users when they are under or over preset inventory ranges.

The CEO's subordinates were very proud of their bright, well-spoken boss, and they often repeated a story he would tell. He described supply chain visibility software as analogous to a bulldozer. You can dig ditches manually, and it will work. But a bulldozer will do the same thing in a fraction of the time. IT was like this—speeding up dramatically work that was previously done by hand.

I was floored by this belief. How does keeping track of inventory on the computer give you any control over making it go away? From my TPS training, I knew that inventory is generally a symptom of poorly controlled processes. Ultimately, manufacturing is about making things. I talked to the boss and gave him my perspective. I explained that software may monitor inventory very quickly, but real people and machines are producing product based on some logic and, in the process, creating inventory. In fact, "supply chain visibility" is more analogous to setting up a video camera at the worksite and hooking up a remote monitor in another state so you can kick back with your coffee and watch the ditchdiggers work. Nonetheless, he pressed on with the technology.

My perspective was confirmed when we were asked to do a parallel project in one plant without the technology for comparison. Without any information technology, we were able to cut inventory by 80 percent on the assembly line, while the pilot plant using the supply chain software had only a marginal impact. We did this by moving from a push system based on schedules to a manual pull system, using kanban. Lead time was reduced by one-third—with no new technology. To eliminate most of the parts inventory required our working with a supplier in Mexico—owned by the same company—that was pushing as much inventory as it could onto this customer plant so its inventory turns metric would look good. Improving the process is how you get to sustainable inventory control.

IMPLEMENTING THE LATEST INFORMATION TECHNOLOGY IS NOT A BUSINESS GOAL AT TOYOTA

Toyota has had a variety of negative experiences with pushing too much automation into processes, as happened in Tahara. One example was an experiment in the 1990s in Toyota's Chicago Parts Distribution Center, where the company installed a highly automated rotary-rack system. At the time the warehouse was built, Toyota's dealers placed weekly stock orders for parts. But soon after the warehouse was completed, the company introduced daily ordering and daily deliveries to reduce lead time and lower inventories in the dealerships. With the change to daily deliveries, it expected to fill the now smaller (one-fifth the size) containers faster and speed up the whole process, but this did not happen. Some quick problem solving revealed the root cause. The center still had a long, fixed conveyor installed, and the person at the end of the conveyor had to wait for the smaller boxes of parts. The technology had created a waste of waiting. The benefit of the technology was short-lived, and the Chicago facility became one of Toyota's least productive warehouses. In 2002, the company again made a significant investment in Chicago, but this time it was to remove the automation and unwind the computer system that supported it. By comparison, Toyota's most productive regional parts depot was in Cincinnati, where there was very little automation.

Jane Beseda, former general manager and vice president, North American Parts Operations, explained:

> When you live in the logistics world, nothing moves without information. But, we're conservative in our approach to applying automation. You can kaizen people processes very easily, but it is hard to kaizen a machine. Our processes got far more productive and efficient, but the machine didn't. So, the machine had to come out.
>
> First work out the manual process, and then automate it. Try to build into the system as much flexibility as you possibly can so you can continue to kaizen the process as your business changes. And always supplement the system information with "genchi genbutsu," or "go look, go see."

Beseda went on to give an example of the power of a simple visual for pull systems. When you set up a kanban, you specify the maximum level of inventory, above which there is too much, and a minimum level that you do not want to go below. The quantity of inventory depends on a number of factors including the takt and the amount of variability in the customer orders and in the process. More variability means a need for more inventory to protect the next customer from shortages. There are mathematical equations to calculate these amounts based on assumptions and that can be computerized. But Baseda was not interested in complex calculations. Instead, she asked her people in one of the warehouses to come up with some numbers based on clear reasoning and then run the system and watch what happens. They should visually mark how many days the inventory exceeds the maximum or goes below the minimum and then take action when they see a consistent pattern, adding or subtracting kanban and then troubleshooting the reasons for having too little inventory. They found this process of adjustment and problem solving based on real circumstances far more effective than trying to guesstimate based on a math model.

In another interesting experience, I visited a Toyota plant in Japan that did machining of engine parts and I was amazed by a simple *chaku chaku* line that used a robot instead of a person. The idea of chaku chaku is to have a semi-automated line, usually two banks of machines lined up in parallel, with a person going up and down the line feeding parts into the machines and removing parts from the machines. The machines are designed to automatically spit the parts out when they are done so the person can simply grab them as they go. The person is taught to follow standardized work that uses both hands so the person can be very productive. But what fascinated me was seeing a simple pick-and-place robot doing the work of the human. It was designed and built by Toyota to be inexpensive and simply picked up a completed part with one "hand" and then inserted it into the next machine with the other. My guide explained that it saved on cost and also on space as the machines could be moved very close together with just enough room for the robot. People required more space for safety reasons.

We then walked to another line where there were a lot of people manipulating parts for a similar product. I asked why that was not robotized. My guide explained that there was much more product variety and the parts were more complex. The tasks required more dexterity and adjustment by people. The plant would like to use robots in the future, but the process and perhaps the product had to be greatly simplified through kaizen, which was being done by the production workers. I remember thinking, "One size does not fit all."

AUTOMATION AND EQUIPMENT CAN ALSO BE IMPROVED BY CREATIVE, THINKING PEOPLE

To be honest, my experience with kaizen was mainly limited to the knowledge and manual work people do, and I had not thought about continuously improving highly automated equipment. This changed when I met Mitsuru Kawai, the first person hired into Toyota as a production team member to rise to the position of executive vice president and board member. He joined Toyota in 1966 after graduating from Toyota Technical Skills Academy, a high school. He spent most of his career in Toyota's Honsha (headquarters) plant where the company machined and forged metal transmission parts. When Kawaii was a member of the production team, Taiichi Ohno took an interest in and personally developed him.

Ohno's teaching always started with a challenge to accomplish something that seemed impossible. Kawai explained that he had a standing order in the plant for 50 years to increase productivity by 2 percent every *month*. Each month he went back to zero. If one month he achieved a 4 percent increase, he still needed to improve 2 percent the next month. He started when the processes were mostly manual and continued for five decades, by which time the processes were almost completely automated.

Kawai was convinced that the same TPS principles applied to manual or automated work. He explained:

Materials will be flowing while changing shape at the speed we can sell the product. All else is waste. Operators need to learn how to use the machine and the materials and their five senses to create a good part at a reasonable price. Then intelligent automation can be developed to reduce as much as possible any transportation or movement that does not change the shape or form.

Kawai expected team members to get inside the equipment and redesign it to eliminate waste, but most were hired after everything was automated. He was deeply concerned by the mentality he witnessed that "you push a red button and a part comes out." Managers, engineers, and production team members needed to develop the following four skills:

- Visualize production.
- Develop explicit knowledge of the process.
- Standardize the knowledge.
- Develop intelligent automation through kaizen.

He did a number of things over the years to develop people. First, people had to get their hands dirty. He required all team members, engineers, and managers to perform the forging and machining jobs manually. Second, Kawai assigned to each equipment operator one piece of equipment, called "my machine." The job of each operator was to hand-draw in detail everything that happened to the part, second by second, as it was moved, oriented, and transformed. He explained to the managers that they needed to teach the workers and answer any questions they had, fully aware that the managers did not know enough to do this. The managers had to go back to the gemba and study the processes intensively. The learning curve was steep, but defects were reduced exponentially over time to almost zero as the footprint of the equipment shrank. Third, he created a manual assembly line so that each employee could experience a traditional application of TPS and improve upon it. There was a primitive transmission plant in Brazil in the 1940s that Toyota wanted to close because the volumes were too low for it to be profitable. Ohno had personally visited the plant and proved that TPS could make it profitable. But 75 years later it had run its course and was shut down. Kawai asked to have the transmission assembly line boxed up and moved to his plant in Japan to use for TPS training.

The task assigned to team members was to work on the line and manually assemble a high variety of low-volume models economically, and to do it without electricity. He called it the "TPS basic learning line." The students received specific assignments for kaizen and learned on the manual line. Then they went to the forging and machining lines to improve the automated processes. Over time, they cut the floor space of what was already an efficient transmission assembly cell in half, while increasing productivity several times over.

There were many innovations born of the challenging objectives on the TPS line with the constraints of using simple, mechanical devices at almost no cost. For example, one of the challenges was to find a way to accurately pick the right parts for a transmission among a large variety of choices manually. With today's technology, this would be done electronically with light curtains, bar codes, and computers. The bin of the next part to pick would light up, and if a worker tried to pick the wrong part, alarms would go off and lights would blink. How could this be done without computers or electricity?

The students came up with an ingenious device that performed two functions: it acted as a kanban and enabled them to replenish parts at low volume, and it acted as a mistake-proof device. They called it the "key kanban." A small number of each part was kept on the assembly line. When the production operators used enough parts that they reached a point to trigger replenishment, a rectangular metal kanban (unique for that part) would be used as a key to open the correct bin. The kanban was color-coded and had identifying information that corresponded to a specific bin where those parts were stored. A plastic see-through cover had a picture of the part and the identifying information. You put the key kanban into a slot and pulled down, and it would lift one and only one bin cover—the one for that part (Figure 8.1).

Figure 8.1   Manual key kanban opens only the cover
of the correct part to pick next.

The implication: trash all the new digital tools and go back to the craft days of manual work and simple machines? Not at all. Kawai was developing people so they could be even more effective in running and improving the automated processes.

WHEN THE TOYOTA WAY MEETS INDUSTRY 4.0

I am by no means an expert on this, but my understanding is that Industry 4.0 uses software to manage assets through the internet of things: data collection devices (e.g., wireless sensors and high-definition cameras), big data mining to identify patterns, predictive algorithms, and artificial intelligence that can learn. There are many applications. One use of the technology is to monitor machines, predict failures, and in some cases take corrective action by automatically adjusting the machines. Another example is smart robots that can adapt to different conditions and learn, simulating human decision-making and motions.

Without realizing it, I experienced the power of this new technology when practicing golf in February of 2020. A friend contacted me to try out a driving range that was the first in the area to install new technology that could track swings and provide data on your smartphone. The driving range had installed radar towers spread over the range to collect data in three dimensions. I downloaded the "Trackman" app, went to the range, entered the number of the bay I was hitting out of, entered the golf club I was using, hit a ball, and then watched on my phone the path of the ball, the distance carried in the air, the distance it continued on the ground, and the height. It could adjust the results based on weather conditions at the time. There was even a measure of variability of my shots by club. How cool was that?

I could then look back and ask questions like "How far do I hit each club on average?" "Which clubs are more reliable?" "Should I use a lesser-distance club in some cases to get the increased reliability?" The key was the data collectors (radar), the connection to the internet to process the data, the analysis of the data, the connection to my phone through the internet, and the application software.

Later I thought some more about this technology and its power. I really enjoyed using it, and it enhanced my overall experience at the driving range, like playing a video game, but did I learn more? The goal of going to the driving range is to practice and get better. Did it aid my practice and skill level? It seemed like a yes in theory, but maybe was a no in reality. It could help if I used it as part of a good regimen of deliberate practice. That meant I had to go beyond just hitting balls and watching on my cell phone what happened. I had to have specific skills I was working toward, a standard for what I wanted my swing to be like, and for each swing of the club I needed to note deviations from the standard and then think of and practice a countermeasure to those deviations. Otherwise it was just fun (not a bad thing). The technology plus the human discipline of deliberate practice could add up to something.

What I saw at Denso was a lot like this technology at the driving range, though on a larger scale and more sophisticated. Denso's culture included the discipline of developing people to think and solve problems based on the gap between the standards and actual conditions, which when combined with IoT, was a very powerful combination.

ELECTRONIC WALLPAPER?*

When I first joined the University of Michigan in 1982, the "factory of the future" was all the rage. I studied the "social impacts" of computer-integrated manufacturing (CIM), which was predicted to disrupt industry, potentially putting millions of workers out of a job. Design something on the computer, create a digital database, upload it to automatic machine tools, and out comes the product. The media was abuzz with this disruptive technology, so I was shocked to learn that at that time it was mostly a myth, and there were far more failures than successes. A group of us studied a small company, a maker of bearings for material handling systems, that advertised itself as an early adopter of CIM. It installed new computerized equipment and displaced the operators of the old equipment; but when the new system failed, it had to put back into use the old equipment and hire back the displaced operators to keep production running.[6] Eventually the company went bankrupt. We wrote an article, "Changing Everything All at Once," and documented why everything turned out so badly. Basically, they were ambitious early adopters, but rushed unproven technology into operation prematurely. Given that experience, I was skeptical when I started hearing all the buzz about Industry 4.0. Meeting Raja Shembekar at Denso both reinforced my skepticism and began to persuade me that this advanced digital technology was the missing piece from those early efforts at computerized manufacturing.

Raja Shembekar, vice president of Denso's North American Production Innovation Center, became the chief architect of Denso's use of IoT. He worked for Ford for 12 years, where he learned the basics of automotive design and manufacture, and then he joined Denso in 2004, learning the culture and system and spending two years in Japan in production engineering. When he was back in the

---

* The term "electronic wallpaper" was coined by Dave Grimmer, who was SVP of Denso's North American Production Innovation Center when he noticed the gap between data displays and use.

United States in 2012, he had an aha moment when he sensed how far the U.S. was ahead of Japan in modern software, particularly in the budding technologies of the internet of things and artificial intelligence. He was determined to bring these technologies to Denso. At the time, he believed Denso was far behind and needed to quickly catch up, so he set out to hire an IoT vendor. Raja explained:

> *Back in 2017 we made many site visits. They showed us great PowerPoint™ presentations and they said we can do this, we can do this. And at that point we really thought we were way behind compared to the rest of US industry. So we talked with five different companies, did actual trials with them, and set up their software inhouse.*

Much like what my research group experienced in the 1980s with the "factory of the future," when Raja and his team delved deeper into supposed Industry 4.0 benchmark companies, he was shocked to learn how little they had done. There was a lot of fanfare and wonderful displays of data, but almost no action to solve real problems. He lamented:

> *We learned a lot but quickly realized that if you go to plants and they show you a lot of monitors and dashboards—I call it electronic wallpaper—unless you show me what action you took from that real time data, and that the data is true data, it is just electronic wallpaper. I visited more than a dozen plants in large prominent companies and many of them had good activities, but they were not fully integrated and those who showed a lot of dashboards, when we started digging deeper into it, we found not much action being taken.*

He visited a plant of another major automotive supplier that was receiving a great deal of attention as a best-practice case of IoT use. The supplier had beautiful data displays with lots of bar charts. He looked at one monitor that was measuring overall equipment effectiveness to gauge uptime of equipment. The numbers on the display for one line said the equipment was running at 135 percent. Raja was surprised by the number and asked if it was accurate. He was told, "No, that's not really true on that line because the software has not been adjusted for the issues we had today." Raja thought, "What would the associates think if they see 135 percent when they know they are not achieving the target output for the day?"

He also found that the software was designed by technology specialists with no understanding of real manufacturing and was often not adaptable to real-world circumstances. An example Raja encountered when checking out possible software vendors:

> *We did proof of concept with 2 companies, one from Germany and one from the US. Let's say your shift starts at 8am and they plug that into the software.*

At 8 it starts to monitor the productivity of your line. But let's say that we have a message from the team leader on some safety issue or something so the line starts at 8:07. Our associates should not be held accountable for this 7 minutes of lost production because management decided to postpone the start for a different reason. Believe it or not, you would think it would be easy, but they could not easily adjust the software so a team leader can go in and say we started at 8:07.

IOT APPLICATIONS AT DENSO, BATTLE CREEK

When I visited in February 2020, many IoT applications were live and working at Denso's testing ground factory in Battle Creek, Michigan. In the hallway entering the plant was a large screen with a map showing various zones. All the zones were green in our winter visit, which meant they were fine on wet-bulb heat-stress indexes. If the temperature is above 95.5°F, associates must legally take a 15-minute break each 4 hours. In the past, people would walk through the plant checking temperatures and calculating an average temperature. If the average temperature was above target, the entire plant would shut down for 15 minutes. Now, continuous data collection by zone will in real time reveal one or more zones going over the limit, and only those zones will be immediately shut down, saving production and wasted labor.

In another area, we saw dashboards based on live data that continuously updated safety, quality, cost, and lead-time measures. If there were official quality claims, the display would show where it happened, what happened, and what countermeasures were taken. If no action was taken within 20 minutes, the problem automatically escalated.

At one workstation, the operator watched a screen that in real time created a quality process control chart with upper and lower control limits. Just glancing at the screen at the time, it was clear that the process had very recently gone out of control, and the operator had seen it, acted, and got it back in control.

One of the biggest successes was the use of predictive maintenance for brazing ovens that are part of the process for making aluminum heat exchangers. The ovens are large and long, and each one has 12 expensive fans that are about the size of a round dinner table and provide a controlled atmosphere for circulation to keep a specific temperature constant through the oven. If a single fan stops, the oven must be brought down, and at almost 1300°F, it takes 12 hours to cool it down, 12 hours to replace the fan, and 12 hours to bring it back up. Each time the fan stops, the plant loses 36 hours of production and 30,000 pieces a day. In addition, 60 people are idled by the production stoppage. There were four to six unexpected stops per year at a cost of about $70,000 to $80,000 each time.

Denso hired a vendor that attached a sophisticated wireless sensor to each fan motor that monitors harmonics in two dimensions (since the fans operate on a dual axis), temperature, and fan speed—and the data are analyzed by predictive analytics software. The software is smart enough to predict not just that a fan is going to fail, but in some cases the cause; for example, the bearing is hot. In one case, Denso data scientists reported to maintenance that a fan was going to fail in 58 hours and that the maintenance people should replace it. Raja explained:

Maintenance did not believe it. But we asked them to change it anyway. They took the fan out. Half the blades on the fan had disintegrated. They were totally shocked that they had no idea this was happening and we could provide that prediction. They became much more accepting of the new technology.

HOW DID DENSO MAKE IT WORK?

After benchmarking presumed leaders in Industry 4.0, it became clear to Raja that Denso had to take control of the technology internally and selectively work with outside vendors with particular expertise. The company needed to do what had been hammered into his head since he joined Denso—solve real problems and take action. It also needed to build consensus around the technology at all levels, and particularly among those people on the production floor who were responsible for production work and maintenance.

Develop Internal Expertise to Develop and Customize Software

Raja assembled a cross-functional team of about 10 programmers at the Battle Creek plant to lead the effort for North America. About half were hired from outside with specific IoT expertise, and about half were internal with extensive manufacturing experience. Three had quality auditor experience, so they knew the problems Denso had in production. North America IoT manager Chad Orbeck had over 26 years of experience, including running a production line. Raja explained:

They are really good at software but they are engrained for over 20 years in how production is to be run the TPS way. That is why I think Denso has been far more successful than any of the companies that I have benchmarked in the US. They could develop software that they knew would work because they knew what the issues would be.

His team even developed the software used to move the data between systems. One of the keys for transforming a company that has many legacy systems is to allow those systems to share data seamlessly. Raja continued:

> *The User Interface is easy to do but getting that data from different legacy systems requires an effective API [Application Programming Interface] so they could pull in the data. The vendors we benchmarked were not able to create good interoperability with our legacy systems. Only our guys could do it because they were the ones that had built the legacy systems. And they learned the new systems so they were able to make the APIs work.*

For big data, Raja hired two data analysts who had expertise in analyzing large data sets. They collaborated with team members on the shop floor and with outside software companies on real projects at the gemba. They began to get great results. At one point, one of their customers, a large American automotive manufacturer, heard about what they were doing and brought a group of people to benchmark their use of data analytics. The customer had made a major investment hiring 50 data analysts. Raja asked one of the group members what the group was working on and described how disappointed he was at the visitor's answer:

> *He laughed and he said, "Not much. We just collect a bunch of data." So 6 months later we were keeping in touch and I showed him some of the examples we are doing with the data scientists, people actually use it, and he was shocked, saying, "You only have 2 people and you already have working examples?"*

Collaborating with a Startup for Motion Technology

Another key to Denso's success has been networking and collaboration. One example was the discovery of a company that developed technology that digitizes human motion and provides real-time data about standardized work. Denso found out about this through a contact at the Stanford Research Institute.

The company is Drishti Technologies, and it was founded by Dr. Prasad Akella. Dr. Akella started with the belief that technology should augment people, not displace them. He partnered with A.T. Kearney who surveyed 100 large manufacturing companies and found that human employees performed 72 percent of factory tasks. He then asked the question: What happens when you combine the creativity and adaptability of people with the cognitive power of AI? The advantage of people is our flexibility and ingenuity. The disadvantage is our variability.

Standardized work is a way to reduce that variability. What if AI could analyze video data, recognize cycles of work, recognize work elements, and alert workers immediately when there is a deviation from standard? It would be like an automatic andon giving the worker in real time feedback on their work. Did they skip a step? Did they grab the wrong part? Did they exceed the timing for the work cycle? Immediate feedback leads to rapid learning.

Drishti's technology has multiple cameras continuously recording work from different angles and storing the data in the cloud and then a proprietary AI system based on neural networks analyzes the video data and identifies times over the planned cycle time, finds bottlenecks, and even generates work balance charts. It also brings traceability to a whole new level. Your customer calls about a defective product they received. You call it up by serial number and you can watch the part being built and look at the data generated by the AI. Root cause analysis is now a real possibility rather than a guessing game.

When Raja visited it was clear that Dr. Akella had experience with manufacturing, but no in-depth training in TPS. Raja and his team taught Dr. Akella and his team about lean systems, and after one year of intensive collaboration, they created something that just may revolutionize standardized work.[7] Raja explains how this breakthrough technology works:

> *There is a camera focused on each associate on a manual assembly line. Videos record action in real time, send the data to the Google cloud where analysis is done using AI, and report back within 2 seconds and it tells the person whether they did the action in the right sequence. Before we had this technology for real time analysis you would have to have video cameras mounted and someone would have to go through it manually taking many hours. This technology digitizes the human motion and provides bottleneck analytics. It is a global first. It covers many of the technical TPS tools including standardized work, not passing defects to the next process, having a pace setter, and achieving the cycle time at each station and reports it back instantly. We've eliminated hand-written hour-by-hour charts. This system recognizes every part by human action and sees how many parts are done. And it tells me where I am against takt. It produces yamazumi [work balance] charts that break down the work elements for each of the functions. The analyst can extract data for any time period and go back to look at videos of interest, across associates, shifts, and at the bottleneck, so it really is a revolution in TPS.*

Perhaps it is no surprise that Drishti has found that the AI system is most useful for customers like Denso and Toyota that already have strong lean systems. Toyota department general manager Akiharu Engo refers to the total system as "TPS+AI," suggesting that the two go hand in hand. For example, the AI is useful when the factory has achieved some level of standardized work that is stable and being used effectively. This depends on a smooth flow of work that depends on all the technical TPS factors in Principles 2 to 7 working together. Visualization continues to be important. Drishti uses a tablet computer hung in front of the operator that shows each step as it is being performed, and it is red if there is a deviation. The role of the technology is alerting people to issues so they can quickly respond with creative problem solving, and as we will learn under Principle 10, lean companies are organized around work groups with members trained in problem solving. Undergirding the system of people and technology is a culture built on mutual trust. The worst situation is when management and workers fight over performance standards and team members believe the AI system is a management attempt to control them and speed up production.

DOES THE TECHNOLOGY DESKILL, REPLACE, OR ENHANCE?

The answer is, it depends on management philosophy. Recall the discussion in the Preface about mechanistic and organic approaches. From a mechanistic perspective, the value of technology is clear—replace people, monitor those remaining, and control them with clear instructions on what to do. Implement the technology quickly and broadly to remove the unpredictable human element.

From an organic systems perspective, the value of the technology is very different. When combined with the ingenuity of highly developed people motivated toward the goals of serving the customer and helping the company, it can multiply kaizen—faster and better.

Raja made it clear what side of the fence he was on. Denso's focus was not on using the technology to eliminate people, though he had no doubt that over time there would be a need for fewer people in the factory. While there would be cases where a closed-loop technical system diagnosed and automatically corrected problems, there would be plenty of issues that required human ingenuity and intervention. In fact, Raja became convinced that the skill requirements of the people need to grow:

> We will always need people, but their skill level needs to be completely shifted over time. The technology provides data that allows the associate and the team leaders at the gemba to provide a far higher level of decision-making. In the past they would just fill out the paperwork, but by the time they did all that, they had either no time or no energy to really comprehend the data. If they want to see trends from say five days ago or across people, that just wasn't there. What this has provided is what we now call fast PDCA. We can't afford to have PDCA that takes three weeks anymore. We want a PDCA done before the end of that shift.

Raja gave an example from the technology to predict failures of fans:

I was able to tell there was a problem with the fan faster and better than the guy with 26 years of experience. Before, he would connect an ultrasonic device and listen and say this vibration is kind of bad. Now, he is looking at time-series data, a Fourier series. Imagine his shift in knowledge from just listening to really understanding an amplitude frequency curve. So you have shifted his skill level significantly up the curve—kind of like a low-level engineer. People will still be there but at that level.

At Denso in Japan, executives and engineers also explained that IoT is not intended to cut people out of the loop, but actually provides superior information to people about the process (see Figure 8.2). The power of big data and artificial intelligence is to give the operator information just in time that they previously could only guess at. But Denso then expects the operator to use that information creatively to find the root cause and solve the problem through kaizen. Denso calls this "collaborative creation and growth of humans, things, and equipment." One irony might come out of this. Historically, a major role of industrial engineers was to reduce the number of workers needed. Now, the technology might enable the workers to the point where they can eliminate the industrial engineers.

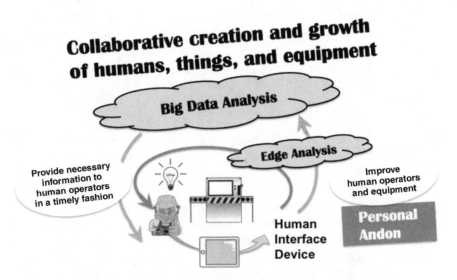

Figure 8.2   Denso depiction of the internet of things supporting people.

BALANCING THE RUSH FOR THE LATEST TECHNOLOGY WITH EFFECTIVENESS

Toyota is a technologically advanced company and has been for decades—shut down its computer systems, and you shut down the company. Now Toyota is putting super computers into its vehicles. But Toyota is not interested in being trendy and making adoption of new technology an end unto itself. Just as Toyota refuses to schedule parts made in one department to be pushed onto another department, Toyota refuses to allow an information technology department or advanced manufacturing technology department to push technology onto departments that do the value-added work of designing and building cars. Any information technology must meet the acid test of supporting people and processes and prove it adds value before it is implemented broadly. And then the ownership for introducing the new technology falls on existing management. Managers are responsible for its operation and for meeting targets, and so they should lead the introduction.

Toyota is willing to spend several years to first pilot the technology in one plant (like Battle Creek) and then spread it globally plant by plant, even though it could get the payback quickly if it were introduced everywhere in the first year led by corporate experts. Each introduction in a new plant is a learning experience to build on for the next plant, and each plant introduction is an opportunity to develop local managers and engineers in that plant to maintain and improve the technology.

The problem as I see it is that people living in the computer software world seem to believe if they can do a demonstration based on a digital simulation, it should translate seamlessly into solving real problems in the outside material world. That is the thinking that got companies in trouble back in the 1980s. And it was the situation that Raja of Denso encountered in the twenty-first century when he was exploring Industry 4.0 software. I was skeptical before talking to Raja about the bold concept of a fully automated factory with everything run by internet connections, big data, and AI—and Raja confirmed my suspicions that it could be a lot of smoke and mirrors. On the other hand, I also was awakened to the strength of the technology. I am still skeptical that completely computerized lights-out factories without people will be practical, but the capability of the technology with AI and the internet is far beyond anything possible in the 1980s. It seems people were not completely wrong about the potential, but just early.

It also became clear in seeing what Raja has been doing at Denso's plant in Battle Creek that Industry 4.0 is not a disruptive force that makes TPS irrelevant, but rather can be an enabler that builds on TPS culture and thinking. After all, the internet of things necessarily includes things. And if the things are poorly designed, poorly laid out, and poorly maintained, software will not solve the problem.

The difference between Denso and the companies that are creating electronic wallpaper seems to be a matter of mindset. Denso starts with the problem and then builds the social and technical systems to help address the problem. It builds on its existing culture of disciplined execution and problem solving. As we discuss scientific thinking under Principle 12, think back to the systematic approach Denso is taking. Without this, companies are left to throwing the technology at the wall and hoping it sticks. The principles of TPS will not disappear from a company like Denso, but the way the factory operates under TPS + IoT will be very different.

I was fascinated by the IoT technologies I saw at Denso, but in the back of my mind I could not help but guess at what Mr. Kawai would think. He was deeply concerned in his highly automated factory that people were not thinking critically. They were happy to push a button and wait for the part to pop out. So he forced them to dig deep to understand the automated process at a very granular level and then improve it. When computers begin to do the thinking, will people abdicate responsibility? A lot of data are coming out of these systems, and with analytics and AI, even some conclusions. But these systems are still primitive compared with the human brain, and they are not creative. How can we marry the powerful information coming out of the computers with the creativity of people in developing and testing ideas for improvement?

Akio Toyoda seems to have similar thoughts. In a speech he said:

Two concepts—automation with people and Just-in-Time—are the pillars of the TPS. What both have in common is that people are at the center. I believe that the more automation advances, the more the ability of the people using it will be put to the test. Machines cannot improve unless people do, too. Developing people with skills that can equal machines and senses that surpass sensors is a fundamental part of Toyota's approach.[8]

KEY POINTS

- Toyota has had bad experiences loading up plants with automated equipment only to find in a business downturn that the company had too much money tied up in fixed capital costs.
- After several such experiences, including in the Great Recession, the mantra became "simple, slim, and flexible," with the right balance of people and automation.

- Kaizen does not end with automation, but rather continuous improvement of automated equipment can help organizations move closer to the lean vision of one-piece flow without interruption.
- The internet of things has the potential to build on TPS principles and take operations to a whole new level of performance, with people being fed real-time and continuous information to accelerate and amplify kaizen.
- People in Toyota are still viewed as master craftsworkers who use all their senses to understand the state of the process and can perform even automated processes manually.

Notes

1. Takahiro Fujimoto, *The Evolution of a Manufacturing System at Toyota* (New York: Oxford University Press, 1999).
2. https://www.toyota-global.com/innovation/partner_robot/index.html.
3. Joann Muller, "Musk Thinks Tesla Will School Toyota on Lean Manufacturing; Fixing Model 3 Launch Would Be a Start," *Forbes*, February 16, 2018.
4. http://www.businessinsider.com/elon-musk-says-model-3-production-using-to-many -robots-2018-4.
5. https://techcrunch.com/2018/04/13/elon-musk-says-humans-are-underrated-calls -teslas-excessive-automation-a-mistake/.
6. Jeffrey Liker, David Roitman, and Ethel Roskies, "Changing Everything All at Once: Work Life and Technological Change," *Sloan Management Review*, 1987, vol. 28, no. 4, pp. 29–48.
7. https://www.prnewswire.com/news-releases/denso-and-drishti-bring-innovation-to-the -production-floor-with-ai-based-action-recognition-technology-301003329.html.
8. Akio Toyoda speech, December 2019, https://global.toyota/en/company/messages -from-executives/details/.

PART THREE

PEOPLE

Respect, Challenge, and Grow Your People
and Partners Toward a Vision of Excellence

Principle 9

Grow Leaders Who Thoroughly Understand the Work, Live the Philosophy, and Teach It to Others

There is no magic method. Rather, a Total Management System is needed, that develops human capability to its fullest capacity to best enhance creativity and fruitfulness, to utilize facilities and machines well, and to eliminate all waste.
—Nampachi Hayashi, Ohno disciple, Toyota Motor Manufacturing

GROWING HUMBLE LEADERS FROM WITHIN

The *Automotive News* wraps up each year by recognizing the biggest newsmakers in the industry. Some time ago, the Newsmakers of 2002[1] included Bill Ford (CEO of Ford), Robert Lutz (GM executive vice president), Dieter Zetsche (Chrysler Group president), Carlos Ghosn (Nissan president), and Fujio Cho (president of Toyota). The contrast in accomplishments between Cho and several of the other recognized leaders revealed differences in culture across companies. Here is what *Automotive News* admired about each leader:

Bill Ford *(Ford CEO): Talks up revitalization, brings back Allan Gilmour, promotes David Thursfield, and stars in TV commercials. But it's tough out there. Ford Motor stock remains mired in the $10 range.*

Robert Lutz *(GM executive VP): At 70, former Marine pilot inspires GM's troops and revolutionizes (and simplifies) product development, giving car guys and designers a bigger voice.*

Dieter Zetsche *(Chrysler Group president): Turns the Chrysler group around a year early with three quarters in the black.*

Carlos Ghosn *(Nissan president): Perennial newsmaker produces more incredible results at Nissan. U.S. market share moves up again. Ghosn truly deserves to be called the "Mailman." He delivers.*

Fujio Cho *(Toyota president): Toyota president presides over rise in operating profit to industry record. Takes lead on hybrids. Grabs 10 points of U.S. market. Joins with Peugeot for plants in Eastern Europe.*

All of the non-Toyota leaders made a positive impact on their companies, at least for some time, until they didn't. They were brought in from outside to turn around ailing companies. They each, in turn, brought in a group of their own handpicked, outside lieutenants to help in the turnaround. They also reorganized the company and brought their own philosophy and approach to transform it. Bill Ford, a Ford employee and family member, is the exception. However, he was appointed largely on a temporary basis to get the company out of trouble; his biggest accomplishment was hiring wizard CEO Alan Mulally from Boeing as his successor. None of these non-Toyota leaders naturally progressed through promotions to become presidents and CEOs at their companies. They abruptly came in from the outside to shake up the culture and to reform the direction of a company that was going bad.

In fact, it seems the typical US company regularly alternates between the extremes of stunning success and borderline bankruptcy. This roller-coaster ride is exciting, and for a time, it's great. Then, when something suddenly goes wrong, the organization turns to a new CEO preaching a very different direction. It is business leadership like the hare in the fable, running madly and then going to sleep—an erratic pattern that leads to uneven results.

In contrast, Cho grew up in Toyota and was a student of Taiichi Ohno. He helped provide a theoretical basis for the Toyota Production System (TPS) and presided over the introduction of *The Toyota Way 2001* to strengthen the culture in overseas operations. Cho was the first president of the Kentucky plants, Toyota's first wholly owned engine and assembly plants in the United States. He was a board member and became president when the company was already successful. He moved into the position naturally and built on the momentum that had been ongoing for decades. At Toyota, the new president does not need to come in and take charge to move the company in a radically new direction or put his imprint on the company. The leadership role of Cho focused more on continuity than change. Perhaps like its vehicles, Toyota leaders are not always exciting, but they are highly effective.

Even when Toyota promoted someone from an unusual part of the company to lead a shift in strategic direction, there was never a sudden change of culture. Think of this as eliminating muri (unevenness) at the executive level. It seems that throughout Toyota's history, key leaders were found within the company, at the right time, to shape the next step in Toyota's evolution. That's been true across the enterprise—in sales, product development, manufacturing, and design.

The first non-Toyoda family member to take the reins in decades, Hiroshi Okuda, became president at a time when Toyota needed to globalize more aggressively. He ruffled some feathers along the way. He pushed forward the development of the Prius, which launched the company into the twenty-first century. After this aggressive period, Fujio Cho, in a calmer, quieter way, continued the globalization of Toyota, building on his experiences in the United States and focusing on reenergizing the internal Toyota Way culture. Despite major differences in personal style, neither of these leaders deviated from the basic philosophies of the Toyota Way.

Eventually Akio Toyoda, grandson of Kiichiro Toyoda, was appointed president. Akio Toyoda explained to me that he did not get a free ride, but had to start at the bottom, working in a boot camp–like environment in the Operations Management Consulting Division. He was challenged to meet a seemingly impossible target in a department of a supplier plant. Like Ohno, his sensei was demanding and punishing. Akio Toyoda struggled, but succeeded in meeting the challenge. The biggest challenge he had to face as president was to position the company for what he proclaimed would be a "once-in-a-century" industry disruption as a result of digital technology and electrification. Along the way he had to deal with crisis after crisis. When asked what he learned, Akio Toyoda emphasized calm and stability, rather than a knee-jerk reaction:[2]

> *The number one thing I have learned and that I am prioritizing from my learning is that I am not panicking. I am managing the company very efficiently and stably. In managing the company during these past 10 years, no years were peaceful. Every year, year on year, we have witnessed and experienced a large, drastic change on the scale of a one-in-a-100-year event. So, I think that the calmer I am, the calmer things are within the company.*

Toyota does not go shopping for "superstar" CEOs and presidents because its leaders must live and thoroughly understand the Toyota culture. Since a critical element of the culture is genchi genbutsu, which means deeply observing the actual situation in detail, leaders must demonstrate this ability and understand how work gets done at the front lines of Toyota. According to the Toyota Way, a superficial impression of the current situation in any division of Toyota will lead to ineffective decision-making and leadership. Toyota also expects its leaders to teach their subordinates the Toyota Way, which means they must first understand and live the philosophy. In his first speech as president, Akio Toyoda vowed to be the most active president at the gemba in Toyota history. He explained:

"Genchi genbutsu" [go and see the actual situation] means imagining what you are observing is your own job, rather than somebody else's problem, and making efforts to improve it. Job titles are unimportant. In the end, the people who know the gemba [where the actual work is done] are the most respected.

The vision for a Toyota leader is well summarized in the *Toyota Way 2001*: lead continuous improvement while treating people with respect. Respect starts with treating people fairly and as part of the team, but goes beyond that to challenging people to grow.

GROWING "LEVEL 5 LEADERS" INSTEAD OF PURCHASING LEVEL 4 LEADERS

I often contrast Toyota to Western companies. If you asked me to describe the common view of the ideal CEO in the United States, I would say we value the rugged individualist who is charismatic and articulates loudly a bold vision for the company, then gets the right executives on board, who either make the vision happen or are pushed out—swim or sink. Since our CEOs tend to be portable, they take some recipe that worked for them in the past and impose it on whatever new companies they take over. CEOs that come from the outside to turn around a company are brought in because the company is not performing to expectations, so the new CEOs are likely to talk about a "broken culture" and how they will install their new performance culture. Often, this includes bringing in consultants they have used in the past to build the leadership team and help drive the new culture.

When I first read Jim Collins' book *Good to Great*,[3] I was shocked by his hierarchy of five leadership levels. What I thought of as Western leaders (which I described above) corresponded to his "level 4" leaders, who run companies adequately over time. But every one of the 11 Western "great companies" had what he called "level 5" leaders, who resembled what I observed at Toyota. It provided some validation that what I observed at Toyota was not unique to one Japanese company. His 11 great companies experienced exceptional growth and superior stock market performance, when compared with 11 average competitors and 6 "unsustained" companies that temporarily appeared great but then declined. The level 5 leaders' characteristics included:[4]

- Intense professional will, yet personal humility
- Understated, yet fearless
- Transformational leaders
- Dedicated their lives to building an enduring and great company

- Selected the best people for jobs, even bypassing family members of the founders
- Founded the company or grew the organization from within
- Looked in the mirror and assigned self-blame, looked out the window to assign credit
- Obsessive about knowing their business in detail
- Brutally honest about reality, even when it is bad news

One example of a level 5 leader was Darwin E. Smith, a relatively unknown CEO. He led the transformation of Kimberly-Clark from a struggling paper company that experienced a 36 percent drop in its stock price into the leading consumer paper products company in the world. Under Smith, cumulative stock returns over the next 20 years were 4.1 times greater than for the general market. Smith had been a mild-mannered in-house lawyer for the company, an unlikely choice for CEO. Collins described Smith's level 5 leader characteristics as:

People generally assume that transforming companies from good to great requires larger-than-life leaders—big personalities like Iacocca, Dunlap, Welch, and Gault, who make headlines and become celebrities. Compared with those CEOs, Darwin Smith seems to have come from Mars. Shy, unpretentious, even awkward, Smith shunned attention.[5]

How successful were these bold, outspoken CEOs that we treated as celebrities? They were usually one-step-down, level 4 leaders, who could be effective to a degree and "catalyze commitment to and vigorous pursuit of a clear and compelling vision and stimulate the group to high standards."[6] But they were leaders of the mediocre companies, and their main goal was splashy short-term results, with most seeing the job as a stepping-stone to their next gig. More than two-thirds of the not-so-great companies had level 4 leaders "with a gargantuan ego that contributed to the demise or continued mediocrity of their company." Collins concludes:

The moment a leader allows himself to become the primary reality people worry about, rather than reality being the primary reality, you have a recipe for mediocrity, or worse. This is one of the key reasons why less charismatic leaders often produce better long-term results than their more charismatic counterparts.[7]

LEADERSHIP AND CULTURE

Every new "level 4" CEO of a struggling company I have met loves to talk about culture change. I hear statements like:

- "This company culture lacked discipline, and I am going to build a culture of disciplined execution."
- "This company became like a luxury resort where underperforming managers could hang out. Those people are gone, and in my culture every manager will earn their keep."
- "Here is my new organizational chart where I have product divisions with their own profit and loss. Every tub must stand on its own bottom."
- "This company was a culture of I, and *I* am making it a culture of we." (The term "I" appears often in their proclamations, even when talking about teamwork.)

These kinds of statements make me doubt that these CEOs really understand culture or what real culture change entails. They do succeed in disrupting the business and scaring legacy executives into leaving or conforming, but is management by fear building a new culture? Edgar Schein, one of the gurus of culture, defines "culture" as "a pattern of shared basic assumptions learned by a group as it solved its problems of external adaptation and internal integration. . . . A product of joint learning."[8]

Creating broadly and deeply held "shared basic assumptions learned by a group" takes time. Think a decade or more, not a month or a year. Changing the culture each time a new leader takes over usually means jerking the company about superficially, without developing depth or loyalty from the employees. The "shared" part is missing, which is the very definition of culture. The problem with an outsider leading radical shifts in the culture is that the organization will never learn—it loses the ability to build on achievements, mistakes, or enduring principles. This affects the ability of leaders to make effective changes. On the other hand, in Deming's terms, Toyota strives for "constancy of purpose" throughout the organization, which lays the groundwork for consistent and positive leadership as well as an environment for learning.

More broadly, Toyota's longstanding culture seems like an amalgamation of many influences, as summarized in Figure 9.1. Japan is known as a society built on people working together and, at least publicly, acting very politely toward each other. Mutual dependence, an obligation to help others, and the determination to reach a goal together are all basic assumptions of Japanese life. One study argues that this aspect of Japanese culture derives in large part from rice farming, which requires a high level of cooperation, interconnectedness, and holistic thinking compared with wheat farming in the West, which can be done independently.[9] The theme of passionate commitment to a cause is characteristic of the samurai who spent a lifetime mastering fighting skills to protect their ruler or die trying. The more reflective mindfulness and deep study of the gemba brings to mind the state of Zen.

- Group identity as rice farmers in Japan

- Samurai tradition: Honor and the leader as protector

- Zen: Empty one's mind and use senses for new insight; mindfulness

- Confucius: Respect elders' wisdom; develop others; contribute to society; rules, and structure

- Deming: Most problems are "management" issues; build in quality; PDCA

- Toyoda family: Strive to contribute (looms); follow Toyota precepts

- Henry Ford: Pragmatism; fairness to working class; integrated flow

Figure 9.1   Some of Toyota's cultural roots.
(Information derived from personal discussions with Dan Prock, PhD.)

The commitment to hierarchy, respect for the wisdom of elders, importance of following standards, and obligation of elders to actively develop younger people are tenets preached by Confucius. Dr. W. Edwards Deming had a profound impact on Toyota in many ways, but one thing in particular stands out: a deep belief that most problems are system problems that are the responsibility of management. Toyota leaders are taught that team members are rarely to blame for an error, but rather there is usually something about the system that allowed the error to occur. Henry Ford introduced many of the core tenets of TPS in *Today and Tomorrow*,[10] and then, of course, there are the cultural roots from the company founders.

I have come to think of leadership and culture as so intertwined that one cannot exist without the other. It is leaders who model the cultural norms and values and encourage adoption of the deeply held beliefs by others through their consistent example. Just as consistency between parents is key to raising children to become healthy adults, consistency across leaders and over time is key to building a healthy organizational culture.

Toyota recognized the difficulty of building a culture when it was launching its joint venture plant with General Motors in 1984. For Toyota, the point of NUMMI was to experiment and learn how to bring TPS culture overseas. For several years, many Toyota people from Japan moved to the United States and taught the Americans, studied what was happening, and called into Japan each evening to discuss what they had observed and learned. It was almost like a research institute of applied anthropologists set up to study some newly discovered tribe, though in this case the Japanese leaders were active participants in creating the phenomenon. The long-term goal was to develop American leaders to the point where they could run North American operations as self-sufficient regional entities that adapted locally but still lived the basic precepts of Toyota culture.

CASE EXAMPLE: DEVELOPING THE FIRST AMERICAN PRESIDENT OF TOYOTA MOTOR MANUFACTURING IN KENTUCKY

When Toyota set up its joint venture plant, NUMMI, and then its Kentucky plant, it needed a president who could model and teach the Toyota Way, which at first meant a Japanese executive. There were armies of expatriate Toyota "executive coordinators" and "trainers" from Japan mentoring American leaders. So it was big news when Gary Convis was hired away from running NUMMI and named the first American president of Toyota Motor Manufacturing in Kentucky in 1999. His selection for this critical position—leading Toyota's largest manufacturing complex outside Japan—represented a coming of age for Toyota in the United States. It took Toyota executives about 15 years to develop Convis into someone they could trust to carry the banner of the Toyota Way, but the result was a true Toyota leader. Yet despite all these years of development, Convis was not hired in as president immediately, but rather he was named executive vice president and was expected to earn his way to the higher position. For the first six months, Toyota retained the Japanese president, while Convis prepared to take over the position. He visited all Toyota North American sites, worked in each department in the plant, and led kaizen activities.

Even when Convis became president of the Kentucky facility, he was as upbeat, energized, and humble about learning from Toyota as if he were a new employee coming to his first orientation.

> *I learn all the time, but I don't think I'll finish developing as a human being. One of my main functions now is growing other Americans to follow that path. They call it the DNA of Toyota, the Toyota Way and TPS—they're all just very integrated.*

Like other Toyota executives, Convis stressed on-the-job experience more than brilliant theoretical insights, which underscores Toyota executives' proclamation, "We build cars, not intellectuals." The fact is, they are as apt to talk philosophy as they are nuts and bolts. But the philosophy driving the principles of the Toyota Way is always rooted in nuts-and-bolts practice. Even after 18 years at Toyota, Convis spoke in the self-deprecating, yet proud way characteristic of his Japanese brethren:

> *I got where I am because of trial and error and failure and perseverance. That trial and error was on the floor under the direction of my Japanese mentors. I'm very proud to have grown up with Toyota. Some people would look at 18 years and say, "Well, gee, you spent 20 years in the auto industry before the 18 you just spent with Toyota; you're sort of a slow bloomer!" But this business, I don't think it's one where there are fast bloomers. There's a lot to be said for experience and, if you enjoy what you're doing, it's not a long day, it's a fun day, and it's something you look forward to doing tomorrow.*

Toyota's approach to developing people grew out of the master-apprentice model that has long been a characteristic of Japanese culture and continues to this day. When Convis was plant manager of NUMMI he saw team members struggling to get body welding robots running to the same level as in Japan. With very little inventory, any equipment breakdowns would quickly shut down the plant. Fumitaka Ito, a finance executive who had been named the Japanese president of NUMMI, remarked that that when walking into the plant each morning he saw the engineers sitting at their desks. He suggested that Convis ask the production engineers to go out to the floor every day and fill out a breakdown report (on A3-size paper) for every breakdown lasting more than 30 minutes. Ito asked that they meet with the engineers every Friday to review the reports.

The engineers diligently prepared the breakdown reports and, with Gary, met with Ito. The downtime was reduced somewhat in the next few weeks, but Ito was not happy. He pointed out to Gary that each week the engineers presented their reports, and each week he had to mark up with red ink all the weak points of the reports. He asked, "Gary-san, what are you teaching these engineers?" Finally, the lightbulb came on. Convis realized it was his responsibility to teach the engineers how to problem-solve. After spending time directly coaching the engineers, the body shop approached Japan's levels, and in the process, Gary learned a great deal about being a Toyota leader.* He also learned the power of the simple A3 report for coaching. Ito was no expert on manufacturing, but through the A3 process he could understand the way the engineers were thinking and teach them a more scientific approach to problem solving.

---

* This and more stories are in Jeffrey Liker and Gary Convis, *The Toyota Way to Lean Leadership* (New York: McGraw-Hill, 2011).

GO AND SEE FOR YOURSELF TO THOROUGHLY UNDERSTAND THE SITUATION

Kiichiro Toyoda learned from his father the importance of getting your hands dirty and learning by doing—and he insisted on this from all his engineers. A famous story about Kiichiro Toyoda has become part of Toyota's cultural heritage:[11]

> *One day Kiichiro Toyoda was walking through the vast plant when he came upon a worker scratching his head and muttering that his grinding machine would not run. Kiichiro took one look at the man, then rolled up his sleeves and plunged his hands into the oil pan. He came up with two handfuls of sludge. Throwing the sludge on the floor, he demanded: "How can you expect to do your job without getting your hands dirty?" [The metal shavings in the sludge offered clues about the problem.]*

When I asked American managers who had worked for another company and then came to Toyota what was different about Toyota leadership, they quickly talked about genchi genbutsu. It would be relatively easy for management attempting to learn from the Toyota Way to mandate that all engineers and managers spend a half hour every day observing the floor to understand the situation, and possibly following "leader standard work." But this would accomplish very little unless they had the skill to analyze and understand the current situation. There is a surface version of genchi genbutsu and a much deeper version that takes many years for employees to master. What the Toyota Way requires is that employees and managers must "deeply" understand the processes of flow, standardized work, etc., as well as have the ability to critically evaluate and analyze what is happening. Analysis of data is also very valuable, but it should be backed up with a more detailed look at the actual condition.

Taiichi Ohno took on a series of "students" over the years, and the first lesson was always the same—stand in the circle and look. It became known as the Ohno circle. I was fortunate to speak in person with Teryuki Minoura, who learned TPS directly from the master and participated in the circle exercise:

> *Minoura:*   *Mr. Ohno wanted us to draw a circle on the floor of a plant, and then we were told, "Stand in that and watch the process and think for yourself," and then he didn't even give you any hint of what to watch for. This is the real essence of TPS.*
>
> *Liker:*   *How long did you stay in the circle?*
>
> *Minoura:*   *Eight hours!*
>
> *Liker:*   *Eight hours?!*

Minoura: In the morning Mr. Ohno came to request that I stay in the circle until supper, and after that Mr. Ohno came to check and ask me what I was seeing. And of course, I answered [reflecting]. I answered, "There were so many problems with the process . . ." But Mr. Ohno didn't hear, didn't hear. He was just looking.

Liker: And what happened at the end of the day?

Minoura: It was near dinner time. He came to see me. He didn't take any time to give any feedback. He just said gently, "Go home."

Of course, it is difficult to imagine this training happening in a US factory. Most young engineers would be irate if you told them to draw a circle and stand for 30 minutes, let alone all day, and then explained nothing. But Minoura understood this was an important lesson as well as an honor to be taught in this way by the master of TPS. What exactly was Ohno teaching? The first step of genchi genbutsu, which is the power of deep observation. He was teaching Minoura to "think for himself" about what he was seeing, hearing, smelling—that is, to question, analyze, and evaluate what he learned through his senses.

I learned a lot about genchi genbutsu from Tahashi (George) Yamashina, former president of the Toyota Technical Center (TTC):

It is more than going and seeing. "What happened? What did you see? What are the issues? What are the problems?" Within the Toyota organization in North America we are still just going and seeing [as of 2001] "Okay I went and saw it and now I have a feeling." But have you really analyzed it? Do you really understand what the issues are? At the root of all of that, we try to make decisions based on factual information, not based on theory. Statistics and numbers contribute to the facts, but it is more than that. Sometimes we get accused of spending too much time doing all the analysis of that. Some will say, "Common sense will tell you. I know what the problem is." But collecting data and analysis will tell you if your common sense is right.

When Yamashina became president, he laid out his 10 management principles (see Figure 9.2), which include principles 3 and 4 that relate to genchi genbutsu:

3. "Think and speak based on verified, proven information and data:

- *Go and confirm the facts for yourself.*
- *You are responsible for the information you are reporting to others."*

4. "Take full advantage of the wisdom and experiences of others to send, gather or discuss information."

- Always keep the final target in mind
  - Carefully plan for your final target
  - Have a clear purpose for meetings
- Clearly assign tasks to yourself and others
- Think and speak based on verified, proven information and data
  - Go and confirm the facts for yourself (genchi genbutsu)
  - You are responsible for the information you are reporting to others
- Take full advantage of the wisdom and experiences of others to send, gather, or discuss information (a form of genchi genbutsu)
- Share your information with others in a timely manner
  - Always consider who will benefit from receiving the information
- Always report, inform, and consult (hou/ren/sou) in a timely manner
- Analyze and understand shortcomings in your capabilities in a measurable way
  - Clarify the skills and knowledge that you need to further develop yourself
- Relentlessly strive to conduct kaizen activities
- Think "outside the box" or beyond commonsense standard rules
- Always be mindful of protecting your safety and health

Figure 9.2 The management philosophy of George Yamashina, president of the Toyota Technical Center through 2001.

There are many great genchi genbutsu stories during the formative years of the Toyota Way in America. When Toyota launched a version of the Camry in 1997, it was discovered that the car had a wire harness problem. Yazaki Corporation, a parts supplier to Toyota in Japan, supplied the problem wire harness. What happened next is not typical of most companies. A quality engineer from Yazaki called Toyota to explain the corrective action Yazaki was taking. Yazaki sent an engineer to the Camry plant. But then the president of Yazaki went to the Camry plant in Georgetown personally to watch how workers assembled the wire harness onto the vehicle.

Contrast this to a story told to me by Jim Griffith, then a vice president of TTC. A problem similar to the wire harness problem occurred with a US parts supplier. In this case, the vice president of the business unit that serves Toyota visited the Toyota Technical Center to discuss what he was doing to solve the problem. He was very reassuring, explaining: "I am deeply sorry about this. Do not worry. This will get my personal attention. We are going to solve this problem. There are no excuses." When Jim Griffith asked him what the problem was and what his plans were, he responded: "Oh, I do not know yet, and I do not get into that kind of detail. But do not worry. We are going to get to the bottom of this and solve the problem. I promise." Jim Griffith looked exasperated as he told the story:

And I was supposed to feel better about that? It would be unacceptable in Toyota to come to a meeting like that so poorly prepared. How could he give us his assurance if he did not even go and see for himself what the problem was? . . . So we asked him to please go back and do this and then return when he truly understood the problem and countermeasure.

Go and see also applies to what we typically think of as office functions. When Glenn Uminger, an accountant, was given the assignment to set up the first management accounting system for the Toyota plant in Georgetown, Kentucky, he decided that he must first understand what was actually happening on the shop floor, which meant learning about the Toyota Production System. He spent six months in Toyota plants in Japan and the US learning by doing— actually working in manufacturing. It became evident to Uminger that he did not need to set up the same complex accounting system he had set up at a former company. He explained:

If the system I set up in the parts supplier I previously worked for was a 10 in complexity, the Toyota system I set up was a 3. It was simpler and far more efficient.

The system was simpler because Uminger took the time to understand the manufacturing system, the *customer* for which he was a *supplier* of services. He needed to build an accounting system that supported the real needs of the actual manufacturing system that Toyota set up. Through genchi genbutsu and hands-on kaizen, he developed a deep understanding of the Toyota Production System in action. He learned that Toyota's system is based on pull and has so little inventory that the complex computerized inventory tracking systems used in his former company were unnecessary. And the arduous and expensive task of taking physical inventory could be greatly streamlined. Toyota does physical inventory twice per year and uses the work teams to facilitate it. Tags are prepared for the work teams for inventory counting, and the team leader does a count in 10 minutes at the end of the shift and writes the numbers on the tags. Someone from accounting collects the tags and enters the information in the computer. That same evening the inventory count is completed. The teams spend a few hours twice a year, and it is done!

HOURENSOU—DAILY REPORT, INFORM, CONSULT

Another of Yamashina's principles (Figure 9.2) is to report, inform, and consult (hou/ren/sou) in a timely manner. Since Toyota leaders know the importance of keeping involved at a detailed level, training and developing subordinates through questioning and giving carefully targeted advice, they make a big effort to find efficient ways to gather information and to give feedback and advice. There is no one magic bullet for accomplishing this, but one important approach is to teach subordinates to communicate efficiently and give brief daily reports on key events that happened during the day. When they can, the executives will still travel to where the work is being done.

For example, George Yamashina, as president of TTC, had the responsibility for five areas: (1) the main technical center in Ann Arbor, Michigan, (2) the prototyping center in Plymouth, Michigan, (3) the Arizona proving grounds, (4) the technical center in California, and (5) product engineers stationed at Toyota's manufacturing plants. Yamashina scheduled meetings with all the departments in TTC once a month, which included all levels, and traveled from site to site to have these meetings in remote locations. Though Yamashina had a great understanding of what was happening by Western standards, that was not enough to satisfy him. He also insisted that each vice president and general manager give him a report every single day, a little update, instead of waiting until the end of the month. This gave Yamashina an opportunity to share live information he got that day across parts of the company. "Maybe you should talk to Fred at the proving grounds about this," he might advise. While Toyota is not the most computerized company in the world, it was learning to use email effectively for hourensou. As Yamashina explained:

> One young engineer explains his test through email and its purpose and asks if others have any experience with similar tests. Suddenly a very experienced engineer sends an email saying "I tried that test under similar circumstances and the test did not work." His advice to the young engineer is to find another way to perform the test or stop the test. If there were no system to share the information, probably that young engineer will waste a lot of time and energy. I insist that those who report to me send me a daily journal. So I get 60–70 emails from VPs or General Managers per day. I insist that they make bullet points in the messages. What are the key things you are doing? It has to be designed in such a way that others will read it. That stimulates thinking and sharing information. It is part of how Toyota does learning.

The first reaction of US managers to hourensou was that it was another form of micromanagement; and they resisted it, that is, until they began to practice and experience the benefits at Toyota. According to several managers I spoke to, over time it became an essential part of their management repertoire, and they could no longer imagine leading without it.

FIRST MANAGEMENT PRINCIPLE—PUT THE CUSTOMER FIRST

Shotaro Kamiya was to Toyota Motor Sales what Ohno was to the Toyota Production System. His leadership defined the sales philosophy of Toyota. Like most Toyota leaders, Kamiya could be described as a self-made man. He joined Toyota in 1935, when the auto company was first started, after working at Mitsui Trading Company (a close partner of Toyota). Kamiya created the Toyota dealer network in Japan and was also responsible for expansion of Toyota sales in the United States. Eventually, he became the honorary chairman of Toyota. One famous quote from Kamiya reflects the "customer-first" philosophy he preached and ingrained in others throughout his career:

> *The priority in receiving benefits from automobile sales should be in the order of the customer, then the dealer, and lastly, the manufacturer. This attitude is the best approach in winning the trust of customers and dealers and ultimately brings growth to the manufacturer.*

Unlike the use of auto showrooms in the United States to boost sales, Japan's tradition is door-to-door sales. In Japan, auto companies have extensive data on customers and know when to come knocking at the door. For example, when a young woman, Mika, is about to become the age to drive, a salesperson will contact her to outfit her with just the right Toyota for her needs. The personal attention creates a bond between customers and the company. If customers need auto repairs, they are likely to call the salesperson for help rather than deal with an impersonal maintenance department. This supports the goal of Toyota to have customers for life . . . and for the lives of their descendants.

Toyota used this practice of door-to-door sales, and later its dealerships, as a way to teach new employees how to see and understand the customer's perspective. I asked Toshiaki "Tag" Taguchi, former president and CEO of Toyota Motor North America, about this, and he recalled an early experience selling Toyota cars:

> *The first assignment I got as a freshman trainee . . . , I had to go through various operating departments of Toyota Motor Sales Company and three of us were sent to the dealerships to see if factory people would benefit by spending a few months at dealerships. So I spent about five months at the dealership in Nagoya, where I visited house to house carrying brochures, and sold a total of nine new and used cars during that time. But the point was learning about our customers. I think Toyota is trying to give freshmen an opportunity to learn about themselves. Even today, freshmen have a baptism to go to the dealership for a month or two to learn.*

This experience also applies to Toyota engineers who, as part of their freshman training, must go out and sell vehicles. Going to the source to see and understand extends to understanding what customers want. It is not sufficient for leaders to pore over marketing data or listen to marketing presentations and get an abstract sense of the customer. Selling door to door is one way to get inside the heads of customers and develop a visceral sense of what purchasing a Toyota means to them. Another is through Toyota's chief engineer system.

The chief engineer is like the CEO of an entrepreneurial venture. He owns the vehicle development program. His first responsibility is to deeply understand the customer and develop a vision for the vehicle.

The 2004 Sienna was pivotal, as it transformed Toyota from a bit player in minivans to one of the leaders. The chief engineer's job of developing this Sienna was assigned to Yuji Yokoya. The primary markets for the vehicle were the United States and Canada with some sales in Mexico. Yokoya had worked on Japanese and European projects, but never a North American vehicle. He felt that he did not really understand the North American market. Other managers may have hit the books on marketing data, but that is only one thing you do at Toyota. Yokoya went to his director and requested to take a trip. He said, "I want to drive all 50 states and all 13 provinces and territories in Canada and all parts of Mexico."

Andy Lund was an American program manager at the Toyota Technical Center assigned to assist Yokoya. He had an opportunity to take part of the trip through Canada with him. He was amazed at how deeply Yokoya observed and learned, and gave an example of his determination to visit even a small town in Canada called Rankin Inlet in Nunavut:

> He arrived at a very small airport and tried to reserve a car, but there were no rental car companies there or in the whole town. So Yokoya-san called a taxi, and a minivan-type taxi picked him up. He tried to speak to the taxi driver to make a request, but the driver did not speak English well enough for Yokoya-san to understand. Eventually the taxi driver's son came out and translated. The taxi driver agreed to Yokoya-san's request to hire the car but drive it himself. As it turned out, the town was so small Yokoya-san drove the taxi through the only roads in minutes and was done.

Yokoya-san achieved his goal of driving in every single US state including Alaska and Hawaii and every part of Canada and Mexico. Often, he was able to rent a Toyota Sienna looking for ways to improve it. As a result, he made many design changes that would make little sense to a Japanese engineer living in Japan. For example:

- The roads in Canada have a higher crown (bowed up in the middle) than in the United States, perhaps because of the amount of snow Canada gets.

Driving through Canada, he learned that controlling the "drift" of the minivan is very important.

■ When driving on a bridge over the Mississippi River, a gust of wind shook the minivan, and Yokoya realized that side-wind stability was very important.

■ When he was driving the narrow streets of Santa Fe, Yokoya found it hard to turn the corner with his Sienna, so he significantly reduced the turning radius, despite the larger vehicle size.

■ By practically living in the Sienna for all these driving trips, Yokoya learned the value of cup holders. In Japan, distances are usually shorter. You may buy a can of juice, but it is more common in Japan to drink this outside the car. In America, on a long trip it was common for one person to have one half-empty cup of coffee or bottle of water and one full one. Therefore, you really need two cup holders per person, or even three if a person wants a cup of coffee plus two bottles of water. He designed 14 cup and bottle holders into the Sienna, as well as numerous compartments and pockets that would be helpful for long trips.

■ Yokoya also noted the American custom of eating in vehicles rather than taking the time to stop and eat. In Japan, it is very uncommon to eat in the car, partly because the roads are narrower and with heavy truck traffic you need to focus on the road and periodically stop to take a break from the stress. He learned the value of having a place for hamburgers and fries and put in a flip-up tray accessible from the driver position.

FROM INTERESTING CONCEPTS TO CONSISTENT DAILY BEHAVIOR

One way to understand what a company values in its leaders is to look at its performance appraisal system. Typically, for managers and executives we expect pay for performance. What business targets did they sign up for, and how successful were they in delivering on those outcomes? How they did it is less important. At Toyota, over half the formal appraisal is based on a clearly stated set of "universal" competencies, so as people rotate and are promoted, there is high consistency in leadership behavior—which sustains a consistent culture. By "universal," Toyota means the competencies apply to every leadership role any place in the company. The other half of the performance appraisal focuses on targets for key performance indicators, but even these look at how the targets were achieved—in other words, was the leader's approach consistent with the core values? Evaluation of competencies ties to an annual merit increase, while the results are tied to a bonus.

Toyota retiree Glenn Uminger progressed within the company over 27 years in many different leadership roles, including executive-level positions in TPS, production control, and North America logistics. In that time, Toyota identified 10 core competencies foundational to the official performance evaluation system for all management levels that are part of Toyota's Global Appraisal Process (nicknamed GAP) for executives (see Figure 9.3). Glenn explained to me:

Each person is required to have a Development Plan registered in the HR Development system. Each person, in agreement with their manager, must choose 3 of the 10 competencies for their development focus. The development plan then includes certain, mostly on the job, activities that will provide opportunities for development. There is a wide range of what these activities can be, but all are within the natural flow of one's job responsibilities. The full range of competencies are looked at, but the three receive closer focus with greater supervisor involvement and coaching.

1. Accurate grasp of the situation: Dig deep, go and see, listen, use facts and data
2. Open and innovative thinking: How to see and lead beyond the status quo
3. Develop and lead improvement activities: Target mid- to long-term goals
4. Make appropriate decisions: Carefully consider the business situation
5. Constantly practice perseverance
6. Allocate and adjust resources based on priorities
7. Establish and improve the business framework and systems
8. Consistent and fair assignments and performance reviews
9. Thorough and fair staff development
10. Achieving personal mission, aligned with company values

Figure 9.3 Toyota core competencies for management (used for performance appraisal, development, and promotion).
Source: TMMK, Georgetown, Kentucky, 1995.

One obvious question is how do you precisely measure each of the 10 core competencies? Each competency has its own matrix describing what "meeting the requirement" and "exceeding the requirement" mean by management level. Of course, the higher the level, the broader and more complex the requirement. The formal evaluation requires the reviewee to write up one specific situational example where each expectation was applied, and that one example needs to be representative of everyday practice. Feedback is gathered from lower-management tiers as a check on subjectivity. Still, it is very important for leaders doing the evaluation to learn about the person they are evaluating firsthand at the gemba, observing and spot-coaching subordinates and developing a concept of strengths and weaknesses. Methods like hourensou are part of the ongoing process of learning about subordinates and coaching just in time.

Toyota leaders share a lot of the basic characteristics of any good leader. For example, in the 10 core competencies, there are elements common to leaders in any field: "leading improvement activities toward mid- to long-term goals," "making appropriate decisions," "allocating and adjusting resources based on priorities," and "consistent and fair assignments and performance reviews." These are basic management responsibilities that any organization would expect from its leaders. But Toyota goes beyond most organizations in its emphasis on teaching, coaching, and constantly developing oneself and others—which are beacons of Toyota's core values. Toyota is a learning organization, and the learning is transmitted through its leaders. The starting point of learning is Competency 1: "Accurate grasp of the situation: Dig deep, go and see, listen, use facts and data." This is the foundation for scientific thinking and moving step-by-step toward any goal, and the way to move step-by-step in developing people.

Glenn also identified from his own experience several daily leadership behaviors, four of which are critical to coaching and developing people:

- Ask challenging and intelligent questions.
- Challenge constantly for continuous improvement.
- Coach and be supportive of your staff . . . give them room to fail.
- Set challenging goals; allow the person responsible to decide method to achieve.

These four behaviors could be taken right out of the Ohno playbook for developing people. This is what Ohno did. He asked questions, rarely even hinting at answers. He was constantly challenging his students to think, think, think and improve, improve, improve. "Try something and do it now." Failure was OK, as long as his students were trying many things and learning from the failures. His challenges were monumental, but his students needed to do the thinking on how to achieve them. One of Ohno's students, Fujio Cho, described to me a bit tearfully this paradox:

Mr. Ohno could be very critical when he saw something wrong. It was very difficult for some people to take. And often we would work into the evening to solve problems. But then at the end of the day, even at 7 pm at night, he would gather us all together and explain why he was critical that day. Everyone, even the junior workers, appreciated that he was trying to teach them. He was interested in developing everyone to their potential.

PRINCIPLE 9: GROW LEADERS WHO THOROUGHLY UNDERSTAND THE WORK, LIVE THE PHILOSOPHY, AND TEACH IT TO OTHERS

The roots of Toyota leadership go back to the Toyoda family, who evolved the Toyota Way. If we look at all the great leaders in Toyota's history, we see they share several common traits:

- Focusing on a long-term purpose for Toyota as a value-added contributor to society
- Staying consistent with the precepts of the Toyota Way DNA and living and modeling the behaviors for all to see
- Going to the gemba—the actual place where the real value-added work is done. Getting their hands dirty and working their way up the organization
- Seeing problems as opportunities to train and coach their people

A common saying heard around Toyota is, "Before we build cars, we build people." The leader's goal at Toyota is to develop people so they are strong contributors who can think and follow the Toyota Way at all levels in the organization. A company growing its own leaders and defining the ultimate role of leadership as "building a learning organization" is laying the groundwork for genuine long-term success. In the next chapter, we will see with granularity how daily leader behavior is formed at the level of the work group and its group leader.

KEY POINTS

- Toyota has a history of great leaders, grown from within, who believe in and model the values of the Toyota Way.
- The core values can be traced back to the company founders, Sakichi Toyoda and Kiichiro Toyoda, and were formalized in the *Toyota Way 2001* under the direction of President Fujio Cho.
- Jim Collins' study identified 11 "great companies," and all 11 had level 5 leaders who shared the duality of personal humility yet intense professional will, and who had many of the same characteristics as those of Toyota leaders.
- Leadership and culture are intertwined—through their behavior and coaching, leaders at all levels spread the culture broad and deep.
- Toyota's longstanding culture has had many influences, including some distinctively Japanese, but the company has had success in spreading the culture in countries where it has set up shop.

- The approach to spreading the culture is through the master-apprentice model in which every leader from the president to team leaders on the shop floor is at the gemba with the people, seizing opportunities to provide challenges and feedback.
- Genchi genbutsu—go and see to understand and learn—is one of the most important core values for coaching and spreading the culture.
- Customer first is reinforced in all parts of Toyota, including among new engineers, who in their first year spend time at a dealership selling cars.
- To achieve consistency of behavior globally, Toyota uses a powerful performance appraisal system that emphasizes universal competencies reflected in behavior. Getting results is not sufficient for a positive review; you must also learn and demonstrate these competencies.

Notes

1. "Newsmakers of 2002," December 20, 2002.
2. https://planet-lean.com/akio-toyoda-crisis-management/.
3. Jim Collins, *Good to Great* (New York: HarperBusiness, 2001).
4. Jim Collins, "Level 5 Leadership: The Triumph of Humility and Fierce Resolve," *Harvard Business Review*, January 2001.
5. Collins, "Level 5 Leadership."
6. Collins, "Level 5 Leadership."
7. Collins, *Good to Great*.
8. Edgar Schein, *Organizational Culture and Leadership*, 4th ed. (San Francisco: Jossey-Bass, 2010).
9. T. Talhelm, X. Zhang, S. Oishi, et al., "Large-Scale Psychological Differences Within China Explained by Rice Versus Wheat Agriculture," *Science*, 2014, vol. 344, no. 6184, pp. 603–608.
10. Henry Ford, *Today and Tomorrow: Special Edition of Ford's 1929 Classic* (Boca Raton, FL: CRC Press, Taylor & Francis Group, 2003).
11. *Toyota Way 2001*, Toyota Motor Corporation.

Principle 10

Develop Exceptional People and Teams Who Follow Your Company's Philosophy

Respect for people and constant challenging to do better—are these contradictory? Respect for people means respect for the mind and capability. You do not expect them to waste their time. You respect the capability of the people. Americans think teamwork is about you liking me and I liking you. Mutual respect and trust mean I trust and respect that you will do your job so that we are successful as a company. It does not mean we just love each other.

—Sam Heltman,* former Senior Vice President of Administration,
Toyota Motor Manufacturing North America

SERVANT LEADERSHIP SUPPORTS THE PEOPLE DOING THE VALUE-ADDED WORK

No matter how progressive the company, most organization charts end up as some type of pyramid. There are relatively few people at the top in executive roles. There is a somewhat larger mass of managers in the middle, and the majority of people are at the bottom. Pay starts at a certain level at the top and gets lower, often by a lot, as you move down the chart.

Toyota often flips the chart upside down on paper—as an inverted pyramid. Now the people assigned leadership roles are at the bottom and middle, and still get paid more, but the people doing the value-added work are at the top. This is sometimes referred to as "servant leadership," a philosophy often attributed to Robert Greenleaf, who admonished leaders to help those served grow as people and as a result "become healthier, wiser, freer, more autonomous, more likely themselves to become servants."[1]

---

* One of the first five Americans hired by Toyota Motor Manufacturing, Kentucky.

Toyota naturally adopted "servant leadership" early in its history based on the commonsense notion that the only people doing value-added work are the workers, and therefore they are at the "top." Toyota calls them team members, and managers speak almost with reverence about how team members contribute to building the product and their devotion to continuous improvement. In the Preface, we heard from a former NUMMI executive who referred to every team member as an industrial engineer.

Why would we think of workers doing short-cycle, repetitive manual jobs as drivers of continuous improvement? After all, they usually have less formal education than management, they may not be as articulate or well read, they are paid less, and they have control over a very limited part of the factory. Toyota's answer is that what really matters is making improvements at the gemba, and the team members are the ones at the gemba, personally experiencing the processes and living with the equipment. Toyota needs team members to be observing, thinking, and experimenting.

Because Toyota expects so much from people, it has an intensive selection process, but like with many other things, it breaks accepted norms. Often, the people hired do not have the experience or technical skills for the job they are hired into. Toyota rarely hires veteran electricians, or mechanics, or welders, or painters. Instead, people are hired for their potential to learn those skills. While work experience in those skills is helpful, the ability to work in teams, and most of all to learn to think critically and solve problems, is more important. Toyota believes it can develop these people to be exceptional.

Carol Dweck refers to this as a growth mindset.[2] The growth mindset assumes we as individuals, even in adulthood, can learn and grow throughout our lifetime. People with a growth mindset are willing to try new things even if they fail at first. Constructive feedback is viewed positively as an opportunity to learn. This reflects beautifully the human-resource philosophy of Toyota. Hire people who are good raw material and then grow them through challenging experiences and coaching to guide them along the way.

I read an interesting opinion piece about how the Scandinavian school system educates the "whole person," which suggested this was a reason for the success of the Scandinavians both economically and as a civilized society:[3]

> *They look at education differently than we do. The German word they used to describe their approach, bildung, doesn't even have an English equivalent. It means the complete moral, emotional, intellectual and civic transformation of the person. It was based on the idea that if people were going to be able to handle and contribute to an emerging industrial society, they would need more complex inner lives. . . . It is devised to help them understand*

complex systems and see the relations between things—between self and society, between a community of relationships in a family and a town.

I quickly connected this to how Toyota builds a culture of respect for people and continuous improvement—how Toyota takes ordinary people and makes them exceptional. Broadly study the environment, set a great challenge, and harness the power of the organization through aligned goals, and it seems they can achieve anything. Education in Toyota's case is what is happening day by day, hour by hour, under the watchful eye of servant leaders who are being developed by their servant leaders. It is at the gemba, and it is not always easy. It is fair and respectful and educates the whole person.

THE POWER OF TEAM MEMBERS AND WORK GROUPS

Talk to somebody at Toyota about the Toyota Production System, and you can hardly avoid getting a lecture on the importance of teamwork. All systems are there to support the team doing value-added work. But teams do not do value-added work. Individuals do. The teams coordinate the work and motivate and learn from each other. Teams can inspire, and even influence through peer pressure. Nevertheless, for the most part, it is more efficient for individuals to do the actual detailed work necessary to produce a product or to advance a project.

Excellent individual performers are required for teams to excel. This is why Toyota puts such a tremendous effort in finding and screening prospective employees. It requires great potential to thrive in the Toyota culture. But Toyota does not leave its new employees alone to perform; they intensively develop them.

Toyota's assumption is that if you make teamwork the foundation of the company and develop strong leaders, individual performers will give their hearts and souls to contribute to the team and make the company successful. As you will read, the Toyota Way is not about lavishing goodies on people whether they have earned them or not; it is about simultaneously challenging *and* respecting team members.

The Upside-Down Organization Chart

In a conventional automotive plant, white-collar or skilled maintenance staff are responsible for problem solving, quality assurance, equipment maintenance, and productivity. By contrast, shop floor work groups are the focal point for daily problem solving in the Toyota Production System (see Figure 10.1).

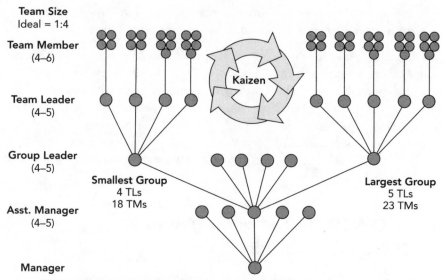

Figure 10.1 Typical Toyota organization of an assembly operation, where TMs are team members and TLs are team leaders.
Source: Bill Costantino, former group leader, Toyota, Georgetown.

As discussed, the *team members* are at the top of the hierarchy, with the rest of the hierarchy there to support them. The next line of defense is the *team leader*, an hourly team member who mastered jobs on the line, was energetic about learning problem solving, and went through an intensive training and development process. The Toyota team leader in most countries is still an hourly employee but gets a small bump in pay per hour. Team leaders are not responsible for performance reviews or disciplinary action but are there to support and develop the team members. The first-line supervisor is the *group leader*, the first management level, who is responsible for leading and coordinating a number of teams in the production work group.

The largest *quantity* of kaizen activity happens at the level of the production work group, although those improvements individually may not generate large impacts. Engineers and managers often lead individual projects, such as introducing new technology or changing the architecture of material flow, that have huge impacts. Once these large changes are made, the system is generally in flux with a lot of nagging problems, and working through all the fine details of production is the responsibility of the work groups. They make the difference between good and great.

The roles and responsibilities for team members, team leaders, and group leaders are summarized in Figure 10.2. (Note that both Figures 10.1 and 10.2 are courtesy of Bill Costantino; Bill was one of the first group leaders at the Toyota plant in Georgetown, Kentucky.) Noteworthy is the progression of responsibilities from team members to group leaders. *Team members* perform manual jobs to standard and are responsible for surfacing problems and aiding in problem solving. *Team leaders* take on a number of the responsibilities traditionally done by "white-collar" managers, though they are not formally managers and do not have formal authority. Their prime role is to keep the line running smoothly to produce quality parts (immediate response to andon) and to resolve problems when there are deviations from standard. *Group leaders* do many things that otherwise would be handled by specialty support functions in human resources, engineering, and quality. They are responsible for HR functions such as performance appraisal, attendance, training, safety, and discipline, but also much more. They are integral to major improvements in the process, even introducing new products and processes. They regularly teach short topics. If needed, they are capable of getting on the line and performing the jobs. There is no such thing as a hands-off leader at Toyota.

Team Members (TMs)
- Perform work to current standard
- Maintain 5S in their work area
- Perform routine minor maintenance
- Look for continuous improvement opportunities
- Support problem-solving small-group activites

Team Leaders (TLs)
- Respond to andon calls by TM
- Process startup and control
- Meet production goals
- Confirm quality—routine checks
- Cover absenteeism
- Training, cross-training, coaching
- Work orders for quick maintenance
- Audit standard work and coach
- Facilitate small-group activities
- Ongoing continuous improvement projects
- Ensure parts/materials are supplied to process

Groups Leaders (GLs)
- Manpower/vacation scheduling
- Monthly production planning
- Administrative: policy, attendance, corrective actions
- Hoshin planning
- Coaching team leaders
- Team morale
- Confirm routine quality and TL checks
- Shift-to-shift coordination
- Process trials (changes in process)
- TM development and cross-training
- Report/track daily production results
- Cost-reduction activities
- Process improvement projects: productivity, quality, ergonomics, etc.
- Coordinate major maintenance
- Coordinate support from outside groups
- Coordinate work with upstream and downstream processes
- Group safety performance
- Help cover TL absence
- Coordinate activities around major model changes

Figure 10.2 Toyota work group roles and responsibilities.
Source: Bill Costantino, former group leader, Toyota, Georgetown.

Four to One: Work Groups and the Mysterious Team Leader Role

This would appear to be a tall hierarchy for a company that prides itself on being lean. After all, many Western companies have "leaned out" their org chart by eliminating layers of management, which inevitably means each frontline supervisor has a very large span of control, perhaps 30 to 50 direct reports. This large span of control is supposedly "empowering" workers to do the right thing based on their own judgment. Managers only need to deal with exceptions and individual discipline problems.

As we discussed in the last chapter, Toyota's view of the role of the leader is quite different. It is not to discipline and react to problems, but rather to plan, lead by example, and coach. And continuous improvement is critical. On their own, team members may not participate in continuous improvement. They need to be coached, and one person cannot effectively coach dozens of people. Toyota's ideal standard is a four-to-one ratio, that is, four team members for each team leader, and four team leaders for one group leader, though in reality there is variation in group size.

The Toyota team leader plays a broader set of roles than team members (see Figure 10.2). The first priority in preparing for the shift is to ensure sufficient resources to staff the production line, and team leaders become potential team members if someone is absent. Once the shift starts, the priority of the team leader is to respond to the andon. As discussed under Principle 6, the team leader has a matter of seconds to respond or the line segment can shut down. The team leader will later use a record of andon pulls for problem solving.

I call the team leader role "mysterious," because when I teach about the Toyota Way, most people sense this role is important but are concerned it means adding expensive indirect labor. One common question is, "Do Toyota team leaders work a full-time job on the line?" because they are wondering if they have to pay for extra overhead to have team leaders. The answer is no and yes.

The no is because team leaders could not possibly fulfill all their role responsibilities if they were working on the line. For example, they could not stop their work and run to answer the andon at a different process because that would cause the line to stop. They could not do all the other offline tasks either, and they certainly could not work on problem solving.

At the same time, the answer is yes. The Toyota standard is to have just enough team members to staff all the positions on the line, with half the team leaders working a production job and the other half offline, and they rotate (though often team leaders spend more time working on the line than is desired). So Toyota gets two team leaders for the price of one, e.g., typically two are working production and two are offline.

This still seems unrealistic to many continuous improvement leaders in companies strictly governed by target ratios of direct labor to indirect labor. As soon as a worker is pulled out of the direct labor headcount and made a team leader, that person adds to the indirect headcount and then gets targeted for elimination. Toyota also has a strict budget, but it is a budget for headcount without distinctions made between the team member and team leader count. The ratio is not the issue, but rather the team leader role is simply considered standard headcount and part of the budget. It would not occur to a Toyota plant manager to question the role and consider eliminating it. Some think it is the most critical role in the plant for the continuous improvement of individual production processes and quality. Later in the chapter, we look at how Herman Miller, an American office furniture company, addressed this issue.

Group Leaders—the Most Challenging Role

The group leader has an even broader set of responsibilities. This is the first management level, the equivalent of the frontline supervisor, but it is much more than that. In the UK plant, people like to refer to group leaders as the managing directors of their own business.

The group leader has many responsibilities, as summarized in Figure 10.2, from planning the day for the teams, to coordinating launches of newly designed vehicles, to developing and working toward an annual plan for improvement through the hoshin kanri process (Principle 13). In many companies, engineers view the factory as their domain. They make plans and execute as they wish. The frontline supervisors need to be informed and involved to a degree, such as communicating what is coming to workers, but then they get out of the way and let the engineers do their jobs. Not so at Toyota. The factory is the domain of group leaders, and anyone who wants to do work on the production line needs to treat the group leaders as customers. After all, group leaders have to make the new system work, and improve it.

Each work group has its own meeting area on the shop floor next to the group's work processes where the group leader's desk sits. It is an "open office" and includes lockers, microwave ovens, and large tables. The team leader boards and some of the group leader boards are here. This is the place for daily briefings before the shift starts, as well as the place for breaks, lunch, and a lot of informal interaction.

Japanese Students in Elementary School Are Socialized to Work Not Just in a Group, but as a Group

Toyota had an advantage organizing around small work teams in Japan because that is how Japanese children are taught all the way back to elementary school. One of my former students, Jennifer Orf, split time between going to school during the regular sessions in the United States and then going to school in Japan during the summers, when Japanese schools are still in session. She wrote about her experiences.[4] She describes how Japanese elementary school students identify with their class and also with their small group (called a "han") of four to six students:

In Japan, students are taught how to work together as a group as distinct from working in a group. . . . This means that not only do the children learn that they can accomplish more as a group than they could individually, but also that they feel a sense of collective identity with the group and recognize the special responsibilities that come from being part of a group, such as the ability to listen to the other members in the group and to delegate responsibility.

Students in han take responsibility for learning through various projects assigned to the groups, such as science projects. Tools like standardized work and visual management are common in the daily lives of these students. Consider Jennifer's description of lunchtime when the classroom is converted by the students into a dining room:

In my experience, groups looked forward to being on lunch duty, and the faces on the other side of the "cafeteria counter" were more often than not beaming under the chef's hats. . . . The student-management of this chore, which even first graders perform daily, is made possible because of the standardized nature of the process. Charts list the responsibilities for the different lunch duties, so that students can check off the steps as they perform their duties.

DEVELOPING TEAMS IN A TOYOTA WAREHOUSE: MORE THAN A ONE-MINUTE PROPOSITION

Toyota started its first North American parts distribution center in California and hired many people without experience, assigning some to team leader and group leader roles. It did not go as well as hoped, and after many years the company was still working to develop these leaders and develop teamwork. So when Toyota started a second North American Parts Center in Hebron, Kentucky, it decided to get teams right from the beginning. Ken Elliott, who launched the new operation, explained to me in 2002:

We are not building a warehouse; we are building a culture. This is why we have been as successful as we are. We had one shot at this to get the culture right.

What he meant is that years out, he did not want to be in a position of trying to fix the culture like he experienced in California. Get it right the first time.

When I visited Hebron, I heard a frequent reference to "situational leadership," which people had learned about from Ken Blanchard, famed author of *The One-Minute Manager*. Blanchard describes four stages of team development (in parentheses are the descriptors from another popular model) and the leader's role for each stage:

Stage 1: Orientation (forming). The group needs strong task direction from the leader and must understand the basic mission, rules of engagement, and tools the members will use.

Stage 2: Dissatisfaction (storming). The group goes to work, which is a lot less fun than talking about great visions of success, and the members discover it is harder than they thought to work as a team. In this stage, they continue to need strong task direction from the leader, but also need social support to get through the social dynamics they do not understand.

Stage 3: Integration (norming). The group starts to develop a clearer picture of the roles of various team members and begins to exert control over team processes. The leader does not have to provide much task direction, but the team still needs social support.

Stage 4: Production (performing), The group puts it all together and is functioning as a high-performing team with little task direction or social support from the leader.

Blanchard was describing a committee or task force and the development takes a few weeks. Combining the concepts of situational leadership with the highly evolved work processes of TPS led to something new that requires far more than one minute. Toyota decided to start out with no team-leader roles. The group leaders were trained in TPS and provided task direction directly to the stage 1 team members. As the group matured through stages 2 and 3, members with leadership potential were identified, and at the same time, TPS matured. After several years (not weeks), the group leaders finally felt the associates had matured to the point that the leaders could assign members to team leader roles and move the group toward becoming more self-directed. But even this happened situationally, and different groups matured at a different pace and started up the team leader role at different times over several years. The level of investment Toyota was making at Hebron in developing people and teams was far beyond anything I had seen before. As we will see at General Motors, too often the team leader is just thrown into the job, as though creating a job title on an organization chart creates the leader.

REENERGIZING THE FLOOR MANAGEMENT DEVELOPMENT SYSTEM AT TMUK

The Toyota plant in Burnaston, United Kingdom (TMUK), the first Toyota plant in Europe launched in 1992, was a mature organization that struggled with work group leadership, despite making huge investments early on. As I am writing this, the plant is building the 2020 Corolla, hybrid and gas engine. TMUK launched with many Japanese executives, managers, and engineers who moved there to train new hires in basic automotive production skills and TPS. After several years, the Japanese members were moved elsewhere, and because of the high visibility of the Toyota plant, British members became hot commodities for poaching by other companies. This started a more challenging period for TMUK, as it lost and had to replace many group leaders and managers. Years later, when the Great Recession took its toll and sales dropped, one of the two lines was closed, and separation agreements were offered and accepted by many members.

Performance across the plant became inconsistent and not up to Toyota standards. Some of the symptoms of this weakness included a drop-off in solving problems revealed by the andon, less rigorous focus on standardized work and job instruction training, less than stellar 5S, more unexpected absences than usual, and quality problems discovered in inspection. The root cause pointed to a weakness in the group leader role, and particularly to the time spent coaching team leaders.

TMUK had Toyota's standard Floor Management Development System (FMDS)—which included daily stand-up meetings, a visual management system, and clearly defined roles and responsibilities and training for team leaders and group leaders. TMUK studied the problem and concluded it needed to further develop FMDS and bring it to a new level. It launched the redesigned FMDS in the paint department as a pilot over several years and spread the practices throughout the plant.

There are, of course, key performance indicator boards for group leaders, the boards being organized around the categories of safety and environment, quality, production, cost, and human resource development. These are reviewed each day in meetings led by group leaders with a focus on red items—those below target. But there is far more to it. The TMUK group defined in great detail the roles for each level of leadership, skill requirements, and training and introduced new visual management boards to stimulate kaizen.

Core Role Definition

Roles were defined and expectations documented on a series of A3-size papers for team members, team leaders, group leaders, and section managers. For team members, 21 roles are defined, including understanding TPS, performing equipment startup-TPM-shutdown, identifying abnormalities, serving as a primary process owner, perfecting the execution of standardized work, knowing the fundamental skills, and using andon. As an example, the A3 for the team member role for andon use is shown in Figure 10.3: to follow standardized work exactly, alert the group to any abnormalities, and actively engage in kaizen through process ownership. The plant uses job rotation between two processes, and each team member is assigned to be the primary process owner responsible for one process on that shift and for communicating across shifts.

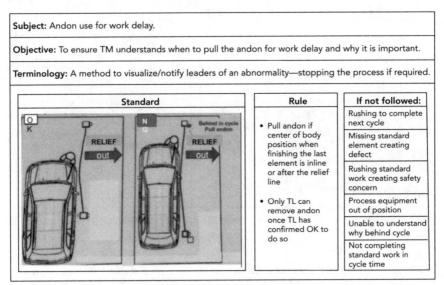

Subject: Andon use for work delay.

Objective: To ensure TM understands when to pull the andon for work delay and why it is important.

Terminology: A method to visualize/notify leaders of an abnormality—stopping the process if required.

Standard	Rule	If not followed:
	• Pull andon if center of body position when finishing the last element is inline or after the relief line	Rushing to complete next cycle
		Missing standard element creating defect
		Rushing standard work creating safety concern
	• Only TL can remove andon once TL has confirmed OK to do so	Process equipment out of position
		Unable to understand why behind cycle
		Not completing standard work in cycle time

Figure 10.3   Team member expectations for andon use.
Source: Toyota Motor Manufacturing UK.

For team leaders, there were 40 core roles defined, including such responsibilities as andon response, andon analysis, safety training, posture confirmation, quality management, preshift team meeting, TPS house knowledge, change point management, 4S leadership, kaizen, quick problem-solving report, and standardized work confirmation. As an example, the A3 for the core team leader role for confirming healthy posture for members is shown in Figure 10.4. Overall, team leaders set up the team members for success, run the preshift meeting, respond to andon, and lead kaizen.

Group leaders have 44 core roles defined. According to one TMUK manager, group leaders have the "toughest job in the business." Their responsibilities include managing the KPI board, managing the production control board (hour-by-hour chart of units produced versus actual with reasons), knowing how to hold meetings, managing personal protection equipment, confirming employees' posture, confirming standardized work, ensuring Toyota Business Practices are followed, managing scrap and reject materials, attaining hoshin objectives, coaching, and giving performance feedback. Group leaders are like managing directors of their business for planning, daily management, personnel management, and kaizen toward annual hoshin objectives.

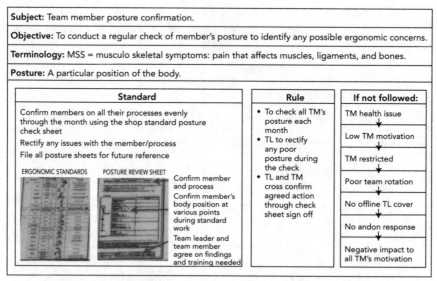

Subject: Team member posture confirmation.

Objective: To conduct a regular check of member's posture to identify any possible ergonomic concerns.

Terminology: MSS = musculo skeletal symptoms: pain that affects muscles, ligaments, and bones.

Posture: A particular position of the body.

Standard	Rule	If not followed:
Confirm members on all their processes evenly through the month using the shop standard posture check sheet Rectify any issues with the member/process File all posture sheets for future reference ERGONOMIC STANDARDS POSTURE REVIEW SHEET Confirm member and process Confirm member's body position at various points during standard work Team leader and team member agree on findings and training needed	• To check all TM's posture each month • TL to rectify any poor posture during the check • TL and TM cross confirm agreed action through check sheet sign off	TM health issue ↓ Low TM motivation ↓ TM restricted ↓ Poor team rotation ↓ No offline TL cover ↓ No andon response ↓ Negative impact to all TM's motivation

Figure 10.4   Team leader expectations for posture confirmation.
Source: Toyota Motor Manufacturing UK.

Section (sometimes called assistant) managers have about 100 to 120 people reporting to them, with about four group leaders as direct reports. They spend an intensive two hours on the shop floor at the beginning of the shift, making sure things are running smoothly, and then have more flexibility for the rest of the shift. The saying at TMUK is "Lose the first two hours, lose the shift." They have only 11 core roles defined, and these are very general and focused on living and modeling the Toyota Way, including finding facts and analyzing problems, engaging in creative and innovative thinking, creating action plans and building consensus, taking action and persevering, monitoring progress, and coaching.

Global Minimum Critical Role for Group Leaders

Toyota Motor Manufacturing in Japan defined in more detail the minimum critical roles that are like standardized work for the group leader. They are checked off and expected to be completed every day (see Figure 10.5). Of course, for this management position, the day will never go exactly according to plan, but as a starting point, these are things that should happen, along with estimates of time. Some are regularly scheduled meetings that have an allotted time. There are four broad categories of activities—gemba (where most of the coaching is done), office, meeting, and breaks. Gemba time is supposed to constitute about half of the time of the group leader, but in reality, group leaders spend much more time on the floor and in meetings (usually on the floor).

I highlighted some examples of standard daily activities in Figure 10.5, such as coaching the Delta S quality audit done by team leaders on the most critical safety items; attending the shipping quality audit (SQA), which is a teardown of a small number of cars each day; attending the team leader meetings to coach; calling the quality gate, which happens after the group leader processes and gives feedback on any quality deviations that arose in his or her area; coaching team leaders on process kaizen; and attending the manager's meeting with the other group leaders. These things need to happen. The group leader keeps track of these items, checking them off, and then the section manager checks the sheet each day.

EXAMPLES

- Delta S quality audit (Coach)
- SQA meeting (Task)
- Team leader meetings (Coach)
- Consumables order (Task)
- Phone call quality gate (Task)
- Break
- TL process kaizen (Coach)
- Paperwork to AM (Task)
- Manager meeting (Task)
- Lunch

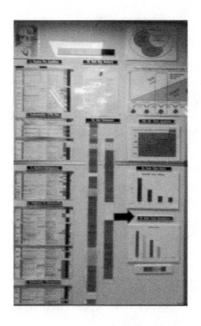

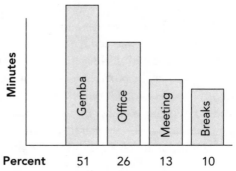

	Gemba	Office	Meeting	Breaks
Percent	51	26	13	10

Figure 10.5   Minimum critical role for the group leader and the Yamazumi chart.
Source: Toyota Motor Manufacturing UK.

Transitional Roles and Structured Learning

Roles were formalized for the transitions between leadership positions: advanced team members, advanced team leaders, and advanced group leaders. These included new titles, pay levels, and role definitions. New training programs were developed for these transitions.

The advanced team member training is 17 weeks of structured learning and focuses mostly on standardized work, including writing out the processes, auditing, and responding to deviations. The advanced team leader also gets 17 weeks of structured learning, focused heavily on leading improvement projects and coaching team leaders. In both cases, these are mainly work-based leadership assignments—acting in the leader role or improving something. They are scheduled day by day and tracked day by day, and there are intensive reviews at various stages. Some are formal training sessions off work time, and many assignments need to be completed by the team member and team leaders off work time, like working on coached kaizen projects. The team members have to be seriously committed to put in this unpaid time.

Visual Boards and Daily Meetings

Arguably the most powerful new innovations at TMUK were new team leader and group leader boards and daily meetings focused on 1x1 problem solving. A prototype "team leader control board" with fictional data is shown in Figure 10.6. This is the board used for daily 5-minute preshift meetings. There are some traditional things on the board, like a place in the upper left-hand corner for quality, safety, and other points to be highlighted to the team in the preshift meeting. Change point management is very important, which highlights anything that has changed in a process that may impact the shift and actions to be taken. Changes could include a temporary team member filling in on a process, a new member being trained, an engineering change in a part, or a new tool being trialed. There is an area for A3s of the bigger team leader problem-solving projects by shift.

The rest of the board is what is new—an emphasis on 1x1 problem solving. Remember the andon is pulled because an abnormality is detected, and the team leader and team member are responsible for abnormality management. There are charts to capture the number of andon pulls, including an overall trend and the number of andon pulls the prior day by process. This data is generated automatically by the computer in real time as the cords are pulled. Team leaders are expected to write down the cause by hand for each pull and then make a Pareto chart of the causes. The biggest problem is then selected for problem solving by writing it on a tag, which is placed in day 1. Each day until the problem is solved, the tag moves from day to day until on day 5 it hits the red spot (gray in this figure), and the card is physically escalated to the group leader "power board."

The new group leader power board was a countermeasure to a problem noted in the old meetings (see Figure 10.7). Group leaders felt left on their own. They had problems to address that required support from engineering, maintenance, or staff specialists, and they had to chase down these people for help. In the power meetings, these people are already in the meeting, every day—engineering,

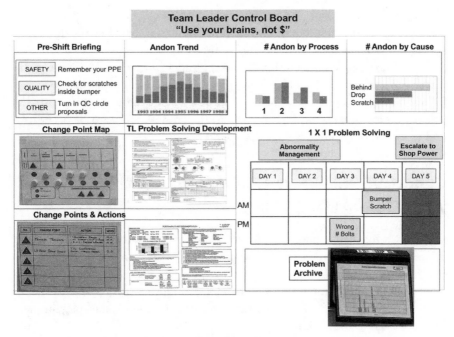

Figure 10.6   Example of a TMUK team leader control board.
Source: Toyota Motor Manufacturing UK.

Figure 10.7   Example of a TMUK group leader power board.
Source: Toyota Motor Manufacturing UK.

maintenance, production specialists, the section manager, quality, and anyone else needed. The group leader has a microphone, and only the one with the mic speaks. Everyone is there as a "servant" to the group leader.

Each card that comes up from the team leader or new cards that the group leader generates for 1x1 problem solving are assigned to the appropriate group. Chronic-complex projects are managed through Gantt charts on the board. The power that the visuals and meeting give to the group leader can't be overstated, and the speed of response is lightning quick.

FORM VERSUS FUNCTION OF TEAMS AT GENERAL MOTORS

General Motors had a unique opportunity through its joint venture with Toyota at the NUMMI plant to learn the Toyota Production System firsthand. The company was not committed to learning for many years, but after about a dozen years it was making good progress. It took this long to move from copying features of TPS to working on an effective culture, and then in 2009 bankruptcy hit, and GM was back to the beginning.

In the early stages of the joint venture, General Motors sent 16 "commandos" to NUMMI to work as managers for a few years and then come back and teach what they learned. The commandos were immersed in TPS culture and had a lot to teach, but they were scattered in different locations and had little power to change the organization. Larry Spiegel, one of the commandos, later lamented:[5]

> The lack of receptiveness to change [at a GM plant on Long Beach] was so deep. There were too many people convinced that they didn't need to change. It's not logical. They just didn't [believe it was necessary to change].

After about a decade, GM formalized its version of TPS in its "Synchronous Manufacturing" program, and where GM did not have leaders experienced in lean, the attempt became more of a carbon-copy activity. Some GM leaders reportedly took photos throughout NUMMI and then worked to make the GM factories look exactly the same. Among the things GM copied was the work group structure, including the team leader role. The company created the job description, worked with the union to get agreement on the role, and deployed it broadly and quickly. The result was GM got the form right—but not the function.

At some point an executive wanted to know how the groups were performing. Industrial engineers conducted a time study to measure how the GM team leaders were using their time throughout the company compared with the NUMMI team leaders' time. The overarching difference between GM and NUMMI team leaders was that GM team leaders didn't really understand or fulfill their role. In fact, only 52 percent of the time were the GM team leaders doing anything that you could regard as work, while NUMMI team leaders were actively supporting the assembly-line workers and spent 90 percent of their time doing work on the shop floor. As examples, NUMMI team leaders spent:

- 21 percent of their time filling in for workers who were absent or on vacation. GM team leaders did this 1.5 percent of the time.
- 10 percent of their time ensuring a smooth flow of parts to the line. GM team leaders were at 3 percent.
- 7 percent of their time actively communicating job-related information. This was virtually absent at GM.
- 5 percent of their time observing the team working in order to anticipate problems. This did not happen at all at GM.

Basically, GM team leaders focused on emergency relief of workers (e.g., so workers could use the restroom) and quality inspection and repair. When there were no immediate problems and no fires to put out, they were not sure of what to do, sometimes going to a back room for a break. What GM was lacking was obvious: it did not have the Toyota Production System or the supporting culture. It merely copied and appended the work group structure onto traditional mass production plants. The lesson was clear: don't introduce work teams unless you also commit to the hard work of developing the system and culture to support them, as we saw at Toyota's warehouse in Kentucky.

TAKING TEAM LEADER AND GROUP LEADER DEVELOPMENT SERIOUSLY AT HERMAN MILLER

In contrast to what General Motors was doing in its early years, office furniture designer and manufacturer Herman Miller made a serious long-term investment in the team leader and group leader roles. Herman Miller began working with the Toyota Production System Support Center, and Mr. Ohba, in 1996. The company began with a model line in one filing cabinet plant and went through the pain and struggles of any student of a Toyota sensei. What does he want? Why doesn't he give us any answers? But the company struggled, and learned, and got remarkable results. For example, it increased production, even though it eliminated one shift and reduced the number of direct production workers from 126 to 30 people with little capital investment.

The sensei had an agreement with the CEO that no people would lose their jobs because of TPS; and so as people's positions were eliminated, the people were moved to other roles, sometimes temporarily on a kaizen team. Later, the productivity increases across the company allowed Herman Miller to keep production in the United States, which saved many jobs, while its competitors were moving to Mexico to chase lower labor costs (more on this in final chapter).

Out of the model line, the Herman Miller Performance System (HMPS) spread across all manufacturing with stunning results. This is not to say the journey was linear and easy. It was filled with ups and downs, and the company learned that the key to sustainability was the management system and people development. In 2004, to address the need for qualified people, the HMPS group piloted development of versions of the team leader and group leader roles with several months of intensive, one-on-one coaching. It called the team leader a "facilitator" and the group leader a "work team leader," but the roles were similar to those at Toyota. The roles were so successful that all the plants started their own version of training, although with inconsistent results.

One of the issues the company encountered early on was getting the sequence of development right. When facilitators were developed before the work team leaders they reported to, they were underutilized and frustrated. Seeing the need for centralized, programmatic development, in 2009 the company introduced a 12-week "Bridge" learning program for facilitators (team leaders) and a program called "Propel" for work team leaders (group leaders) run out of the HMPS group. Note that 13 years passed from when Herman Miller first started learning from Toyota until it introduced formal training for this new role of facilitator, so the company was already quite mature in its use of the tools and systems. It also had skilled "continuous improvement leaders" in each plant.

At Toyota, these roles are ingrained in the culture, but there was a bit of a sales job needed at Herman Miller since operations divisions had to pay the cost. At first, senior leadership had some struggles accepting the facilitator role, believing that it would add wasteful overhead. The programs' creators believed otherwise. As explained by Matt Long, vice president for continuous improvement at the time:

> *Early on in this journey when we were developing the Bridge program we were challenged about the funding for those positions, because it looks like just more overhead and your indirect to direct ratio seems to be going the wrong way. But when we tracked the payback for those students in the first Bridge class, two members of the Bridge class paid for the whole class [10 people] within six months of coming out of the Bridge program.*

This is not a bad return on investment for a training program. The cost was simply the payroll of the 10 people who attended the first class. This was a full-time assignment for three months, and "students" were intentionally placed in a different plant so they were not held back by familiarity with the people and processes—one of the best decisions made at Herman Miller. As it became clear that there was a great payback and as senior leaders began to believe in the program, they did not press for tracking costs and return. They just wanted more trained facilitators.

The HMPS group had learned enough from Toyota to understand the difference between classroom training of concepts and on-the-job development of actual skills. It wanted skills and people who would behave appropriately for the situation. The agenda for the 12-week Bridge program for facilitators is shown in Figure 10.8. Nothing was taught without a specific purpose, and almost everything was immediately applied and assessed.

Week 1 is general orientation and some "soft skills training," and then each of the students is sent to an assigned work area to do production jobs for a week and get familiar with the area and the people and experience what a team member experiences. The students begin to learn about the "stability" of the operation with the goal of identifying struggles that impact the smooth operations a team member needs in a standardized work condition. When the Bridge students learn about standardized work, they practice it: they time work elements, they develop standardized worksheets, and they look at the balance between the cycle times of the jobs in the area and the takt. Where are there light jobs? Where are there heavy jobs? They develop in this early stage a "critical eye." As described by Jill Miller the leader of the program:

> They learn and apply tools, like identifying waste, cycle time versus takt time, building a work-balance chart, prioritizing problems to solve, standardized work. With these tools they are building a current condition and looking at the work differently than they had ever looked at the work before.

Weeks 2–12 are spent in the learning area, practicing all the skills they were taught in the classroom, under the overall theme of problem solving through PDCA. The work team leader in the area assigns them a problem to work on, and the trainees need to define the problem and then work on rapid problem solving. The problems are generally small and specific, like items in the hour-by-hour chart that caused underproduction. The students are not on their own for any of this. In addition to the support given by the team members and leadership in the learning area, they are assigned a continuous improvement leader who is part of the staff of the plant and spends two to three hours per day with the trainees.

After the three months of training, the trainees spend another three months as interns practicing what they have learned and taking on greater facilitator responsibility. If they pass, and a large majority do, then they are eligible for a facilitator position when one opens up, perhaps in the plant they came to for learning or in their original plant.

As a result of the program, processes are improved, costs are paid back, and most importantly, there is a fundamental transformation in the trainees. It is an

WEEK	MONDAY	TUESDAY	WEDNESDAY	THURSDAY	FRIDAY
1	Bridge Orientation	Bridge Orientation	Bridge Orientation	Soft Skills–Relationship Building	Soft Skills–Relationship Building
2	HMPS–Experience the Operator	HMPS–Experience the Operator	Stability Module / HMPS–Experience the Operator	HMPS–Experience the Operator	HMPS–Experience the Operator
3	HMPS–Waste	HMPS–CT/TT	HMPS–CT/TT	HMPS–CT/TT	Soft Skills–Communicating with Others
4	HMPS–Standardized Work Day 1	HMPS–Standardized Work	HMPS–Standardized Work	HMPS–Standardized Work	HMPS–Standardized Work
5	HMPS–POCA and Standardized Work Day 2	HMPS–Problem Solving	HMPS–Problem Solving	HMPS–Problem Solving	Soft Skills–Gaining Influence
6	HMPS–JI Training / JI Prep and Practice HMPS–Problem Solving	HMPS–JI Training / JI Prep and Practice HMPS–Problem Solving	JI Prep and Practice HMPS–Problem Solving	JI Prep and Practice HMPS–Problem Solving	JI Prep and Practice HMPS–Problem Solving
7	JI Prep and Practice HMPS–Problem Solving	HMPS–JI Training / JI Prep and Practice HMPS–Problem Solving	HMPS–JI Training / HMPS–Problem Solving	HMPS–Problem Solving	Soft Skills–Managing Conflict
8	Jidoka / Visual Management/HR x HR	Visual Management/HR x HR	HMPS–Problem Solving	HMPS–Problem Solving	HMPS–Problem Solving
9	HMPS–Problem Solving	HMPS–Problem Solving	HMPS–Problem Solving	HMPS–Problem Solving	Soft Skills–Managing Change
10	Shadow the Facilitator	Experience the Facilitator	Experience the Facilitator	Experience the Facilitator	Experience the Facilitator
11	Experience the Facilitator	Experience the Facilitator	Experience the Facilitator	Experience the Facilitator	Group Reflection / Experience the Facilitator
12–26	Internship	Internship	Internship	Internship	Internship

Basic Skills

Improvement Challenge 1

Improvement Challenges 2, 3, 4

Improvement Challenge 4

Group HMPS Training   Soft Skills Training

Group Reflections for Students:
12–1pm on:
Soft Skills Day 2
Soft Skills Day 3
Soft Skills Day 4
Soft Skills Day 5
Last Day of Bridge

Figure 10.8 Herman Miller facilitator Bridge program schedule.

222

experience that will change the rest of their lives, and their level of enthusiasm is off the charts. Jill gushed:

> *I tell people all the time I have the best job ever getting to watch these people learn and grow week after week. The students even talk about the impact it has on their families because their families can see how much they have grown and changed. It's really amazing. It's a life changing opportunity for these people.*

An unexpected benefit of the Bridge program is that it created a leadership pipeline that didn't exist before. Previously, Herman Miller looked outside the organization for work team leader candidates, but now the company develops them from within. There are numerous examples of team members that have moved through the ranks of facilitator, work team leader, continuous improvement leader, and even manager. It has also helped drive diversity in leadership by intentionally developing diverse candidates.

The Propel program for work team leaders begins with a one-week review of the skills taught in facilitator training and with identifying any weaknesses. It is important that work team leaders have the fundamental skills of the people they are leading. They learn additional concepts and skills such as writing a monthly A3 plan, developing a cadence for management, and charting material and information flow. These skills are used to understand the current condition of an area and effectively manage it. Problem-solving training is learned on the job, again with intensive coaching from the continuous improvement leader.

The problem solving in this case is a bigger project for the trainees and follows Toyota's eight-step process called Toyota Business Practices (discussed under Principle 12). In this case, the trainees are defining a big problem, including identifying the gap between the ideal state and the actual state and breaking the problem down to manageable chunks working in the direction of the ideal state. Along the way, they learn to teach the classroom sessions that were taught to the facilitators, develop presentation skills, and learn more deeply by being forced to think about the tools and concepts and how to explain them to others. After their HMPS training, the learning shifts to human resources skills and how to apply them situationally. There is a three-month internship, but Propel students are in such demand that they often are grabbed by operations before they complete the internship.

We asked graduates of Bridge and Propel about the highlights of the program, what they are most proud of, and how it changed them and helped them grow. In all, 27 people answered with heartfelt and glowing essays that went far beyond the specific lean tools to the relationships they built, how they learned to become leaders, and a new way of thinking about solving problems. Here are examples from facilitators:

- Making improvements in our assigned areas and having it become successful is the most rewarding feeling. Also successfully making people's ideas come to reality especially when it's a problem that's been around for a while. I am also proud that I was able to change people's perspective about facilitators, that they are someone you can trust, to see them as support where they are doing things in your best interest.
- My coach was a highlight of mine. He sensed my ambition but tempered it with making sure to focus on fixing the smaller problems first. It was really quite humbling since I think almost everybody wants to solve the world's problems the moment they have the freedom to. . . . The nice thing is that a coach is always there beside you to make sure you have the support when you need it, a challenge to keep you engaged, and someone to remind you that it's alright to make mistakes.
- I am most proud of how confident the process made me. I knew no one . . . I challenged myself to forge relationships and friendships I still have to this day. It drove me out of my comfort zone, but I like myself a lot more for it. The program taught me to be me . . . I learned to lead with what was inside of me. To show compassion, a willingness to assist and a side of humbleness that everyone loves in a leader. I learned to be a forward thinker and to work with character as if no one was watching.
- Prior to the development, "leader" would have been one of the last words I would have used to describe myself. Now, it is in my job title. I didn't just develop in learning the tools of HMPS, but also being put out of my comfort zone, practicing presentation and communication skills, and learning to network in different plants—all of which has helped put me on the career path I am on now.

Then there were Work Team Leaders:

- Bridge taught me to not be arrogant and prideful but to be a servant leader. It continues to teach me to ask for help. To have ownership for everything I do whether it is good or bad. It continues to teach me . . . people are your most valuable resource. They are not to be blamed, they are valuable and we need to make their job easier.
- Personally, I honestly did not see myself practicing lean in manufacturing. I did think about gaining a better understanding, perhaps developing a greater appreciation for lean principles but not really DOING IT! It's been challenging to put pencil to paper, go see, measure, and collectively with team members solve problems and sustain improvements.
- The amount of personal growth I've noticed in myself and others, both as a leader and as a human of the earth. A great leader at Herman Miller is a great leader across the world. In a nonintentional way we develop not just

business leaders to accomplish a demand but also community leaders to guide the world into a better tomorrow. In every single facet of my being, every nook and cranny of my character I have learned and developed into a strong leader and support. . . . Bridge not only gives you the skills, tools, and proficiency in those tools to lead a business but also grows you in a moral and logical way.

Herman Miller has many visitors who come to learn about these programs, and Matt and Jill realized that few have experienced such an intense learning program. Most leadership development programs are five days or less—primarily classroom training with some experiential exercises. Herman Miller has been working on this for over 23 years since it first started learning from Toyota in 1996; yet the Bridge and Propel training are both still being refined, and even after all this development, not all lines have facilitators. It is a long-term effort, far longer than the life span of most corporate programs. And the program is effective because the basic tools and management systems are in place and working for leaders to learn from and improve upon. This level of commitment may not be realistic for all companies, but Herman Miller is providing one model of what it means to take developing leadership skills seriously.

MOTIVATING WORK GROUPS THROUGH INTRINSIC REWARDS OR EXTRINSIC OR BOTH?

How do you motivate team members to care about their work enough to continuously improve it? I often hear that "workers are only interested in getting through the day and getting paid." I am asked how to motivate them to go beyond the minimum effort and make suggestions for improvement. What seems to automatically come to mind is extrinsic rewards and punishments—which means you give people something if they perform well, or you take something away if they do not. For example, American auto companies used to provide a bonus for implemented suggestions proportional to the cost savings. Some workers even got cars. It led to conflict over whose idea it was and union grievances over the proper amount of the bonus, but it did produce some good ideas.

Karl Duncker published a study in 1945 that looked at how extrinsic versus intrinsic rewards impacted how subjects performed a task focusing on speed. The challenge was to attach a candle in some way to a wall as fast as possible. He divided subjects into an experimental group that received intrinsic rewards—doing this for the benefit of science—and a control group offered extrinsic rewards—money if the subject won. In experiment 1, he provided some supplies laid out, as in Figure 10.9, including tacks in a box. Subjects ended up trying

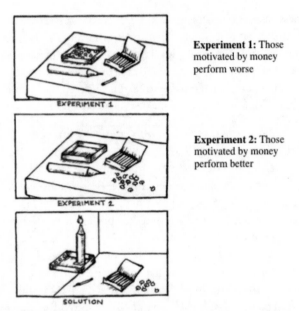

Experiment 1: Those motivated by money perform worse

Experiment 2: Those motivated by money perform better

Figure 10.9 Candle experiments with extrinsic rewards and intrinsic rewards. (Drawing by Karyn Ross, based on Karl Duncker, "On Problem Solving," Psychological Monographs 58, American Psychological Association.)

various things that failed, like melting wax and trying to use the wax to stick the candle to the wall. Nothing worked until they discovered the simple solution of removing the tacks from the box, tacking the box to the wall, and using it as a holder for the candle. Who did better? Surprisingly, those with intrinsic motivation won, by a lot. Money actually hurt performance, and the financially incentivized subjects on average took longer to discover the secret.

In experiment 2, the box was empty and the tacks were laid out separately. In this case, it was more apparent how the box could be used, and subjects often went right to the correct solution, with those incentivized by money easily beating out subjects not offered money.

His conclusion was that extrinsic rewards can be powerful motivators when the work to be done is very clear and creative thinking is not required. When "outside the box" thinking is needed, money causes people to try to rush toward the goal, and they think less deeply.

There have been many other studies with similar conclusions—for creative tasks, extrinsic rewards are less helpful and can actually reduce discretionary effort, and subjects enjoy the work less.[6] Since people are getting paid per unit of activity, they tend to do the minimum required to get the reward.

With repetitive manual work, you would think rewarding people with pay per piece would make sense. Or if you want creative ideas for improvement, why not pay per idea? Yet Toyota works hard to avoid extrinsic rewards when possible. Everyone gets competitive pay for their positions, but there are no performance-based bonuses for production workers. Even for managers, discretionary pay is small and mostly tied to how well the company does and how well the organization, e.g., the factory, performs. A small part is an individual bonus.

Toyota wants more than a lot of pieces produced or ideas generated quickly. It wants production work done with high quality to the takt, not overproduction. It wants workers thinking about how to improve their work. It wants problems to be solved thoughtfully, usually as a team. It wants creative contributions by everyone.

One exception to only giving intrinsic rewards is using recognition as a reward. For example, at the TMUK plant these include an eagle eye award for spotting a hard-to-notice quality problem, recognition and small awards for the best quality circles, and recognition for particularly good kaizen activities. Moreover, all leaders are taught to identify positive behaviors and recognize individuals and teams.

TRUST IS THE FOUNDATION FOR RESPECT FOR PEOPLE, AND JOB SECURITY AND SAFETY ARE THE FOUNDATIONS FOR TRUST

Toyota leaders are firmly committed to respect for people and job security. It is nonnegotiable. A human resource model that's taught at TMUK puts job security as the foundational item and *essential* for all the other levels (see Figure 10.10). This is one of the most difficult Toyota concepts to transfer. I frequently hear, "We understand Toyota is committed to job security, but we have too much instability in demand to make that kind of commitment to our workforce."

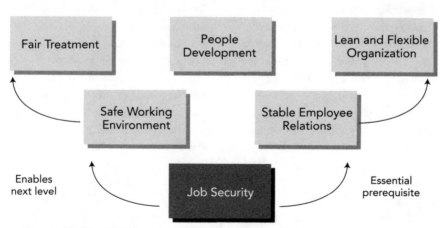

Figure 10.10   Building blocks of respectful human resource management.
Source: Toyota Motor Manufacturing UK.

The problem is the assumption that the current condition is fixed and cannot be changed. Most people are correct that if they take their system as it is and then try to simply guarantee job security, they will have a problem. Their systems are not designed for this. Toyota, with an improvement mindset, has evolved systems to support job security over time, not just because the leaders are nice people, but because job security becomes a design constraint. If a cultural assumption is that both long-term employment *and* cost competitiveness are necessary for survival, then there is little choice but to find creative ways to do both. For the long term, a strong support for ensuring job security and keeping plants open is Principle 4 on heijunka. One reason (not the only one) that Toyota wants to make multiple vehicles on the same production line and to level the production schedule is to stabilize volumes and thus employment. The passenger car is not selling well, but the sport utility version is going gangbusters, or vice versa. If they are made on the same line, there will be stable work over time.

One important tool for adjusting to demand changes is the "variable" workforce, as opposed to the regular work force that has tremendous job security. All Toyota plants use a temporary workforce as a buffer, adding or dismissing based on need. A common Toyota standard is that 20 percent of team members are from the temporary workforce. Pay policies for temporary workers vary by country and may be lower than or equal to the pay of regular team members, and Toyota does its best to treat the temporary workers with respect; the company even invites them to participate in quality circles and invests in their training. Those that perform well become first in line for hiring if there is a long-term upward trend in demand.

In the short term, Toyota uses a variety of tools for flexing working time (see Figure 10.11). Many visitors wonder why Toyota is not running production around the clock and prefers two shifts with several hours in between. In addition to using the third shift for preventative maintenance, it provides flexibility for scaling up and down work hours. At TMUK, when sales increase temporarily— for example, when a new model is first introduced—Toyota can add up to 1½ hours of overtime per shift. When volume goes down, the company can cancel the ½ hour of overtime it pays per shift in normal conditions to cover line stops. At TMUK, management has negotiated with its union partners various policies, such as adding nonproduction members to do production work and banking up to five shifts in a month. Banked hours work this way: If volume is down and Toyota would like to reduce the hours in the week, it might shut down production for two shifts in a week. It still pays team members who stay home, but then at another time, it can add a Saturday and pay only the overtime premium.

The combination of the variable workforce and tools for short-term hours adjustments leads to flexibility to shift work hours up or down by about one-third each way to adjust to sudden demand changes. I am not suggesting that

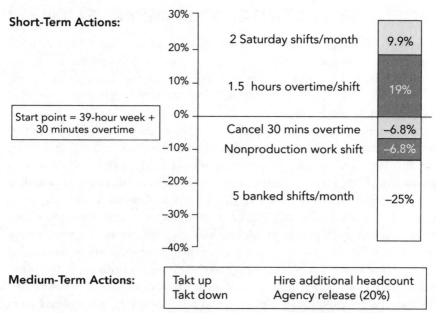

Figure 10.11   TMUK: Working time flexibility = protect job security.

these are generic solutions for all companies. I often hear, "Our union does not have that kind of flexibility, and our laws do not permit temporary workers." The point is that because of its commitment to job security and its belief it is critical for success, Toyota has developed local solutions to achieve flexibility in the very difference conditions of each country where it has manufacturing operations. The principle remains the same: establish mutual trust between management and team members and construct a win-win partnership. If team members think management is playing games it is over.

Job security enables other key elements of human resources as shown in Figure 10.10. The most important, safety, is a given at Toyota and has evolved over time. At TMUK, every meeting begins with a personal safety commitment from whoever speaks. Warning signs against unsafe practices are everywhere. Personal protective equipment is a must. Standardized work builds in key points on how to do the job safely. Single-point lessons on safety are a regular occurrence. Team members stop and point in the direction they will walk in the plant every time they make a turn in the plant. The number of days without a lost-work incident is posted prominently and is usually in the hundreds of days. Any safety incident is instantly sent to the cell phones of senior leaders. A safety culture communicates to everyone that "we value you and your health, and safety comes above anything else."

PEOPLE DRIVE CONTINUOUS IMPROVEMENT

Toyota invests in people and in return gets committed associates who show up to work every day on time and are continually improving their operations. On one of my early visits, I found that in the past year at the Toyota, Georgetown, assembly plant, associates made about 80,000 improvement suggestions. The plant implemented 99 percent of them.

So how can you get your employees to work diligently to do their jobs perfectly and strive to improve every day? Build a system that follows Toyota Way Principle 10: "Develop exceptional people and teams who follow your company's philosophy." First, look at the system dynamics of your organization. Building excellent people who understand and support your company's culture is not a matter of adopting simple solutions or an afterthought of applying motivational theories. Training exceptional people and building high-performing work groups need to form the backbone of your management approach—an approach that integrates your social systems with your technical system. Throughout this book, you have seen how one-piece flow drives positive problem-solving behaviors and motivates people to improve. However, you need a social system and culture of continuous improvement to support this behavior.

Of course, you cannot pull a ready-made culture out of a wizard's hat. Building a culture takes years of applying a consistent approach with consistent principles. You must design jobs to be challenging. People need to feel they have a degree of control over their job. Moreover, in a supportive context, there seems to be nothing as motivating as challenging targets, constant measurement and feedback on progress, and meaningful recognition for effort. The rewards can be symbolic and not all that costly. In the end, building exceptional people and teams derives from a culture of respect for people.

KEY POINTS

- Toyota culture is based on a growth mindset that with the right leadership anyone can develop and grow to face new challenges with dedication and passion.
- Toyota embraced servant leadership long before it was fashionable, turning the organization chart upside down, with value-added workers at the top.
- The Toyota standard is to develop work groups who own their processes and are served by support organizations.
- The standard structure is a group leader who is viewed as a managing director of a company's small businesses with team leaders who lead their small work teams.

- The "mysterious" team leader is a pivotal role responsible for supporting team members, ensuring standardized work, responding to abnormalities, and leading kaizen, with a small enough team (ideally four people) to allow for daily coaching.
- Developing and sustaining effective leadership is even challenging for Toyota, and the company is regularly experimenting with new approaches to reenergize the work group.
- Some organizations make the mistake of assuming if they create a version of the team leader and group leader roles on paper, their work groups will function the same way Toyota's do, but they usually fail.
- Herman Miller committed to developing high-performing teams and trains facilitators and work team leaders in a rigorous hands-on program over a three-month period plus a three-month internship.
- Toyota work groups are supported by a human resource system that focuses on a fair, safe, and secure environment with job security as the foundational element.

Notes

1. Robert Greenleaf, *The Servant as Leader* (pamphlet), Greenleaf Center for Servant Leadership, 2015.
2. Carol Dweck, *Mindset: The New Psychology of Success* (New York: Ballantine Books, 2007).
3. David Brooks, "This Is How Scandinavia Got Great: The Power of Educating the Whole Person," *New York Times*, February 13, 2020.
4. Jennifer Yukiko Orf, "Japanese Education and Its Role in Kaizen," in Jeffrey Liker (ed.), *Becoming Lean: Inside Stories of U.S. Manufacturers* (Portland, OR: Productivity Press, 1998).
5. https://www.linkedin.com/pulse/30-years-later-original-nummi-commando-shares-lessons-mark-graban/.
6. Daniel Pink, *Drive: The Surprising Truth About What Motivates Us* (New York: Riverhead Books, 2012).

Principle 11

Respect Your Value Chain Partners by Challenging Them and Helping Them Improve

Toyota is more hands-on and more driven to improving their own systems and then showing how that improves you. . . . Toyota will do things like level their production systems to make it easier on you. Toyota picks up our product 12 times per day. They helped move presses, moved where we get the water from, trained our employees. On the commercial side they are very hands-on also—they come in and measure and work to get cost out of the system. There is more opportunity to make profit at Toyota. We started with Toyota when we opened a Canadian plant with one component and, as performance improved, we were rewarded, so now we have almost the entire cockpit. Relative to all car companies we deal with, Toyota is the best.

—An automotive supplier

We have been looking at lean processes and people development within Toyota. Let's consider the broader value chain that links inputs from suppliers to the company and to customer-facing distributors. In the auto industry, it is common that 70 percent or more of vehicle content comes from outside suppliers, so the automobile is only as good as the supplied parts. With the new world of innovative technologies to support connected, autonomous, shared, electrified vehicles, partnerships are increasing in importance. Distribution for many industries is done through outside agents or dealers. In the US automotive industry (with the exception of Tesla), the dealers are independent business owners who have been selected by the automakers to represent them. Toyota views outside companies it does business with as "partners," whether they are suppliers, dealers, IT providers, lawyers, or you name it. Long-term partners are entitled to the same respect afforded to team members—treat them fairly based on mutual trust, challenge them, develop them, and help them grow. Let's look first at auto suppliers, and later in the chapter we'll look at developing dealers who sell and service the vehicles.

SUPPLIER PARTNERING

Auto industry suppliers consistently report that Toyota is their best customer—and also their toughest. We often think of "tough" as difficult to get along with or unreasonable. In Toyota's case, it means it has very high standards of excellence and expects all its partners to rise to those standards. More importantly, it will help all its partners rise to those standards.

Let's start with an example of an *ineffective* (but sadly typical) approach to supplier relationships. In 1999, one of the Big Three US auto companies, which I'll call "American Auto," decided it wanted to make its supplier relationships the best in the industry. American Auto was tired of hearing how great Toyota and Honda were at teaching and developing their suppliers to be lean. American Auto decided to create a supplier development center that would become the global benchmark for best practice. Even Toyota would benchmark American Auto.

This became a highly visible project with champions for its success at the vice president level. From the start, the vice presidents had a vision for a supplier development center, including preliminary blueprints for a state-of-the-art building with the latest instructional technology. The building would be the biggest and best, and suppliers would come together to learn best practices, including lean manufacturing methods.

I joined as a consultant to help design training programs for the center, so I got an inside look—which beyond the blueprints was not pretty. The first step in the project was to collect data on the current situation by interviewing 25 American Auto suppliers to understand their training needs. Most of these suppliers already had internal lean manufacturing programs that surpassed American Auto on lean. We listened to supplier after supplier as they angrily railed against their customer. Typical example:

> *Tell American Auto not to waste their money building a big expensive building to train us, but instead to get their own house in order so they can be a capable and reliable partner we can truly work with. Fix their broken product development process and ask them to implement lean manufacturing internally. We will even help teach American Auto.*

And another supplier:

> *The problem is American Auto has inexperienced [supplier] engineers who think they know what they are supposed to do. I would rather have those who realize they need to learn and train them. I have worked with American*

Auto for almost 18 years and saw the wave of good people back then who were trying to help you. Now relationships have deteriorated tremendously.

Clearly, American Auto needed to do a great deal of work before any benefit would come from constructing a fancy supplier development building. The basic problems were inherent in the weaknesses of American Auto's own internal systems, the lack of development of its own people, and its focus on mechanistic carrot-and-stick management without understanding its suppliers' processes. It needed to earn the right to be a leader before it could expect its suppliers to be followers and learn from it. Ultimately, cost-cutting killed the whole effort to build a supplier development center.

In the meantime, Toyota has spent decades building a strong lean enterprise in Japan and later building a world-class global supplier network. Suppliers typically react positively to Toyota's demanding but fair partnership approach. For example, John Henke has developed a "working relations index" that measures relationships between auto companies and first-tier suppliers.[1] Toyota is almost always on top. From 2012 to 2019, Toyota was number one in working relationships. A close second was Honda. North American–based automakers were far behind. Toyota regularly leads in several areas, perhaps most importantly in supplier trust. The study looks at how the index relates to performance outcomes and concludes:

The Working Relations Index® is highly correlated to the benefits that the OEM receives from its suppliers, including more investment in innovation and technology, lower pricing, and better supplier support, all of which contribute to the OEM's operating profit and competitive strength.

Toyota has been rewarded time and time again for its serious investment in building a network of highly capable suppliers. Much of the award-winning quality that distinguishes Toyota and Lexus vehicles results from the excellence in innovation, engineering, manufacturing, and overall reliability of Toyota's suppliers. Toyota suppliers will often give Toyota access to new technology ahead of selling it to competitors. And Toyota suppliers are integral to the just-in-time philosophy, both when it is working smoothly and when there is a need to address breakdowns in the system.

While many companies would abandon just-in-time when the first crisis hits, Toyota works its way through the rare crises, working hand in hand with suppliers. For example, on February 1, 1997, a fire destroyed an Aisin factory.[2] Aisin is one of Toyota's biggest and closest suppliers. Normally, Toyota dual-sources parts, but Aisin was the sole source for something called a "p-valve," which was an essential brake part used in all Toyota vehicles worldwide—at that time producing 32,500 per day. Toyota's vaunted JIT system meant only two days of inventory were available in total in the supply chain. Two days and disaster would strike. Was this evidence that JIT is a bad idea? Instead of faltering, 200 suppliers self-organized to get p-valve production started within two days. Sixty-three different firms took responsibility for making the parts, piecing together what existed of engineering documentation, using some of their own equipment, rigging together temporary lines to make the parts, and keeping Toyota in business almost seamlessly. Toyota's reflection did not include abandoning JIT, but rather avoiding the mistake of sourcing a critical part from only one location.

THE PRINCIPLE: RESPECT YOUR VALUE CHAIN PARTNERS BY CHALLENGING THEM AND HELPING THEM IMPROVE

Go to a conference on supply chain management, and what are you likely to hear? You will learn a lot about "streamlining" the supply chain through advanced information technology. If you can get the information in nanoseconds, you should be able to speed the supply chain to nanosecond deliveries, right? Perhaps you will learn of the benefits of shifting your supply to low-wage countries. It is all based on a mechanistic view of the supply chain as a predictable, technical process that can be instantly redesigned to meet any needs. What you are not likely to hear about is the enormous complexity of coordinating detailed, daily activities to deliver value to the customer. You are not likely to hear about relationships across firms—about how to work together toward common goals.

When Toyota started building automobiles, it did not have the capital or equipment for building the myriad components that go into a car. One of Eiji Toyoda's first assignments as a new engineer was to identify high-quality parts suppliers that Toyota could partner with. At that time, Toyota did not have the volume to give a lot of business to suppliers. In fact, some days it did not build a single vehicle because it did not have enough quality parts. Toyoda understood the need to find solid local partners for the company's major complex component systems (this is less the case for commodities like nuts and bolts). All that Toyota could offer was the opportunity for all partners to grow the business together and to mutually benefit in the long term. So, like the associates who work inside Toyota, suppliers became part of the extended family who grew and learned the Toyota Production System.

Even when Toyota became a global powerhouse, it maintained the principle of building partnerships with high-value-added suppliers. In general, Toyota likes to have two to three suppliers of a given part type in each region of the world. Competition is encouraged, though long-term partners tend to get a consistent share of the business over time. Once a supplier earns the position of partner in a region, it becomes a long-term supplier, which means it is difficult for new suppliers to break into the business. Toyota views new suppliers cautiously, and initially it tests them with small orders. If they dedicate themselves to quality and reliable delivery over several years, new suppliers are rewarded with bigger orders.

One very grateful Toyota supplier is Avanzar, which produces seats and other interior parts in sequence, just-in-time, right across the wall from Toyota's truck plant in San Antonio, Texas. Avanzar is part of a grand experiment to create a supplier park on Toyota's truck plant site and to source from minority suppliers. There are 23 suppliers on-site, and Avanzar is one of the largest. It was founded in 2005 as a joint venture between established supplier Johnson Controls (now Adient), and a minority Latino group, headed by Berto Guerro, who had majority ownership.

Avanzar, which means "to move forward," has embraced the Toyota Production System and has grown several times in size, even adding a location in Mexico. With Toyota right across the wall, there is a constant stream of managers and engineers teaching Avanzar. And Avanzar is a hungry student. Gradually, over the years, Avanzar has developed an entire system of people, processes, and problem solving based on a philosophy of long-term development and commitment to all team members. When the Great Recession hit, Avanzar decided to follow Toyota's lead and keep its people employed. On the verge of failing to meet payroll, Berto approached partner Toyota and asked for relief. Toyota paid ahead tooling costs and agreed to a retroactive price increase based on a strong rationale. Avanzar made payroll, and Berto was further committed to becoming the best partner Toyota ever had. Avanzar regularly wins J.D. Power awards for quality seats, including highest-quality seat supplier in 2010–2012 and 2017 (with Adient).

There is always fear suppliers will take advantage of customers who treat them well. Berto, and every other Toyota supplier I know of, has great respect for Toyota, but none would say working as a Toyota supplier is easy. Toyota challenges its suppliers to improve, just as it does its own people. One example of this is the target cost system. Large system suppliers participate in the vehicle development process, designing their part of the vehicle in collaboration with Toyota engineers. There is a bidding process, but it is often pretty clear up front that Toyota has designated a supplier for the business. That supplier is invited to "design in" its system collaboratively. Like Toyota's own engineers who develop systems and components, each suppliers is given a target cost. Toyota develops an overall price for the vehicle based on the market. Then it takes out its profit, and what is left over is what the vehicle must cost. Suppliers get a "checkbook" for what their part can cost. "Please design the component with these characteristics and at this cost," they are asked. The target will require intense engineering work to figure out how to achieve the challenging target and to make money. After the vehicle is in production, Toyota asks for annual price reductions. It assumes that with kaizen, the cost should continually come down.

This is not to say that Toyota closely partners with all of their hundreds of suppliers. Think of the supply chain like a hierarchy on an organization chart. Participation in product development, and close working relationships, are mostly focused on the "first tier" of suppliers who build and ship major component systems like instrument panels, seats, exhaust systems, brake systems, and tires, directly to Toyota plants. These suppliers in turn have a second tier they work with directly, and there is a third tier as well.

Toyota has many people who can add real value in teaching suppliers how to achieve their targets, whether in purchasing, the quality department, or the manufacturing plant, and is not concerned that benefits may spread to parts sold to competitors. Suppliers want to work for Toyota because they know they will get better and develop respect among their peers and other customers. From Toyota's perspective, having high expectations for their suppliers, treating them fairly, and teaching them is the definition of respect. And simply switching supplier sources because another supplier is a few percentage points cheaper (a common practice in the auto industry) would be unthinkable. As Taiichi Ohno said, "Achievement of business performance by the parent company through bullying suppliers is totally alien to the spirit of the Toyota Production System."

PARTNERING WITH SUPPLIERS WHILE MAINTAINING INTERNAL CAPABILITY

These days, a management buzzword is "core competency." Define what the company needs to be good at so it can outsource the rest. Toyota has a clear image of its core competency, but seems to look at it quite broadly. This goes back to the creation of the company when Toyota decided to go it alone instead of buying designs and parts of cars from established US and European automakers.

One of the philosophical roots of Toyota is the concept of self-reliance. It states in *The Toyota Way 2001* document: "We strive to decide our own fate. We act with self-reliance, trusting in our own abilities." So handing off key capabilities to outside firms would contradict this philosophy. Toyota sells, engineers, and makes mobility vehicles. If Toyota relied on the technology of its suppliers and outsourced 70 percent of its vehicles to the same suppliers that worked with its competitors, how could Toyota excel or distinguish itself? If a new technology is core to the vehicle, Toyota wants to be an expert and best in the world at mastering it. It wants to learn with suppliers, but never transfer all the core knowledge and responsibility in any key area to suppliers.

Under Principle 14, I discuss the development of the Prius. One of the core components of the hybrid engine is the insulated gate bipolar transistor, or IGBT (a "semiconductor switching device [IGBT] boosts the voltage from the battery and converts the boosted DC power into AC power for driving the motor").

Toyota engineers were not experts at making electronic parts, but rather than outsource this critical component, Toyota developed it and built a brand-new plant to make it—all within the tight lead time of the Prius development. Toyota saw hybrid vehicles as the next step into the future. The company wanted "self-reliance" in making that step. Once it had that internal expertise, it could selectively outsource. Senior managing directors insisted on making the transistor in-house because they saw it as a core capability for the design and manufacture of future hybrid vehicles and beyond that to any electrified vehicle. Toyota wants to know what is inside the "black box." It also did not trust other companies to put the effort into cost reduction it knew it could apply.

Also, in developing the Prius, Toyota decided to work with Matsushita (Panasonic) on the development and manufacture of the battery, which is central to successful hybrids and future energy-efficient vehicles. Toyota sorely wanted to develop this capability in-house but concluded it did not have the time. Rather than simply handing off responsibility to Matsushita, Toyota established a joint venture company—Panasonic EV Energy. This was not Toyota's first experience working with Matsushita. The Electric Vehicle Division of Toyota had already codeveloped with Matsushita a nickel-metal hydride battery for an electric version of the RAV4 sport utility vehicle, so Toyota had a prior relationship with Matsushita, and the two companies had a track record of successfully working together.

Even with this history of working together, the joint venture tested the company's differing cultures. Yuichi Fujii, then general manager of Toyota's Electric Vehicle Division and Prius Battery supervisor, at a point of frustration, said:[3]

I have a feeling that there is a difference between an auto maker and an electric appliance maker in the way they feel the sense of crisis about lead time. A Toyota engineer has it in his bones to be fully aware that preparing for production development should occur at a particular point in time. On the other hand, I feel that the Matsushita engineers are a little too relaxed.

There were also concerns about Matsushita's quality control discipline and whether the level of quality required for this new, complex battery was too high for Matsushita's normal practices. Fujii was reassured when he found a young Matsushita engineer one day looking pale. He learned the engineer had been working until four in the morning to finish some battery tests. Yet he had come back the next day to "make sure of just one thing."[4] At that point, Fujii realized that there was a "Matsushita style" that could work together with Toyota's style.

WORKING WITH SUPPLIERS
FOR MUTUAL LEARNING OF TPS

One way that Toyota has honed its skills in applying TPS is by working on projects with suppliers. Toyota needs its suppliers to be as capable as its own plants at building and delivering high-quality components just in time. Moreover, Toyota cannot cut costs unless suppliers cut costs, lest Toyota simply push cost reductions onto suppliers weakening the supplier's financial condition, which is not the Toyota Way. There are many methods Toyota uses to learn with its suppliers, and in the Toyota Way style, these are all "learning by doing" processes, keeping classroom training to a minimum.

All key suppliers are part of Toyota's regional supplier associations. These are core Toyota suppliers that meet throughout the year sharing practices, information, and concerns. There are committees that work on specific things, including joint projects. In the United States, BAMA (Bluegrass Automotive Manufacturers Association) was created in the Kentucky area, since Toyota suppliers started there, and has since expanded to a North American association. BAMA members are core suppliers, representing more than 65 percent of Toyota North America's annual purchases and accounting for 60 percent of the total vehicle cost. Members of BAMA can participate in many activities, including study groups that meet to develop greater skills in TPS. These are called "jishuken," or voluntary study groups.

The jishuken was started in 1977 in Japan by the Operations Management Consulting Division (OMCD). OMCD is the elite corps of TPS experts started by Ohno in 1968 to improve operations in Toyota and its suppliers. At that time, this included six senior TPS gurus and about fifty consultants—some of whom were fast-track, young production engineers on a three-year rotation who were being groomed to be manufacturing leaders.

Only the best TPS master trainers have directed OMCD. About 55 to 60 of Toyota's key suppliers (representing 80 percent of parts in value) were organized into groups of 4 to 7 suppliers by geography and part type. TPS trainers rotated across companies, working on three- to four-month projects in each company, one by one. They chose a theme and went to work. Representatives of the other suppliers visited regularly and made recommendations. The OMCD TPS expert visited the plant every week or so to give advice. The projects involved radical transformation, not incremental improvement, often tearing up the floor and creating one-piece flow cells, leveling the schedule and the like, to create huge improvements in cost, quality, and delivery. Strict targets were set and achieved.

Kiyoshi Imaizumi, an executive with seat supplier Araco Corporation, one of Toyota's most sophisticated suppliers in Japan, explained that jishuken taught TPS in the spirit of the harsh approaches originally used by Taiichi Ohno:

Toyota's suppliers' jishuken in Japan is completely different from that in the U.S. It is compulsory. You cannot say no. Toyota picks suppliers to participate. From each supplier they pick three to five members. Toyota sends their own TPS expert to the target plant and they review this plant's activity and give a theme, e.g., this line must reduce 10 people from the plant. The supplier's member has one month to come up with a solution. The TPS expert comes back to check to see if the supplier has met the target. In the past some of the participants had a nervous breakdown and quit work. Toyota has a gentler version of TPS in the U.S. Once you clear Toyota's jishuken in Japan, you can feel so much more confidence in yourself. One of the former Trim Masters presidents went through this and became so confident he never compromised anything with anybody.

Toyota has gradually changed its style to one that is more supportive and less punitive, particularly in the United States. The closest thing in America to OMCD is what used to be called the Toyota Supplier Support Center (TSSC) and is now called the Toyota Production System Support Center (still referred to as TSSC). It was established in 1992 and led by Hajime Ohba, a former leader of OMCD and an Ohno disciple. A variation on the theme of OMCD was created to fit the American culture, while continuing the focus on real projects. Suppliers, and even companies outside of the auto industry, like New Balance Shoes, Viking Range, and Herman Miller, had to petition to be accepted as clients. The service was originally free, but then became a pay-for-service consulting arrangement in which private companies covered costs only.

The TSSC identifies a business need and then picks a product line for a project. The project consists of developing a "model line." A typical model line includes a manufacturing process that makes parts that go to an assembly process. A full TPS transformation is done by the company's management with all the elements of JIT, jidoka, standardized work, visual management, daily management, total productive maintenance, etc. Toyota mentors teach and demonstrate TPS as a system. Over time, TSSC was set up as an outside, not-for-profit corporation, which was the time it changed its name to the Toyota Production System Support Center. It targets one-third of the business to private companies, one-third to not-for-profits, and one-third to charitable organizations. Only private businesses pay for the service.

The TSSC results were spectacular right out of the gate. From 1992 to 1997 TSSC completed its first 31 projects, getting impressive results in every case. It had reduced inventory an average of 75 percent and improved productivity an average of 124 percent. Space was reduced, quality improved, and emergency freight shipments were eliminated.[5] In 25 years of service, TSSC served over 320 organizations, including food banks, hospitals, schools, charitable home-building organizations, software development companies, and more.

For example, the Community Kitchen & Food Pantry of West Harlem, New York serves over 50,000 free meals to clients each month. In the past, lines were long, even on freezing cold days, yet dining room space was only 77 percent utilized. Community Kitchen went to TSSC for help. TSSC looked at the operation as an assembly process, focusing on improving flow and eliminating waste:[6]

> *The team quickly determined that instead of serving 10 clients at one time, it is more efficient to serve clients one-by-one. The team also suggested the idea of creating an on-deck area for the next batch of customers to wait on stand-by and assigned a "point person" to ensure customer flow by assisting clients to open seats. With these changes, once a client finished eating, the Community Kitchen was able to more quickly and efficiently serve the next client.*

After teaching and supporting the leaders of the service over an eight-week period, the waiting lines outside dropped from 1½ hours to 18 minutes and the number of people served dramatically increased. The transformation continued to spread across the vast New York City Food Bank network of 900 agencies.

One thing I had noticed while visiting Toyota suppliers was that they often served multiple auto companies in the same plant—and even with the same labor practices throughout, the Toyota production line seemed to perform better. To test this, we collected data on 91 supplier plants that served both Toyota and at least one US-based automaker, thus holding many variables constant. Sure enough, on the Toyota line, inventory turns were higher, work-in-process inventory was lower, cost reduction was greater, and on-time delivery was superior.[7] We believe this had to do with Toyota's logistics policies like heijunka, multiple deliveries daily, and the steady stream of teaching the suppliers got from Toyota on TPS. A separate study by Jeffrey Dyer and Nile Hatch got similar results which they attribute to knowledge sharing and faster learning.[8]

PARTNERING WITH DEALERS BY TEACHING, NOT FORCING

Any manufacturer is only as good as its relationship with its distribution network. In the auto industry, this means the dealers who are the face of the company to customers. Toyota dealers are independent businesses that Toyota respects

---

* This is described in detail in Yoshio Ishizaka, *The Toyota Way in Sales and Marketing* (Tokyo: Asa Publishing, 2009).

as partners. Bullying is no more effective with dealers than it is with suppliers. Toyota has developed a version of its *Toyota Way* document for sales and service* and writes: "Set up dealer networks for pleasure, convenience, and high value and provide integrated 3S services (sales, spare parts, service), engaging in direct communication with customers to develop a long-term relationship."*

Toyota long ago developed a version of the Toyota Production System for dealers—but it does not impose it. It offers it and teaches it. One example in the United States is Toyota Express Maintenance. Repair bays are dedicated to oil, lubrication, and routine service visits. The maintenance system resembles what happens in separate quick oil change businesses. Toyota developed the system and certified a network of consultants to teach it by helping the dealer set it up. The dealer pays for the consultant, but then when the dealer has achieved a milestone, it is reimbursed by Toyota.

One of the best examples I have seen of developing a comprehensive lean dealer system was outside Toyota in Volvo Sales and Service. Einar Gudmundsson was the vice president for sales and service globally and read *The Toyota Way to Lean Leadership*. Gudmundsson decided to go all in, starting with developing himself with a top-notch external coach. He never let up from there. He developed an obeya to plan the year, the month, and the day and met with his staff daily to review progress. This visual daily management spread through all functions, and sales of vehicles, accessories, and service parts increased.

One area the company deep-dived in was the redesign of dealerships. The starting point was the customer experience. Customers buy a vehicle once, but then they repeatedly go back to the dealership for tire rotation, scheduled service, and repairs. Volvo pays for any warranty work, but after the warranty period is up, customers can go to other repair shops, which means they possibly lose the connection to the vehicle manufacturer.

The Volvo team used its own form of value stream mapping to display the journey of a customer bringing a car in for service (see Figure 11.1), and it was far from excellent. First, you called and described the problem and scheduled an appointment with a booking clerk. Then you braced yourself for a long day, drove into the dealership, and checked in (and probably needed to repeat what you told the booking clerk on the phone). Next, if you didn't have a ride, you likely sat in a waiting area for much of the day. At some point, you learned that the dealer did not have the parts needed for your car but they would be in the very next morning. So you drove your vehicle home and brought it back the next day or perhaps left it at the dealership. Finally, the vehicle was serviced, and you were asked to go to a separate part of the dealer to pay the bill.

---

* An explanation of the Toyota way philosophy for sales and service dealers can be found in Jeffrey Liker and Karyn Ross, *The Toyota Way to Service Excellence* (New York: McGraw-Hill, 2016).

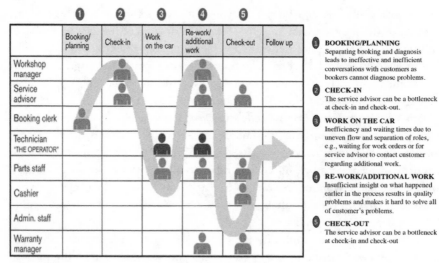

Figure 11.1   Customer value chain in a traditional Volvo auto repair workshop.
Source: Volvo.

Volvo rethought everything from the customer viewpoint. What would be ideal? The answer: the vehicle is repaired and ready to go in one hour, and you only deal with one person from your first explanation of the problem through paying and driving off (see Figure 11.2).

	Booking/ planning	Check-in	Work on the car	Re-work/ additional work	Check-out	Follow-up
Workshop manager						👤
Service advisor						
Team/Andon						👤
Booking clerk						
Technician "THE OPERATOR"	👤	👤	👤		👤	👤
Parts staff	👤					
Cashier						
Admin. staff						
Warranty manager						

Figure 11.2   Lean customer value chain in one-hour-stop Volvo auto repair workshop.
Source: Volvo.

After a good deal of experimenting and learning, Volvo redesigned the customer experience. Rather than calling in to a clerk, the customer directly calls a technician—assigned to the customer when the car was purchased—who understands the issues, asks diagnostic questions, and schedules the appointment. If the technician suspects you need parts, he or she calls the service parts warehouse and orders them, where they are put on trays organized by type of service or repair. The trays arrive in time for the repair and are put on carts on wheels, along with needed tools. You check in and talk to the technician and may choose to wait in a well-appointed living room environment with lattes and snacks and a play area for children. Within one hour you get briefed by the technician, pay the technician, and are on your way.

Gudmundsson put together a team of lean leaders who traveled the world to help dealers set up the system. The system had great success, usually more than doubling the throughput of each repair bay, very important in urban centers where there was no room to expand. But Gudmundsson was still not satisfied. Dealers picked and chose what to implement and only got a portion of the potential benefits of the system. When he got an opportunity to become CEO of a business with two Volvo dealerships in Halmstad, Sweden, he decided to leave Volvo for that job in order to introduce the whole system and use it as a teaching laboratory for Volvo and other dealerships.

Behind the scenes (through large windows visible to customers), the repair area is organized like a set of cells run by Toyota work groups. When Gudmundsson first took over, one technician was assigned to each bay. The technician spent more time walking around and around the vehicle than repairing. Experiments showed that two technicians, one on each side of the vehicle, were more than twice as productive . . . if they followed standardized work and communicated effectively. The technicians are supported by a team leader who schedules, tracks, and responds to andon calls.

The team leader is aided by a "pulse board" to visually plan the day and respond to deviations (see Figure 11.3). Across the top of the pulse board are the names of the pairs of technicians, and underneath are their appointments and how long each job is predicted to take. Color-coded magnets display the status of the job, such as whether the customer is waiting or leaving the car, whether the car is new or used, or whether there are special problems that need investigating. Time between customers is also scheduled for things like training, 5S, and planning. The times can be predicted and achieved because standardized work was developed for common types of service and repairs.

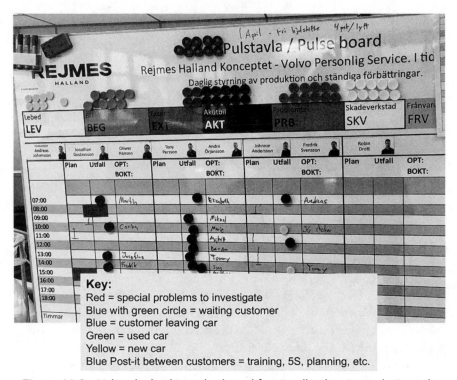

Figure 11.3   Volvo dealership pulse board for visually planning a day's work.
Source: Volvo dealer.

Lean management is used throughout the dealership including visual planning and daily stand-up meetings for salespeople. When Gudmundsson first took over the dealership was in a shambles, losing money with among the worst customer satisfaction scores among Volvo dealers in Sweden. Within a few years it became one of the most profitable with the highest customer satisfaction scores of any Volvo dealership in Sweden. As Gudmundsson hoped, his shop became a destination for dealers from around the world to learn. It holds training classes, and he has continued to advance the understanding of lean dealerships.

BEYOND SUPPLIERS, TOYOTA SEEKS HARMONY AND MUTUAL LEARNING WITH SERVICE PROVIDERS AND IN THE COMMUNITY

If you have bought a house, you probably signed a zillion documents at closing, trusting and hoping that they were all standard documents and none would come back to haunt you. Perhaps your lawyer reviewed the documents and told you that everything was in order, and you faithfully signed each document. This seems like a natural way of doing business in most companies, but not if you are following the Toyota Way.

Richard Mallery was engaged by Toyota in 1989 as its lawyer to help acquire 12,000 acres just northwest of Phoenix. Today, it is the Toyota Arizona Proving Ground, where vehicles are driven on test tracks and evaluated. The acreage comprised the northern one-fourth of the Douglas Ranch. Mallery has handled much larger transactions, and from his perspective, the acquisition was routine. But he had not worked for a client like Toyota. As Mallery explained:

> *I came away with a far more complete knowledge of the legal history of Arizona and the development of its statutory and common law than I ever had before* (laughing), *because I had to answer all of the Toyota team's questions. I could not just point to the title policy and say either, "That is how we have always done it" or "Do not worry; the seller will indemnify us." To answer all of their questions, I became a student again and learned a lot about the federal system that established Arizona first as a territory and then as a state.*

Toyota wanted to know how the seller acquired title and how the title traced back to the original owner, the federal government. After supporting Toyota for 14 years, Mallery concluded, "Toyota stands out as the preeminent analyst of strategy and tactics. Nothing is assumed. Everything is verified. The goal is getting it right."

Richard Mallery had another profound learning experience in 2002. Toyota became aware that a planned mega-housing development near its Arizona Proving Ground threatened the long-term water supply of the entire surrounding area. Toyota took legal action to stop the developers and worked to get a citizens' committee organized to protest the plan. But instead of taking an adversarial approach, Toyota tried to get consensus from all the parties involved—the developer, the surrounding towns, and their local governments. And they all searched for a solution to benefit everyone. Ultimately, the developers agreed to set aside 200 acres and pay several million dollars in infrastructure costs to create a groundwater replenishment site. Basically, for every gallon of water they used, they would purchase a gallon to replace it in the aquifer. As Mallery, who led the consensus-building process, explained:

> *The Mayor, the developers, and the citizens' committee—all of the contending parties agreed that Toyota had served each of them well and had satisfied all of the parties from each of their perspectives. The town ended up with a more responsible, long-term solution to groundwater subsidence concerns,*

the problem was solved for the developers, who would have had to address it eventually—maybe 30 years from now. It is the what and the how that makes the difference—protecting the land for the next 50–100 years, not just for the short term.

Now let's translate this consensus-building behavior into a company's day-to-day business. Inside most companies, everyone is expected to be on the same team. There does not seem to be a reason to act in an adversarial way. Yet the most common problem I hear in large corporations is the "silo" phenomenon. Many different groups are in their own silos and seem to care more about their own objectives than about the company's success. These groups could be functional departments like purchasing, accounting, engineering, and manufacturing, or they could be project teams that are implementing new software or even implementing lean manufacturing. The groups often seem to act as though they want their particular department or project to get all the resources and that their perspective should dominate decision-making. Sometimes, it appears they want to win at all costs, even if other groups lose in the process.

Not so in Toyota. The same process used to gain consensus with these outside community groups in Arizona is used every day to get input, involvement, and agreement from a broad cross-section of the organization. This does not mean all parties get what they personally want, but they will get a fair hearing.

DEVELOPING AN EXTENDED-LEARNING ENTERPRISE MEANS ENABLING OTHERS

While musing over American Auto's debacle with suppliers and wondering why it wanted to take an elevator to the top without stopping at any of the floors in between, I began to conceptualize the problem as a pyramid or hierarchy. Thinking back to college social psychology, I thought of Maslow's needs hierarchy, which assumes humans can work on higher-level needs like self-actualization (developing themselves) only if lower-level needs like food and shelter are satisfied. So I developed a value chain needs hierarchy that can extend up and down the value stream (see Figure 11.4).[9]

The message suppliers were desperately trying to get to American Auto was that they were not interested in supplier development help until more fundamental issues were addressed. As a starting point, they wanted fair and equitable commercial relations. A lot of American Auto's practices were simply unfair. For example, American Auto had adopted the Toyota practice of target pricing, setting targets for suppliers instead of relying on competitive bidding, but they had not executed it effectively. One supplier explained:

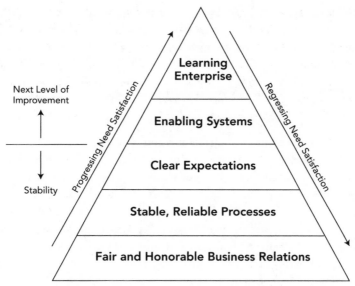

Figure 11.4   Value chain needs hierarchy.

We have gone through a different target cost process for every group we deal with [in American Auto]. If you are above target, they cannot issue a purchase order. We have gone around and around and reached launch without a purchase order.

American Auto also developed a long and complex process of certifying that a supplier's process is capable from a quality perspective. Although it was burdensome, suppliers accepted it—but American Auto kept changing it. In fact, it changed it multiple times during a new vehicle program, and every time it extended out the supplier certification process. Until they were certified, suppliers did not get reimbursed for investments in production tooling, even when they were already in production supplying parts that met American Auto's quality standards.

This comes back to the concept of "coercive" versus "enabling" bureaucracy discussed in the Preface. Both American Auto and Toyota are very bureaucratic in their dealings with suppliers. By this, I mean there are extensive standards, auditing procedures, rules, and the like. While suppliers view American Auto as highly coercive, they rarely view Toyota that way. Even though Toyota uses similar quality methods and procedures, its bureaucracy is generally viewed favorably as enabling. For example, an American automotive interior supplier described working with Toyota in this way:

When it comes to fixing problems, Toyota does not come in and run detailed process capability studies 15 times like American Auto. They just say, "Take a bit of material off here and there and that will be OK—let's go." In 11 years, I have never built a prototype tool for Toyota. Knee bolsters, floor panels, instrument panels, etc. are so similar to the last one it is not necessary to build a prototype. When there is a problem, they look at the problem and come up with a solution—focus on making it better, not placing blame.

Beyond their customers using fair and honorable business practices, suppliers need their customers to have their own processes in order. This starts with stable, reliable processes—including what is often the elephant in the room, heijunka—discussed under Principle 4. If the customer is not level, the supplier is constantly being jerked around and cannot have strong lean systems. The supplier has little choice but to build a wall of inventory to ship whatever product the customer happens to request, while replenishing it through internal pull systems. One supplier showed me a huge amount of inventory for one unleveled customer, calling it the customer's "wall of shame."

The value chain needs hierarchy in Figure 11.4 suggests that until the relationship has stabilized to the point where the business relationship is fair, processes are stable, and expectations are clear, it is impossible to get to the higher levels of enabling systems and truly learning together as an enterprise. The same principles apply to the sales side of dealer networks. I do not know how many times I have heard dealers of American automakers complain that sales were sluggish for particular vehicles but that they were forced to buy more of those vehicles anyway to make the sales numbers for the automakers look good. They felt more pressure than help from the automakers and did not feel the automakers were even capable of helping. Programs by American automakers to give their dealers some sort of rewards, like a star ranking, were viewed by dealers as another form of external pressure without any support. By contrast, Toyota regularly has people coming to the dealers who can actually help. These people provide exceptional local marketing data and offer programs to truly help the dealers learn lean methods, and in a crisis, they will even financially support their dealers.

Toyota Way Principle 11 is "Respect your value chain partners by challenging them and helping them improve." What really cements Toyota as the model for value stream management is its approach to learning and growing together with its partners. It has achieved, in my view, something unique: an extended learning enterprise. This is, to me, the highest form of the lean enterprise.

KEY POINTS

- Toyota carries respect for people and continuous improvement to the value chain, challenging and developing its key outside partners.
- From the customer's perspective, it is a Toyota vehicle, and so all supplied parts have to be of the same quality of design and function as Toyota parts. Similarly, independent dealers are still viewed as Toyota by consumers, and they must reflect the Toyota brand.
- Toyota challenges suppliers with perfect delivery of parts and aggressive cost targets.
- The first-tier suppliers of large component systems are engaged early in the cycle to design in components, collaborating with Toyota engineers and working toward the same aggressive targets of cost, quality, weight, and functionality.
- Toyota has a variety of ways to develop suppliers, including regional supplier associations; direct support from knowledgeable professionals in purchasing, quality, and manufacturing; and model-line projects coached by master TPS trainers.
- Despite the pressure of Toyota challenges and high standards, suppliers typically rate Toyota the most trusted and respected customer.
- Toyota carefully selects new suppliers with small bits of business, building over a period of years to full partnership, and rarely "fires" a supplier.
- Toyota extends respect and challenge throughout the value chain including to dealers who are the direct point of contact to customers.
- The foundation of strong supplier relationships starts with their customer's fair and honorable business practices and stable, reliable processes.
- The ultimate goal is to build a stable learning enterprise across the value chain.

Notes

1. https://www.plantemoran.com/get-to-know/news/2019/06/working-relations-study -shows-uphill-road-for-oems.
2. T. Nishiguchi and A. Beaudet, "The Toyota Group and the Aisin Fire," *Sloan Management Review*, Fall 1998, vol. 40, no. 1.
3. Hideshi Itazaki, *The Prius That Shook the World: How Toyota Developed the World's First Mass-Production Hybrid Vehicle* (Tokyo, Japan: The Nikkan Kogyo Shimbun, LTD, 1999).

4. IHideshi Itazaki, *The Prius That Shook the World: How Toyota Developed the World's First Mass-Production Hybrid Vehicle*.
5. Jeffrey Dyer and Nile Hatch, "Using Supplier Networks to Learn Faster," *Sloan Management Review*, Spring vol. 45, no. 3, 2004.
6. https://www.tssc.com/projects/nfp-fbny.php.
7. Jeffrey Liker and Yen-Chun Wu, "Japanese Automakers, U.S. Suppliers, and Supply-Chain Superiority," *Sloan Management Review*, 2000, vol. 41, no. 2.
8. Jeffrey Dyer and Nile Hatch, "Relation-Specific Capabilities and Barriers to Knowledge Transfers: Creating Advantage through Network Relationships," *Strategic Management Journal*, vol. 27, no. 8, August 2006, pp. 701–719.
9. Jeffrey Liker and Thomas Choi, "Building Deep Supplier Relationships," *Harvard Business Review*, December 2004, pp. 104–113.

PART FOUR

PROBLEM SOLVING

*Think and Act Scientifically to Improve
Toward a Desired Future*

IV. Problem Solving
12. Observe Deeply
and Learn
Iteratively (PDCA)
13. Align Goals
14. Bold Strategy,
Large Leaps,
and Small Steps

Principle 12

Observe Deeply and Learn Iteratively (PDCA) to Meet Each Challenge

During the testing of the 200 looms (to test if they would work in real world operating conditions) I came out with various suggestions, and [Father] tried every single one of them. Humans come up with a surprising number of useless ideas; when you actually try them out, the ones you thought were good ideas sometimes prove to be unexpectedly useless, and the ones you thought were bad ideas sometimes turn out to be unexpectedly good. This is the principle that practice is number one. In a discussion about a certain thing with my father, I won the discussion. The conclusion to be drawn from our discussion was that it was not worth trying it out. But Father said, "Anyway, let's give it a try," so I tried it. Contrary to what I had expected, the thing worked well. From that time on, I stopped putting discussion first.[1]
—Kiichiro Toyoda, Toyota Motor Company founder

The beginning of the twenty-first century has continued the turbulence, uncertainty, and intense competition that marked the end of the twentieth century. Long gone are the days when a company could set up shop, make a product or offer a service well, and then milk that product for years, hanging on to its original competitive advantage. Adaptation, innovation, and flexibility have knocked this old business approach off its pedestal and have become necessary ingredients for survival as well as the hallmarks of a successful business. Even nonprofits and charitable organizations must compete for resources to stay afloat. To sustain such organizational behavior requires an essential attribute: the ability to learn. In fact, the highest compliment we can pay to any organization in today's business environment is that it is a true "learning organization."

Peter Senge popularized this concept in his book *The Fifth Discipline*, in 1990, defining a learning organization as:[2]

a place where people continually expand their capacity to create the results they truly desire, where new and expansive patterns of thinking are nurtured, where collective aspiration is set free, and where people are continually learning how to learn together.

Senge focused on "expansive patterns of thinking," with systems thinking at the very top, and learning to learn. In other words, a learning organization not only adopts and develops new business or technical skills, it evolves a second level of learning—*how to learn* new skills, knowledge, and capabilities. To become a true learning organization, the very learning capacity of the organization should be developing and growing over time, as it helps its members adapt to a continually changing competitive environment.

Of all the institutions I've studied or worked for, including world-class companies and major universities, I believe Toyota is among the closest to Senge's learning organization. Toyota did not read about systems thinking in Senge's book on the "fifth discipline." Nor did Toyota offer seminars on how to be a learning organization. Toyota did it the hard way—years and decades of practice developing the mindset of scientific thinking and learning, one person at a time. Toyota recognized that learning organizations are built on learning individuals, and individuals need to develop the mindset through repeated practice, with a coach. Taiichi Ohno was the consummate coach, training his students to observe, try, reflect, and learn. The greatest sin under Ohno was to take things for granted and assume you know—"Back to the gemba!" he would shout.

LEARNING TO DELIBERATELY WORK TOWARD BIG CHALLENGES*

Steven Spear had a unique opportunity to experience firsthand the Ohno way of teaching and developing people as part of his doctoral research. He traveled with the Toyota Production System Support Center and met and interviewed many people, including Dallis (pseudonym), who was hired from outside to be a manager in the plant in Georgetown, Kentucky. This bright, young manager with two master's degrees in engineering already believed he understood TPS, but even so, his orientation in Toyota started with going to the gemba to learn the Toyota approach to kaizen.

His Japanese mentor (code named Takahashi) asked him to help a group of 19 team members at the Georgetown engine plant assembly line to improve labor productivity, operational availability, and ergonomic safety. For six weeks,

---

* This section is summarized from Steven J. Spear, "Learning to Lead at Toyota," *Harvard Business Review*, May 2004, pp. 1–9.

he was asked to perform short cycles of observing and changing work processes, over and over. He worked with the group leader, team leaders, and team members and identified small problems, made changes, evaluated the changes, rinse and repeat. On Mondays, Dallis regularly met with his mentor, who would ask him to explain what he observed about work processes, what he thought the problems were, what changes he and others had introduced, and what was the expected impact of his recommendations. On Fridays, the mentor reviewed what Dallis had done during the week, comparing *expectations* with *results*. (We will see this pattern again later in the chapter on Toyota Kata).

In six weeks, 25 changes were made to individual processes along with 75 recommendations for redistributing the work that required a larger reconfiguration of the equipment, which was done over a weekend. In week six, Dallis and his mentor reviewed the changes and their impact. The results were impressive, including reducing the number of people needed to do the work from 19 to 15 team members.

After Dallis focused on team member work, his mentor had him do the same thing for six weeks focusing on machine work, with a target of reaching 95 percent operational availability (runs as designed 95 percent of the planned run time). Dallis managed to achieve 90 percent, an accomplishment but still below target.

By now Dallis had studied more intensively than he could have imagined, but the training was not done. He was shipped to Japan to do similar work in Toyota's famous Kamiga engine plant. Spear explains:

After 12 weeks at the US engine plant, Takahashi judged that Dallis had made progress in observing people and machines and in structuring counter-measures as experiments to be tested. However, Takahashi was concerned that Dallis still took too much of the burden on himself for making changes and that the rate at which he was able to test and refine improvements was slow. He decided it was time to show Dallis how Toyota practiced improvements on its home turf.

Dallis was assigned an area for three days with the target of making 50 changes (or 1 change every 22 minutes). In the first shift, Dallis, with help from a Japanese member of the production cell, generated seven ideas, of which four were implemented. He then was humbled to learn that two lower-ranking Japanese team leaders were also going through this training and had generated 28 and 21 change ideas, respectively, in the same shift. Dallis picked up the pace and kept working and learning, with great results.

Still not done, Dallis was sent back to the American engine plant to try to close the gap on the operational availability. Why did he get to 90 percent and not 95 percent? What was he missing? He continued the relentless kaizen he had been trained in and achieved 99 percent. More important, Dallis's image of his role as a leader and problem solver and his respect for the work group had changed dramatically. Spear reflected on Dallis's life-changing experience and what he learned:

Lesson 1: There is no substitute for direct observation.
Lesson 2: Proposed changes should always be structured as experiments.
Lesson 3: Workers and managers experiment as frequently as possible.
Lesson 4: Managers should coach, not fix.

Lessons 1–3 all acknowledge that we don't fully understand the problems or solutions and have to go and find out. In fact, managers cannot sit in meetings or in front of a computer and do any of the four. All require time at the gemba observing, testing ideas, and collaborating with people at the front line.

UNDERSTANDING THE CURRENT CONDITION— ASK WHY FIVE TIMES

Toyota's famous five-why analysis has become almost synonymous with how Toyota solves problems, but it is misunderstood. Taiichi Ohno emphasized that true problem solving requires identifying "'root cause' rather than 'source'; the root cause lies hidden beyond the source." For example, a simple five-why example often used as a teaching case in Toyota starts with an oil spill on the floor. You could simply clean it up, but without your solving the root cause of the problem, it is likely to keep returning. As you dig down through successive whys, you get deeper and deeper into the cause until you discover that without changing how purchasing agents are evaluated, you will keep having similar problems (see Figure 12.1). Asking five whys does not give you a deterministic right answer. Even in this seemingly simple case of the oil change, one might argue that after we agree the gasket has deteriorated, we might have asked why the design allowed this to happen, which could lead to thoughts of redesigning the part and perhaps eliminating the gasket. What I think is most important is that the answers to why are grounded in deep observation and even trying some experiments, rather than abstract understanding. Ohno disciple Nampachi Hayashi emphasizes that to get to the root cause, we must go the gemba: "Use your feet to investigate processes and not your computer; use your hands to draw the flow."[3]

A life-and-death example* of the importance of going to the gemba to understand the actual cause revolves around a problem that arose in 2013 at a Midwest US pediatrics hospital. The presenting problem was three blue babies, meaning

---

* As conveyed to me by Edward Blackman who led continuous improvement for this healthcare provider.

Level of a Problem	Corresponding Level of Countermeasure
There is a puddle of oil on the shop floor	Clean up the oil
Because the machine is leaking oil	Fix the machine
Because the gasket has deteriorated	Replace the gasket
Because we bought gaskets made of inferior material	Change gasket specifications
Because we got a good deal (price) on those gaskets	Change purchasing policies
Because the purchasing agent gets evaluated on short-term cost savings	Change the evaluation policy for purchasing agents

why why why why why why

Figure 12.1 "Five whys" cause investigation questions.
Source: Peter Scholtes, *The Leader's Handbook* (Toyota Motor Company).

they stopped breathing and turned blue. Sensors were attached to the babies, and there was an elaborate signaling system run by computer. When a signal indicated a problem, the expected response time was 30 seconds, but the average was an alarming 150 seconds. This was a crisis—heads would roll; serious changes needed to be made. It was serious enough to rise to the attention of the president of the hospital, who convened a group of 30 subject-matter experts to fix the problem.

The team set aside four hours to discuss this serious issue. Unfortunately, the members of the team began with a conclusion in mind: "We need a new computer system to fix the problem." Their main rationale was "our clinicians were highly trained and good people. They would not intentionally harm babies." Therefore, the fault must rest with the computer system. The estimated cost for the new computer system was a hefty $5 million. Nonetheless, they felt certain they knew the root cause and this was the necessary solution, and they were angry at the existing IT vendor for doing this to them. At that point, expecting the group to ask the five whys would have quickly devolved into the five whos, getting them even angrier as they identified more and more people to blame.

Edward Blackman, who headed up continuous improvement for IT, had been asked to the meeting. He was pretty certain he was invited just to rubber-stamp the team's conclusion, but he could not stand by idly and let the hospital spend millions of dollars on computer technology that might not even solve the problem. He had to find a way to get this powerful group to reopen the investigation of the causes of the problem, and he had always learned important things by going to the gemba. What he did not want to do was to go off on his own and investigate and then have to report back to the team members that they were wrong—which would almost certainly lead to defensive reactions. Instead, he respectfully asked them if they would be willing to go to the gemba to investigate the problem further. The actual clinic was just a walk upstairs, so they agreed as long as it was quick. They had plenty of time since the meeting had been scheduled for four hours, and they had spent less than an hour getting to what they were sure was the root cause and solution.

Before beginning to study the gemba, Blackman gathered key stakeholders, including the director of the wing, nursing managers, nurses, IT analysts, quality coordinators, technicians, and administrative assistants, and spent 10 minutes in a conference room discussing what was really going on. The driving question was "What is actually happening?," not just what should be happening according to procedure. It was clear that nobody really knew, so they hit the gemba and proceeded to investigate for two hours. They interviewed people responsible for the process, they videotaped and timed responses, they played the roles of patients and responding clinicians, and they value-stream mapped the current-state process.

A picture started to emerge, and it became clear to all that the problem had little to do with a bad computer system. It was an issue of how the existing software was set up and how people, including patients' families, were trained. The map of the floor in Figure 12.2 gives a picture of what was happening. On one side of the oval-shaped floor are the patient rooms for babies. In the center of the oval, out of the line of sight and sound of the patient rooms, is the registration desk, where the alert messages were received.

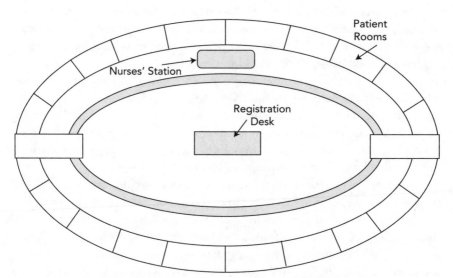

Figure 12.2   Hospital floor layout for babies.

When the group went to talk to the administrative assistant at the desk, Edward asked to do the questioning, as he did not want a bunch of high-powered people intimidating her and casting blame. He asked what happened when she received an alert. The answer: "I turn it off." The crowd was getting restless. He calmly asked why. Answer: "Because they are always false alarms." The murmuring of the crowd grew louder. Edward asked how she knew that. Answer: "When there is an alert, I am supposed to get a voice follow-up. If there is no voice follow-up, I assume it is a false alarm. The parents can signal for help or I can get an automated signal from sensors on the babies detecting a breathing problem. The babies roll around all the time and trigger the sensors stuck onto them, causing mainly false alarms" (see the process flow in Figure 12.3). The crowd started questioning whether they really understood what was going on and were now more open to investigation.

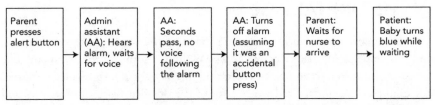

Figure 12.3   Current process for parents alerting of blue baby to get action.

There were other discoveries. For example, purchasing had ordered the wrong sensors, ones designed for adults, which were less sticky than the version for highly active babies. When they came off the baby, they would automatically trigger. In addition, the sensors were supposed to be changed out every 12 hours, but there was no way of telling if the 12 hours had passed and the sensors were expired. There were multiple colored lights outside each patient room to alert responders to what was happening in the room, but nobody seemed to know what they all meant.

Two short-term changes with the biggest impact were made that same day: (1) The administrative assistant could no longer remotely turn off alarms; only a clinician in the patient room could turn off an alarm. (2) All parents/guardians of children were trained in how to use the manual bedside alarm along with instructions posted bedside.

Longer term, other inexpensive changes were made to engineer and pilot a new process, like simplifying the light system and getting proper sensors for the babies, but none involved buying a new computer system. Results: post-intervention response time went down from 150 seconds to 20 seconds (better than target), and no babies turned blue. In addition, some of the changes were then introduced in other areas of the hospital that were experiencing similar problems.

What is the lesson from this case? It was clear that very intelligent and well-meaning people sat in a conference room and dreamed up a nonexistent scenario with no real evidence. At this point asking why five times would not have moved their knowledge threshold forward and gotten them closer to real understanding.* They had to seek answers to why based on real facts and data, which required going to the gemba.

Ohno admonished his students to "observe the production floor without preconceptions and with a blank mind. Repeat why five times to every matter." The real lesson was not to ask why a specific number of times, but to get facts and somehow wipe away preconceptions of both what is happening and what we assume is the solution.

GENCHI GENBUTSU AND THE FIVE WHYS IN THE DIGITAL AGE

Let's consider how new technologies are changing the way we approach learning and problem solving. In Principle 8, we saw how a sophisticated company like Denso is using IoT to enhance people thinking deeply, not to replace thinking. For example, in standardized work, a lot of the detailed work of observing and recording data can be done with Drishta's intelligent computer systems. Data are collected in real time and can be cataloged and analyzed by AI. People can call up videos and see what happened at a specific point. That allows them to focus on improvement, but it does not let them off the hook on going to the gemba. Armed with the information from the computer systems, people can arguably be more intentional about what they look for at the gemba.

As part of the annual financial results presentation on May 12, 2020, Akio Toyoda was asked what he wants to protect in this time of once-in-a-century transformation of the mobility industry. He replied:

> We have a "genba" or frontline where work gets done. That genba is real, and what we have been able to cultivate in our genba over these many years is something that no digitization or telework system, no matter how advanced they become, can ever replace in the real world. It is the real world where people have work to do, doing the work only people can, and where Toyota people capable of further kaizen or improvement are trained. With this ability to improve, I would like to make Toyota into a company that all people can have high expectations from into the future.

---

* Some people harshly refer to trying to solve a problem by talking and not actually moving one's knowledge threshold as "breathing our own exhaust."

However, he did qualify that in the digital age some aspects of genchi genbutsu have to be rethought based in part on his experience with online tools in the Covid-19 crisis. For example, he noted that he has found some benefits to virtual meetings:

> *[By staying in Toyota City], I have reduced 80% of my travel time, also 85% the number of people I meet, 30% of time in meetings and 50% of the documents that were prepared for meetings.*

He further explained:

> *For Toyota's "genchi genbutsu" philosophy, going to the actual site, looking at the actual goods, I believe that we have to make a clear definition of this once again. Up to now, we placed importance on, first of all, going to the actual site, go to the "genchi," and it was done as a matter of course. Even if we look at products, we will always have to look at the actual product and place it in front of our own eyes. No one questioned this philosophy up to now. But in the past month, we have been looking at products more through images on monitors. I think at certain stages, it is fine to see the product on the monitor but there will always be times that you will have to see the actual product. Some things can only be felt when you are at the gemba. So, for those kinds of things where you need to feel the actual products, the actual people, then that should be done at the actual site. I think we should not just say we do "genchi genbutsu" everywhere, but we need to clarify under what conditions it is necessary to actually go see.*

I do not believe Akio Toyoda abandoned understanding the current condition in detail. I discussed this with former Toyota manager John Shook, who aptly pointed out the difference between the principles and the specific methods for gathering information and analyzing it:

> *I believe Akio Toyoda is talking about getting back to purpose, not only in terms of being selective about when to literally go and see, but clarifying the purpose of going to see. Genchi genbutsu (or the shortened "genba") means grasping the real situation. How you get facts and grasp the situation is actually secondary. It doesn't mean you must always literally go and see. It means confirm what's really happening. Same with genba's matched pair of the five whys. The point is not to literally ask why 5 times; it means pursue understanding of causality. As for how to understand reality, use the simplest means possible, starting with the five whys. When you need more than simply asking why a few times, pull out your more sophisticated tools. Together genchi gembutsu and five whys, defined as confirm what's really going on with any situation and understand the causes of it, must surely remain foundational.*

Once again, we see a distinction between the tools and the way of thinking. The tools, in this case digital tools, can be blunt instruments if the human using the information is not thinking scientifically and solving real problems, or the tools can be fantastic enablers when coupled with critical thinking and experimentation. We saw in the case of the blue babies how computer systems were first thought of as the problem and solution, which actually could have prevented uncovering the actual causes and solving the problem.

WHEN FEASIBLE, GO BACK TO FIRST PRINCIPLES OF SCIENCE

When Charlie Baker was in Honda R&D, he also learned about problem solving.[4] He brought that model with him when he left for other companies—but with one critical difference. The problem-solving steps were similar, except in place of "Find the root cause" was "Understand the physics." For many of the physical hardware problems that engineers face in the automotive industry, there are opportunities to ask why in a deep technical sense. The root cause is often some known physical phenomenon. Medical doctors, engineers, and physicists draw on hundreds of years of study to identify the root cause for a given case.

When Baker left Honda to become VP of automotive seat engineering for Johnson Controls (JCI), he brought this thinking with him. Often, this did not lead to a complex mathematical model, but rather a trade-off curve; for example, as you use more of this, you increase the cost according to this curve. When it came to meeting a challenge to reduce costs for making seats, he started with first principles. What are the raw components of seats, and how much does each component cost for our competitor to make? After looking at those data, he looked at the gap between the lowest cost competitor and the JCI cost for each component. He then created a "Frankenstein" model of a seat. Theoretically, if JCI used all of the lowest-cost components, it could build a seat for about half of what it cost the company at the time. This might not be feasible since these components may not work together, so Baker set the challenge to a design team at a 30 percent cost reduction. Going a step further, Baker worked with finance to develop cost models. What in the manufacturing process influenced the cost of a component? Then reversing the logic, what would the manufacturing process need to look like to achieve the best-practice cost targets? The design team achieved the 30 percent cost-reduction target through creative product and process engineering.

I found it interesting that Elon Musk was using the same type of first-principle logic for his breakthrough engineering of electric car components. "What are the physics of it? How much time will it take? How much will it cost?"[5] For example, batteries are one of the biggest costs of an electric car and one of the key constraints is having enough battery power for the desired range. Musk became impatient with generic talk about what batteries cost from vendors and pushed his engineers to go back to first principles. When they broke the battery down to its raw materials, they concluded they ought to be able to build one at about half the cost of purchasing one and could control the supply of the huge numbers of batteries they would need—leading to the huge gamble of building Tesla's famous battery Gigafactory 1.

WHAT ARE OBSTACLES TO SCIENTIFIC THINKING, AND HOW DO WE OVERCOME THEM?

I have not found it difficult to convince executives and managers that scientific thinking is a good thing. "Management by fact," as preached by Dr. Deming, is widely accepted and easily embraced. But what this ends up meaning in the context of a high-control organization is "get the data on key performance indicators and hold people accountable for results."[6] Accountable means extrinsic motivation—tie results to rewards and punishment—get on the bus or off the bus.

What Toyota is doing is something different—developing in people a way of thinking to clearly understand the direction; go and see and ask why to deeply understand the current condition; and experiment and learn on your way to the goal. This can be thought of as "practical scientific thinking" and fits the model of the improvement kata that is explained later in the chapter. In a sense, we can view the practice of coaching people to think scientifically as a countermeasure to our natural inclination to jump to conclusions, assume we know, and commit to solutions before we have evidence that they work.

Our neurological apparatus was formed over millions of years through an evolutionary process of survival of the fittest. Some researchers suggest that evolution may have started with the reptile brain that has basic life preservation functions like breathing, eating, procreating, and the the fight, flight, or freeze survival responses. Then evolving on top of that was the mammal brain and the limbic system, where memories and emotions live—pleasure, pain, fear, defensiveness, and seeking safety. These emotions tend to be reflexive and do not lead to well-thought-out plans. Finally, the neocortex is the distinctively human part of the brain, where we evolved language, self-consciousness, abstract thought, a sense of time, reasoning, and the ability to imagine things.

For most of the time period that the human brain evolved, survival meant gathering food, fighting off human and animal predators, and procreating to spread our genes. Deep reflection and "scientific thinking" did not ensure survival and the spreading of genes as well as quick reactions and physical prowess. It is therefore not surprising that cognitive psychologist and Nobel Prize winner Daniel Kahneman found in humans a natural tendency toward "fast thinking." Slow thinking, he found, comes much less naturally and can even feel painful.[7] Those who succeeded in passing on genes had brains that discouraged slow thinking, punishing them with pain for thinking too deeply. Kahneman suggests the useful simplification of thinking of the brain as having two systems operating in parallel:

- "System 1" (FAST) thinking is *intuitive thinking*—fast, automatic, and emotional—and based on simple mental rules of thumb ("heuristics") and thinking biases (cognitive biases), that result in impressions, feelings, and inclinations. Fast thinking dislikes uncertainty and wants the "right answer" now.
- "System 2" (SLOW) thinking is *rational thinking*—slow, deliberate, and systematic—and based on considered evaluation that results in logical conclusions. Slow thinking requires concentration and broad consideration of problem definition and possible solutions.

He also introduced the "law of least mental effort," which was a requirement for survival in more primitive times. Slow thinking takes a lot of working memory and is an energy hog. Natural selection did not favor slow thinkers who wasted a lot of energy thinking instead of taking actions needed to survive. So our genetic background produced in us a desire for certainty, *knowing* what will happen and what did happen and why. As Mike Rother put it in the book *Toyota Kata*:[8]

> . . . *humans have a tendency to want certainty, and even to artificially create it, based on beliefs, when there is none. This is a point where we often get into trouble. If we believe the way ahead is set and clear, then we tend to blindly carry out a preconceived implementation plan rather than being sensitive to, learning from, and dealing adequately with what arises along the way.*

This subjects us to a litany of cognitive biases that have been well researched. With confirmation bias we seek information to confirm our predetermined attitudes and beliefs. Hindsight bias is the belief in retrospect that we knew what would happen all along. One of the most potentially damaging for society is the Dunning-Kruger effect where people who are beginners in a particular skill greatly overestimate their ability—when people are low in mastery they tend to think they are at least average or above.[9] This is dangerous because if we assume we are already skilled, there is little incentive to submit ourselves to the struggle of developing skills and understanding. Think of Dallis earlier in the chapter who thought he was already expert at TPS before being subjected by his coach to the harsh realities of solving real problems.

In part, these biases reflect a physiological limitation of our brains. While remarkably we can process 11 million bits of information every second, our conscious minds can only handle 40 or 50 bits of information per second.[10] We are almost forced to simplify to understand the world and act on that oversimplification. Therefore, we naturally develop templates that fill in the gaps. We see someone with certain physical traits in a certain context, then we layer onto this relatively small amount of information we can quickly process a lot of assumptions about their other characteristics. That is the basis for stereotyping people based on such things as race, religion, and gender. See a big, strong man wearing tattered clothes in an isolated alley, and you might assume he is someone violent who is on the hunt to rob or abuse you. See a young woman with a baby, and you may assume you are safe. It was also the basis for those medical staff assuming they knew the cause of the blue babies.

So what are we to do in a day and age where slow, scientific thinking is often more effective for dealing with modern-day complexity than our initial off-the-cuff conclusions? The answer is practice, practice, practice what does not come naturally, to make it more natural. As Toyota grew and globalized, with too many people for the TPS masters to coach, how could this discipline continue to be developed?

TOYOTA BUSINESS PRACTICES TO DEVELOP SCIENTIFIC THINKING

President Fujio Cho led the creation of *The Toyota Way 2001*. While the document laid out Toyota's philosophy and principles, Cho realized that wasn't enough. People needed something to practice, with a coach, to develop the mindset for continuous improvement and learn how to respect and develop people. Within a few years, he introduced Toyota Business Practices (TBP)—which, on the surface, was an eight-step problem-solving process. But Cho did not set out to create a rigid problem-solving method that always has to be followed; rather his intention was to provide a framework for developing Toyota Way thinking through practice on real-world problems:[11]

> *The Toyota Business Practices—a standard approach of business processes and a common language for all of Toyota. Such a standardized approach is not intended to limit an individual's way of conducting business. Rather, the standard approach provides a basic framework from which the individual can express their unique talent.*

The steps of TBP, along with the drive and dedication the coach is trying to instill, are summarized in Figure 12.4. A good TBP project is not intended to fix a nagging issue, but rather to strive in the direction of an aspirational challenge—typically with a target of four to eight months in the future. In the original version of this book, we talked about the seven-step "practical problem-solving" method. The new version of TPS has eight steps, and the largest differences are comparing the current state with the ideal state in step 1 and breaking down this big gap into tractable, smaller subproblems in step 2:*

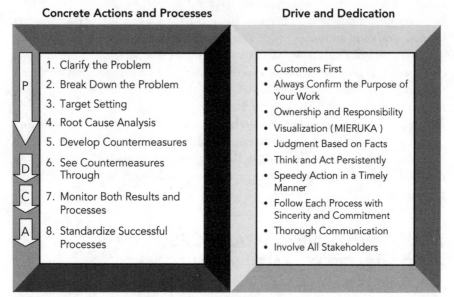

Concrete Actions and Processes   **Drive and Dedication**

P
1. Clarify the Problem
2. Break Down the Problem
3. Target Setting
4. Root Cause Analysis
5. Develop Countermeasures

D
6. See Countermeasures Through

C
7. Monitor Both Results and Processes

A
8. Standardize Successful Processes

- Customers First
- Always Confirm the Purpose of Your Work
- Ownership and Responsibility
- Visualization (MIERUKA)
- Judgment Based on Facts
- Think and Act Persistently
- Speedy Action in a Timely Manner
- Follow Each Process with Sincerity and Commitment
- Thorough Communication
- Involve All Stakeholders

Figure 12.4 Toyota Business Practices—Toyota's kata for people development.
Source: The Toyota Business Practices (Toyota Motor Company, 2005).

1. **Clarify the problem.** This starts with a big challenge that is appropriate for the person leading the activity and learning TBP. Then, the learner must grasp the current condition. Finally, the learner defines the ideal condition, which is compared with the current condition to visualize the large gap. In this step, there is no root cause analysis because the gap is too large and multifaceted.
2. **Break down the problem (to a set of subproblems).** The gap between the big challenge and the current condition is too large and vague to get started. So the learner goes to the gemba to learn and break down the problem into smaller, more tractable problems—and prioritizes, selecting one to start. Learning to prioritize is important in this step.

---

* Based on *The Toyota Business Practices* booklet, Toyota Motor Company, 2005.

3. **Set a target (for the prioritized subproblem).** According to the booklet, "With enthusiasm and commitment, set challenging targets."

4. **Analyze the root cause (for the prioritized subproblem).** This is not to be done by asking why five times in a conference room. Go to the gemba and thoroughly investigate the process involved, based on actual facts.

5. **Develop countermeasures.** "Broadly consider all stakeholders and risks involved." The learner should think creatively, beyond preconceived ideas or one's own position. It is also critical at this stage to engage key stakeholders and work to build consensus. This is where you get signoffs on your plans.

6. **See countermeasures through (by coordinated and speedy implementation).** This is a collaborative process with those directly affected by the change as well as about informing, reporting, and consulting key stakeholders outside that group.

7. **Monitor both results and processes.** Learn from the success and failure of the countermeasures and the effectiveness of the process you used. Be objective and consider the perspectives of the customer, company, and personal development.

8. **Standardize successful processes.** The learner is not done until these become the new way of operating and the new processes are shared with other people across the company who might benefit.

The term "countermeasure" is an important one at Toyota. You will hear there are no solutions, just countermeasures. These are measures that members hypothesize might help counter (reduce) the gap between the desired condition and the current condition. The measures are tested, and if they help to reduce the gap, they are continued until better ones are developed. Proven countermeasures lead to standards—the best we know today until we set a better, perhaps more challenging, standard.

Even though the problem-solving process as it is laid out in documents appears to be very linear, in practice it is intended to be about iterative learning. In the first pass, the learner breaks down the challenge into subproblems, prioritizes, and then starts with number one. Addressing this first subproblem rarely gets you to the challenge. The learner goes back to review the new current condition and selects the next prioritized subproblem, and so on. As we discuss Toyota kata later in the chapter, we will see similarities to TBP. For example, the subproblem being addressed and its targets are similar to the "target condition."

When Toyota began to use TBP for teaching, it started at the top executive level with senior sensei as coaches. You cannot coach something you have not yourself experienced. The executives, after a career of learning how to problem-solve, humbly followed the process, typically over eight months, for very large issues appropriate for their level. Then, they had to report out to a board of examiners, including Fujio Cho. In about 80 percent of the cases, they were asked to go back and do some more work. Having completed the work, they began to teach their subordinates who worked through TBP projects, acting as coaches and serving on the board of examiners—and this continued to cascade down the company. This mirrors the approach Steven Spear observed, mentioned earlier in this chapter.

The goal of TBP is to develop the management hierarchy into a chain of coaching, so that developing people becomes a core responsibility of managers, and managers do not wait for someone from the staff to do the teaching. I was at a Toyota plant where TBP had finally gotten to the level of group leaders eight years after it was first introduced to senior executives. It is a long-term process at Toyota with proven staying power.

In Figure 12.4, notice the competencies listed under "Drive and Dedication," including "Customers first," "Ownership and responsibility," "Visualization," "Judgment based on facts," "Thorough communication," and "Involve all stakeholders." It is not enough for the learner to execute the eight steps well. The learner should be learning these competencies and demonstrating them to others. The apparent task of the learner is to follow the eight steps and achieve the goal, but there is a deeper, parallel process of developing this set of leadership competencies. The coach (manager) takes advantage of being with the learner who is following the steps to find occasions to provide feedback on all these competencies.

Some keys to effective feedback are to give it immediately after the behavior, focus on the behavior not the person, and do this in a context of true compassion for the person you are coaching. The coach cannot artificially create behaviors in the learner, so the coach must identify them when they occur and immediately provide feedback. That is why it is so important that the manager of the person is the coach and is around the person enough to observe behaviors in real time and provide feedback.

The TBP pattern is something that Toyota leaders should follow for addressing any complex project. It encapsulates a way of thinking that should be learned at a deep level so that it becomes the natural way to approach any problem, large or small. At the Toyota plant in the United Kingdom, taking part in a formal, coached TBP project is done at each level of a person's career as the person is promoted, typically once every three to four years. A person undertaking a TBP is mentored by someone who has passed at least the level the person is aspiring to as "ready to mentor." The report-out is presented as an A3 summary in a strict 15 minutes to a panel of three people, who quiz the person on the document and then pass or fail the person (pass can be "ready to mentor," and fail can be "requires level up").*

---

* Explained to me by Rob Gorton, Corporate Planning & External Affairs, describing what people do at Toyota Motor Manufacturing United Kingdom.

Some years later Toyota developed a third phase of training focused on on-the-job development (OJD), which was designed to develop the coach. The training starts with a few days of classroom training but then is learned by coaching a TPB project. The coach in training picks a subordinate to coach through a TPB project and is coached on how to coach. So you have the learner, the coach in training, and what Toyota kata refers to as the "second coach."

Having started in 2001, the training on the Toyota Way, TPB, and OJD is still going strong in 2020 and has become an institutionalized part of building Toyota culture.

QUALITY CIRCLES TO DEVELOP SCIENTIFIC THINKING IN TEAM MEMBERS

I am often asked how Toyota provides time for production team members to practice kaizen. The short answer is it does not during the workday—at least for the most part. In a sequential build process like an assembly plant, every worker is tied to the line, and if a worker leaves the process, the line will shut down. As we discussed under Principle 10, there are members who have been given the responsibility of a team leader, and there are always team leaders offline, where they have more flexibility to run experiments, collect data, and engage team members. And they can take over performing a job to allow that team member a little time to work on kaizen. But for team members to experience the entire life cycle of problem solving, Toyota uses "quality circles."

Quality circles were introduced in Toyota in the 1960s as part of total quality control, but evolved to addressing any problem—quality, productivity, safety. These are offline activities with meetings generally after hours. Every Toyota plant in the world has an active program, and some service jobs, such as in call centers, also use quality circles. Since Toyota rarely dictates exactly how programs should be run, different plants have different ways of structuring quality circles. In Japan they are "voluntary," though the expectation is that all production team members participate, and for the most part they do. In the US plants, they are voluntary, and participation rates are generally lower than in Japan, perhaps half the members participating at a given point in time.

The United Kingdom plant makes quality circle participation an expectation, and nearly all members are in one. In this case, the circles consist of intact teams. Each circle is led by the team leader, and the members are that person's team. The group leader must agree on the problems selected and coaches the team leader. The members of the circle work on a given problem for six months and thus have two significant problems per year. Section managers and managers regularly check in. Quality circles do not follow the eight-step TPB process. Rather they follow a simplified six-step version with less time spent on problem definition or breaking down the problem, since the problems are relatively straightforward, for example, reducing scratches on painted vehicles.

It is an important developmental experience. As Andy Heaphy, general manager of body manufacturing at TMUK, explained:

> *If we get away from the paper side of it and they start to follow the steps in everyday business, they may solve many more problems. That is what we are after.*

Competition and recognition are fostered by selecting the best projects in each section and providing public recognition. Then each plant selects two of the best projects: One winning team will represent the plant in a regional presentation to the European CEO, and the other will go to Japan and present in a global forum with a senior VP presiding. The winners get awards and an all-expense-paid trip.

In addition to participating in quality circles, some team members are taken offline for a period of two to three years to work on special kaizen activities with managers, and in some cases they are placed on a pilot team to launch new products. This can become a pathway for promotion to team leader and then group leader.

KATA TO HELP DEVELOP THE HABIT OF SCIENTIFIC THINKING: WHAT ARE THE IK AND THE CK?

Toyota has been investing in hands-on development of people since its inception and has many people highly developed as problem solvers and coaches. That is fine, but how can those organizations outside Toyota that have not been doing this for decades get started on the journey of developing a scientific mindset? That is the challenge Mike Rother set out to address. He had written two popular workbooks on lean methods, *Learning to See* (with coauthor John Shook) which introduced value stream mapping and *Creating Continuous Flow* (with coauthor Rick Harris).[12] Mike worked with many organizations to put these ideas into practice, but he wasn't satisfied with the results. He did not want to leave behind just tools or one transformed process, but rather a way of thinking he was beginning to uncover from studying Toyota, as well as a way of practicing that at any gemba. So he went back to the drawing board and began a six-year research project that included testing all findings and ideas at the gemba of five companies that agreed to participate and learn together. There were two research questions:

1. What are the unseen managerial routines and thinking that lie behind Toyota's success with continuous improvement and adaptation?
2. How can other companies develop similar routines and thinking in their organizations?

The first question led to identifying an underlying pattern of thinking that Rother observed, particularly among Toyota sensei and how they taught TPS through model-line projects. We have seen examples throughout this book in the work of TSSC, and we saw it earlier in this chapter in how Dallis was introduced to Toyota leadership by working intensely with guidance from a coach to achieve challenging goals. This pattern led to the improvement kata (IK) model of scientific thinking. The second question led to the conclusion that people change their habitual ways of thinking by deliberately practicing new ways, initially with some simple practice routines, aka kata.

Mike Rother discussed with me how he came upon the idea of using the term "kata." Near the end of his research, he came across a little book about martial arts that highlighted the concept of kata. "Kata" has two meanings: One is the form, or way of doing things.* The second is the pattern of movements to be practiced to develop fundamental skills. Martial arts black belts will teach one kata at the time that the student practices until they can naturally duplicate what they are shown. Rother describes a deep physical and emotional response when he first read about kata because it so remarkably fit what he had come to learn by studying Toyota and was trying to define for a non-Toyota audience. The improvement kata (IK) model represents a practical, everyday way of thinking scientifically, the form, and Rother then developed practice routines, or what he calls "starter kata," for the learner and the coach. The IK is designed to be more fundamental and less complicated—more meta—than specific problem-solving methods like TBP. It represents the underlying pattern of thinking. The IK is not intended to replace problem-solving methods, but to teach a fundamental scientific pattern of thinking with the result that any method will be used in a more effective way.

The model of scientific thinking is represented in Figure 12.5, which is an intuitive visual summary of the desired pattern:†

---

* One translation of "Toyota kata" is "Toyota Way." My former student Mike and I still laugh about this and smile at what has turned out to be an interesting confluence in our investigations around Toyota.

† An intuitive and visual guide is found in Mike Rother, *Toyota Kata Practice Guide* (New York: McGraw-Hill, 2017).

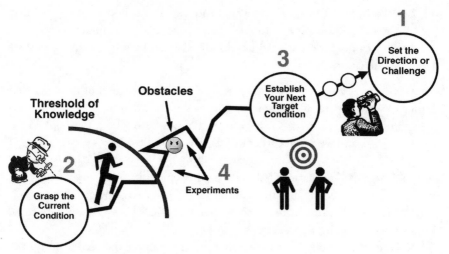

Figure 12.5 The improvement kata pattern.
Source: Mike Rother, *Toyota Kata Practice Guide* (New York: McGraw-Hill, 2017).

1. **Set the direction or challenge.** The challenge, usually set by management, may often seem out of reach, maybe even impossible, and thus forces the learner to break down the problem and learn through shorter-term target conditions. It is typically six months to one year out.
2. **Grasp the current condition.** Where are we now in relation to the challenge? It is useful, but not sufficient, to calculate statistics describing the current condition. Rother recommends a routine, a starter kata, for process analysis that includes understanding the current process steps and making run charts—repeatedly observing the current process pattern and documenting the variation across trials and identifying reasons for the variation.
3. **Establish your next target condition.** Based on the learner's initial grasp of the current condition, the target condition is a shorter-term next goal that is a significant step beyond the current condition on the way to the challenge. It includes a target (outcome metric) and a condition (desired process characteristics, or operating pattern, and a process metric). This is typically one to four weeks out. Shorter is better for novices, as it is easier to envision the condition. Smaller, short-term goals have been shown to be more motivating than big long-term challenges, and the beginner learner gets more repetitions of the entire improvement kata cycle. *Warning:* Do not attempt to plot out all the target conditions in advance, because that is way beyond your threshold of knowledge. Start with one, and when you reach it, reflect back and then set the next one in light of what you have learned, and so on.

4. Experiment. Go crazy! Have fun! Be creative! This is the most enjoyable part for most people. Most of the planning to this point has been holding the learner back from trying out their ideas. Finally, some doing. Test one factor at a time if possible, predicting what will happen, running the experiment, and reflecting on what you learned. Repeat rapid cycles of PDCA until you reach the target condition, set your next target condition, and continue toward the challenge.

It is recommended this be done in pairs—a learner with a coach. The learner is leading the project and often acts as the leader of a team. The coach meets regularly, ideally daily, with the learner. Rother also developed a coaching kata (CK) that helps get the coach engaged with a "five-question" starter kata (see Figure 12.6). The learner documents his or her IK process on a storyboard, which itself is one of the starter kata routines. The coach asks questions from each category, which mirrors the IK pattern. They are nested questions beginning with the target condition and actual condition, and on the flip side are questions to reflect on the last experiment that the learner has run. Each experiment is practiced via another starter kata, following the pattern of description, prediction, results, and reflection (PDCA). The comparison between prediction and actual results provides an opportunity for learning.

Asking the predefined questions on the card is a starting point, a mental patternmaker, as they demarcate phases of a coaching cycle. As the coach matures, he or she will ask deeper and deeper clarifying questions and eventually develop an individual style. There is research under way by Tilo Schwarz to build on the coaching kata and address specific ways to respond to the learner, with the opportunity to practice in rapid cycles offline in a dojo (simulated environment for practice).[13]

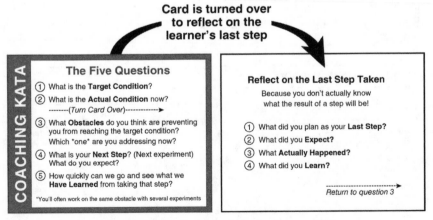

Figure 12.6   A starter kata for the coach.
Source: Mike Rother, *Toyota Kata Practice Guide* (New York: McGraw-Hill, 2017).

A CASE EXAMPLE: ZINGERMAN'S MAIL ORDER

Practicing Toyota Kata Through Collaboration Between UM and ZMO

For several years I taught a University of Michigan course focused on the IK and CK for graduate students in industrial and operations engineering who were working on projects with local companies. Zingerman's Mail Order (ZMO), a business discussed earlier in the book that sells online artisan foods, was the most active. The projects were done at the ZMO warehouse where it picks items, assembles gift boxes, and ships to customers. The company started its lean journey in 2004, and as I write this, it is still an avid practitioner and the UM course continues.

Students teamed with Zingerman's production associates. ZMO management would select pressing problems and assign them to groups. One group got the most pressing problem—that of running out of items that were to be picked. Food items were organized in a market where the pickers would select the items ordered and put them in bins. This group had the challenge of reducing instances where the company ran out of an item at the picking line. The company was using a kanban system to replenish what it set out in the market for order pickers. It was highly effective most of the time, but there also were some serious failures that disrupted the timing of the order. The challenge was zero OOMs, or zero out of markets, meaning the pickers would always have what they need. This challenge was revisited for three classes of my students over three years. Experimenting records for experiments 1, 2, and 4 done by the first class are presented in Figures 12.7, 12.8, and 12.9. As you can see, there were experiments that supported hypotheses and others that did not. For these high-achieving engineering students, it was surprising when they were wrong—and very helpful in building their scientific thinking skills. Here is a broad summary of the project and results:

EXPERIMENTING RECORD					
Obstacle: Lost Meat Kanban		**Process:** Kanban Audit Process			
		Learner: Group		**Coach:** Betty	
Date and Step	**What Do You Expect + Metric**	Coaching Cycle	Run Experiment	**What Happened**	**What We Learned**
Start: 2/22/16 to 2/28/16 **Step:** A daily audit to detect lost meat kanban in real time and take corrective actions. **Metric:** % meat OOM as a % of work orders	25% reduction in meat OOM			• No change in % meat OOM as a % of work orders	• Lost kanban are not a significant cause of OOM. • A system to quickly detect lost kanban has some value

Figure 12.7   Out-of-market experiment 1.

EXPERIMENTING RECORD				
Obstacle: Frequency of Kanban replenishment for meat route not scaled to match takt		**Process:** Meat Replenishment Route		
		Learner: Group		**Coach:** Betty & John
Date and Step	**What Do You Expect + Metric**	Coaching Cycle / Run Experiment	**What Happened**	**What We Learned**
Start: 2/9/16 to 3/11/16 **Step:** Scale frequency of meat route to meet takt **Metric:** % meat OOM as a % of work orders	80% reduction in meat OOM from .67% to .17% by 3/11		• Meat OOM increase on 3/9 and 3/10 when club demand had spiked. Variability persists and target is not achieved.	• Club meat demand might be the reason for variability that may cause OOM.

Figure 12.8 Out-of-market experiment 2.

EXPERIMENTING RECORD				
Obstacle: Frequency of Kanban replenishment for meat route not scaled to match takt		**Process:** Market Sizing		
		Learner: Emma		**Coach:** John
Date and Step	**What Do You Expect + Metric**	Coaching Cycle / Run Experiment	**What Happened**	**What We Learned**
Start: 3/24/16 to 4/4/16 **Step:** Have a flexible market size estimation for clubs through coordination between marketing and routes teams	Meat OOM as a % of work orders should drop below .17%		• Meat OOMs ranged from zero to 1.2 % of work orders. • 3 of 5 days OOMs at zero • Target condition exceeded.	• Adjusting market sizing based on varying demand reduced OOMs

Figure 12.9 Out-of-market experiment 4.

1. **2016 Challenge: Zero OOMs.** While zero was the long-term aspirational vision, management set a more realistic shorter-term challenge of "limiting the stock-out defect occurrences to 0.75 percent of the total number of work orders across all product groups over an eight month period." The project continued over several years.

2. **Current condition (start of semester): 3 percent OOMs with continued backups at checking.** Mapping the process led to identifying kanban replenishment as the bottleneck, and the team chose to focus on one of the biggest offenders—meat products. The students spent many hours observing the process steps, following material handlers, and performing the material handling route. Among other things, the team observed that there was little connection between changing customer demand (takt) and changes in the material handling frequency or routes, that products were sometimes in the wrong locations, and that kanban were lost.

3. **First target condition (set on February 29, 2016).** A target of 1 percent OOMs (outcome metric) by semester's end on April 15 with the following operating conditions (desired process characteristics):

- The frequency of replenishment is aligned to the established takt.
- Number of material handlers and routes are scaled to changing takt.

4. Experiment. The team conducted five experiments over the semester. Some failed to support the hypotheses, but the team learned from each one. The three experiments summarized in the figures illustrate the step-by-step learning process.

In experiment one the kata team worked to overcome the obstacle of lost kanban which they hypothesized was a significant cause of OOM. They set up a system to audit kanban and take corrective actions immediately when lost kanban were detected. There was no reduction in OOM and the team learned lost kanban were not a significant cause. (A good example of how learning via experiments works!)

In experiment two they found a way to scale the frequency of the meat route to takt and expected a big improvement, but OOM actually increased on two of the days when demand spiked. They observed that the cause of the increases on those two days was an increase in "club demand." Food clubs are subscriptions that are shipped to customers monthly. When marketing holds a club sale it can create a sudden bump in meat orders. Experiment three focused on testing the idea that club demand was a major source of variability and supported that hypothesis.

It was in experiment four where marketing and the route team communicated directly about the club orders and adjusted the size of the market based on demand that the team hit a home run with zero out of market for three of five days. Experiment five focused on a different obstacle—gaps between the planned material handling route and what actually occurred—but the team ran out of time to collect all the data needed.

By the end of the semester, the team saw an 80 percent reduction in OOMs for meat products and reached its target condition. The project continued in subsequent years adding product groups to the scope, and although OOMs continued to peak when the temp workers started each year in December, progress was clear:

- December 2016 = 2.6%
- December 2017 = 2%
- December 2018 = 1.6%

More importantly from the perspective of the students' future roles as managers and leaders, their thinking was changing. As the students ran experiments and participated in coaching sessions, I could see that they were moving away from their deterministic mindset, where they assumed with certainty they had the right answer, to taking a more provisional and exploratory scientific outlook. They were moving away from an "implementation" mindset, for example, viewing kanban as a solution to implement, to a learning mindset, seeing kanban as a way to help make problems visible. I also observed a marked increase in scientific thinking among management at ZMO.

Scientific Thinking to Adapt to Covid-19

In March 2020, ZMO, like most businesses in the world, faced a great deal of uncertainty about what Covid-19 meant for the company. As an "essential business" selling food, it was not forced to shut down operations, but initially it shrank staff and daily capacity. Staffing was inconsistent, and day to day the company did not know if it would be allowed to remain open. But then something unexpected and delightful happened. ZMO was now receiving orders in droves from customers who would normally go out to stores and restaurants, resulting in a record number of orders. The company was used to huge increases in demand around Christmas time and planned for it all year, but high demand in the spring overwhelmed it; on some days the demand was double what it had been the year before. With spacing of people and no easy way to instantly bring on more staff, fulfilling orders was getting behind. The standard practice was to fulfill orders the same day they were received, but over a three-month period, the company was now at filling capacity and quoting wait times of 8 to14 days—horrifying! Yet customers continued to buy.

Sales and finances were not a problem, but ZMO had to overcome many obstacles to create a safe and productive work environment. It was an opportunity to see if the years of learning lean and practicing scientific thinking led to a responsive, learning organization.

ZMO did not put up kata storyboards or hold daily coaching sessions, as it had to immediately react. But it had internalized the patterns and did to a great degree follow scientific thinking. This illustrates the role of any starter kata. The point is not the starter kata themselves, but the patterns of thinking and acting—fundamentals to build on—that practicing them leaves behind. Commonplace in sports and music, this deliberate-practice approach to skill and mindset development is now finding its way into the business world.

As one example, in the early stages the three managers were in disagreement on expected capacity (number of boxes that could be shipped each day) and how much they could reasonably expect people to work. One manager felt that the staff didn't want to work full-time hours. When the discussion heated up, one manager pointed out, "Kata has taught us to look at the facts; we are assuming the staff don't want to work. Let's ask them." They took a poll that day—everyone except two staff members wanted to work full-time. The power of facts.

Following the improvement kata model, the managers set long-term goals and short-term target conditions. The big challenge was to be prepared by the Christmas rush to meet demand safely using the prior year's demand as a target. Shorter-term target conditions focused on nearer-term holidays—with goals to safely meet the increased demand for the spring sale, then Mother's Day, then Father's Day, then the summer sale. Each event had its unique current condition and mix of orders.

Warehouse managers deeply trained in lean and scientific thinking led the way. For example, one manager led the effort to define how to sanitize work stations every two hours. She decided to develop a safety checklist, but she realized two things. First, she should not assume there was a one-size-fits-all set of practices that could apply to all areas of the warehouse. Different practices were needed for preparing bread, picking orders, filling boxes, and material delivery, because each faced different task requirements. Second, the area leads were already overwhelmed trying to get work done, and each area could not be expected to develop its own standardized practices. So she did what a good lean manager does; she headed out to the gemba observing and even doing the jobs herself in each area to see what was being touched. She developed initial checklists and then met with staff, and for three days they tested and refined and learned, resulting in customized checklists for each type of process that then required almost no additional changes.

Beyond these checklists, problem after problem was addressed at the gemba, by studying the current condition and testing ideas—at breakneck speed. One manager, Betty Gratopp, explained:

What did we try? Physical changes to stations, adding stations in some areas, mothballing stations on others, rescheduling when we start prep work for the next day's orders, additional fulfillment happening at an offsite location. Screening and cleaning processes were created and documented and handed off to frontline staff. Our staffing levels were more variable than ever with quarantines and people simply opting for unemployment. We had to figure out how and when it was ok to hire. We don't have orientation or training classes or huddles right now. We created a message board and information share wall in place of the huddles and classes.

The results were impressive. The delays in fulfilling orders shrank and shrank until most days got close to same-day shipping. Even more impressive, nobody got the virus at work. Betty described the calm she felt through this crisis:

The scientific approach brought a calmness to how we adapted. What do we improve today? The problems we tackled were more bite size.

Management wanted to reward the employees who were taking risks each day coming to work. The company gave each employee, even temporary staff, a $3 per hour raise, and it increased profit sharing to 10 percent of the large profits earned—resulting in a more than a 10-fold increase in payouts from the prior year.

A survey of many businesses by the Barret Values Centre conducted from April 21 to May 5, 2020, resulted in responses from over 2,500 people around the world and suggested ZMO was not alone in accomplishing remarkable feats in the face of the virus.[14] Many of the companies reported making changes in a fraction of the normal time, at one extreme making changes that would have required five to seven years in just six weeks. The survey asked the respondents to rate a set of values and behaviors as they were before the crisis, then as they were during the initial adaptation to the crisis, and finally as they were after things had calmed down a bit. There was significant movement in the reported strength of these values. From the perspective of the Toyota Way, there was both good news and bad news.

The good news was that at the middle level of staff, there was a shift from a focus on performance, control, and hierarchy (mechanistic characteristics) toward a focus and values placed on people, adaptability, and working together (organic characteristics). Engagement, trust, and communication increased in importance to mid-level staff. But the bad news was that this shift was not evident among the C-suite respondents, who increased their focus on external strategic and performance issues. The C-suite people wanted increased adaptability and innovation, but they did not increase their beliefs in the importance of engagement, trust, or communication or in general the culture of the workplace. You could say they were blind to the transformation that was taking place at the gemba and were only focused on results—a recipe for great short-term adaptation but little long-term culture change.

PDCA AS LEARNING VERSUS IMPLEMENTING WHAT WE ASSUME WE KNOW

Underlying assumptions of scientific thinking are that we cannot know the future in advance and that uncertainty is a fact of life, while our fast-thinking brain desires certainty and assumes we know. Repeated practice of the Toyota kata patterns helps us make the scientific-thinking zone, where we question our assumptions, more habitual. As with any new skill, scientific thinking is deliberate and slow when first practiced, which eats up a lot of our limited conscious brainpower and feels awkward. But as the scientific-thinking patterns grow more automatic, slow-thinking brain capacity is freed up and we can focus more on the details of a particular situation to address the problem at hand. Through practice your brain is trained to automatically react in a more scientific-thinking way, often without conscious thought.

Problem solving is central to the Toyota Way, but what I see all too often is the steps of the *method* being viewed with an implementation mindset. We define the problem, collect some data about the current condition, brainstorm a root cause, and then select "lean solutions" to be implemented. Or in some lean circles, we "countermeasure the problem." We quickly become committed to what we think is the root cause and to our pet solutions, mostly solutions we have used in the past with some success. In this version of PDCA (see Figure 12.10), we make commitments to implement our guesses about what will work, before we have even tried anything—in fact, this is the point of maximum uncertainty.

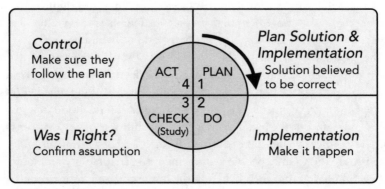

Figure 12.10   PDCA with assumed certainty to implement known solutions.

A more scientific way to think about PDCA is shown in Figure 12.11. A plan leads to direction and to a series of hypotheses, which are each tested through experiments. In this way, we are learning and extending our threshold of knowledge step-by-step. Rother advises we might better think about the journey as navigating with a compass that shows a direction instead of starting with a detailed road map that we then follow. John Shook recalls at NUMMI that people used

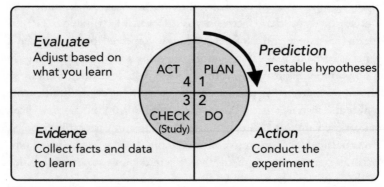

Figure 12.11   PDCA to scientifically learn your way to a challenge.
Source: Mike Rother, *Toyota Kata Practice Guide* (New York: McGraw-Hill, 2017).

to say there is no GPS for getting to TPS. Many consulting firms offer their road maps to lean, but that ignores the complexity and unpredictability of the journey. Training our brain to accept uncertainty and creatively test ideas to overcome unexpected obstacles as we discover them is a fundamental skill in today's complex, rapidly changing world. We are learning how to learn.

As President Cho warned, TBP was not intended to create a rigid way of thinking, but rather build a foundation for creative problem solving. Similarly, Mike Rother sees the IK in this same way. Here are a few key points about practicing the IK pattern with starter kata:

1. It represents a practical, scientific thinking approach. It's practical because it is about pursuing specific goals as opposed to the basic science purpose of understanding the nature of something.
2. It starts with an aspirational challenge—usually six months to one year out. What big improvement will make an important difference in achieving our vision?
3. It assumes uncertainty. If the challenge is well conceived, the solutions will not be clear at the outset, and any presumed "solutions" will quickly move beyond our threshold of knowledge.
4. It makes rapid, iterative learning cycles explicit. Each target condition is intentionally short, such as one to four weeks. Each experiment tests one idea quickly and cheaply and includes a prediction and reflection.
5. There generally is one coach and one learner; the learner is accountable and often leading a team to follow the process and results, and the coach is accountable for developing the learner's skill and mindset.
6. The practice is a small amount per day (e.g., 20 minutes), fits into busy people's schedules, and is best for learning—by doing something every day and constantly expanding your threshold of knowledge.

Too often we problem solve in batches—a batch of specific issues leads to a batch of root causes and then a batch of solutions that get "implemented" and checked as a batch. Then we broadly deploy the batch of solutions everywhere. This is often done in a batch of time, such as full-time for one week in a kaizen event. I started to think of the Toyota Kata pattern as one-piece flow problem solving. Break down the problem into pieces, set one target condition at a time, run one experiment at a time, learn from each experiment to inform the next. Spend a little time each day learning something new. The benefits of one-piece flow should be clear by now.

CHANGING THINKING
BY CHANGING BEHAVIOR

The term "scientific thinking" can be confusing in a number of ways. First, as we mentioned, it brings to mind trying to make everyone into a professional scientist. We are actually trying to develop people who work to achieve difficult goals in a scientific way. Second, when people imagine how to change thinking, they often think of communicating. What can I tell this person to persuade the person to think differently?

Decades of research have shown that it is difficult to change behavior by telling people things. Even successfully getting them to repeat what you said, with intellectual understanding, is not likely to impact daily behavior, which is governed more by habits. To get to habits we need to change behavior through deliberate practice, repeatedly. What matters is what we do, not what we think we *should* do.

As we look at how Toyota develops people, we see that the company creates conditions that foster certain behaviors, like reducing inventory so problems surface quickly and visibly, which puts pressure on problem solving. But challenging people is not enough. The company also teaches managers how to coach—to find opportunities in the course of daily work to give corrective procedural feedback to their team members as they strive to move toward a goal.

Toyota kata is a structured approach for getting started with practice and feedback; it does this by utilizing small "starter kata" practice routines. You are put in a situation in which you deliberately practice working toward a challenging goal facing real-world obstacles. The more you practice the behaviors of scientific thinking, the more you develop in your brain the neurological pathways that make this a habit you are likely to repeat in the future (see Figure 12.12). Corrective feedback, preferably from a coach, is key to deliberate practice so you do not develop the wrong pathways that lead you to skip over defining goals, grasping the current condition, and testing your ideas, and instead jump to conclusions. The coach will explain some concepts but mostly will ask questions to trigger thoughts and if necessary interject a focused learning point when the time is right. Kata for practicing an intellectual task like problem solving may seem unusual, but it is much like using kata to develop a variety of skills such as a playing a musical instrument, cooking, dancing, martial arts, and sports.

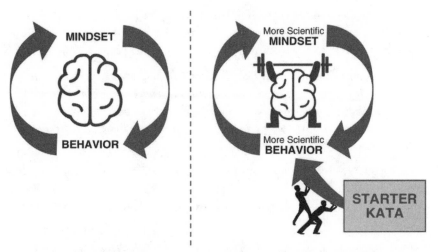

Figure 12.12 Increase scientific thinking by increasing scientific behavior.
Source: Mike Rother, *Toyota Kata Practice Guide* (New York: McGraw-Hill, 2017).

THE ROLE OF HANSEI (REFLECTION) IN KAIZEN

Ultimately, the core of kaizen and learning is an attitude and way of thinking by all leaders and associates—an attitude of self-reflection and even self-criticism, a burning desire to improve. Westerners view being criticized and admitting to a mistake as something negative and a sign of weakness. People with a "fixed" mindset will see it as an attack on who they are, on their competence. So we blame others, defend ourselves, or hide the problem. In Japan, people learn the art of reflection, called "hansei," at a young age.

Toyota found teaching hansei to American managers to be very challenging, but it is an integral ingredient in Toyota's organizational learning. George Yamashina, past president of the Toyota Technical Center (TTC), explained it as something like the American "time-out" for children:

In Japan, sometimes the mother and the father say to the children, "Please do the Hansei." Some child did a bad thing. It means he or she must be sorry and improve his or her attitude—everything is included, spirit and attitude. So once the child is told, "Please do the Hansei," he understands almost everything about what the mother and the father want him to do.

Toyota finally introduced hansei, translated as "reflection," to its US managers at TTC in 1994 as part of introducing hoshin kanri and A3 thinking. According to Yamashina, it had to be introduced at some point:

Without hansei it is impossible to have kaizen. In Japanese hansei, when you do something wrong, at first you must feel really, really sad. Then you must create a future plan to solve that problem and you must sincerely believe you will never make this type of mistake again. Hansei is a mindset, an attitude. Hansei and kaizen go hand in hand.

At Toyota, even if you do a job successfully, there is a "hansei-kai" (reflection meeting). Bruce Brownlee, retired general manager of the Toyota Technical Center, helped clarify this, drawing on his experience as an American who grew up in Japan:

Hansei is really much deeper than reflection. It is really being honest about your own weaknesses. If you are talking about only your strengths, you are bragging. If you are recognizing your weaknesses with sincerity, it is a high level of strength. But it does not end there. How do you change to overcome those weaknesses? That is at the root of the very notion of kaizen. If you do not understand hansei, then kaizen is just continuous improvement. We want to overcome areas of weakness.

INDIVIDUAL LEARNING AND ORGANIZATIONAL LEARNING GO HAND IN HAND

The concept of a learning organization can quickly become a theoretical abstraction. What does it mean for an organization to learn? The organization is not a creature, but a concept. When we think of a learning organization, it might be more useful to think about a learning culture. Culture ties people together toward shared beliefs, values, and assumptions. In mechanistic organizations, learning becomes difficult. Some parts of the organization become the keepers of learning for their specialty and then dictate standards to the rest of the organization to be obeyed, not questioned. A learning culture brings to mind a more organic organizational form. Learning becomes a pattern. For individuals we think of "habits," and for organizations we can think of "routines" that help people learn to work in a synchronized way.[15]

There are a number of ways to learn:

- Grasping a concept
- Storing information

- Retrieving and applying information
- Developing new habits or routines

This seems pretty clear when applied to an individual. And we saw how this applies to scientific thinking. You can grasp a model, like the improvement kata. You can try to simply store the *model* in memory. You can even try to retrieve the information and apply it from time to time. But the purpose of the starter kata is to deliberately practice until elements of thinking scientifically become *habit patterns* in your memory and then continue to evolve.[16]

When applied to an organization, if we take the view that the goal is simply to store and retrieve information, we can utilize all sorts of online computer programs to capture and disseminate "best practices." Unfortunately, just because I see what you have done as a best practice does not mean that I can do it, or that I really understand it, or that it applies to my situation. At Toyota, people use the term "yokoten," which means "gain widespread adoption," but in practice it is more than that. I like Alistair Norval's description:

> *Yokoten is horizontal and peer-to-peer, with the expectation that people go see for themselves and learn how another area did kaizen and then improve on those kaizen ideas in the application to their local problems. It's not a vertical, top-down requirement to "copy exactly." Nor is it a "best practices" or "benchmarking" approach. Rather, it is a process where people are encouraged to go see for themselves and return to their own area to add their own wisdom and ideas to the knowledge they gained.*[17]

LEARNING ORGANIZATIONS EVOLVE; THEY ARE NOT IMPLEMENTED

It took Toyota several decades to build an organization in North America that bears a resemblance to the learning enterprise it built over most of the last century in Japan. Moving people from firefighting and short-term fixes to long-term improvements is an ongoing process at Toyota.

The Toyota Production System itself embodies the learning cycle of plan-do-check-act. The house in Figure 12.13 depicts the cycle. In the plan stage, you develop a vision of one-piece flow, something to strive for. Then, in the do stage, you experiment and learn in the direction of the targets in the roof. Jidoka is the check, comparing the actual to the target to surface problems, including unexpected problems arising from the changes you made. Every andon pull signifies a new problem to address. The foundation is where we standardize the new practices with the goal of developing new routines. And the cycle repeats.

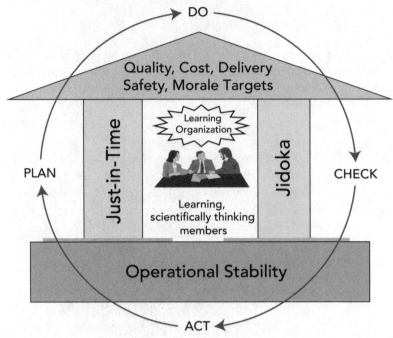

Figure 12.13   The Toyota Production System as cycles of plan-do-check-act.

When he became president of Toyota, Fujio Cho saw the company devolving into local cultures around the world, without strong bonds or common language and thinking. The countermeasure was to develop a global standard of principles and ways of thinking, along with coached practice routines—Toyota developed some kata. These were the Toyota Way 2001 model, Toyota Business Practices, and on-the-job development, and they were transformational.

Mike Rother has created more universal kata for scientific thinking for the rest of us outside of Toyota, which can even apply in everyday life. These days he spends a lot of his time with elementary, middle, high, and vocational schools showing teachers how to coach their students in an everyday scientific way of thinking. It is a way to learn with a purpose. And it can lead to a common vocabulary and way of thinking that is the basis for shared culture.[18] In the next principle, we consider how cascaded planning can clarify the direction of the company and connect the improvement goals and efforts of scientific-thinking individuals and teams horizontally and vertically.

KEY POINTS

- In the rapidly changing environment of the twenty-first century, organizational learning and adaptation are becoming critical for success.
- The concept of a learning organization can remain an abstraction until it is translated into a mindset and behavior of scientific thinking. People naturally prefer certainty and want to believe they are right, without taking the time to think deeply or study the actual condition.
- Fujio Cho recognized this and realized that as Toyota grew and globalized, it needed to develop people through practice and coaching. He led the creation of the Toyota Way 2001, Toyota Business Practices, and OJD. Individuals were coached in these methods through projects, one by one.
- Mike Rother has developed a non-Toyota-specific approach for developing scientific thinking based on his research into Toyota's management system. It includes a practical, scientific thinking model and "starter kata," which are practice routines. Using this approach and through repetition and corrective feedback from a coach, the learner builds the neural pathways to think and act scientifically.
- There is some evidence that the shock of Covid-19 pushed many companies to cut through coercive bureaucracy and become more people centered, quickly adapting and learning and even changing values toward higher levels of trust, engagement, and communication. Unfortunately, those changes often did not reach the thinking in the C-suite, which makes them unlikely to sustain over the long term.
- Think of iterative learning as one-by-one problem solving where you break the problem into pieces and learn from each experiment informing the next. It is not just that small changes can make a difference, but many small changes with a clear direction toward a big challenge.

Notes

1. Kazuo Wada and Tsunehiko Yui, *Courage and Change: The Life of Kiichiro Toyoda* (Toyota Motor Corporation, 2002), p. 130.
2. Peter Senge, *The Fifth Discipline* (New York: Doubleday Business 1990).
3. https://vimeo.com/300443389.
4. Charlie Baker, "Transforming How Products Are Engineered at North American Auto Supplier," in J. Liker and J. Franz (eds.), *The Toyota Way to Continuous Improvement* (New York: McGraw-Hill, 2011), chap. 11.

5. Ashlee Vance, *Elon Musk* (New York: Ecco Press, 2017).

6. W. Edwards Deming, *Out of the Crisis*, MIT Center for Advanced Engineering Study (Cambridge, MA; 2nd Edition, 1988).

7. Daniel Kahneman, *Thinking, Fast and Slow* (New York: Farrar, Straus and Giroux, 2011).

8. Michael Rother, *Toyota Kata* (New York: McGraw Hill, 2009), p. 9.

9. Justin Kruger and David Dunning, "Unskilled and Unaware of It: How Difficulties in Recognizing One's Own Incompetence Lead to Inflated Self-Assessments," *Journal of Personality and Social Psychology*, 1999, vol. 77, no. 6, pp. 1121–1134.

10. https://www.britannica.com/science/information-theory/Physiology.

11. Fujio Cho, *The Toyota Business Practices* (Toyota Motor Corporation, 2005).

12. Mike Rother and John Shook, *Learning to See: Value Stream Mapping to Create Value and Eliminate Muda* (Cambridge, MA: Lean Enterprise Institute, 1998); Mike Rother and Rick Harris, *Creating Continuous Flow: An Action Guide for Managers, Engineers & Production Associates* (Cambridge, MA: Lean Enterprise Institute, 2001).

13. https://www.kata-dojo.com.

14. https://www.valuescentre.com/covid/.

15. Robert E. Cole, "Reflections on Learning in U.S. and Japanese Industry," in Jeffrey K. Liker, W. Mark Fruin, and Paul S. Adler (eds.), *Remade in America: Transplanting and Transforming Japanese Production Systems* (New York: Oxford University Press, 1999), chap. 16.

16. Charles Duhigg and Mike Chamberlain, *The Power of Habit: Why We Do What We Do in Life and Business* (New York: Random House, 2012).

17. https://www.leanblog.org/2011/05/guest-post-what-is-yokoten/.

18. Mike Rother and Gerd Aulinger, *Toyota Kata Culture: Building Organizational Capability and Mindset Through Kata Coaching* (New York: McGraw-Hill, 2017).

Principle 13

Focus the Improvement Energy of Your People Through Aligned Goals at All Levels

Life is what happens to you while you're busy making other plans.
—John Lennon, lyrics from "Beautiful Boy (Darling Boy)"*

I first learned about hoshin kanri, aka policy deployment, in the 1980s when consulting for Ford as it adopted it as part of a package of Toyota management practices. The concept was simple. At the top of the company, develop the policy that will allow the company to perform well in the business environment (mainly profits in Ford's case), deploy the policy down into the organization with some give-and-take discussions called "catchball," and when all the people in the organization have their targets aligned to the top-level policy, let it rip. Those who met their targets were rewarded, and those who didn't . . . well. What sane CEO would not want that? In a command and control organization, which Ford was at that time, it was like giving candy to a baby. And to make it even more sweet, it was all done in the name of collaboration and participative management. After all, the little people got to play catchball.

After spending more time studying the philosophy behind hoshin kanri (HK) at Toyota and how it operated, I realized there was a night-and-day difference in the thinking at Toyota compared with what I saw at Ford. Toyota had introduced HK as part of total quality control in the early 1960s. By then TPS was spread across Toyota plants, and quality at the plant level was good. But senior executives wanted excellent, and they realized it was necessary to develop aligned quality improvement plans vertically and horizontally across the company. They set as a challenge to win the prestigious Deming Prize for Total Quality Management, which they did in 1965. Toyota never looked back. HK became a core part of Toyota's culture.

---

* The expression of this sentiment can be traced to a 1957 *Reader's Digest* article, which attributes it to Allen Saunders.

The way of thinking was clarified for me about 25 years later when I was working with the vice president of sales and service at Volvo, Einar Gudmundsson. Gudmundsson took my work with Gary Convis on developing lean leadership[1] to heart and worked on transforming his leadership approach to stimulating improvement through coaching. As part of this work, his organization adopted hoshin kanri. He had been at the nexus of Volvo's traditional command and control style and this new way of leading. He modified the Toyota diagram of HK from our book and contrasted it to Volvo's traditional way of planning (see Figure 13.1).

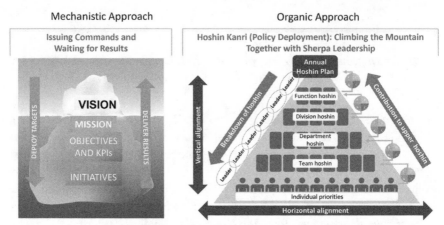

Figure 13.1   Mechanistic versus organic view of hoshin kanri
(aka policy deployment).
Sources: Volvo Car Corporation (left); adapted from Toyota Motor Company (right).

The CEO of Volvo developed the strategy and led an annual planning process with something they thought of as catchball with vice presidents, leading to a business plan for each business unit. The vice presidents then deployed their objectives down through the organization. Once the objectives were determined, the senior executives met in a classy boardroom to review the results and issue orders. Gudmundsson realized that the executives' approach was unsatisfactory. It made him think of an iceberg metaphor. The senior executives could only see as far as their own desired goals and the results that were rising above the water level. What was happening in the larger part of the iceberg, below the water level, was largely invisible, and the executives did not believe the details concerned them.

Gudmundsson started to think about hoshin kanri in a different way. It was like mountain climbing. Selecting the mountain, setting the schedule, getting the resources, and planning the climb happened from the top, but then as a senior leader in the execution stage, he had to climb down the mountain and act as a sherpa—guiding, supporting, and developing leaders. Climbing a mountain never goes as planned, so the initial plan is just a starting point. The ability to adapt and respond to the obstacles faced is the difference between success and failure, sometimes life and death.[2]

In an organic approach, the leaders are connected through interlocking goals and plans, and the ability to achieve results is as strong as the weakest link, so leadership development must be a priority. In fact, the intense discussion of challenging goals and plans and the process of working to achieve these objectives are a great opportunity for leadership development. Hoshin kanri is as much a process of developing people and culture as it is a tool for deploying strategy and getting results. Gudmundsson informed the CEO that his chair in the executive meetings would often be empty because he was out at the gemba. He proceeded to deliver record profits from his sales and service organization that helped at a time when auto sales were losing money.

HOSHIN KANRI IS AN ANNUAL PROCESS OF WORKING TOGETHER TOWARD A VISION AND STRATEGY

The overall flow of the annual process is summarized in Figure 13.2. Hoshin planning starts at the top of the organization with an environmental scan and a strategic plan. What are the risks? What trends will influence the organization's

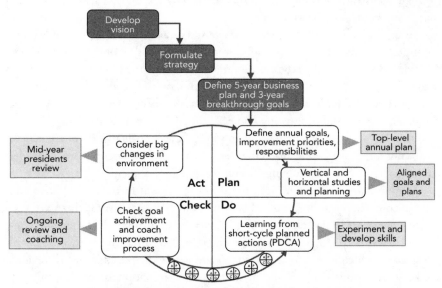

Figure 13.2   Overview of the hoshin kanri process.

success? How can we position the organization for long-term success? What is the distinctive competence of the organization? We discuss the role of strategy and how it relates to effective execution under Principle 14. Suffice it to say at this point, many companies we have worked with do not have much of a strategy other than—sell more, lower the costs, and make more profit. In contrast, the strategy should tell me why customers should prefer your products and services over those of competitors. What is distinctive? What will you focus on doing, and what will you not do?

Toyota creates a ten-year global vision roughly every decade, which is converted into more concrete goals in a five-year business plan and then gets translated into one-to-three-year breakthrough objectives. At the time of this writing, the company's Global Vision states, "Toyota will lead the future mobility society, enriching lives around the world with the safest and most responsible ways of moving people." It will do this by "engaging the talent and passion of people who believe there is always a better way."

A key milestone of hoshin kanri is the president's address at the beginning of the fourth quarter of the year when he presents the global hoshin items and launches three months of hoshin planning across the company. However, individual units have a good idea of what is expected in advance and work in the third quarter on reflection and preparation. The detailed hoshin process across the company involves planning, communicating horizontally and vertically, building consensus, and committing to targets (see "Hoshin Kanri at TMUK" later in the chapter). The end result of this annual planning is many A3 reports that cascade through the organization and become increasingly focused on specifics the further down in the organization you go.

At the end of this planning period, it would be a mistake to send people off to go implement. As Gudmundsson discovered at Volvo, it's more effective to view achieving challenging objectives as mountain climbing. You have a plan, you have made all the preparations you can, and now you have to face all the unanticipated obstacles of climbing the actual mountain. This is a process of many PDCA cycles; it requires a great deal of learning and scientific thinking. It is also where leaders take the time to develop their people and coach and challenge them to achieve great things. In Toyota, they teach that the keys to effective hoshin kanri are leader competencies in problem solving and on-the-job development.

In a mechanistic organization, the review process is formally scheduled and usually complex—but at Toyota this is not the case. At Toyota, there are two major reviews for the whole company, midyear and year-end. But there are constant reviews and dialogues throughout the year, including within Toyota's board of directors, which is mostly an internal board led by the president. Most reviews are local in various parts of the organization, from shopfloor work groups to engineering product groups to sales groups focused on particular vehicle segments. There are checkpoints and daily reviews of progress nested within the management hierarchy. In Toyota manufacturing, each level of the management hierarchy from group leaders to the plant manager meets daily in standup meetings next to visuals on a board and wall to discuss yesterday, today, and tomorrow and consider overall progress. As a result, there are no big surprises in milestone reviews; mostly, they are reflection events. At the halfway point in the year, there may be some major changes in the environment that call for adjusting the hoshin. For example, the coronavirus pandemic greatly affected the original 2020 hoshin.

THOROUGH CONSIDERATION IN PLANNING AND DECISION-MAKING (NEMAWASHI)

Throughout the hoshin process many decisions must be made. Employees outside Japan who joined Toyota after working for another company faced the challenge of learning the Toyota approach to planning and decision-making. Because Toyota's process of consensus decision making deviates so dramatically from the way most other firms operate, this is a major reeducation process. New employees wonder how an efficient company like Toyota can use such a detailed, slow, cumbersome, and time-consuming process. Some Americans jokingly refer to Toyota Motor Manufacturing as "Too Many Meetings." But all the people I have met who have worked for or with Toyota for a few years become believers in the process and have been greatly enriched by it—even in their personal lives.

For Toyota, *how you arrive at the decision is as important as the results of the decision*. Taking the time and effort to do it right is mandatory. In fact, management will forgive a decision that does not work out as expected if the process used was a good one. A decision that by chance works out well, but was based on a shortcut process, is more likely to lead to a reprimand from the boss. Toyota's secret to smooth and often flawless implementation of new initiatives is careful, up-front planning. Underlying the entire process of planning, problem solving, and decision-making is careful attention to every detail. Often part of the planning process is running experiments in a pilot. This behavior is associated with many of the best Japanese firms, and Toyota is a master at it. No stone is left unturned.

Thorough consideration in planning and decision-making follows a scientific approach similar to what we saw with problem solving. It includes five major elements:

1. Understanding the problem or issue and explaining its importance and priority.
2. Understanding the current condition including possible causes for the issue, asking "Why?" five times.

3. Broadly considering alternative approaches and developing a detailed rationale for the preferred approach.

4. Building consensus within the team, including Toyota employees and outside partners.

5. Using very efficient communication vehicles to execute steps 1 through 4, preferably one side of a sheet of paper (A3 size).

There are a variety of decision-making methods used at Toyota in different situations. These range from a manager or expert making a decision unilaterally to a group developing a consensus. As shown in Figure 13.3, the preferred approach at Toyota to making important decisions is group consensus with management approval. But management reserves the right to seek its own group input and then make and announce a decision. The manager will generally decide only if the group is struggling to develop a consensus and there is an urgent need for a decision. The philosophy is to seek the maximum involvement appropriate for each situation when there is time available and the quality of the decision is important, and to seek the least involvement if there is urgency to the decision or it is a straightforward issue.

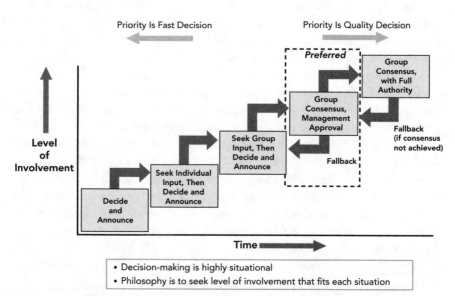

Figure 13.3   Situational involvement and consensus
in planning and decision-making.
Source: Glenn Uminger, former general manager,
Toyota Motor Manufacturing North America.

Getting consensus is done through "nemawashi," which translates to "going around the roots," a process of digging around the roots to prepare the tree for transplant. At Toyota, it means gathering broad input from people with a stake or with special knowledge and, in the process, building consensus. You are preparing the people, and generally by the time the final decision is made, all have agreed to it even before a formal meeting. Consensus does not mean everybody agrees 100 percent, but it does mean that everybody's input is considered. It's expected that everyone involved will support the final decision 100 percent.

One example of the nemawashi process is the way the broad circulation of ideas works in the early stages of product development. Before the styling of a vehicle is even determined, Toyota puts an enormous amount of effort into evaluating the early designs and thinking through possible engineering and manufacturing issues. Each design is meticulously analyzed, and countermeasures are developed through "study drawings"—sketches that include possible problems and alternative solutions. When the study-drawing phase is completed, the collective drawings across all engineering departments are put together into a binder called the K4 (shorthand for "kozokeikaku"—a Japanese word referring to a structure plan—the study drawings that collectively address the structure and integration of the vehicle). One day I met with Jim Griffith, who at the time was vice president of technical administration. He looked frazzled. I asked him why, and he told me he had just gotten a K4 on a new vehicle to review. Griffith is not an engineer, so I asked why an administrator would get this document. He seemed surprised I would ask and responded that Toyota is always looking for broad input, and he, too, will have opinions about the vehicle.

He was frazzled because this was clearly a challenging task for a nonengineer, and he felt obliged to take it seriously and provide some useful input. As it was, well over a hundred signatures were required on the K4. Jim was a vice president and very well established at Toyota, so he could have just blown off the assignment. But he knew that if the chief engineer was asking for a nonengineering opinion and he had to sign off on the document, there was a reason. The process matters, and every member must take the process seriously. Perhaps he might see things that others missed. In any event, he knew his opinions would count.

Alan Ward was a professor of mechanical engineering but prior to that was a practicing product development engineer. He had endured the trap of getting committed to a particular idea, creating the engineering drawings, and then discovering problems in the test stage which required many design iterations to fix the original idea. He thought of this as "point-based design" and believed it was a trap. Better, he thought, was "set-based design" where you consider a broad set of alternatives, then systematically narrow the alternatives considering a range of factors and a range of perspectives. Alan and I traveled through Japan to see if Japanese engineers were more likely to think in terms of sets of alternatives. We hit gold at Toyota where set-based design seemed to be everywhere.[3] This same way of thinking applies to any complex decision. Toyota prefers a broad and creative search process at first, to avoid getting locked into an inferior plan or solution that has to be corrected through wasteful iterations. Like a funnel, they start broadly with many alternatives and then narrow toward a decision.

THE A3 STORY FOR COLLECTIVE WISDOM AND MAKING THINKING VISIBLE

The inconspicuous A3 report is documented on A3-size paper, about 11 inches by 17 inches (ledger size) in the United States. At Toyota many years ago, it became the standard for telling a story with facts—one side of one sheet of paper to tell a story, preferably with figures and diagrams and few words. At Toyota, it is a key tool for nemawashi, a crisp and clear explanation of the current thinking that is used to get critiques and generate ideas.

Most commonly adopted outside Toyota is one type of A3: problem-solving stories. If you type "A3 problem-solving template" into your search engine, you'll find bunches of free downloads. The formats are abundant, but effective use is scarce. What many organizations miss is that the A3 is not just a problem-solving report that summarizes what happened, but also the start of a problem-solving process that unfolds over time with give-and-take with the coach and other stakeholders. Looking at it through the lens of kata, instead of viewing the steps on the A3 as a method, think about these processes as practice routines for developing a scientific way of thinking. Perhaps the most important use of an A3 is to make the thinking of a learner visible for coaching. This was well explained by John Shook in *Managing to Learn*.[4] Shook encountered A3 in 1983 when he became the first American manager for Toyota in Japan. His first boss emphasized that he needed to learn how to "use the organization" to get anything important accomplished. His boss coached him on how to use A3 as a tool for using the organization.

The A3 report came to be a hot tool for lean practitioners outside of Toyota. After all, Toyota was the benchmark and used A3, so lean companies should use A3 too. When Shook saw how it was being used, he shuddered. He had gone through so many years of training and practice on how to define a problem, how to deeply observe the actual process, how to ask questions, and how to conduct nemawashi—all the while constantly responding to questions and challenges from his various coaches. It was typically intense and exhausting.

Shook wrote *Managing to Learn* to introduce the Toyota management process. He was not trying to teach the format of an A3 report, but rather he said the

A3 should be thought of as a hook or an artifact to assist a manager in coaching others. As John writes in the book:

I discovered the A3 process of managing to learn firsthand during the natural course of my work in Toyota City. . . . My colleagues and I wrote A3s almost daily. We would joke, and lament, that it seemed we would regularly rewrite A3s 10 times or more. We would write and revise them, tear them up and start over, discuss them and curse them, all as ways of clarifying our own thinking, learning from others, informing and teaching others, capturing lessons learned, hammering down decisions, and reflecting on what was going on.

There are versions of A3s for problem solving, proposals, status reporting, and information sharing. Sobek and Smalley discuss these various A3s with many examples drawn from Toyota in *Understanding A3 Thinking*.[5] Whether problem solving or planning or proposing, the point is to reflect and embed PDCA into the entire process. Good A3s have PDCA built in, except perhaps "information sharing" or status report A3s, and in those cases, they are often interim stages to support a broader PDCA story.

As we will see later in the chapter in the example from Toyota in the United Kingdom, A3 reports are key tools throughout the planning and execution of hoshin kanri, including the initial stage of reflecting on the previous year's hoshin and results. The proposal story becomes central in the planning phase. One example of a proposal A3 is in Figure 13.4. This was not driven by hoshin; rather it originated from a problem brought up by engineers at the Toyota Technical Center and championed by the head of purchasing.

The problem was that most purchases were for less than $500, yet these small purchases required the same arduous paperwork as major equipment costing hundreds of thousands of dollars. It seemed like a reasonable request, but at Toyota the executives want the facts and data and rationale, and they want to know that this was all well thought through with input from key stakeholders. The A3 report recommended Toyota issue credit cards for minor purchases. It included a description of the various controls to be put in place to prevent misuse, such as blocking out personal purchases from grocery stores and jewelry stores. They had already started a pilot to test the idea. By the time the proposal was formally presented, the executives involved had already contributed to the process and knew well what was in the proposal. It was approved in a few minutes. What was important was the process. We do not see here all the ideas that were considered, rejected, and refined; the torn-up A3s; the nemawashi; and the research done—but it is evident there was careful thinking about many details. The person who created the A3 was self critical about all the words in the document and would have preferred more figures.

PURCHASING CARD PLAN FOR TOYOTA TECHNICAL CENTER

Date: August 20, 1996

CURRENT SITUATION

Cost to process PO (labor & mat'l):
Purchasing = $57   Acct = $39   Tech Dept. = $27   TOTAL = $105/PO

Cost to process invoice for labor & mat'l:
Purchasing = $0   Acct = $27   Tech Dept. = $27   TOTAL = $54/Invoice

1995			
# of Purchases:	<=$250 = 813	<=$500 = 1200	<= $1000 = 1525
# of Invoices:	<=$250 = 2516	<=$500 = 2740	<= $1000 = 3026
Time Required:	<=$250 = 5525 Hrs.	<=$500 = 7184 Hrs.	<= $1000 = $8489 Hrs.

Percentage of Purchase Orders
Percentage of Purchase Order Dollars

23%   34%   43%

<=$250   <=$500   <=$1000

PROPOSAL

Implement use of purchasing credit cards for purchases < = $500.00 to incur the following savings and increases in efficiency:

Labor hours saved—Tech Groups, Purchasing, Admin
Labor and Material Cost Savings
Reduced P.O., RFP, expense reports, invoiced paperwork
Customer Service to T/As through reduction of time spent on paperwork
Easy of performing spot transactions—Test Trips, Emergency Purchases, etc.
Helps to maintain existing ADM & AFD headcount while TTC grows over next 5–10 years
Reallocated time used on higher ticket buys, priority projects, etc.

LABOR COST & TIME ANALYSIS

LABOR & MAT'L SAVINGS:		P.O.	INV.
	Current Cost/Transaction	$103	$54
	Purchasing Card Costs	$20	$20
	Savings/Transaction	$83	$34

TIME SAVINGS:		P.O.	INV.
	Current Process:	3300 Hrs	3900 Hrs
	Purchasing Card:	650 Hrs	1550 Hrs
	Potential Annual Time Savings	2650 Hr/Yr*	2350 Hr/Yr*

* Approx. 1/3 of time savings is to Tech Grps

PLAN

• Pilot program starting with Facilities, Purchasing, Tech. Groups.
• Dept. GM determines which T/As are issued cards for specific dept. purchases.
• Acceptable business-related purchases using card:

Small Tools	Seminars	Photo Processing & Film
Auto Supplies	Office Supplies	Postage
Minor Equip Repairs	Printing Services	Copy Services
Electrical Supplies	Safety Supplies	Bld. Maint. Supplies
Catering	Florists	Coffee Services
Hardware	Signage	

• Unacceptable uses of card (blocked):

Cash Advance	Travel & Entertainment	Independent Contract Services
Computer Hardware	Personal Use	Capital Purchases
Jewelry, Personal Clothing		

IMPLEMENTATION

1. Card user obtains approval from Dept. Manager for each purchase.
2. Card user contacts vendor, places order and provides vendor with appropriate information.
3. Goods shipped as specified and labeled "Purchasing Card" —Cardholder Name.
4. All packing lists and receipts are retained by requestors and matched against monthly statement.
5. Card user reviews statement, attaches appropriate packing lists and receipts, records, JRN #'s, signs and forwards to Dept. Manager.
6. Dept. Manager reviews statement for accuracy and initials and dates statement.
7. Dept. Manager forwards to Accounting to audit statement and supporting docs. for compliance, sales tax, 1099.
8. Accounting pays from master invoice received directly from the purchasing card bank.

CONTROLS

The following controls are set up prior to the card being issued:
  • Monthly dollar limits per card
  • Single transaction limit is ($500)
  • Limited number of transactions per card per day
  • Merchant Category Blocking (i.e., cash advances, jewelry, appliances entertainment, etc.)

TTC requires all card users to sign a P-Card Agreement stating that all use of the card will be for business purposes within the procedures set forth.

TIME LINE

9/3	9/4-9/20	9/16-11/15	11/15-3/31	11/15-3/31	4/1-4/15	4/16-4/18
Present Proposal	Policy Guide/ Vendor enroll	Training Pilot	Pilot Program	Finalize Policies	Audit 3 Mo Pilot	Report Results	Training Corp. Wide	Corp. Wide Implement.
4/21-5/20 6/2/97						

Figure 13.4 Example A3 proposal story for planning at Toyota.

HOSHIN KANRI AND DAILY MANAGEMENT GO HAND IN HAND

Let's return to hoshin kanri. Technically speaking, hoshin kanri focuses on breakthrough objectives led by senior management, while the work groups focus on smaller improvements directed toward targets on key performance indicators (KPIs), but at Toyota they are blended together (see Figure 13.5).* Within TMUK, people use an analogy that identifies the strategic plan as the intended "road" to the desired future state of the organization and the boulders and rocks as the obstacles to get through. The boulders make the journey uncertain and detailed road maps unrealistic, although in most cases even the road is not clearly laid out in advance. At TMUK people are taught that "big boulders require organizational hoshin to remove, while small rocks can be improved through daily kaizen." The heavy lifting of the big boulders, which generally cuts across individual work groups and even departments, is the responsibility of managers as they have the authority and the access to resources to make systemic changes. Managers are taught to lead PDCA to overcome obstacles on the way to the hoshin targets.

Daily Deviation Management SDCA Cycles

To sustain breakthrough improvements and to continue with daily small kaizens through SDCA cycles

Hoshin Management PDCA Cycles

To deliver breakthrough improvements at all levels through continuous PDCA cycles

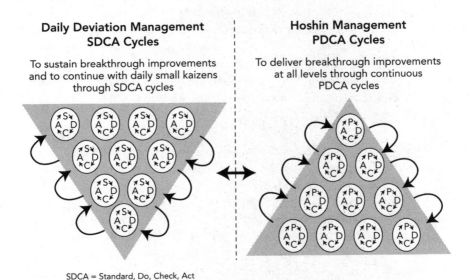

SDCA = Standard, Do, Check, Act

Figure 13.5   Hoshin kanri and daily management work together.

---

* For a discussion of four types of problem solving—troubleshooting, gap from standard, open-ended, and target condition—see Art Smalley, *Four Types of Problems: From Reactive Trouble Shooting to Creative Innovation* (Cambridge, MA: Lean Enterprise Institute, 2019).

For the smaller rocks you will often hear in a Toyota plant, "We are an abnormality (or deviation) management company." When Toyota talks about abnormality management, what the company means is a gap from a standard. In fact, Toyota's definition of a "problem" is a deviation from standard.

As you go into a factory and observe the production line where work is short cycle and regimented, you'll find that there are standards for everything. At the front line, most of the problem solving is to remove the small rocks by finding and solving deviations from existing standards. Examples might be that the filters are not being changed on schedule or that there are scratches on the product that violate quality standards; or perhaps process 5 keeps getting behind the planned cycle time, or the person on process 3 is repeatedly violating ergonomic posture standards, or there was a missing bolt on one vehicle for process 6. Thus, Toyota uses the acronym SDCA (standard-do-check-act), where the starting point is not defining a big problem and breaking it down into smaller problems, but instead focusing on individual deviations from a standard. As you solve problems one by one at the root cause, you will have fewer abnormalities and can spend less time fixing specific deviations and more time focusing on daily kaizen toward KPI targets. The KPI targets are a form of a standard.*

I have found the distinction between PDCA and SDCA helpful at a high level of abstraction. More ambitious projects based on large challenges require a good deal of time in the plan stage to define the problem, as we saw in the last chapter with Toyota Business Practices, while smaller, more constrained issues in a specific process often can be defined more easily as a deviation from a specific standard. In reality, it is all PDCA, and includes understanding the goal versus the actual condition, getting the facts, identifying causes, and then experimenting to reach the target. This may happen more quickly for SDCA, but it still needs to happen.

Toyota developed a conceptual model to illustrate how SDCA and PDCA work together and what happens when one is missing (Figure 13.6). The model shows a disruptive process of breakthrough changes driven by hoshin, followed by a period of SDCA, and then gradually working toward KPI targets. Life, of course, is not so orderly, but it illustrates an important point. When there is a big change, there is a lot of disruption, which means a lot of variation. To reduce the variation and get closer to the standards requires a great deal of SDCA at the front line.

As we discuss TMUK's approach to hoshin kanri and daily management in the next section, an important context is that the plant had recently launched a new model Corolla, gas engine and hybrid, based on a recently developed global architecture that was very different from the previous models—new equipment, changes in all processes, and a new product. Predictably, this led to an expected

---

* A standard for comparison could be a rule, specification, procedure, or even a target.

increase in deviations from quality, safety, and productivity standards—life got crazy—and a good deal of kaizen was focused on addressing these issues through daily kaizen. The plan was for people to do what they could in the launch according to plan and then deal with all the unexpected deviations through daily problem solving at the front line.

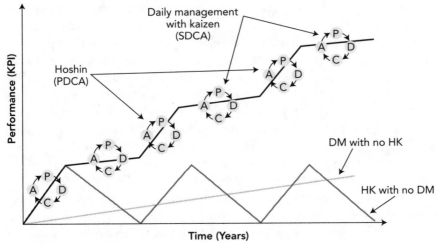

Figure 13.6   Relationship between hoshin kanri and daily management: how top-down and bottom-up meet.
Source: Toyota Motor Corporation.

At the bottom of this graph is an illustration of what can happen when a company introduces HK without effective daily management (DM). It looks like the sawtooth effect: a big jump on selected measures to meet the challenge until senior management changes the focus to the next big, new thing, and the initial effort degrades. On the other hand, killer daily management with frontline teams passionately engaged in SDCA will lead to steady improvement, but not the breakthrough architectural change needed to adapt to changing products, technology, and environments.

The idea that HK and DM go together has received widespread acceptance in the lean community. Yet there are many consulting groups that will come in and simultaneously "implement" both HK and DM broadly and rapidly. They will generally promise large cost savings that are several times their hefty fees. Usually neither will be effective for the long term. As I write this, one of my clients is facing this issue, as it was forced by headquarters to shift from a more gradual approach of developing people to what I call a smashmouth get-the-numbers-now approach. Don't get me wrong; the company will get results, and the consultants will get paid and move on to their next engagement, with all parties happily counting their money. Many big ideas will be generated quickly by managers, long action lists with associated names and dates will be created, and the CEO will watch and pressure for results. Big changes will get done, some people will get promoted, and others will be asked to leave. Production workers will be laid off. And the processes will be in turmoil—there will be lots of variation.

The problem with rapid implementation of so many things at once is that people have not been developed to continue to improve the systems and the culture has not changed. Most of the ideas that managers under extreme pressure will generate will be big, transactional changes, like automating processes, pressuring suppliers, cutting anything or anybody not needed to get production out the door, focusing attention on large losses like scrap, changing layouts, and pressuring people to work harder. The daily management system will include lots of KPI boards and daily meetings led by leaders who do not know how to run meetings or how to improve processes. I have seen it repeatedly. It is a crude application of the technical side of lean. What the executives do not realize is that even the lean tools have both a technical dimension and a social dimension. Using only half—either half—loses effectiveness.

On a more optimistic note, I have seen companies that made some significant architectural changes such as creating flow lines, developing value stream managers, setting up kanban systems, writing lots of standardized work, and taking out a lot of low-hanging waste—and then they realized things had started to go backward. At this point, they decided to go a bit slower and deeper and start with pilots to develop effective daily management systems and train managers in problem solving—an approach that helped them evolve in a positive direction. We will discuss different approaches to change management in the final chapter.

HOSHIN KANRI AT TMUK

Let's take a tour of one year of hoshin kanri at TMUK, starting at the senior management level—the plant hoshin. It starts with studying the environment. There were a number of factors that influenced the environment for TMUK. These included:

1. **Profit contribution.** A new CEO for Toyota of Europe made a serious commitment to profit contribution, which for TMUK meant it had to compete on cost with lower-wage countries. For a three-year period, the hoshin focused on reducing total controllable cost by 10 percent per year, which TMUK accomplished through relentless kaizen in all parts of the operation—and no layoffs of regular team members.

2. **Great Recession impact.** In this tumultuous period, TMUK closed one of its two assembly lines and offered separation incentives, which many long-service members and managers took, therefore losing a good deal of bench strength and leaving a whole line available for new business.

3. **New-model launch.** As mentioned, TMUK launched a new Corolla that was reengineered from the platform up and required a lot of new equipment. As expected, a major launch like this is always disruptive.

4. **Brexit.** This creates uncertainty, as most of the plant's vehicles are sold in Europe, and customs costs could damage profitability.

5. **CASE.** As Toyota shifts to connected, autonomous, shared mobility, and electric vehicles (see Principle 14), TMUK wants to be prepared for the new mobility technology and competitive in winning the right to produce these new vehicles.

Top-Level Hoshin

Based on these conditions, TMUK developed the top-level hoshin (level 1) for 2019, summarized in a diagram in Figure 13.7. From the point of view of all the members of TMUK, the aspirational goal was to become a "Globally Admired Plant—Ready for Any Future Business." They all want the plant to stay alive in the future and continue to provide a living for all the members and their families. Toyota allocates vehicles to plants, and so in a sense, TMUK's competitors are other Toyota plants, mostly in Japan and some in Europe. TMUK wants to be at the front of the line for new vehicles, as they come on board. Successfully launching the new Corolla, meeting cost, timing, and quality targets, would show what the folks at TMUK were capable of so this was the "year of the launch."

The plan for achieving both objectives included three themes, with some enabling systems. Theme 1 was to become the number 1 producer of the Corolla based on the global vision of three bests—best management, best member, best process. These were all defined and put into practice through the revamped floor management development system described under Principle 10.

Theme 2, "Brains not money," is about daily kaizen with minimal capital spending. Toyota believes that "if members have the thinking of kaizen, we can take on anything." Larger steps—steps that involve more fundamental innovation—are led principally by managers and engineers. Business targets come from the ACE 1000 European program launched in 2015 to create a more sustainable business through profit contribution that includes reducing costs, improving productivity, and increasing revenue.

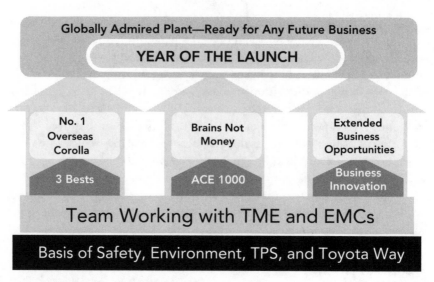

KEY: 3 Bests = best management, member, process
      ACE 1000 = European profit target
      TME = Toyota Motors Europe
      EMCs = European manufacturing companies

Figure 13.7   2019 Toyota Motor United Kingdom plant hoshin.

Theme 3 focuses on the available capacity and ways to increase profit margin beyond building the Corolla. This was assigned to a TMUK executive who had to think outside the box and move up and down the supply chain. Moving down the supply chain included bringing manufacturing of supplied parts in-house, and moving up included doing some work on sold vehicles like additional options and refurbishment. He even investigated building the vehicles of competitors, like Nissan, though that did not work out.

The foundation is safety (zero accidents) and protection of the environment (for example, 100 percent recycling, zero landfill use, 100 percent water reuse). And TPS and the Toyota Way are a core part of the foundation—the how. This conceptual vision is shown as a house and is then broken out into company targets.

Note that nobody from Toyota corporate was taking a lead on any of these issues. There were ideas like the three bests developed in corporate, support from many people, including a TPS master trainer, and key decisions like assigning the Corolla, but in many ways TMUK was expected to do and think for itself. Even generating new lines of business was an idea from within TMUK and managed internally.

Deploying Hoshin to the Shops

A Toyota plant is set up as a series of shops—body panel stamping, welding, paint, plastic molding, and assembly. Each shop, or sometimes a combination of shops, is led by a general manager. The general manager develops a hoshin strategy for that shop, which gets deployed to the manager level for sections within the shop.

At TMUK, Andy Heaphy was general manager of body manufacturing, which includes both press (stamping) and body (welding). He developed the shop hoshin (level 2) with input from his managers (see Figure 13.8). His hoshin is also on a (blown-up) A3, but in this case organized as a table. The top level includes a vision and commitments that align with the TMUK concept—to become "the most admired press and body shop globally" through motivating and engaging team members, developing team members to deliver outstanding results, and aiming for the three best. The group decided to have a special focus on best member and has described how it will achieve that goal through highly developed and motivated team members.

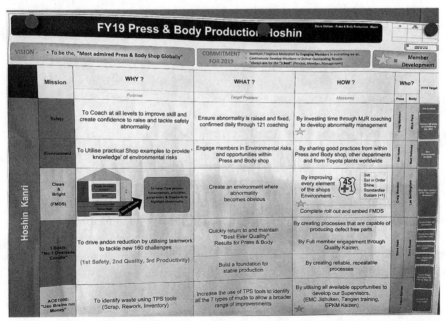

Figure 13.8   General manager's hoshin for press (stamping)
and body (weld) production.

The meat of the hoshin is five missions that align with the top-level hoshin: safety, environment, clean and bright (FMDS); the three bests ("no. 1 overseas Corolla"); and ACE 1000 ("use brains not money"). Each mission gets broken out into a general plan with aspirational challenges like zero accidents and zero environmental incidents and some more specific targets like improve green mapping by 5 percent and achieve the FY19 cost target.

The green mapping target (called "process diagnostics" in some parts of Toyota) is related to "best process." It is a comprehensive audit of the process against standards for areas like safety, ergonomics, walking percentage, number of returns to get parts, and complexity of member decision-making. Originally an engineering tool for developing processes at new-product launches, it is time consuming and takes training. Group leaders do this audit twice per year, and gaps provide a clear focus for kaizen. Best member includes following standardized work, proper andon use, and versatility of learning multiple processes. Best management is measured twice per year by a macro-level standardized-work audit; e.g., a job instruction sheet is in place and up to date; the team member followed standardized work and used andon correctly; and all basics are in place and used correctly. Every process gets an in-depth audit twice per year. To find areas for improving the group leader role, group leaders do a separate audit twice a year focused on the minimum job role discussed under Principle 10. It is labor intensive and requires that the section manager follow the group leader around for a day.

The "whos" named for each mission, one for press and one for body, are then responsible to develop an even more detailed hoshin plan (level 3). We see the hoshin plan for weld quality in Figure 13.9. In this case, there is a Gantt chart for timing of the elements of the plan. Below this on the wall (not shown in the figure) are even more detailed plans at the activity level, such as managing quality standards, reducing scrapped car bodies, and introducing a new process for control of standardized work. Even further down are targets for the three main quality outcome measures—shipping quality audit (SQA), defects per unit, and direct run rate. SQA is a global KPI, and a small number of finished vehicles are randomly picked each day and subjected to exhaustive inspection and testing—this reflects what the customer will experience and is the most important measure. The direct run rate is the percentage of car bodies that go through all welding stations without having to be pulled offline for repair. Then there is another board with a three-month quality improvement plan that is even more detailed; for example, one plan focuses on "clean body," which is a body with zero defects.

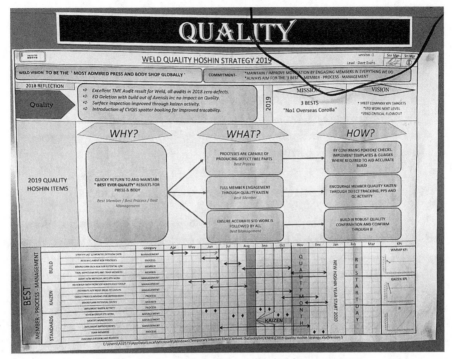

Figure 13.9   Body weld quality hoshin strategy.

Notice that as we work down the levels, the higher-level conceptual direction is translated to detailed and actionable targets and plans. The translation requires a great deal of thought, study, and discussion. It is not just a mindless cascading of outcome targets such as "we need 10 percent cost reduction for the plant so your portion is 3 percent." It is this difficult translation process to identify the causal factors that can influence the desired outcomes that is at the core of hoshin planning. The general manager and managers are asking: "What should I work on to deliver the results the plant needs?"

As general manager, Heaphy views every aspect of this process as an opportunity for coaching. He could create his hoshin and then deploy it by giving orders, but he understands that would not develop anyone. Instead, he presents his ideas or his hoshin, gathers input, revises, and then requests of his team: "Please develop a plan to help me achieve my objectives." Each member then presents a plan on an A3, and that begins a coaching process.

It should be clear by now that Toyota uses a lot of paper, often A3 size. I asked Heaphy why:

First, we are not very good at technology, and second, to see everything in an easy way is very hard to do on a computer. And when you have a meeting with a multitude of people, you need a very big screen; otherwise you are not going to share it. So, we tend to put things out on boards so you can share it with the group, and other people like managers and my director can come in my shop and they can have a look themselves. It is genchi genbutsu, and that can't easily happen if it is in a database with a password. I also think it is very effective from an engagement point of view and also following the progress, having the plans on the board. It makes you wonder, what is the status of that? You are asking that question. If it is hidden away from you, what triggers you to ask the question?

Putting Hoshin Kanri into Action in Work Groups

When hoshin gets to the group leader level, the concepts and overall targets are set. There is no separate group leader hoshin strategy. The group leader focuses on FMDS, including a KPI board. The KPI board has a standard layout globally (Figure 13.10). The missions rarely change: safety and environment, quality, productivity, cost, and human resource development. While the KPIs rarely change, the targets and priorities will change. For example, since TMUK was in a launch year, there were a certain number of in-line quality defects caught in the plant and ergonomic issues as group leaders and team leaders worked out the details of the new processes with team members, so safety and quality were priorities.

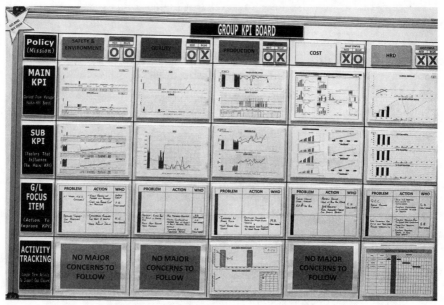

Figure 13.10   Group leader KPI board.

The "main KPIs" are the outcomes derived from the manager's hoshin KPI board. The "sub-KPIs" are factors that influence the main KPIs. This is critical. The group leaders cannot significantly influence outcomes by simply focusing more and trying harder; they need to have something to work on. They can work on improving the causal factors that influence the outcome. This is similar to the idea of the target condition in kata—you need both the outcome and the desired process condition. This involves causal reasoning, which is much more difficult for people than simply giving them a target to hit. As an example, in safety, the main KPI is lost time incidents, but these are rare and cannot be directly controlled. The sub-KPI is near misses in getting injured, which can be observed and are more numerous. As metrics, there are regular safety audits to assess all safety risks associated with the job, and these audits measure near misses. For example, when I toured the plant in December 2019, it had only 6 lost-work accidents in all of press and body for the year, with the target for the year being 10. But there were a larger number of near misses to work on.

Then at the bottom of the board are the focus items—actions to improve the sub-KPIs—for example, properly wearing all personal protective equipment or designing the jobs for the right posture to avoid musculoskeletal disorders. The KPI boards and power boards are used in the daily group leader power meeting held with the section manager, shown in this case for the quality group in weld (see Figure 13.11).

Figure 13.11   Body weld quality shop power meetings.

This is a long chain of visions, missions, metrics, targets, and plans. As mentioned, the planning really starts in the third quarter with reflection (hansei), which adds columns to the A3 hoshin plans to note the gaps that still exist and actions for closing the gaps. In addition, reflection is done every day and week in one-on-one meetings at all levels. This is where the most important dialogue and the short-term planning take place.

USING HOSHIN KANRI WITH TOYOTA KATA THINKING: SIGMAPOINT EXAMPLE

Let's consider one more example of hoshin kanri, this time moving outside Toyota. SigmaPoint Technologies in Ontario, Canada, provides end-to-end electronic manufacturing services for use in telecommunication, industrial controls, alternative energies, medical devices, defense, and more. Its core product is surface-mount circuit board assemblies. With annual sales in 1999 of US$80 million and 350 employees, the company operates two sites, with quick-turn prototyping in Kitchener, Ontario, and full-volume services in Cornwell, Ontario. Like many organizations, it became intrigued by lean manufacturing and investigated it. Like few organizations, it made lean a reality without receiving any consulting support. The company's standard approach was to study the method, try it, refine it, evolve it, and continue learning. The leaders seem to be natural scientific thinkers. It all worked, with tremendous results for quality, cost, and lead time. Lean systems became the organizing philosophy of the company.

For example, the leaders organized their production lines into value streams by product families. They shifted from organization by type of machine to flow lines for product families ranging from small-lot engineered to order, to relatively large lot standardized boards. To make this transition, they started with a pilot. They decided to move across the street to a new facility and first tested the cell concept for the high-volume value stream with less variety, and then one by one they organized the whole site in value streams. All the lean principles discussed earlier in the book were integrated and functional: flow, pull, leveling, standardized work, visual management, error proofing, andon, and technology to support people.

Each end-to-end value stream is run by a value stream manager who has the level 2 responsibility. The value stream manager acts as the business owner and connects to all service groups, including engineering, sales, and accounting. Reporting to the value stream manager is a value stream coordinator who is similar to Toyota's group leader and has level 3 responsibility. The equivalents of the Toyota team leaders are "value stream group leaders." Daily huddles around visual boards are a combination of A3 problem solving and the improvement kata, which evolved from formally coached practice sessions to the way they scientifically approach daily improvement.

When the leaders felt they were ready for alignment from strategy to operations, they studied popular books on hoshin kanri and went to work to try it, evolve it, and learn. They attended a workshop and started with the popular

X-matrix at the top level of the company. I will not go into details about the X-matrix since it is in almost every book about hoshin kanri, and it is not used in Toyota. In summary, it is a matrix on a single page with an X in the middle, and you move around the four edges writing (a) three-to-five-year breakthrough objectives, (b) annual objectives, (c) top-level improvement priorities, (d) improvement targets, and (e) the people who will be responsible for the targets. In the corners, you put X's to show how the objectives and priorities and targets are linked to each other. SigmaPoint found this a useful way to visualize its top-level plans, although for deployment it preferred A3 documents like those Toyota uses, and then at the action level it linked the plans to the kata approach to scientific thinking.

As a medium-size manufacturing company, it was able to go from strategic plan to deployment with three levels of leadership (see Figure 13.12), not unlike the approach used in the TMUK manufacturing plant. The level 1 strategic deployment plan took information from the X-matrix and laid it out in greater detail as a hierarchical breakdown chart (see Figure 13.13). The company began with two 3- to 5-year breakthrough challenges: "Be World Class in Operational Excellence" and a challenging level of "Earnings Before Taxes"—both of which were broken down to a set of 1- to 3-year goals. For example, in year one the goals were to win the AME Prize for Operational Excellence (as a way to focus operational improvement efforts), achieve profit targets, increase inventory turns, improve production efficiency, improve integration of business systems, improve

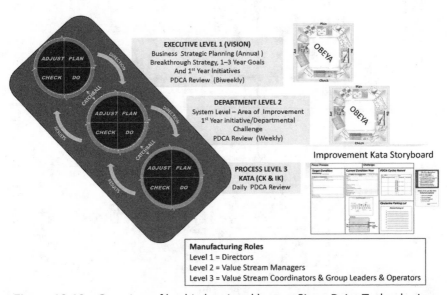

Figure 13.12   Overview of hoshin kanri and kata at SigmaPoint Technologies.
Source: SigmaPoint Technologies.

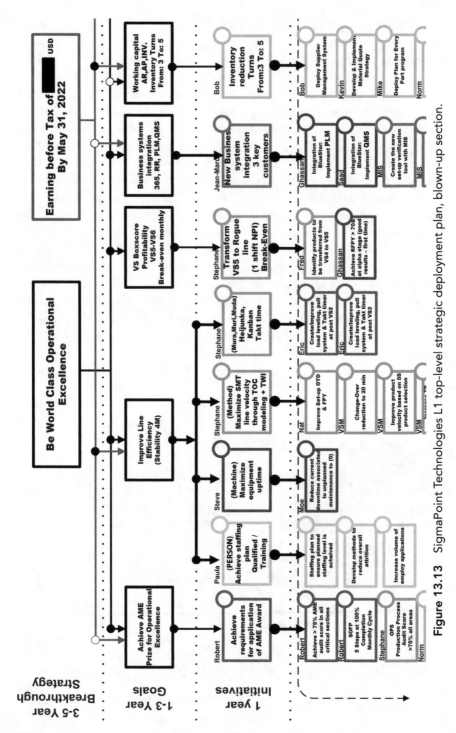

Figure 13.13 SigmaPoint Technologies L1 top-level strategic deployment plan, blown-up section.

quote accuracy, increase account management services and skills, and achieve aggressive revenue targets. This broad set of goals touches every function in the company.

The goals are further broken down to level 2 challenges, which include targets for departments. The departments then deploy down to the process level 3 through daily management systems. Catchball, throwing a ball back and forth, is a metaphor of a give-and-take exchange. For many companies, it is used in the planning stages to agree on the hoshin objectives. At SigmaPoint, the executive teams hold a biweekly meeting in the obeya and biweekly catchball meetings with department heads. Level 2 then has regular catchball sessions with level 3, so catchball is an ongoing coaching and learning process.

Let's follow one part of the chain linked to the manufacturing department's one-year goal at level 2 to "maximize SMT velocity through theory of constraints modeling and training within industry" (standardized work and job instruction), where SMT means "surface mount technology." In Figure 13.14, we give an example of one A3 focusing on increasing throughput through SMT. SMT is an automated process that includes robotics and is the bottleneck of each value stream. The A3 is organized around the improvement kata pattern. The challenge target is to free up four hours of capacity per day for the 80 percent highest-volume items with minimum capital investment. There are target conditions, current conditions, obstacles, and "active" PDCA cycles at the time this A3 was produced. The A3, which keeps evolving, was the responsibility of a value stream manager who was experimenting in the high-volume value stream. The value stream managers meet weekly to discuss their various A3s, and they also are responsible for catchball with value stream coordinators.

Moving down to the process level 3 (Figure 13.15), we see the daily management board for a cell leader, which is organized like a kata storyboard. This has been cleverly designed to include both PDCA driven by hoshin and SDCA. The level 2 challenge is in the upper left-hand corner. Then we see the target condition, current condition, various other charts and graphs, and the PDCA cycle record. Each experiment designed to move closer to the level 2 challenge is documented on this record—plan, prediction, results, learning. In the lower right, there is a process health check sheet for items like buffer locations, conveyor operation, SMT pallets, theory of constraint balancing, and staging of materials.

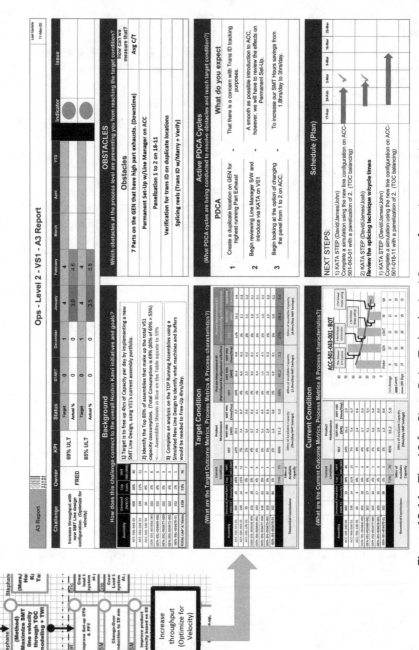

Figure 13.14 The A3 for SigmaPoint Technologies L2 manufacturing operations.

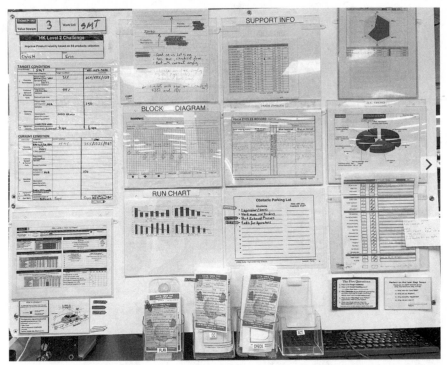

Figure 13.15   SigmaPoint Technologies L3 process level
daily management board (based on Toyota Kata).

At the bottom is an interesting addition to document SDCA. First, there is
a running list of obstacles that are mostly quick-hitter items (see Figure 13.16).
But instead of having the usual action register—problem, countermeasure, when,
who—the board has a modified version of the improvement kata on idea tags. If
an obstacle turns out to be a bigger problem than originally thought, the leaders
staple PDCA cycle records onto the idea tags. These tags are then moved through
slots for plan-do-check-act. So the scientific approach is used even for SDCA.
The result—the direction set at the executive level of the organization is linked
and cascaded to action through experimenting and learning at the gemba.

Figure 13.16   Obstacle parking lot generates idea tags for SDCA.

HOSHIN KANRI IS A PROCESS FOR ORGANIZATIONAL LEARNING

Toyota long ago realized that hoshin kanri is the connective tissue between organizational learning and the achievement of business objectives. Continuous improvement based on problems that pop up can accomplish a good deal, but to get everyone involved in continuous improvement in a way that adds up to huge corporate improvements requires aligned goals and objectives and daily measurement of progress toward those objectives. Thus, Principle 13 states "focus the improvement energy of your people through aligned goals at all levels." The motivational benefits of setting specific, measurable, challenging goals that matter and then measuring progress are huge—even when there is no tangible reward associated with success.

Toyota managers have become highly skilled at setting challenging goals jointly with their subordinates and are passionate about frequent measurement and feedback. This is the basis for hoshin kanri. It is Toyota's process of cascading objectives while incorporating into that downward cascade the upward "cascade" of understanding the reality, generating innovative ideas, and taking initiative. It is a highly interactive and dynamic process of getting consensus (nemawashi), reflecting (hansei), going to see the actual condition (genchi genbutsu), and experimenting (PDCA).

In my experience, most of the companies attempting to adopt hoshin kanri miss the essence of this dynamic process. Planning remains at a high level; senior executives remain above the water level and are not in touch with the reality of the workplace. "Solutions" are defined prematurely in the plan stage, and they miss the process of aligning by concurrent top-down and bottom-up contributions. Catchball is often a few meetings in the planning stage to throw targets and ideas back and forth.

At Toyota, people do a great deal of planning to create visions, missions, and themes for actions and translate the desired outcomes to what they believe to be the drivers of those outcomes at operational levels. Outcome metrics are achieved by focusing on actionable process metrics. In the execution phase, they are madly doing PDCA and experimenting and learning. They combine PDCA with SDCA, using PDCA to remove the large boulders on the road to the challenges and using SDCA through daily management to remove the smaller rocks. PDCA and SDCA reinforce each other.

SigmaPoint has been even more formal than Toyota in developing initial plans and then using a scientific approach to learn its way toward creating and meeting challenges. The company is building on Mike Rother's kata model to coach and learn through aligned daily activities across levels. What SigmaPoint is doing looks like the model in Figure 13.17, which makes explicit that the main result of hoshin planning is to create aligned challenges. But in scientific logic

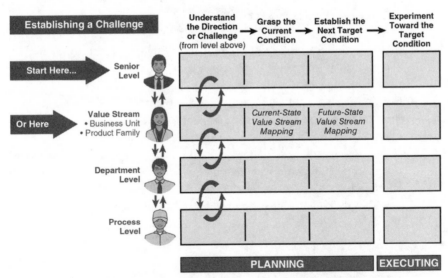

Figure 13.17 Hoshin kanri connects to the improvement kata.
Source: Mike Rother, *The Toyota Kata Practice Guide*
(New York: McGraw-Hill, 2017), p. 83.

these plans are all preliminary. Once execution starts, the first step is to revisit the challenges; then go back to the gemba to focus on some area and set the first target condition; then experiment to meet that target condition; then reflect and define the second target condition; and so on. PDCA is embodied in a dynamic up-and-down cascade. This requires a different mindset than deploying plans and solutions. As Rother explains:[6]

> *Although learning new skills involves a certain amount of discomfort, it's quite amazing what you can achieve through practicing a practical form of scientific thinking. The more scientific capability you develop in your teams, the more you can empower them to meet challenges that you may have once considered impossible. Managers play a key role in this, because it is their job to create the creators.*

As the famous military saying goes, "No battle plan survives first contact with the enemy."* Or as John Lennon sang, "Life is what happens." All bets are off once deployment starts; there is a great deal of uncertainty, and the best organizations learn their way to the challenge in bite-size steps. Every attempt to "implement" something becomes an experiment to reflect on and learn from, guided by the direction and plan. In the last and final principle, we will focus even more deeply on the direction. It begins with what few companies do well— develop a well-thought-out strategy and commit to it.

KEY POINTS

- Hoshin kanri (aka policy deployment) is Toyota's approach to jointly aligning goals and plans at all levels to lay out the challenges and targets for the year.
- Hoshin kanri is more than a business realization tool: it is a process for developing people through coaching and problem solving.
- Hoshin kanri uses a planning period to lay out challenges and milestones, which provide a framework for the step-by-step improvement process of experimenting and learning.
- The process of working toward breakthrough objectives to achieve new standards (PDCA) is supported by daily management to identify and eliminate deviations from standard (SDCA).

---

* This saying (and variations of it) is usually attributed to Helmuth von Moltke the Elder, chief of staff of the Prussian army before World War I. https://blog.seannewmanmaroni.com/no-battle-plan-survives-first-contact-with-the-enemy-966df69b24b9.

- The simple A3, one side of an 11-inch x 17-inch sheet of paper, is a great way to summarize thinking about plans, actions, and results, so leaders can coach and develop people and build consensus around plans and actions.
- Use constant hansei (reflection) to openly identify weaknesses and prioritize areas for improvement.
- As we move from the executive suites to the work groups that execute, each level takes responsibility for its own business—planning and working to meet the plan.
- The cascading process is far more than breaking down desired outcomes and assigning them to groups. The planning requires causal reasoning. What do I need to work on to help my boss achieve his or her targets?

Notes

1. Jeffrey Liker and Gary Convis, *The Toyota Way to Lean Leadership* (New York: McGraw-Hill, 2011).
2. Jim Collins, *Great by Choice* (New York: Harper Business, 2011).
3. Alan Ward, Jeffrey Liker, Durward Sobek, John Cristiano, "The Second Toyota Paradox: How Delaying Decisions Can Make Better Cars Faster," *Sloan Management Review*, Spring, 1995: 43–61.
4. John Shook, *Managing to Learn: Using the A3 Management Process to Solve Problems, Gain Agreement, Mentor, and Lead* (Cambridge, MA: Lean Enterprise Institute, 2008).
5. Durward Sobek and Art Smalley, *Understanding A3 Thinking: A Critical Component of Toyota's PDCA Management System* (Boca Raton, FL: CRC Press, 2008).
6. Mike Rother, *The Toyota Kata Practice Guide* (New York: McGraw-Hill, 2017).

Principle 14

Learn Your Way to the Future Through Bold Strategy, Some Large Leaps, and Many Small Steps

You've got to think about big things while you are doing small things, so that all the small things go in the right direction.
—Alvin Toffler, author, *Future Shock*

Toyota's history of growth from start-up to global powerhouse has been a challenging journey filled with turns and twists. Internally, Toyota developed the winning culture of the Toyota Way, continually improving in every nook and cranny of the company. Externally, Toyota has largely grown through incremental innovation, that is, keeping up with competitors in product technology, combined with exceptional quality and reliability. Everything works as it should, but exciting is not an adjective often applied to Toyota. There have been sports cars like the Supra and Lexus LF that have been plenty exciting. The Lexus brand focused on "the relentless pursuit of perfection" with high value for the price and changed the luxury car industry. The Prius was a breakthrough in technology that changed the industry and moved it in the direction of all-electric vehicles. But these breakthroughs seem periodic, not the norm.

As Toyota faces the twenty-first century, Akio Toyota envisions vehicles that connect with customers, making them smile, and wants to "lead the future mobility society, enriching lives around the world with the safest and most responsible ways of moving people." Seems pretty bold to want to "lead" and beyond automotive to "mobility." But exciting? The way Toyota will do it is "by engaging the talent and passion of people who believe there is always a better way." The engine driving the company forward remains the Toyota Way of respect for people and continuous improvement.

In the meantime, anyone who can spell mobility seems to be starting an electric vehicle company that will disrupt the industry, displace out-of-date

323

"legacy automakers" like Toyota, and entice investors to throw money at them. Obviously, this is an exaggeration, but the leader is Tesla, which already has successfully disrupted the industry, has exceeded the market capitalization of any other automaker, and has become the new model other automotive startups are aspiring to. This leads to the question: Has the Toyota Way lost its luster and usefulness as a model for this new age?

By 2020 some analysts already declared the game is over and Tesla has won.[1] The argument of Tesla superiority does make some sense. "Tesla is not making cars, it is selling an iPhone with wheels. The vehicle itself is merely a medium to market the software undergirding the iTunes-like community that Tesla is building."

As I write this, Toyota and Tesla are not really in a competition to the death for the same customer base. It is not clear they are even playing the same game. Toyota is serving most vehicle segments, most global markets, selling about 10 million vehicles per year and investing capital earned through profits, compared to Tesla selling about ½ million targeting very specific markets, mostly in the United States, and using the money of investors who hope it will be the next Amazon or Apple. Where this goes long term we can only speculate.

Toyota and Tesla do have in common that they have bold strategies, have taken some big leaps, and have struggled through many small steps. Behind the scenes of the big-bang Tesla, which seemed to appear overnight as the next great car company, was over 15 years of very hard work with successes and many failures. The original Tesla company was launched in July, 2003, and much of the core technology we see today was developed by two brilliant engineers, before Elon Musk got involved as an investor in 2004. It took 17 years to become the phenom we see in 2020. The message of Principle 14 is that turning strategy into execution is a struggle and you cannot simple copy the strategy of another company. Unfortunately, each company will need to define its own strategy based on its unique circumstances and work toward this vision with some large leaps and many small steps.

One thing is clear. The success of any organization is far more than continuously improving processes (now you tell us!). Every organization needs a strategy for the products and services that will bring in customers. And we also need a strategy for our operations—what capabilities do we need to deliver on our business model? What customers want is a product and/or service that connects with them—solves their problems, excites them, makes sense to them, and does something important for them that competitive products or services do not. Customers who can afford it will pay extra, and even be inconvenienced, for a next-generation product or service that satisfies their needs at a higher level.

A strategy consists of a vision, a plan, ideas about the product or service, the target market, the means of delivery, and the service levels; it then needs to be put into action. For simplicity, let's distinguish between strategy, which is the vision and plan, and execution, which is how we actually do things. Execution can be excellent, OK, or poor. If the strategy leads to a uniquely useful product or service, or you have a monopoly on it, or it is in short supply, then execution does not have to be as great. Consider how people put up with the first iPhone, buggy and featureless, yet waited in line to get it. Or more recently, how people would do anything to get sanitized wipes during the Covid crisis. At these times, refined execution was not the priority for these products.

Then there are companies like Amazon, that combine a disruptive business strategy with excellent execution. The original model in 1994 was a user-friendly website with direct shipments of books to customers. This grew to the mission to be "Earth's most customer-centric company, where customers can find and discover anything they might want to buy online." To deliver, Amazon had to get really good at fulfilling customer orders by building a superior logistics system and a world-class supply chain.

On the other hand, some company strategies focus on delivering commodities, and executing at superior levels of quality, cost, and delivery—what we usually think of as lean. Execution is everything. One of the worst situations can be when a company's strategic plan includes being great at execution, but the reality is the opposite. Pfeffer and Sutton talk about the "knowing-doing gap" and give many examples of organizations that think they know how to be excellent but fail in daily practice.[2] What they believe they know is not what they are able to do.

As an example of a company with a unique product strategy and offering, Tesla is shaking up the auto industry by dominating the small, but growing, battery-electric market. It has one highly-focused strategic direction: CASE, which is connected (through the Internet), autonomous, shared (with other paying customers), and electric battery-powered vehicles. Unencumbered by old-line vehicles (self driving), supply chains, and business models, Tesla is off and running toward CASE with a level of innovation not seen in the automotive industry since early breakthroughs in gas-powered vehicles. Before Tesla, entering and surviving this capital-intensive industry with a history of low margins seemed difficult, if not impossible. But Tesla has been successfully blazing new trails and disrupting the auto industry in the process, and the barrier to entry of building factories for complex powertrains are all but gone for electric vehicles.

Corporate strategy guru Michael Porter warned in a classic 1996 *Harvard Business Review* article that "operational effectiveness is not strategy."[3] He also warned in that article that Japanese companies had turned cars into a commodity and were competing on cost and quality, cannibalizing each other's margins:

> *The dangers of Japanese-style competition are now becoming easier to recognize. In the 1980s, with rivals operating far from the productivity frontier, it seemed possible to win on both cost and quality indefinitely. . . . But as the*

gap in operational effectiveness narrows, Japanese companies are increasingly caught in a trap of their own making. If they are to escape the mutually destructive battles now ravaging their performance, Japanese companies will have to learn strategy.

Since Porter prophetically wrote that, many auto companies throughout the world have struggled, hovering near or ending up in bankruptcy. Toyota has not been one of them, charging premium prices, relentlessly cutting costs, and earning robust profits year after year, and with plenty of cash available. The Toyota Way is as much about studying the environment and developing long-term strategy based on facts as it is about taking cost out of manufacturing processes. Toyota is showing no signs of sticking its head in the sand and pretending all this new technology shall pass. As President Akio Toyoda made clear in a speech on "becoming a mobility company" in December 2019:[4]

Toyota's growth to date is within the established business model of the automotive industry. In light of technological innovations in "CASE," the very concept of the automobile is on the verge of major change. Given this situation, we must transform our business model into one that is in line with the CASE era. Therefore, rather than focus solely on passenger cars and individual customers, we can spread these technologies via commercial vehicles and vehicles for government offices and fleet customers. Rather than conduct development on our own—without friends and partners—we can partner and collaborate with others who share our aspirations. Rather than sell only cars, we can provide various services in which vehicles are incorporated into a system.

Contrary to popular belief, continuous improvement means more than small, incremental changes in processes. As we learned from Principle 13, it simply means improving continuously, sometimes with breakthroughs driven by hoshin and other times more gradually through daily management—PDCA and SDCA can go hand in hand. For Toyota, a well-thought-out strategy and excellent execution are not alternatives, but a necessary combination. The foundation of *The Toyota Way 2001* starts with breakthrough *challenges*, not small incremental improvements. Toyota evolved out of innovation, originally in developing power looms and then in designing automobiles, and ever since, its executives have preached about the next existential crisis around the corner while the company repeatedly breaks new performance records.

Toyota disrupted the industry in the 1970s with the Corolla. Eiji Toyoda could have been satisfied by a car that pleased the Japanese consumers Toyota knew well, but he wanted a global car to rival the Volkswagen Beetle. In studying US consumer tastes at the time, the company realized that with rising fuel costs, Americans wanted a smaller, fuel-efficient vehicle at low cost, but expected many of the luxuries of a big, expensive vehicle. Toyota's Corolla hit the sweet spot of fuel efficiency, size, upscale features, and power and became the bestselling vehicle in the world. Toyota succeeded again with the Lexus when nobody thought of luxury and Japanese cars in the same sentence. The Prius, discussed in the next section, was another example, successfully taking a bold step into the twenty-first century before any other automaker. And when we look back, we may view Toyota as the disruptor that created the hydrogen fuel cell market for various types of mobility services.

At this point, Toyota is focused on building competencies in the technologies for the future, and as usual Toyota is happy to stay under the radar. It likes to let its "products speak for themselves." The company is definitely methodical, like the tortoise, but it can also move at a crisp pace and arguably works on more fronts than any other automaker. Having built a strong brand known for reliability, generated strong sales and profitability, and amassed boatloads of cash, Toyota has the luxury to think long term and execute based on a strategy and a bold vision that looks out to 2050 and encompasses major milestones in environmental friendliness. When asked what he has learned from the many crises he has faced, including the transformation of the industry and Covid-19, Akio Toyoda responded with an answer that stressed keeping calm and managing stably:[5]

The number one thing I have learned and that I am prioritizing from my learning is that I am not panicking. I am managing the company very efficiently and stably. In managing the company during these past 10 years, no years were peaceful. Every year, year on year, we have witnessed and experienced a large, drastic change on the scale of a one-in-a-100-year event. So, I think that the calmer I am, the calmer things are within the company.

THE PRIUS THAT SHOOK THE WORLD*

The Prius provides a window into how Toyota approaches breakthrough innovation through large leaps and small steps. In retrospect, it can be difficult to imagine the obstacles a company had to overcome to achieve a successful innovation, but at the time nobody outside Toyota seemed to think a gas-electric hybrid was a viable product—or a wise business decision. The Prius shook up the industry and paved the way for electric vehicles (EVs). How did it happen? In the early 1990s, when Toyota was earning record profits from gasoline-powered vehicles

---

* This section is based on personal interviews with Takeshi Uchiyamada as well as the book by Hideshi Itazaki, *The Prius That Shook the World: How Toyota Developed the World's First Mass Production Hybrid Vehicle* (Tokyo: Nikkan Kogyo Shimbun, 1999).

and appeared unable to do anything wrong, chairman Eiji Toyoda asked at a board meeting:

> *Should we continue building cars as we have been doing? Can we survive in the 21st century with the type of R&D that we are doing? . . . There is no way that this [economic boom] situation will last much longer."*

When Eiji Toyoda spoke, everyone listened. Toyota was practically printing money at the time, but it challenged itself to think and act long term for fear of eventually facing extinction (see Principle 1).

In response to Eiji Toyoda's challenge, Yoshiro Kimbara, then executive VP of R&D, formed Global 21 (G21), which ultimately led to the Prius. Kimbara launched a "Business Revolution Project" in September 1993 that was tasked with researching new cars for the twenty-first century. The only real guidance was to develop a fuel-efficient, small-size car—exactly the opposite of the large gas guzzlers that were selling at the time. A committee of about 30 senior executives met weekly for three months and developed a concept, including a full-scale drawing. In addition to the small size, a distinguishing feature of the original vision was a large, spacious cabin that turned out to be critical to the success of Prius. The committee also set a target for fuel economy. The then current engine in a basic Corolla got 30.8 miles per gallon, and the target was set at 50 percent more, 47.5 miles per gallon.

High-level executives then pondered who should lead the effort of developing a prototype vehicle and settled on the unlikely choice of Takeshi Uchiyamada, who later was tasked as chief engineer for the production vehicle. The chief engineer role in Toyota is sacrosanct as the super engineer and business mind leading the program as if it were a startup. Uchiyamada hadn't been groomed to be a chief engineer and never even aspired to this role. His technical background was in test engineering, and he had never worked in vehicle development. Uchiyamada described to me his dilemma:

> *As a chief engineer, if there are supplier problems it is the responsibility to visit the supplier and check the line and solve the problems. I did not even know what I was looking for to know what to do in many cases. One of the personifications of the chief engineer is that they know everything, so even when developing different parts of the vehicle you know where the bolts can go together as well as what the customer wants.*

So what could Uchiyamada do since he did not "know everything"? He surrounded himself with a cross-functional team of experts and relied on the team. One of the most important results of the Prius project from an organizational design perspective was the creation of the obeya system of vehicle development, which to this day is the standard for Toyota. "Obeya" means "big room." It is like the control room, but using visuals on the walls to show the actual condition compared with the target condition on key metrics. In the old vehicle development system, the chief engineer traveled about, meeting with people as needed to coordinate the program. For the Prius, Uchiyamada gathered a cross-functional group of experts who worked together full-time in the "big room" to review the progress of the program and discuss key decisions. He also introduced a higher-level use of email and brought CAD terminals into the room. Toyota executives achieved their goal of reinventing the company's vehicle-development process by selecting a nonexpert chief engineer.

The goal for the G21 was stated as a "small, fuel-efficient car." An all-electric vehicle certainly would have been fuel efficient and would have produced almost zero emissions, but it was not considered practical or convenient. You needed a separate infrastructure to recharge the batteries, the range between charges was short with the known technology at the time, and the batteries needed would be huge and expensive. Executives feared the car would be a "battery carrier." Fuel cell technology, on the other hand, had great promise, but the technology was not nearly developed to the point of being viable and there was no infrastructure for refueling.

Even a hybrid was initially rejected by the team by 1994. It was considered too new and a risky technology. In September 1994, the team met with Executive Vice President Akihiro Wada and Managing Director Masanao Shiomi, and the hybrid technology came up, but no conclusion was reached. What did come up was an unexpected request by Wada to develop a concept vehicle for the Tokyo Motor Show. When Uchiyamada went to brief Executive VP Wada on progress, Wada not so subtly pulled the rug out from under him:

> By the way, your group is also working on the new concept car for the Motor Show, right? We recently have decided to develop that concept car as a hybrid vehicle. That way, it would be easy to explain its fuel economy. We are not talking about production here, so show us your best ideas.

This seemed impossible, particularly since there were only two months until the auto show. Despite this incredible time pressure, Uchiyamada followed the Toyota process of set-based design—first broadly considering alternatives, asking his team to consider all the possible known hybrid technologies, and converging on a selection.[6] The team met the challenge, and the hybrid concept won top awards and was the talk of the show. It was not terribly surprising after the show that Wada increased the fuel economy target for the Prius, and it became obvious that a hybrid was the only practical alternative for the production version. It was fitting that a car named Prius, which is Latin for "go before," would be a hybrid.

In the meantime, in August 1995, Toyota named a new president, Hiroshi Okuda, and he was an unusually aggressive leader for Toyota. When he asked

Wada when the hybrid vehicle would be ready, Wada explained that he and his team were aiming for December 1998, "if all goes well."

Okuda said, "That is too late; no good. Can you get it done a year earlier? This car may change the course of Toyota's future and even that of the auto industry."[7]

The Prius launched in October 1997, two months ahead of the new December target date. Despite the time pressures and doing so many things for the first time, Uchiyamada made the critical decision to develop in-house all the core technologies that would make up the Prius—electric motors, switching circuits to change between DC and AC, computer systems to optimize the use of the gas engine and electric motors, and regenerative braking systems to convert mechanical energy to electric energy stored in the battery. The company could not go it alone on the battery itself, and so it partnered with Panasonic, a partnership that to this day is still researching and improving battery technology for Toyota and ultimately for sale to other companies—in this case, breakthrough solid-state batteries.[8]

At launch, the Prius took first place in the two most prestigious automotive competitions in Japan, winning both the coveted Japan Car of the Year and RJC New Car of the Year. It was actually beat to market by the Honda Insight hybrid, but Toyota's initial vision of a roomy interior for families won out over Honda's two-door, two-person vehicle. The Prius hybrid timeline is summarized in Figure 14.1. At a big-picture level, we see Toyota's philosophy of breakthrough vehicle development followed by incremental improvement. Toyota developed a vision for the twenty-first century and made a big leap into the new technology, developing in-house many new technical capabilities leading to refining the Prius through successive generations and then expanding hybrids to most other models. We can think of each generation of the Prius as a PDCA loop, and Toyota has gone through more of these learning loops than any other automaker.

With each generation, cumulative annual unit sales went up in leaps—to 1 million by 2008 and 3 million by 2013. By 2017, the Prius was being hailed as one of the most important cars since the Model T.[9] Meanwhile, Toyota had been working hard in R&D to bring down the cost of the hybrid synergy drive and branched out making hybrid versions of most of its bestselling models for just a few thousand dollars more than the gas engine equivalent. By January 2017, the company reached cumulative sales of 10 million hybrids, and by early 2020, Toyota had sold over 15 million hybrids in the 23 years since the launch of the first Prius.[10] In the UK market in 2019, hybrids accounted for two-thirds of all Toyota-Lexus sales.

Year	Milestone
1990	Japanese bubble economy peak; Eiji Toyoda proclaims need for cars for the twenty-first century
Sept. 1993	G21 Business Revolution Team formed to create concept
Nov. 1993	Uchiyamada to head concept-vehicle development team
Oct. 1995	Hybrid concept shown at Tokyo Motor Show
June 1995	G21 is official project with people, budget, timing; Uchiyamada named Chief Engineer
Dec. 1997	First Prius sold in Japan
2000	Prius goes global
2003	Second-generation Prius launched
2008	1 million Priuses sold*
2009	Third-generation Prius launched
2010	2 million Priuses sold*
2012	Prius bestselling car in Japan 4 consecutive years; bestselling car in California
2013	3 million Priuses sold*
2015	Fourth-generation Prius launched
Jan. 2017	Prius is 6.1 million of 10 million hybrids sold by Toyota worldwide*
2018	15% of Toyota global sales were hybrids; 1.6 million vehicles**

*Volume sales are cumulative.
** Growth in hybrid sales continued in 2019 and Toyota could sell many more—except the constraint was the supply of batteries.

Figure 14.1 Prius key milestones.

Meanwhile, electric vehicle sales were still a small percentage of vehicles sold, though creeping up. In 2017 in the United States, electric cars, including the plug-in Prius Prime, accounted for 200,000 vehicles out of 17 million vehicles sold (1 percent).[11] In 2019, that increased to 2.2 percent, and in the United States about three-quarters of those sales came from Tesla.[12] The enthusiasm for producing battery-only electric vehicles has been through the roof, and stock prices soared for startup companies making electric vehicles, though doing so profitably and at high volumes has been a struggle to this point.

Toyota has been criticized for being one of the last auto companies to produce all battery-powered vehicles. Is it finally dead wrong about the future and missing the market? I think the answer is that it has an equally bold strategy, but its strategy is just different from that of Tesla and some other automakers because Toyota is in a different position financially and in the market. Toyota has been following Principle 14: "Learn your way to the future through bold strategy, some large leaps, and many small steps." The Prius is a great example of this, pursuing a seemingly impossible challenge at breakneck speed, coupled with steadfast step-by-step execution via PDCA doing and learning. As I write this, Toyota introduced the first Mirai hydrogen fuel-cell vehicle, and like the original Prius, is refining the range and features of the second generation with a long-term goal of bringing it within the price range of hybrids. And it has a number of battery-electric vehicles nearing production through joint ventures, focusing at first on the large market of China.

Toyota has spent decades learning the new technologies of the future and introducing these technologies into mass-produced vehicles. With its technology capability and rapid product-process development systems, it can pivot quickly, shifting focus to plug-in hybrids with varying range, battery vehicles, hydrogen fuel cell vehicles, or whatever else the market demands.

COMPARING TOYOTA AND TESLA ON STRATEGY

For Nokia's phone business, the big disruptor was the Apple iPhone, which ultimately drove it to bankruptcy and reemergence with a different product line. For the auto industry, the not-so-big disruptor appears to be Tesla. Tesla did one thing really well, but it is the one thing that matters. Tesla developed a new kind of car that customers love. With the bold vision of Elon Musk, the company started with a clean sheet of paper and envisioned what would excite customers in the twenty-first century.

Elon Musk was a child prodigy and grew up loving science fiction, physics, and computer programming, but not necessarily working with other people.[13] He grew up socially awkward and a loner who believed he was always the smartest person in the room, and probably was in most cases. He cofounded PayPal as a software innovator, but he made the remarkable shift to automobiles and spaceships—innovating in hardware at the pace of software innovation. Elon Musk is like a CEO and chief engineer combined who is involved in every important decision and whose motto seems to be "no compromise."

With Musk's vision, Tesla designed into automobiles anything it could imagine a customer wanting—all at once. It made the car all electric, innovated on batteries to extend the range; engineered the car to be superfast, even "ludicrous"; created a simple, clean interior with no buttons; used one computer instead of many; designed in a grandiose screen; updated the software over the air; designed and built its own comfortable seats; allowed stopping the vehicle by releasing the gas pedal without even touching the brake pedal; offered an autopilot that the company claims will quickly morph into full autonomy; set up operation by your smartphone; sold reservations for vehicles before they were in production; created cool stores and avoided independent dealerships—and the list goes on. The company took product risks, for example calling the autonomy features "autopilot" at a time when the auto industry had become almost paranoid from repeated recalls and was avoiding terms that suggested a car could drive itself.

This does not mean all went well for Tesla. Execution was hectic, even chaotic. The company promised unrealistic launch dates and broke one promise after another. There were quality problems, launch problems, production problems, problems in introducing technologies that were not ready for prime time, spectacular crashes with autopilot, and failures to deliver on promises to customers, and yet passionate early-adopter customers still fought their way to getting their Tesla.

Elon Musk himself called attempts to manufacture Model 3s at volume "production hell" and learned manufacturing was a lot more difficult than he initially thought. A few months after proclaiming that Tesla's real product was the automated factory that would run competing automakers out of business, he backtracked and declared: "Yes, excessive automation at Tesla was a mistake. To be precise, my mistake. Humans are underrated." The solution was to set up a makeshift, mostly manual, assembly line under a "tent" in the parking lot of the plant in Fremont, California. Read Edward Niedermeyer's book *Ludicrous*[14] about the showmanship of things that were promised but did not exist at Tesla and how the company narrowly avoided multiple bankruptcies, and you will wonder how the company survived, let alone prospered.

Tesla's strategy, as I can intuit it, is straightforward (see Figure 14.2). Create a disruptive computerized product powered by a self-renewing power system made with a disruptive computerized factory. Tesla's ultimate purpose is to help save the planet through 100 percent renewable energy. It is clear Elon Musk cares deeply about humanity and has a long-term vision greater than short-term profits.

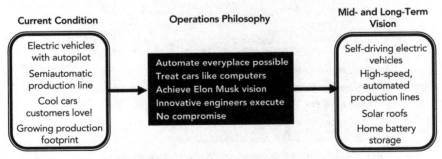

Note: Highly-simplified view of Tesla strategy

Figure 14.2 Tesla's disruptive strategic vision.
Source: James Morgan and Jeffrey Liker, *Designing the Future*
(New York: McGraw-Hill, 2018).

Anyone who in any way diminishes the accomplishments of Tesla is not paying attention—it's the first automotive startup since Chrysler that looks like it will survive and even prosper, bringing to life a whole product family of all-electric vehicles and making them cool, dominating sales of battery electric cars globally, achieving a market capitalization greater than that of established automakers many times its size, and causing all existing players to scramble to compete.

Toyota's strategy is more complex and subtle and is fitting of Toyota's situation. Toyota has been at its best as the determined tortoise, step-by-step, carefully evaluating each step. Historically, Toyota wanted to hold about 80 percent of vehicle design constant from established model to new model, while focusing on key innovations in the other 20 percent. Toyota has not been the leader in vocalizing a commitment to battery electric vehicles, though it is rushing a bunch to market as I write this, with some based on a joint e-platform with a nine-company consortium including Subaru. Toyota is moving toward all-electric vehicles, but sees for itself a more extended transition period where hybrid and plug-in hybrid sales will continue for years, taken over later by a combination of battery-electric and hydrogen-powered vehicles (Figure 14.3). These may occupy different niches, for example, with hydrogen focused on larger commercial vehicles.

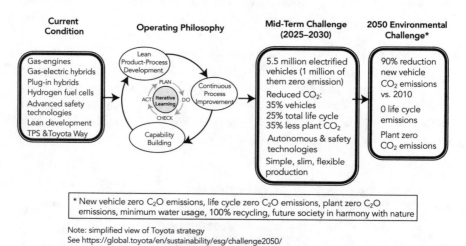

Figure 14.3 Toyota's environmental strategic vision and operating philosophy.
Source: James Morgan and Jeffrey Liker, *Designing the Future* (New York: McGraw-Hill, 2018).

Even with the rising popularity of battery-only vehicles, Toyota decided someone had to take the lead on hydrogen, so in 2014 the company launched the Mirai (meaning "the future"), and later Toyota made hundreds of its hydrogen patents open and free to anyone. Interestingly, the Mirai is a hybrid with a battery and electric motors alongside the fuel cell. Toyota realized that the first-generation Mirai would sell in small quantities (10,000 total), as it was expensive and the refueling infrastructure was limited to just a few places. Since then, the company has made major investments in hydrogen infrastructure on its own and working with governments and other companies such as Shell. Toyota announced the 2021 Mirai as a luxury sedan with sleek styling and a longer range of 400 miles. Toyota anticipates sales of 30,000 units in the first year. The company is also working with subsidiary Hino on a commercial truck with a heavy-duty hydrogen fuel cell.

Battery efficiency and cost have progressed at a remarkable rate but have remained heavy and expensive and, as of 2020, in limited supply. In 2019, Gerald Killmann, Toyota's vice president of research and development for Europe, explained that Toyota was able to produce enough batteries for 28,000 battery-only vehicles each year, or 1.5 million hybrids. And selling 1.5 million hybrids reduced carbon emissions by one-third more than 28,000 electric vehicles, while also providing its customers more practical vehicles (because of no range or charging anxieties) at more affordable prices.[15]

Toyota's "Environmental Challenge 2050," announced on October 2015, provides a road map of the plan to work toward harmony with the environment.* Challenge 2050 is more than a vision; it contains specific goals. The six challenges for 2050 are zero carbon emissions, zero life cycle carbon emissions, zero plant carbon emissions, minimizing and optimizing water usage, establishing a recycling-based society and systems, and establishing a future society in harmony with nature. To move in that direction, Toyota has set intermediate goals for 2030, which are summarized in Figure 14.3.

By 2025, Toyota expects to sell 55 percent of its vehicles as electrified, which includes a hybrid version of almost every vehicle, plug-in hybrids, EVs, and hydrogen fuel cells.[16] Nearly 1 million are expected to be fully electric EVs (including battery only and hydrogen fuel cells), which will include a range of six body types from compact to a crossover. Toyota has set up a separate engineering group called the Toyota ZEF factory with about 300 people to create the Toyota versions of the e-platform from the nine-company consortium. It is also working on small electric vehicles with Toyota-owned Daihatsu and through a tie-up with Suzuki, as well as with Chinese joint-venture partner BYD. And the list of partnerships goes on.

Does Toyota or Tesla have a better strategy? Who is a better model to copy? The answer is neither. Remember strategy is based on forecasting (informed guessing) what will happen and what the situation is in a particular company.

---

* By the time you read this, the challenge may have changed, but at this point you can read about it at https://global.toyota/en/sustainability/esg/challenge2050/.

Both companies have a strategy that fits their circumstances. Tesla is a startup working toward becoming a more mature and financially healthy company. As a startup with no existing product lines, it is highly dependent on investor capital. Its lofty stock valuations are based on the image of Tesla as a technology company that is disrupting the mobility market.

Toyota is a large, established multinational company and already has large investments in gas, hybrid, plug-in hybrid, and hydrogen vehicles. Toyota has a balanced portfolio—a combination of products designed for the near term, mid-term, and long term. The current cash cows generate funding to support investing in other companies and R&D. Some organizational theorists have argued the most successful firms are "ambidextrous," with some parts of the organization focused on incremental improvement in the current product lineup and other parts focused on long-term technology development.[17] One study published in 2012 found that successful firms allocated on average 70 percent of their innovation funds to incremental innovation (short term), 20 percent to adjacent innovation (mid-term), and 10 percent to radical/breakthrough initiatives (long term). Google is an example of one firm that worked toward the 70-20-10 balance. At the time the study was done, firms with this portfolio balance historically realized a price/earnings premium of 10 to 20 percent.[18]

Tesla cannot be Toyota, and Toyota cannot be Tesla. Tesla has the advantage of being a young, entrepreneurial company with only one voice that matters—that of Elon Musk. It can be very nimble and only has to invest toward its limited focus. Toyota has a lot of balls in the air, including "legacy products" that pay the bills and many mouths to feed internally. And with its extensive network of established suppliers, it needs to tread more carefully. But Toyota also is a learning organization and has retained many of its entrepreneurial characteristics, including passionate leaders who will take on even seemingly impossible challenges with energy and focus. Not only should Toyota and Tesla not imitate each other, but your organization should not imitate either of them.

TOYOTA STRATEGY FOR AUTONOMOUS VEHICLES

You are just preparing to leave your home for a business appointment. You open an app on your phone and call your favorite ride-sharing service for your ride. A robotic car pulls up, no driver, and takes you wherever you want to go. Science fact or fiction? For the foreseeable future both. The technology exists for self-driving under certain limited conditions, certainly the media hype is loud, but most believe the reality is far off.

The problem with the myth that self-driving cars will soon be found everywhere is that it assumes what is called level-5 autonomy, or what Toyota calls "chauffeur" mode. You trust chauffeurs to safely drive you wherever you want to go while you text, sleep, read, and pay no attention to the road. There are three core competencies that chauffeurs need to accomplish this. The first is perceiving the environment, including other vehicles, pedestrians, animals, and bicycles. Computers are good at this. In fact, with cameras located in prime places and with lidar (laser-based radar) that can sense three dimensions, in many situations computers are better at this than humans. The second chauffeur competency is planning, basically figuring out in advance where to go and what to do. Again, with so much data available, such as high-resolution maps, computers are very good at this. The third competency is prediction, and this is where computers are weak. We might notice two kids with skateboards on the street corner and become suspicious about what they might do, so we adjust our driving accordingly. There are many situations where we predict possible danger because we read the motivations of people. Computers are not good at this. Because of the weakness of computers in making predictions, Toyota concluded that full level-5 autonomy is beyond current technological capability, and no one knows when it will be available and trusted, perhaps a decade or more in the future.

Meanwhile there is a lot that can be done with the current capabilities, and Toyota is focusing heavily on the other extreme, which it calls the "guardian function." The guardian looks over the shoulder of the human driver and detects whether the person is drowsy, distracted, drunk, or disabled and will work to prevent an accident—even taking over driving if necessary. As the technology evolves, Toyota is going farther into what it calls the "mobility teammate concept" (MTC), which can alternate between guardian and chauffeur.

> *MTC is a philosophy built on the belief people should have choices. Rather than removing humans from any engagement with their own mobility, this allows people to enjoy the fun and freedom of driving when and if they choose, while also benefiting from the capabilities of automated driving when they wish. Indeed, under MTC, individuals can choose Chauffeur capability in some situations, such as highway and long-distance travel, or the support of Guardian capability in others, such as at lower speeds or on shorter trips.*[19]

In MTC, the relationship between the human driver and the automated system is symbiotic, with each monitoring while the other drives. Human drivers do not get to go to sleep or be distracted. Toyota's motto is "Guardian first," which means Toyota vehicles will be biased toward guardian mode and only cautiously move to chauffeur mode.

By the time you read this, Toyota will, at least in some Lexus vehicles, offer a version of this more advanced teammate level, which some refer to as level-2 autonomy, on highways where the driver can take both hands off the wheel and let the computer drive from on-ramp to off-ramp, including some lane changes, merges, and splits. To get to these capabilities, Toyota has to build into each car an advanced supercomputer.

As the computer systems advance, the computer can take over more of the driving in more situations. Self-driving at level 4 is already possible under limited circumstances, called "operational design domains" (ODDs), such as low-speed urban shuttles (less than 25 miles per hour), some private roads, dedicated lanes for automated driving only, and the last mile of delivery where there is not a lot of human traffic. As the technology further develops, the ODDs that are safe will expand.

Toyota is collaborating with many different companies in "sharing" vehicles, including major investments in Uber, Chinese ride-sharing giant Didi, and a Singapore ride-sharing company, Grab. It has also created an open-source vehicle platform to sell to third-party companies, which it calls "e-Palette," to open up new commercialization opportunities. It is designed to be a safe, reliable platform that other companies can build on with their own technology and their own body shape for diverse applications like food trucks, mobile offices, and last-mile delivery vehicles (like the choices on an artist's palette).

So how did Toyota make the shift from a conservative, legacy automaker that is great at electromechanical systems to one that is developing autonomous-vehicle software? The answer is that it broke with its long-established practices and made a radical decision to go outside and invest billions in establishing two subsidiaries—Toyota Research Institute (TRI), to do advanced research on autonomous driving, and Toyota Research Institute–Advanced Development (TRI-AD), to bring that research from the prototype stage to the preproduction stage. In 2020, Toyota also created an $800 million global investment fund, led by TRI-AD, focused on growth-staged companies developing new technologies and business models.

The company went even further. Rather than assign Toyota lifers to run those institutes, Toyota went outside to hire brilliant Americans who are experts in artificial intelligence and robotics. Dr. Gill Pratt is CEO of TRI with offices in Silicon Valley; Ann Arbor, Michigan; and Cambridge, Massachusetts. Dr. Pratt came from DARPA of the US Defense Department and earlier from MIT, where he was a professor of robotics and artificial intelligence. Dr. Pratt hired a colleague, Dr. James Kuffner, as CTO of TRI, who was later appointed as CEO of TRI-AD in Tokyo. Dr. James Kuffner, a Stanford PhD, was an associate professor in Carnegie Mellon's Robotics Institute and then joined Google to work on its self-driving car.

To further amplify their influence, Toyota named Dr. Kuffner to the Toyota Motor Corporation's board of directors in March 2020 and appointed Dr. Pratt as Toyota's chief scientist. Both new Toyota executives love cars, AI, and robotics and studied and admired Toyota long before they were hired. They were attracted to the opportunity to lead well-funded subsidiaries within a global giant like Toyota, with the opportunity to commercialize on a mass scale what they develop. You could say that Toyota, instead of contracting out autonomy to a Silicon Valley startup, built its own technology startups.

Toyota's strategy is not to maximize profit from autonomy as fast as possible, but rather its strategy is driven by its core values. Dr. Pratt explained:

> Our motivation starts with trying to make the car safer and then more fun to drive. When I first interviewed Akio Toyoda, he explained that people love cars, but do not love refrigerators. I think the difference is that the refrigerator is useful, but it is passive . . . you don't control what it does. A car is an amplifier. It multiplies what you make it do by hundreds of horsepower. In autonomy we want to make cars that are more fun to drive and safer as a primary goal, and if a secondary side effect pops out of that where in some situations the cars can drive by themselves, that is perfectly fine, but that is not the driving goal.

Dr. Kuffner has a compatible view, and I asked him if Toyota's strategy means the company is intentionally going slower in autonomy to avoid risks, to which he replied:

> For Toyota, the most valuable asset that we have is our brand. Therefore, if a smaller company doesn't have as much to lose, then they can certainly be more aggressive, which is an advantage that startups will have. We are looking for something that will scale to millions or tens of millions of customers every year and have the reliability and robustness expected of a company like Toyota, so the bar is higher for us. Is Toyota lagging? Not necessarily. I think other competitors market their technology more aggressively. But Toyota's approach is to let our products speak for themselves more than some others. There are trade-offs to both approaches.

COMPETING VALUES AND STRATEGY

Robert Quinn illuminated the world of strategy and how it relates to internal culture in the 1980s with his "competing values model."[20] I saw him present when this chapter was in progress and realized it is a great framework for understanding the relationship between strategy and execution. He began with two dimensions—control versus flexibility and internal versus external. The concept of control is a characteristic of the mechanistic model, while flexibility is characteristic of the organic model. An external focus is on the environment while an internal focus is on how a company runs its own operations. Quinn put these together into a 2 × 2 table and named the four cells (see Figure 14.4).

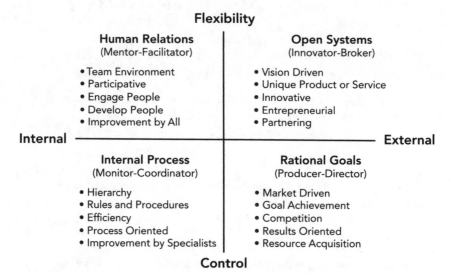

Flexibility

Human Relations (Mentor-Facilitator)	**Open Systems** (Innovator-Broker)
• Team Environment • Participative • Engage People • Develop People • Improvement by All	• Vision Driven • Unique Product or Service • Innovative • Entrepreneurial • Partnering

Internal ———————————————————————— **External**

Internal Process (Monitor-Coordinator)	**Rational Goals** (Producer-Director)
• Hierarchy • Rules and Procedures • Efficiency • Process Oriented • Improvement by Specialists	• Market Driven • Goal Achievement • Competition • Results Oriented • Resource Acquisition

Control

Figure 14.4   Competing values framework for strategy and culture.
Source: Robert Quinn, Beyond Rational Management: Mastering the Paradoxes and Competing Demands of High Performance (San Francisco: Jossey-Bass, 1988).

Externally, the company can focus on control (rational goals) or flexibility (open systems). Internally, the company can tend toward control (internal process) or flexibility (human relations). So which quadrant is best? The answer is, it depends. First, "best" depends on the company's strategy and environment. Second, competition among values can be broken, leading to a paradox where an organization can be seemingly opposite things at once—this, yet that. In fact, some of the most successful organizations are strong in multiple areas. Think of a spider diagram giving you a profile where you can be weak in all areas, or strong in all areas, or any other combination.

I used a spider diagram to roughly plot—that is, guesstimate—the profile of Toyota, Western auto companies, and Tesla (see Figure 14.5). Quinn and his associates developed various assessments that are more sophisticated than my guesses. Historically the Western auto industry has been preoccupied with control to the exclusion of flexibility—internally and externally. The companies in this industry want rules, structure, people obeying orders, and the freedom to hire and fire people at will, and then the goal externally is to grow, make a profit, and satisfy shareholders. To Western auto companies, lean programs have been attractive not for continuous improvement, but as cost-reduction tools within a coercive bureaucracy. The external strategy seems to be "Make money through high sales and low cost." As I write this there is a shift in Western auto companies toward more technological innovation in the direction of open systems.

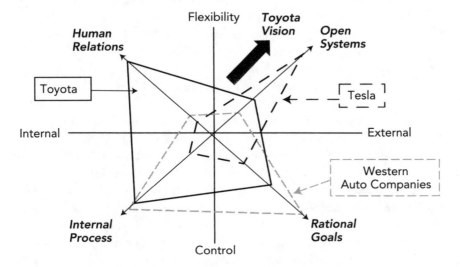

NOTE: Based on Liker's subjective assessments

Figure 14.5 Competing values framework and auto companies.
Source: Robert Quinn, Beyond Rational Management: Mastering the Paradoxes and Competing Demands of High Performance (San Francisco: Jossey-Bass, 1988).

Toyota is different and I believe has the widest range of any automaker. Internally, continuous improvement for Toyota combines high-value-added internal processes with strong human relations, thus combining high levels of control with high levels of flexibility. The control of processes is what Paul Adler called "enabling bureaucracy." One might think that the future belongs to the purely innovative companies that do not need any bureaucracy, just brilliant teams of innovators. That misses the majority of work that a company does when it is grown up, much of which is relatively routine and needs some structure and stability.

For example, Dr. Pratt and Dr. Kuffner have been pushing Toyota toward applying TPS to IT. The amount of code that needs to be written now and well into the future is overwhelming—the two colleagues cannot hire enough people to write it based on conventional models of writing a lengthy program and then spending as much time debugging it. So they are borrowing from TPS and focusing on designing in quality. Under Principle 6, I discussed how Menlo Innovations builds in quality through breaking the software into tiny bits and designing unit tests for each bit to confirm that it works. TRI and TRI-AD do this, and every night the researchers compile and test all the coding done during the day, hoping not to find any more problems. When they do find an issue, they rely on root cause problem solving to prevent the problem from reoccurring. You can find similar methods throughout Silicon Valley under the rubric of "agile development," originally inspired by Toyota. It seems being strong at execution is also the key to our innovative digital future—internal control *and* flexibility.

Externally, Toyota is very good at planning and achieving rational goals, which has fueled 70 years of profitability, including a run of record profits for the industry: the company has had only one year of loss, and that was in the Great Recession. Toyota's strategy for the future is bold in many ways, but also pragmatic.

Toyota has its share of ventures into the open systems quadrant with the paradigm-breaking Lexus, Prius, and Mirai, and even building its "Woven City" of the future at the foot of Mount Fuji that will act as a "living laboratory" to experiment with advanced technologies.[21] The Prius seemed like a dangerous gambit and a guaranteed money loser, but it made lots of money and changed the auto world. And at this point, major investments in hydrogen vehicles may surprise many people and be a significant part of our environmentally friendly future. On the other hand, historically Toyota's lean machine has been fine-tuned for incremental innovation on dependable new models, so I showed it as less strong in open systems. The open systems quadrant is the area Akio Toyoda is working hardest to strengthen, through TRI, TRI-AD, and all the various technology partnerships.

How does Tesla rank on these competing values? From my off-the-cuff assessment, Tesla is firmly ensconced in the open systems quadrant, while doing just enough to build and distribute product in the other three. It is relatively unidimensional and weaker everyplace Toyota is strong. Fortunately, or more likely by plan, Tesla is strong in the one area that really matters for Elon Musk's strategy and style of leadership. I also give him credit in the human relations quadrant for hiring exceptional engineers who have done a good job of innovating. Elon Musk certainly thinks long term and has a vision well beyond earning a paycheck. Save the planet and colonize Mars are very long-term objectives. But long-term thinking for Toyota includes building a highly-adaptive learning organization internally at all levels. And innovative thinking at Toyota applies to everyone, even the person attaching the windshield wipers.

Not every company can act like a startup, but it is critical that the internal capabilities and external challenges are well aligned. As Robert Quinn put it in his book *Deep Change*:[22]

> *The process of formalization initially makes the organization more efficient or effective. As time goes on, however, these routine patterns move the organi-*

zation toward decay and stagnation. The organization loses alignment with the changing, external reality. When internal and external alignment is lost, the organization faces a choice: either adapt or take the road to slow death.

Has your environment shifted so much that you need to radically adapt or die? Are you a startup that needs to attract large amounts of investment capital? Then it may be that Tesla is a useful role model, at least in the near term. If you want to view Tesla as a role model, what are some of the key features you need to imitate?

1. The CEO should be a bold, visionary, genius who thrives on risk taking and has total control.
2. The visionary leader gathers together brilliant people willing to work around the clock to achieve the leader's targets and goals.
3. The key to success is a breakthrough product or service that is so different and appealing that quality, on-time delivery, and cost are secondary considerations.
4. Great optics for the most important customers—investors—are paramount.
5. The leader is the leader and is not to be challenged—dedicate your life to changing the world toward the leader's vision or get off the bus.
6. All managers, other than the top visionary leader and perhaps a small group of close confidants, are replaceable parts whose main task is to get the results they are assigned.
7. People that do the detailed work are also replaceable parts that are to do as instructed and are laid off and hired as needed.
8. Build a utilitarian and goal-oriented culture, and soft values like "respect for people" are lower priority.

These are characteristics of a number of highly successful entrepreneurial startups. Great entrepreneurs are different sorts of animals. And few corporate leaders can imitate what goes on in the mind of a brilliant entrepreneur. There has been speculation that if you could put Toyota and Tesla together, you would have an unbeatable combination. Jim Womack concluded that this will never happen, but they could learn from each other:[23]

The Toyota/Tesla Way sounds like a great idea. But . . . not in one company. Toyota and Tesla have already learned about each other from Toyota's brief investment in Tesla and their project to produce an all-electric Toyota RAV4. And they decided to admire each other from a distance. The most practical way forward is for Toyota to be bolder in pursuing first principles and for Tesla to be less ludicrous, showing respect for each other as they share the road.

STRATEGY AND EXECUTION ARE NOT SPECTATOR SPORTS

We can debate who are the greatest sports figures of all time in tennis, soccer, basketball, golf, or whatever. Are conservatives or liberals best for the country? What is the greatest movie of all time? And we can debate who will be the leading mobility provider in the future—Tesla, Toyota, another legacy automaker, or perhaps one of the many other EV startups? In the game of strategy for our own organizations, we are more than spectators. Few of us will be on a championship team or win a gold medal at the Olympics . . . or start a company that disrupts an industry. In fact, as many as 75 percent of venture-backed companies never return cash to investors, and the most likely outcome is bankruptcy.[24]

I do not pretend to be an expert on strategy. There are many courses and books just on this topic, and it is a core field of study in business schools. I do have a few bits of advice though:

First, develop your own strategy based on your products, services, markets, and unique situation. As former IBM CEO Ginni Rometty deftly put it: "You build your own strategy. You don't define it by what another competitor is doing."

Second, the competing values framework is a useful way to map your future strategy to strike an appropriate balance between external and internal, flexibility and control. The question is not which quadrant is best, but rather, what capabilities does your organization need to be successful in the future, considering your risk threshold, the market you face, trends in technology in your field, the broader environment, and what you think will excite your customers. Your strategy should be specific to *your* organization and *your* relevant environment. If we consider the automotive industry, there is more consensus than I have ever seen before in the industry about CASE. All agree they need to move toward this future, but how fast and with what approach? For Toyota, it's clear that maintaining its strong foundation in safety and reliability is paramount as the company moves forward.

The strategic vision starts in the external environment portion of the competing values model. What is your ideal vision for your products and services, and how will it connect with customers(open systems)? What is your vision for making a living (rational goals)? Then there is the internal portion. How developed do you need to be in execution? Is the delivery of those products and services a differentiator? Do you need flexible people continually improving toward excellence? Or is a moderate level of internal control enough?

Third, do not fall into the trap of thinking that just because you have a well-articulated strategy, with informative figures and charts, that you are done. You have only started. The difference between developing the strategy and executing against it is night and day. The vision is just that, a vision, based on our best guesses about the future. We will not really know what is going to happen until it happens. The execution should be done in bite-size pieces, learning from each experiment.

Mike Rother's model connects strategy to the step-by-step learning approach of the improvement kata (see Figure 14.6). What is your long-term strategic vision for your product or service? What competencies and distinctive processes are needed to support delivery? For the shorter term, say one to three years, what are the concrete challenges you need to take on to move in the direction of that strategy? That bounces you to the current condition—what are your current competencies, strengths, and weaknesses? Then identify, not all, but the first of your short-term target conditions and experiment toward that, and so on. This approach mirrors Alvin Toffler's opening quote advising thinking "about big things while you are doing small things, so that all the small things go in the right direction."

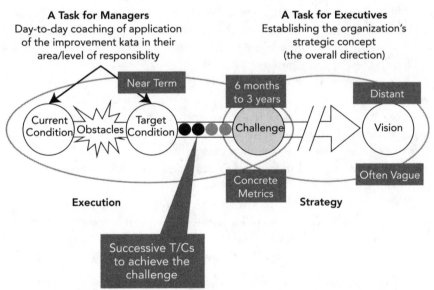

Figure 14.6   Connecting strategy to continuous improvement through successive target conditions and iterative learning.
Source: Mike Rother, *Toyota Kata Practice Guide* (New York: McGraw-Hill, 2017).

Sometimes strategic direction and a lean model for daily operations fit together hand in glove. Merillat was a market leader in kitchen cabinets, a low-margin business, but saw competition from all sides, and cost was a critical factor. The company hired a great lean leader, Keith Allman, as its COO, and he convinced the board that the company needed another way to compete—lead time and service quality. Merillat's largest client base consisted of builders who wanted the cabinets delivered on time at the same time. They had the people ready to do the installation, and they wanted all the cabinets there with perfect quality at that time, not too early or too late. Keith set as the visionary challenge "A kitchen at a time." Build a kitchen; ship a kitchen; get it to the right place on time. This required a lean transformation in the assembly plant, fabrication plants, and supply chain. This became a winning formula.

Some companies, a very small percentage, will legitimately conclude that the great disruptor with a radically better business model is right around the corner, and they either radically change or go out of business. In that case, for the short term, excellence in how they get things done may not be the top priority. If you survive this tumultuous transformation as you rebuild and mature and shift to mass distribution, I submit that excellence in execution and the internal culture to support and improve execution will become increasingly important. In *The Toyota Way to Lean Leadership*, Chapter 6, we described how Gary Convis as CEO helped lead a turnaround of truck-parts supplier Dana as it emerged successful from chapter 11 bankruptcy, by reducing costs, boosting market share, and developing people internally. After Dana was again profitable, the company worked on the Dana Operating System.

For the rest of us in the 99 percent, a better model than the pure open system disruptor is the more balanced Toyota Way. That does not mean it is a waste of time to do environmental scans, or that it is safe to assume there is no digital-based disruptive force for your business. It does mean most of us probably have some time to work our way there and probably can do it best with a strong culture of excellence and motivated, capable, and flexible members committed to the company.

The Toyota Way highlights the struggle of turning strategy as a plan into execution. The gemba is a tough taskmaster. Can I say with certainty that Toyota's strategy and execution will be effective in the future as the industry undergoes radical transformation? As Yogi Berra famously said, "It's tough to make predictions, especially about the future."

KEY POINTS

- To be successful, organizations need a well-thought out strategy to provide a distinctive product or service executed with appropriate operational capabilities.
- Each firm must develop its own strategy based on its unique situation and characteristics of the environment it faces.
- In the auto industry, Tesla was the first to develop an exciting battery-electric vehicle and took a first-mover advantage with sufficient sales and pricing to overcome production, quality, and delivery problems.
- Toyota has the size and resources to develop a more nuanced strategy, selling in parallel battery electric, hybrid, plug-in hybrid, and hydrogen fuel cell vehicles, with the proportions shifting over time.
- The Prius is an example of how Toyota took a bold step, developing the first mass-production hybrid, and then refined it through large leaps and steps to make it a bedrock for profitable growth.
- The competing small values model can help conceptually identify where a firm needs to be externally and internally and how the strategy relates to execution.
- For a startup firm, it is most important to be strong in the open systems quadrant with a breakthrough product or service, while as the company matures, it becomes increasingly important to have strong internal capability for execution.
- Each organization is in a unique position and needs its own strategy; copying benchmarked companies can stunt creative thinking and set you back.

Notes

1. https://asia.nikkei.com/Opinion/Has-Elon-Musk-s-Tesla-already-won.
2. Jeffrey Pfeffer and Robert Sutton, *The Knowing-Doing Gap: How Smart Companies Turn Knowledge into Action* (Brighton, MA: Harvard Business Review Publishing, 1999).
3. Michael Porter, "What Is Strategy?," *Harvard Business Review*, November–December 1996.
4. https://global.toyota/en/company/messages-from-executives/details.
5. https://planet-lean.com/akio-toyoda-crisis-management/.
6. Allen Ward, Jeffrey Liker, Durward Sobek, and John Cristiano, "The Second Toyota Paradox: How Delaying Decisions Can Make Better Cars Faster," *Sloan Management Review*, Spring 1995, pp. 43–61.

7. Hideshi Itazaki, *The Prius That Shook the World: How Toyota Developed the World's First Mass Production Hybrid Vehicle* (Tokyo: Nikkan Kogyo Shimbun, 1999).

8. https://www.caranddriver.com/news/a33435923/toyota-solid-state-battery-2025/.

9. http://www.businessinsider.com/toyota-prius-is-most-important-car-last-20-years-2017-12.

10. https://media.toyota.co.uk/2020/04/toyotas-global-hybrid-vehicle-sales-reach-15-million-units/.

11. Jonathan M. Gitlin, "2017 Was the Best Year Ever for Electric Vehicle Sales in the US," *ARS Technica*, January 4, 2018.

12. https://qz.com/1762465/2019-was-the-year-electric-cars-grew-up/.

13. Ashlee Vance, *Elon Musk: Tesla, SpaceX, and the Quest for a Fantastic Future* (New York: Ecco, 2017).

14. Edward Niedermeyer, *Ludicrous: The Unvarnished Story of Tesla Motors* (Dallas, TX: BenBella Books, 2019).

15. https://www.caranddriver.com/news/a26703778/toyota-why-not-selling-electric-cars/.

16. https://www.reuters.com/article/us-toyota-electric/toyota-speeds-up-electric-vehicle-schedule-as-demand-heats-up-idUSKCN1T806X.

17. Charles A. O'Reilly III and Michael L. Tushman, "The Ambidextrous Organization," *Harvard Business Review*, April 2004.

18. Bansi Nagji and Geoff Tuff, "Managing Your Innovation Portfolio," *Harvard Business Review*, May 2012.

19. https://automatedtoyota.com/automated-driving-technology-deployment-strategy.

20. Robert Quinn, *Beyond Rational Management: Mastering the Paradoxes and Competing Demands of High Performance* (San Francisco: Jossey-Bass, 1988).

21. https://www.youtube.com/watch?v=ng3X39Ienvg.

22. Robert E, Quinn, *Deep Change* (San Francisco: Jossey-Bass, 1996), p. 5.

23. https://www.lean.org/LeanPost/Posting.cfm?LeanPostId=581.

24. Faisal Hoque, "Why Most Venture-Backed Companies Fail," *Fast Company*, December 12, 2012.

PART FIVE

CONCLUSION

Be Thoughtful and Evolve Your Enterprise

Grow Your Own Lean Learning Enterprise—Getting Ideas and Inspiration from the Toyota Way

One man did his part, and the other his, and neither even had to check to make sure both parts were getting done. Like the dance of atoms Alvin had imagined in his mind. He never realized it before, but people could be like those atoms, too. Most of the time people were all disorganized, nobody knowing who anybody else was, nobody holding still long enough to trust or be trusted, just like Alvin imagined atoms might have been before God taught them who they were and gave them work to do. . . . It was a miracle seeing how smooth they knew each other's next move before the move was even begun. Alvin almost laughed out loud in the joy of seeing such a thing, knowing it was possible, dreaming of what it might mean—thousands of people knowing each other that well, moving to fit each other just right, working together. Who could stand in the way of such people?

—Orson Scott Card, *Prentice Alvin: The Tales of Alvin Maker, Book Three*

In the series by renowned science fiction and fantasy writer Orson Scott Card, Alvin can see the tiniest bits of matter and detect when they are out of their natural pattern, e.g., bones broken or a fault in a piece of iron. He can imagine the correct pattern in his mind and make the matter form itself back into that pattern, thus healing the bone or making the iron strong again. In the quote above, Alvin observes two men who appear to be strangers, but then observing as they work together that they fit together in a pattern because for years they had been secretly working together to free slaves. This breakthrough in his thinking leads him to realize that social bonds between people can be as powerful as physical

351

bonds between atoms—creating a whole much greater and stronger than the sum of the individual parts.

The lesson— and secret—of the Toyota Way is just as clear as this: it creates bonds among individuals and partners such that they are "moving to fit each other just right, working together" toward a common goal. "Who could stand in the way of such people?" It is in stark contrast to most companies, which are made up of individuals who are, in Alvin's words, "disorganized, nobody knowing who anybody else [is], nobody holding still long enough to trust or be trusted." The question is how to get from here to there, if in fact we want to.

All I am asking of your organization's leadership is learn to think longer term through systems thinking; focus on a clear purpose for society and customers; develop lean processes; blow up your culture and make it more people centered; develop leaders who understand the gemba, think scientifically, and teach others; engage all employees in continuous improvement; develop value stream partnerships; and let strategy and deployed goals guide your improvement activities. Are you overwhelmed yet? Fortunately, you do not have to do it quickly in a single step, and this image is a future vision to strive for, not something you can quickly implement.

THE COMFORTABLE TENDENCY TOWARD MECHANISTIC IMPLEMENTATION

General Equipment (fictitious) is a global manufacturing company with multiple product lines including woodworking tools, power washing equipment, and vacuum cleaners. Each product line is a market share leader. Competition from lower-wage countries has pressured General Equipment to cut prices to maintain share. To reduce cost and maintain high quality, it decides to launch a global lean manufacturing program across its 32 plants. The company hires consulting firm Mechanistic Lean to create and deploy the General Equipment Operating System (GEOS). It is represented as a house with six pillars: value-added flow, built-in quality, total cost management, total productive maintenance, an engaged workforce, and safety. The foundation is stable operations (see Figure C.1). Senior management wants GEOS to be deployed fast and furiously across the enterprise—no holds barred.

The consulting firm sets a recipe for "lean conversion." The firm develops "lean metrics" associated with each pillar and the foundation and recommends a minimum score for all plant managers in year one. The scores are tied to the bonuses of the managers to motivate them to commit to lean. The consulting firm leads a demonstration project, called a lighthouse, in the factory nearest headquarters. It then aggressively moves across plants, using its 4x4 approach: four parallel "kaizens" at a time, once per month, for four months. The kai-

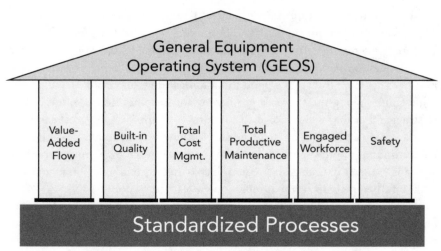

Figure C.1 The General Equipment Operating System.

zens are five-day events orchestrated by a senior consultant, with each of the four workshops led by a local manager or engineer. The results are stunning. The plants are cleaner and better organized, flow cells are created, inventory is reduced, and the plants run better than ever before. The senior executives are ecstatic with the results. They purchased lean, and the investment paid for itself in the first year.

And for additional fees they can purchase the "communication package" and the "change management package" to get their employees on board. What could be better?

The internal director of continuous improvement was impressed, but confessed:

I have noticed that the early lighthouse projects are slipping backward. When the consultants leave, the great new processes they introduced are not sustained by our managers. Even the lean assessments and bonuses do not seem to be enough to get the managers to take ownership. That is on us. We have to do a better job of developing our managers or getting the right people into the right management positions.

TPS sensei in Toyota would not be surprised that the changes were not sustained. Some would call this "consulting nonsense." After all, the consultants may have understood what they were trying to do, but the people running the operations did not take ownership or have time to understand all the tools introduced, and certainly the shop floor workers did not develop new, disciplined habits. Trying to motivate managers with extrinsic rewards and punishments only means they will comply, not lead.

In contrast to the approach of General Equipment and its consulting firm, Toyota sensei would instead go slower in a model area (the first "lighthouse project") and put managers in charge from the beginning. They would challenge, and ask questions, and expect the managers to struggle to figure out what to do next at each step. Struggle is a good thing for learning. Successful struggle, with some failures along the way, is a great thing for learning. It is comfortable not to struggle, but that will not lead to anything even approaching excellence. The lighthouse would become an incubator for learning by other managers and internal continuous improvement leaders who would start their own projects, possibly with a C.I. leader in each global region. Deployment would take longer to begin with, but then pick up steam as more leaders learned by doing.

The problem goes back to my original distinction between mechanistic and organic philosophies. Figure C.2 contrasts the myth of TPS from a mechanistic perspective as a set of tools to make short-term improvements on the shop floor with real TPS from an organic perspective as the basis of a total management philosophy.

Myth: What TPS Is Not (Mechanistic)	Reality: What TPS Is (Organic)
A tangible recipe for success	A consistent way of thinking
A management project or program	A total management philosophy
A set of tools for implementation	A focus on total customer satisfaction
A system for production floor only	An environment of teamwork and improvement
Implementable in a short or mid-term period	A never-ending search for a better way
	A process for built-in quality
	An organized, disciplined workplace
	Evolutionary

Figure C.2   Myth versus reality of TPS.
Source: Glenn Uminger, former general manager,
Toyota Motor Manufacturing North America.

The attraction of the "myth" of mechanistic lean is that it is comparatively easy and natural for command and control organizations. Forget uncertainty. Don't worry about all those messy people issues. Don't try to change the thinking of senior management. They already know how to issue targets and go after them by hiring outside expertise and holding everyone's feet to the fire. Get it done or else! The problem is that over the long term it does not work. Lean processes degrade and when there is a downturn in demand or change in leadership the lean program is dropped and replaced with the next new thing.

APPROACHING LEAN TRANSFORMATION SCIENTIFICALLY

Most companies desire a road map for lean—a "tangible recipe for success." When you contract out to a consulting firm that has a road map, like Mechanistic Lean, you are assuming the firm can predict what is going to happen, and in fact, the firm's representatives typically are pressured to pretend this is true in order to sell their services. Most internal lean consultants are expected to develop a plan and business case based on reading the future. Get out your crystal ball.

What I have seen work is approaching lean deployment scientifically, based on facts and data, learning as you go, with a compass but no road map. Hard to imagine? Dr. Deming taught us with his Point 7, "Adopt and institute leadership," to "expect your supervisors and managers to understand their workers and the processes they use." Toyota kata provides a way to teach managers to "understand their workers and the processes they use" and to approach achieving challenging goals scientifically. Now imagine a C.I. leader who has experience with real TPS, was trained in Toyota Kata, and is given the assignment to transform a plant to lean based on the model in Figure C.1. Rather than charge off and start implementing solutions, she would step back and approach it scientifically using something like the improvement kata model:

1. **What is the challenge?** What are we really trying to accomplish with the lean transformation? What is our long-term vision? What would success look like one year out, and how would we measure it?
2. **What is the current condition?** Where are we now in our processes and people?
3. **What is the next target condition, and what are the obstacles to that target condition?** Let's get started, but not following a laid out plan, or trying to achieve the challenge in one step. Let's break it down and work toward one target condition by overcoming obstacles. When we reach this we can reflect, define our next target condition, and so on.
4. **What is the next experiment I will run to overcome an obstacle?** Experiment, learn from each experiment, and have fun!

Mr. Hajime Ohba of TSSC used the same basic model when coaching Herman Miller—no surprise since the IK was based on how people like Ohba approached transformation (see Figure C.3). The journey started in 1996 when Mr. Ohba walked the gemba to understand the process and issued his challenge: Without major capital investment, and building the same number of file cabinets, go from 2 assembly lines, 3 shifts, and 126 people to 1 assembly line, 2 shifts, and 15 people. This of course was unimaginable to the group of people

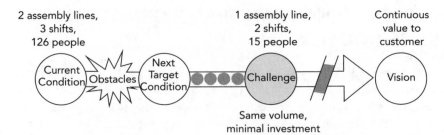

The coach is developing people by challenging and questioning, not telling!

Figure C.3 Scientific pattern of TSSC's Hajime Ohba
leading the model line in the Herman Miller file cabinet plant.

assembled, but they played along. Two young managers present had some experience and understood the power of lean. While waiting and hoping to get support from TSSC, they had been sent for several months on an internship in an auto supplier that Mr. Ohba had worked with. Matt Long was one of them, and he ultimately led the development of the Herman Miller Performance System as vice president of continuous improvement until he retired in 2020.

The next step after getting the challenge was to "stand in the circle" and observe assembly of the file cabinets. Then the people Mr. Ohba was teaching were asked to identify where they wanted to begin to focus their attention (sort of like a target condition), generate some ideas for improvement, and test them out. It was not as structured as Rother's starter kata format of trying one thing at a time and writing down expectations and reflections on each experiment, but Ohba returned regularly to coach, asking similar questions, gave similar assignments, while not giving answers. The people in the group had support from Toyota members who were interning at TSSC, and they were also learning from Ohba.

As usual for TSSC projects, the results were stunning. The company never completely achieved Ohba's challenges, but there were impressive results in the first year, and the employees continued working on the file cabinet plant for the next 15 years with coaching from TSSC (until it was shuttered for other business reasons). It became a model for TSSC to use in TPS workshops. The coaching started with assembly, then moved through the value stream, step-by-step. For example, when it because clear that the constraint was sorting through the inventory of painted panels that came in large batches the team moved back to paint. The Herman Miller people did not do value-stream mapping and "implement the map," yet the resulting system ended up looking like a very good future-state map. After 15 years, the company had achieved one assembly line, two shifts, and 30 people, at a higher level of units produced per week—a 483 percent improvement in productivity (see Figure C.4) with no investment in automation.

Many people rotated through the model-line area and brought what they learned to other parts of Herman Miller. Continuous improvement leaders were developed for each plant, and as we saw for Principle 10, this then extended to versions of Toyota group leaders and team leaders. There were ups and definite downs, but the long-term result was the Herman Miller Performance System, which became a deep part of the culture, still fragile, but with staying power beyond most lean deployment attempts. The long-term results across all of manufacturing were equally stunning (see Figure C.5).

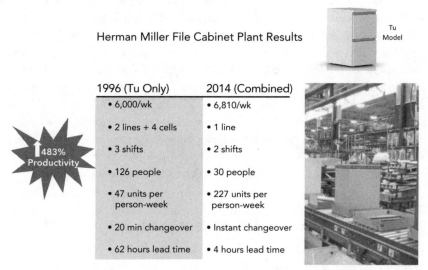

Herman Miller File Cabinet Plant Results

Tu Model

↑483% Productivity

1996 (Tu Only)	2014 (Combined)
• 6,000/wk	• 6,810/wk
• 2 lines + 4 cells	• 1 line
• 3 shifts	• 2 shifts
• 126 people	• 30 people
• 47 units per person-week	• 227 units per person-week
• 20 min changeover	• Instant changeover
• 62 hours lead time	• 4 hours lead time

Figure C.4   TSSC supports Herman Miller in first model-line project.

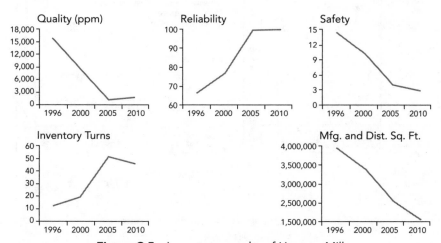

Figure C.5   Long-term results of Herman Miller Performance System across all manufacturing.

When we think of a model line, we often think of the challenge statement as a big financial result, but the more difficult challenge is developing the capability of people. In fact, process improvement and people development go hand in hand. In Rother's model there is a key role for managers as coaches who develop scientific thinkers who practice the improvement kata. The chicken-and-egg problem is that those managers need to be coaches, but first they have to be learners to build their competencies and know-how by taking on a business challenge and practicing the improvement kata pattern to work scientifically toward it. We saw an example of this in the way Dallis was trained when he entered Toyota (see Principle 9 on leadership). The constraint at first is that there are few or no qualified coaches inside the organization. The ideal state is to have all coaching done internally with managers coaching their own teams. Figure C.6 provides one example of how this might work following the kata model. The job of the "advance group" (AG) of leaders is to monitor and guide the process (PDCA). First these leaders scout out what the kata is to see if they are interested, and then they practice it themselves with an experienced (possibly external) coach. With that experience they are then in a position to develop a plan for the next 6 to 12 months for how many coaches they will develop. This is not the usual plan with a series of milestones and dates. Rather it is a challenge to the organization.

**Don't try to expand improvement kata practice faster
than you can develop internal coaching kata proficiency!**

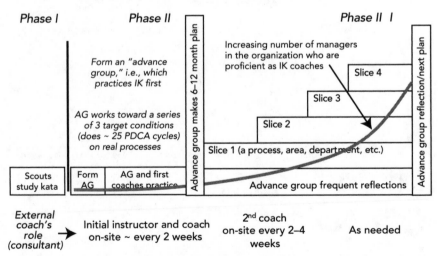

Figure C.6   One model for deploying practice.

Source: Mike Rother.

As with any other challenge, the next step is to understand the current condition. How many people in the organization have the propensity for scientific thinking? And who are open to learning? What are good projects to start on? Then start your model lines and the role of the AG is to study, reflect, learn and adjust. Every day is an experiment! The AG should go first as learners, meet regularly, and between meetings monitor the process so it can make informed decisions about how to provide support and when to spread the process to other areas. Notice that the process of developing coaches is not linear, but exponential: 1 begets 2 begets 4 begets 8, and so on. Zingerman's Mail Order called this advance group activity "kata the kata." The company applied the improvement kata pattern in deploying improvement kata practice.[1]

The reason for starting small and piloting is for learning. Piloting is built into Toyota's culture. They rarely deploy much of anything broadly before it is tested. It is easy to assume that our ideas must work because they make so much sense to us. Yet, when we actually confront our assumptions with reality we almost always find some surprises. The surprises are the basis for learning and improvement, before broadly deploying unproven ideas.

THE EVIL OF ENTROPY AND HOW TO BEAT IT

There have been many companies that seemed to get off to a good start with lean, like the case of General Equipment, but the effort lost steam. The most common question I am asked is, "How can we sustain the gains of lean?" This is itself the wrong question. By now in the book, it should be clear that lean is not something you can mechanically do to processes and then expect the changes to stick. There are no quick-fix sustainment tools. Organizational entropy (a tendency toward decay of systems) will naturally cause regression from the new state, because it requires more energy than the old, steady state; the old state is more natural and easier to sustain (see Figure C.7). Lean transformation pulls the organization out of its steady state. Then, like pulling on a rubber band, if we let go, it snaps back to its steady state. And contrary to the notion that lean processes fix problems, the truth is they reveal problems and place a higher burden on leaders, managers, and team members to keep on improving. We saw, for example, that inventory can hide problems, while one-piece flow makes the problems visible and can quickly shut down processes. When the main source of energy for change comes from the team of external "experts" who stop in to "fix" things and then leave, the capability and energy simply are not available to counter entropy.

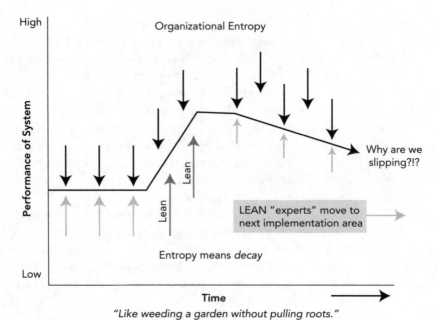

"Like weeding a garden without pulling roots."

Figure C.7   Entropy will always lead to backsliding after "lean tool implementation" if local management does not take ownership.
Source: David Meier.

A useful analogy is our personal fitness. We go to a class that teaches us to go on a strict diet and exercise intensely every day and in six weeks we lose a bunch of weight. We feel great and never want to go back. But the chances are high we slip backward. The new regime was unnatural to us and our bodies, and we have to push ourselves way beyond what feels comfortable to maintain it. When we stop making the extreme effort we did under the pressure of teachers and structure of the class, we fall back to our steady state of overeating and poor exercise habits. Karen Gaudet experienced something similar at Starbucks when the company mass-spread "Playbook" (discussed under Principle 5) and she observed backsliding:[2]

> *No matter how superior the new way seems, people fall back into old patterns. . . . Whenever partners fell back into ad hoc work routines, we found, they had a hard time going back to their playbook routines. . . . What we lacked was leadership resolve to remain a lean operation, to train all incoming employees in the basics, and to push ourselves further in understanding. . . . As one concession or adjustment after another was made, the level of lean capability began to slide.*

We saw under Principle 13 how Toyota combines hoshin-driven PDCA of big changes with daily management changes of SDCA, because both are essen-

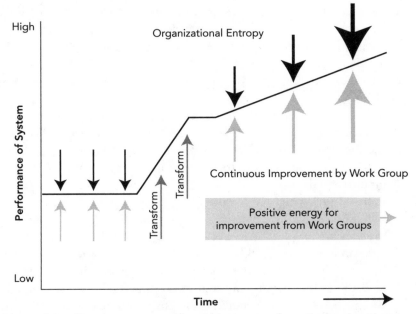

Figure C.8   Counter entropy with positive energy from the local work group.
Source: David Meier.

tial to continuous improvement. Big changes throw people and processes out of a
stable state and have not been fine-tuned. Our new processes at this point are still
a tentative desired state. When the new concept of a process meets reality, reality
wins, unless there is at least an equal and opposite force to beat entropy. The positive energy to counteract entropy comes from work groups improving and taking
ownership of the standards and continuously identifying and correcting deviations
from the standards as conditions change and more is learned (see Figure C.8).

In this model, we see the importance of piloting the new ideas to learn what
happens when they bump up against reality. Run the experiment and study what
happens. The new approach can then be spread gradually from work group to
work group, in each case training group leaders and team leaders to understand
the new processes and goals and helping them to become trainers for team members. This creates a very different dynamic, one of having local control, rather
than having change imposed from senior management and "lean specialists"
doing all the thinking. Unfortunately, this approach takes more time and effort,
just as developing new eating and exercise habits takes more time and sustained
effort than a short-term extreme diet.

I have personally participated in many lean transformation efforts and witnessed many others. All too frequently, a great and exciting start peters out.
Reasons include:

1. **Lack of senior management commitment.** Senior executives delegate lean down to continuous improvement specialists, but are nowhere to be found at the gemba and wait for the results to come up (see the Volvo hoshin diagram, Figure 13.1).

2. **Changing of the guard.** More than once, when we did have an enthusiastic CEO and thought "This is the one," the CEO soon was pushed out and a new one brought in who had a mechanistic view of lean to get quick financial results. The party was over. One of the challenges at Starbucks was the rapid turnover of store managers and shift supervisors and partners, even though the lean transformation led to less turnover than the industry standard.

3. **Political jockeying.** Great things were happening at the gemba while staff specialists in departments like quality and HR, who were far from the gemba, were plotting to take over lean.

4. **Great pilots, then quickly go live everywhere at once.** We strongly believe in the model-line approach of Toyota, but what happens after the model line? Too often when executives see the results, say for one value stream of one plant, they multiply the expected benefits across all operations and order the lean folks to "make it happen" by the end of the year.

5. **Little or no focus on developing desired skills and mindset.** The transformation is viewed as a technical problem, rather than also a process of brain training.

The recurring theme is that even starting out strong organically will go bad if the executive level sees lean implementation as an independent variable: do lean (independent variable); get results (dependent variable). This is far from system thinking. A better model is: strive for appropriate lean systems (dependent variable) taking a scientific approach (independent variable). Coming out of this will be competitive advantage and profits.

Still there are a number of good examples in this book of companies working to build a culture of excellence for the long term that have had staying power. And organizations like TSSC, LEI, and various high-quality consulting firms around the world all have long-term success stories. Here are a few examples:

- **Herman Miller.** I described the heroic effort the Herman Miller office furniture company has been making to develop work team leaders and facilitators under Principle 10. Starting with TSSC in 1996, HMPS is persisting through ups and downs, still going strong in 2020. The immense performance gains are credited with keeping manufacturing in the United States, while competitors fled to low-cost labor in Mexico.
- **SigmaPoint.** This is a smaller, single-plant company, so perhaps it is easier for the management team, from the CEO to middle managers, to be

completely aligned as a lean enterprise. The focus has been on developing people to think scientifically, and this learning organization has continued to evolve month by month, improving sales and profits.

■ **Zingerman's Mail Order.** This is an even smaller company, which operates out of a warehouse–call center. My student Eduardo Lander began consulting to Zingerman's in December 2003, and as of 2020, he continues to return regularly to coach. After growing out of space every few years before the lean journey started, the company has generated double-digit annual growth while staying in the same facility (with some additions) since 2003, saving millions of dollars. The partners and managers are all in on lean and have brought scientific thinking to frontline associates through practice of starter kata. They adapted quickly and innovatively to the Covid-19 crisis and fulfilled records sales, earning record profits that they shared with all team members.

■ **Nike.** Nike brought in former Toyota managers as external consultants to run the company's global lean program dating back to 2001. Nike manufactures very little itself, but focuses on creating lean value streams back to suppliers and strives to be connected, synchronized, and stable, with continual improvements in quality, productivity, and lead times. The approach was similar to how TSSC worked with Toyota suppliers on model-line projects. Nike set up regional "Innovation and Technical Centers" starting in 2004 to support supplier partners, and it helped partners to learn through short-run projects ranging from 3 months' to 12 months' duration. In 2019, Nike lean leaders clarified expectations for suppliers to develop their own internal lean capability and moved on to looking more broadly at the value chain increasing speed through lean and digitization from purchase order to delivery.

Each of these firms went beyond lean tools and has worked hard at developing people in the skills of continuous improvement. Their visions go beyond making a profit and focus on doing an excellent job serving customers. There were differences in the specifics of how they approached change, but all used a similar pattern:

1. Started with a pilot and a challenge of some sort and deployed incrementally and thoughtfully without going too fast for people to absorb
2. Thought long term and had a vision of excellence through a Toyota-like philosophy
3. Focused on internal managers learning, mostly with, and sometimes without, external consultants who acted as coaches rather than experts
4. Took an experimental learning approach, rather than an implementation approach

5. In some way created a coaching culture with repeated feedback so that a disciplined way of acting and approaching problems became habitual
6. Maintained continuity of lean leadership by developing and retaining leaders
7. Provided job security and would not lay off anyone because of kaizen

GETTING TO THE ROOT OF SUCCESS: CULTURE CHANGE

The toughest and most basic challenge for companies that want to learn from Toyota is *how to create an aligned organization of individuals who each have the DNA of the organization and are continually learning together to add value to the customer.* It seems that whatever the starting point of discussions of lean transformation, we end up talking about culture. Perhaps this is an indication that culture is at the root of everything I have been discussing.

Culture change is a complex topic and the subject of many books. The tricky part is that culture is all about people *sharing* values, beliefs, and ways of approaching problems. What you see and hear when you walk into a company for the first time are only surface manifestations of culture. Figure C.9 depicts a culture as being like an iceberg. If you tour a "lean plant," you might learn about the mission statement and guiding principles, perhaps see it on a poster in the lobby. Then you will see tools and formal structures—perhaps 5S, cells, KPI charts, kanban, team structures, daily standup meeting areas, and the like. At

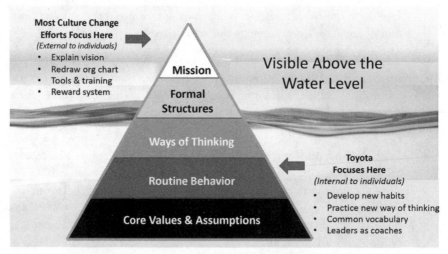

Figure C.9 A misunderstanding of culture change leads to superficial change—change only at the visible level.

this point, you only know what management intends to be happening, not what is really happening. These are what anthropologists call artifacts. Patrick Adams calls this "continuous appearance" as opposed to "continuous improvement."* To really understand the culture, you must dig deeper in the gemba to see if individuals are changing the way they are thinking and acting.

Below the surface at Toyota is the Toyota Way culture. I mentioned Edgar Schein's perspective on culture under Principle 9 on leadership. Let's delve a bit deeper. He defines culture this way:[3]

> *The pattern of basic assumptions that a given group has invented, discovered, or developed in learning to cope with its problems of external adaptation and internal integration, and that have worked well enough to be considered valid, and, therefore, to be taught to new members as the correct way to perceive, think, and feel in relation to those problems.*

This is a remarkably apt description of the Toyota Way culture in a number of ways:

1. The Toyota Way has a depth that goes down to the level of basic assumptions about the most effective way to "perceive, think, and feel" in relation to problems. These include genchi genbutsu, people working together as a team toward a series of challenges, respect for people, daily improvement through kaizen, and the focus of Toyota on long-term survival.

2. The Toyota Way was "invented, discovered, and developed" over decades, as talented Toyota managers and engineers, like Ohno, "learned to cope with its [Toyota's] problems of external adaptation and internal integration." The history of Toyota is very important because we understand the challenges and context that led to active on-the-floor problem solving, not theoretical, top-down programs.

3. The Toyota Way is explicitly "taught to new members." Toyota does offer training classes on the Toyota Way and TPS, but that is a limited part of the learning process. The Toyota Way is explicitly taught in the way you should transmit culture—through action in day-to-day work where leaders model the way and coach. As Jane Beseda, former vice president of Toyota Sales, explained:

> *The Toyota Way matches everything that they [team members] do every hour of the day. So, they are swimming in this culture and this philosophy. We're always doing kaizen projects. It's a part of who we are.*

---

* Patrick Adams in his self-published book, *Avoiding the Continuous Appearance Trap*, contrasts the cultures of two companies he worked with. Though each started with similar lean models and visions, one was mechanistic and only gave the appearance of lean, while the other evolved a culture of continuous improvement.

When Toyota began seriously globalizing in the 1980s, it quickly realized the challenges of creating the Toyota Way in cultures that were not naturally aligned with the company's values. The approach to globalizing, while developing Toyota Way culture was:

1. All executives were assigned Japanese coordinators and all managers and group leaders were assigned trainers. The coordinators and trainers had two jobs: coordinating with Japan, where there are continuous technical developments, and teaching employees the Toyota Way through daily mentorship. Every day was a training day, with immediate feedback shaping the thinking and behavior of the employees.

2. Toyota sponsored many trips to Japan, which turned out to be one of the most powerful ways to influence the cultural awareness of employees. The success of NUMMI started with managers, engineers, group leaders, some workers, and union officials working in Toyota factories in Japan and experiencing the system firsthand.

3. Toyota used the TPS technical systems, or "process" layer of the Toyota Way, to help reinforce the culture Toyota sought to build. For example, we discussed how large-batch manufacturing with lots of inventory supports the Western culture of short-term firefighting and systems problems being allowed to fester. By connecting processes, problems are surfaced all the time and made visible so there is a sense of urgency to solve them.

4. Toyota sent senior executives to each operation to ingrain the Toyota DNA in new leaders. This started with managers from Japan and evolved to homegrown leaders.

The original North American plants were assigned a mother plant in Japan that sent leaders to the states to teach the local leaders. As Toyota expanded operations in the United States, local veteran plants took on the mother plant role. In each country, Toyota adapts, particularly in human resource practices. For example, adaptations in the Toyota Technical Center (TTC) in Ann Arbor, Michigan, included:

1. Toyota put a cap on work hours and became more flexible. In Japan, Toyota engineers historically worked as needed, even if it was 12 hours a day, nights, and weekends. TTC capped work hours and introduced a flextime system including one day of working at home.

2. Toyota changed how it provides performance-based rewards. Traditionally, Toyota in Japan pays a large portion of salary in semiannual bonuses, but these are tied to company performance, not individual performance. In TTC, the company developed an individual bonus system based on performance.

3. Hansei events at TTC were modified to provide more positive feedback in addition to critiques and opportunities for improvement.

Companies that approach lean mechanistically usually do a lot of talking, but the lean philosophy only superficially penetrates into the culture. Buying those communication and change management packages from Mechanistic Lean won't be enough. Building culture through kata starts with a focus on mindset and behavior; and only through a long process of repeated practice can you create a culture of scientific thinkers.[4]

Some of my best clients have recognized that successful lean transformation means "winning the hearts and minds of all members." In Figure C.9 we see that surface-level lean focuses on easy levers external to the individual—explaining the vision, redrawing the organization chart, teaching about tools and concepts in a classroom, and manipulating the reward system. On the other hand, deep culture change gets to the level of individual change, developing a new mindset and coaching a shared way of thinking, speaking, and acting.

At the core of any successful culture change effort is mutual trust. If team members don't trust managers, or if managers don't trust team members, the words of continuous improvement and respect for people will be empty. Mutual trust comes from actions, not words. When I see you behaving consistently over time showing competence, understanding, concern for me, and fairness, I will trust you, until you act in a way that violates that trust. Unfortunately, it is much easier to destroy trust than to build it.

A COMMITMENT FROM THE TOP TO BUILD A DELIBERATE CULTURE FROM THE GROUND UP

Will Rogers, American humorist and social commentator, said, "We are a great people to get tired of anything awful quick. We just jump from one extreme to another." I am afraid that is what most companies are doing with lean manufacturing. It is just one more thing to jump into and one more thing to jump away from when the next fad comes along. "The world is digital; what's next after lean? Oh yes, Industry 4.0. Let's do that." If there is anything to learn from Toyota, it is the importance of developing a system and sticking with it and improving it. You cannot become a learning organization by jumping willy-nilly from fad to fad.

What do we know about changing a culture?

1. Start from the top—this may require an executive leadership shake-up.
2. Involve from the bottom up.

3. Use middle managers as change agents.

4. Don't expect instant changes. It takes years to develop people who really understand and live the philosophy.

5. Don't expect it to be easy. Just the opposite—on a scale of difficulty, it is "extremely" difficult.

The Toyota Way model was intentionally built from the ground up, starting with a philosophy that has been deeply embraced by the chief executives of the organization. What was the goal? To build an enterprise for the long term that delivers exceptional value to customers and society. This requires long-term thinking and continuity of leadership. For organizations looking to emulate the Toyota Way, understand that there is no quick fix. It may take 10 years or more to lay the foundation for radically transforming an organization's culture.

What if the top does not understand and embrace the new philosophy? I asked Gary Convis the following question:

If you were a middle manager or even a vice president passionate about implementing the Toyota Way in your company and the senior executives did not strongly support it, what would you do?

His answer was blunt:

I would be out looking for better pastures (laughter), *because the company may not be around long enough for me to get my pension. Actually, that's a good question. Now, there could be a change in the top management. Maybe somebody up in the board recognizes that lean is not happening and needs to. Like General Motors did. . . . I think the board said, "Wait a minute, we've been giving these guys rope and we've been giving them time and we don't see the direction." At some point in time they decided enough is enough. The new direction was set and new priorities were set and resources were established.*

A prerequisite to change is for top management to understand and commit to leveraging the system and philosophy to become a "lean learning organization." And it needs to follow the principle "Grow your own lean learning enterprise," getting ideas and inspiration from the Toyota Way. Don't copy; think! What is your situation and vision, and how can you translate this to fundamental principles you will work to follow?

This insight led me to develop the model shown in Figure C.10, which illustrates the minimum level of leadership commitment needed to effectively start on the lean journey and to learn from Toyota's model of a lean learning enterprise. Look at the figure, and answer these three questions:

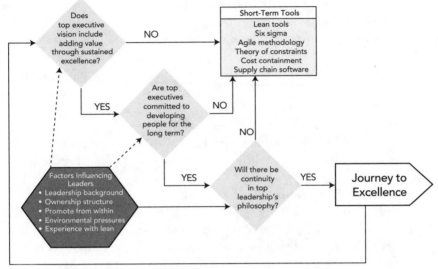

Figure C.10 Top leadership commitment to the lean journey.

1. **Does top executive vision include adding value through sustained excellence?** If the commitment is simply to short-term profitability, the answer is no, so go directly to the "Short-Term Tools" box (the equivalent of "Go directly to jail" in the game Monopoly).

2. **Are top executives committed to developing people for the long term?** This includes key suppliers. If people are viewed as expendable labor and suppliers are viewed as sources of cheap parts, the answer is no, so go directly to the "Short-Term Tools" box.

3. **Will there be continuity in top leadership's philosophy?** This does not mean the same people need to run the company forever, but they need to develop their successors with the company's DNA to continue the philosophy. If new leaders with a different philosophy are brought in every time there is a crisis or if the company is bought out every decade with a new cast of characters installed as leaders, the answer is no, so go directly to the ""Short-Term Tools" box.

Note that there is a feedback loop from "Journey to Excellence" back to the original question of top leadership's commitment to a long-term vision that must be continually challenged. Figure C.10 also shows a set of factors that will influence whether top executives are committed to the lean vision. These include:

1. **Leadership background.** It starts with who the leaders are. What is their background? What have they learned through their careers about what

works and does not work, and what is to be valued? What are the underlying assumptions they grew up with?

2. **Ownership structure.** Who owns the company and how it is financed has a major influence on the ability of the company to focus on the long term. Looking good to Wall Street for the quarter may conflict with long-term investments in excellence. Toyota clearly has a unique situation with only one board of directors led by the company president (Akio Toyoda at present) and a structure of interlocking ownership within the Toyota Group among like-thinking organizations that grew up together. With this insulation, being publicly traded has not prevented Toyota from taking a long-term perspective.

3. **Promote from within.** Develop future leaders from within, or there is little chance of sustaining a long-term vision. Generally, Toyota has been conservative in bringing in managers and executives from the outside, because of the possible threat to the culture. But the culture is so strong and there are so many people with the Toyota Way DNA, that any "outside" manager will be socialized to learn the Toyota Way or decide to leave. Recently, there have been exceptions, as Akio Toyoda led a major shake-up to position Toyota for the once-in-a-century transformation of the industry as a result of digital technology. Toyoda understood the company would need leaders who are experienced in the digital world, like the recently appointed CEOs of Toyota Research Institute and Toyota Research Institute–Advanced Development—both of whom were selected because they admired the Toyota Way and were natural learners.

4. **Environmental pressures.** Unfortunately, there are factors beyond the control of any lean leader that can make it difficult to sustain the lean learning enterprise. One is the equity market, which can take major downturns independent of the enterprise; another is the market for the particular product the company makes, which can deteriorate for a host of reasons. Other external factors that can negatively impact a company are wars, radical new technologies, government policy changes, pandemics, and on and on. Clearly, Toyota's strong culture and philosophy have helped it navigate through these treacherous environments to survive and prosper in many different business and political environments.

5. **Experience with lean.** The best lean leaders in my experience worked for Toyota, or for someone who worked for Toyota, or for a company that worked closely with Toyota—the common theme being direct exposure to the Toyota gene pool. They practiced a new way of managing. Obviously, as more and more companies develop real lean systems, there are broader opportunities for learning lean thinking outside Toyota and its affiliates.

What can you do if you are not the CEO and top management is interested primarily in short-term financial results? There are three things I know of:

1. Find greener pastures, as Convis suggests.
2. Participate in playing the game of applying tools for short-term gains, learn what you can, and hope you share in the gains.
3. Work to build a successful lean model and educate top management by blowing them away with exceptional results.

The third alternative is generally going to be the most productive for those with a passion for lean. "True believers" of lean will have to do their best by creating lean models with great results that executives can learn from and then sell upward. But no matter what the approach, it will take time for management to understand lean and for the old system and culture to evolve. Even within Toyota, Convis noted:

> *The Toyota Way and the culture—I think it takes at least 10 years to really become in tune with what is going on and be able to manage in a way that we would like to sustain. I don't know as you can come into Toyota and in three or four years have it in your heart and your spirit with a deep understanding.*

IS IT WORTH THE EFFORT AND LONG-TERM COMMITMENT?

Having said all this, the question remains, can a company transform and sustain a culture to become a lean learning organization? If a company can maintain continuity of leadership over time, I see no reason why it cannot profit from its version of the Toyota Way principles.

National culture throws up its share of challenges. There is a litany of cultural traits that differ between Japanese and Americans and French and Germans, etc. For example, we saw that the philosophies underlying hansei that Toyota considers necessary for kaizen are rooted in Japanese upbringing. There is even some evidence that Asians more naturally perceive systems of interacting parts, while Americans are more likely to see the parts as independent.[5] Yet the Toyota Way is working and prospering within Toyota affiliates around the world, albeit with a great investment of time and energy by Toyota in growing its unique culture in each locale. And the Toyota Way is evolving as it adapts to other cultures, probably making Toyota an even stronger company.

The only way I know to make lean sustainable is to make scientific thinking a habit. If someone is not already wired this way, which he or she is probably not, this means practice with corrective feedback over a long period of time. I can understand the impatience of executives who are reporting to impatient boards and shareholders. It is hard to keep saying "We are working on it; we do not have a road map, but do not worry because we are taking a scientific approach to pursuing our business challenges." And it may be frustrating to have to go through all this effort and pay so much attention and to think so much without immediate homerun results. Why can't it be easier? It can be easier. Just hire the folks at Mechanistic Lean and pay their hefty fees, and they will turn things upside down and get results enough to pay for their cost and then some. What you will not get is a culture of continuous improvement that respects people and generates sustainable value. I have seen this movie many times before, and it does not end well.

The greatest struggle I see in companies is the tension between deploying lean deeply in a slice of the business, as in a model line, and then spreading it out systematically to the rest of the organization on the one hand, and deploying lean as widely and as rapidly as possible to get big results fast on the other (see Figure C.11). In my consulting work I have always advised going deep to build competency. This almost always has led to local success, but then orders would often come down from the top to move fast across the company with a proven methodology—which meant our consulting team was out. I was convinced these companies would go backward and entropy would win, but in some cases I was wrong. I have seen companies that started out mechanistic have long-term success by later shifting to a more organic approach. Often, after going broad in a lean race against time, they discover that the changes are not being sustained and

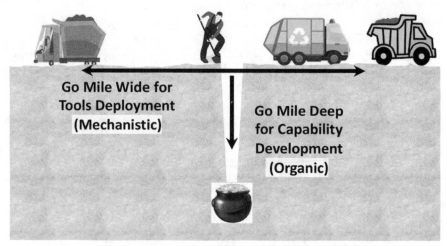

Figure C.11   Balancing mile wide for efficiency
and mile deep for culture change.

shift to a more focused approach of developing leaders. "Implementing" lean tools was not time wasted, but provided some skills and common vocabulary for deeper learning in a later phase.

The good news is that there are examples throughout the world and across types of organizations of great success on the lean journey. Many have experienced a level of performance and satisfaction they never thought possible. There is enthusiasm and excitement, and work is actually fun! The tough news is that there is no guarantee of eternal success. It continues to take work, even at Toyota. It's a lifetime of interesting challenges.

Let's go back to the short-term fitness program that was not sustained. You try a new one that focuses on creating a long-term healthy lifestyle. You meet weekly at a gym for one year, along with a group that provides support and positive feedback. You are taught a series of exercises that you are asked to practice at home. A high-protein, low-carb diet is presented with weekly suggestions for meals. Gradually you lose weight and your body is toned. You never looked and felt so good. For four years after the fitness program ended, you sustain the diet and exercise. Life is great! Does that mean you will stay fit for the rest of your life? It is possible, but it is also possible that life will get in the way and you will revert to old bad habits. Does this mean the healthy lifestyle program was a failure? It certainly succeeded, but it still depended on continued effort. Lean management is like that—sustainment does not come from coasting. You need to keep working at it. Continuous improvement and respect for people are an eternal quest, because the journey to excellence never ends.

Even though there are plenty of uncertainties and challenges, my advice is to consider Toyota Way principles as you envision and work on your future organization. The Toyota Way is to do the hard work of striving for excellence. It is a call to treat people with respect. It is a call to develop in people the ability to lead with respect. It is a call to plan, but ultimately to accept the uncertainty of the world and navigate through the obstacles with a scientific mindset, and even enjoy the trip. It is a call to action, but reading this book or benchmarking Toyota is not action. Action is doing. Improvement requires developing a picture of where you want to go, experimenting with some large and many small changes, noticing gaps between what you expected and what happened, and a lot of reflecting. Go beyond trying to copy or spread best practices, to evolving your own lean learning enterprise.

───────────────────────── **KEY POINTS** ─────────────────────────

- The starting point is a vision of what you are trying to accomplish.
- The Toyota Way vision is to engage the total organization toward adding value to customers and society, continually adapting, improving, and learning.
- Mechanistic implementation feels more comfortable for companies focused on short-term profitability.
- Entropy causes much of the gains from short-term mechanistic deployment to decay over time.
- The best antidote to entropy is the positive energy of continuous improvement by work groups at the gemba.
- Organizations with long-term success on the lean journey start with a commitment from the top to work toward a long-term vision and then organically grow from model lines to broader deployment led by local management.
- A scientific approach to deployment starts with developing scientific thinkers and coaches organically and expanding as skilled coaches mature.
- Most culture change programs focus on artifacts and what people say, but do not penetrate deeply to how people think and act.
- Toyota kata focuses on repeated practice to change actual behavior and ways of thinking and create a scientific-thinking culture.
- The Toyota Way provides inspiration and ideas for creating your own vision and direction.
- If your organization's success depends on excellence, a serious commitment to long-term development will be worth the patience and effort.

Notes

1. Eduardo Lander, Jeffrey Liker, and Tom Root, *Lean in a High-Variety Business: A Graphic Novel About Lean and People at Zingerman's Mail Order* (New York: Productivity Press, 2020).
2. Karen Gaudet, *Steady Work* (Boston: Lean Enterprise Institute, 2019).
3. Edgar H. Schein, "Coming to a New Awareness of Organizational Culture," in James B. Lau and Abraham B. Shani, *Behavior in Organizations* (Homewood, IL: Irwin, 1988), pp. 375–390.
4. Mike Rother and Gerd Aulinger, *Toyota Kata Culture: Building Organizational Capability and Mindset Through Kata Coaching* (New York: McGraw-Hill, 2017).
5. Richard Nisbett, *The Geography of Thought: How Asians and Westerners Think* (New York: Simon & Schuster, 2004.)

Appendix

An Executive Summary and Assessment of the 14 Principles

THE TOYOTA WAY IS MORE THAN TOOLS AND TECHNIQUES

The more I have studied TPS and the Toyota Way, the more I understand that it is a technical *and* social system working together. The Toyota Way leads to more dependence on people, not less. On a daily basis, engineers, skilled workers, quality specialists, vendors, managers, team leaders, and—most importantly—team members are all engaged in continuous problem solving and improvement, which over time trains everyone to think scientifically and become better problem solvers.

This Appendix provides a synopsis of the 14 principles that constitute the Toyota Way. The principles are organized into four broad interrelated categories:

- **Philosophy**—Long-term systems thinking.
- **Process**—Struggle to flow value to each customer.
- **People**—Respect, challenge, and grow your people and partners toward a vision of excellence.
- **Problem solving**—Think and act scientifically to improve toward a desired future.

I have also included Figure A.1 for you to do a very rough assessment of where you are on the 14 principles. I developed descriptors for a baseline of top-down management and control, compared with companies at the tool level of lean and then with the ideal of the Toyota Way principles. You can simply circle where you are on each principle. If you believe you are between two levels, put an X in between. If you connect the circles and Xs, you will have a visual profile. You might want to reword some of the principles with your version for your company.

You could also use this for planning, marking where you want to be over the next year or so. The point is not to develop desired targets on each principle and then try to implement them all. As you learned about the scientific way of thinking in this book, think about the future state as possible challenges. As in hoshin planning, pick the critical few. Don't take on too many at once. Then approach them iteratively, one target condition at a time. Experiment, learn, have fun!

Instructions: Circle maturity level for each principle that best fits. If between two levels, put an X on the border. Then mark your desired future state, where you would prefer to be.

#	Principle	Command and Control	Lean Tools Approach	Toyota Way Vision
		Level 1	Level 2	Level 3
Philosophy				
1	Long-term systems thinking	Short-term performance	Lengthen payback horizon	Long-term, holistic impact on society and key stakeholders
Process				
2	Continuous flow	Individual-process focus	Connected processes	Tighten coupling through kaizen
3	Pull	Scheduled push	Visual or electronic kanban	Buffers that shrink through kaizen
4	Level	Erratic ups and downs	Leveling method	Continually reducing unevenness and overburden
5	Standardized processes	Imposed by staff specialists	Staff specialists responsible for standardized work with input	Standardized work owned by work groups to support kaizen
6	Design-build in quality	Find and fix problems	Apply quality techniques	Designed-in quality and in-station control
7	Visual control	Hidden from view	5S and visual management	Visual standards within work process
8	Technology supports people and process	Latest technology pushed	Right-sized technology to support flow	Simple, slim, and flexible technology supports kaizen
People				
9	Develop leaders	Fast-track training	Leader standardized work	Leaders coach and develop others

10	Develop people and teams	Introduce job, then learn on own	Lean short courses and practice	Semiautonomous teams of highly developed people
11	Partner with value stream	Adversarial cost-reduction focus	Long-term relationships with key partners	Cross-enterprise learning
Problem Solving				
12	Observe deeply and learn iteratively	Plan solutions, implement, confirm	Standard problem-solving methodology	Develop mindset of scientific thinking
13	Aligned goals	Top-down targets, delegated execution	Top-driven hoshin kanri tools	Collaborative planning and ongoing improvement and reflection at all levels
14	Bold strategy, large leaps, small steps	Strategy divorced from execution	Connect strategy to lean processes	Long-term strategy with appropriate flexibility and control in execution

Figure A.1 Maturity levels for Toyota Way principles.

EXECUTIVE SUMMARY OF THE 14 TOYOTA WAY PRINCIPLES

Part I Philosophy—Long-Term Systems Thinking

Principle 1. Base your management decisions on long-term systems thinking, even at the expense of short-term financial goals.

- Have a philosophical sense of purpose that supersedes any short-term decision-making. Work, grow, and align the whole organization toward a common purpose that is bigger than making money. Understand your place in the history of the company and work to bring the company to the next level. Your philosophical mission is the foundation for all the other principles.
- Generate value for the customer, society, and the economy—it is your starting point. Evaluate every function in the company in terms of its ability to achieve this.

- Think of your organization as a living sociotechnical system rather than simple and direct cause-and-effect relationships. Investing in developing people allows them to locally control complex system dynamics.
- Be responsible. Strive to decide your own fate. Act with self-reliance and trust in your own abilities. Accept responsibility for your conduct and impact on society, the environment, and the communities where you do business.

Part II: Processes—Struggle to Flow Value to Each Customer

Principle 2. Connect people and processes through continuous process flow to bring problems to the surface.

- Design work processes to achieve high-value-added, continuous flow at the pace of customer demand. Strive to cut back to zero the amount of time that any work project is sitting idle or waiting for someone to work on it.
- Strive for one-piece flow to move material and information fast as well as to link processes and people together so that problems surface right away. Benefits include productivity gains, better quality, shorter lead time, enhanced responsiveness to customers, higher morale, and better safety.
- Make flow evident throughout your organizational culture. It is the key to progress toward a true continuous improvement process and to developing people.

Principle 3. Use "pull" systems to avoid overproduction.

- Provide your downline internal and external customers with what they want, when they want it, and in the amount they want.
- When one-piece flow with zero inventory is not practical, use small inventory or information buffers and initiate replenishment based on consumption. Over time work to reduce or eliminate these buffers.
- Minimize your work in process and warehousing of inventory by stocking small amounts of each product and frequently restocking based on what the customer actually takes away.
- Be responsive to the day-by-day shifts in customer demand rather than relying on computer schedules and systems to track wasteful inventory.

Principle 4. Level out the workload, like the tortoise, not the hare (heijunka).

- Eliminating waste is just one-third of the equation for making lean successful. Eliminating overburden to people and equipment and eliminating unevenness in the production schedule are just as important as eliminating waste—yet generally not understood at companies striving for lean flow.
- Work to level out the workload of all manufacturing and service processes as an alternative to the stop-start approach of working on projects in batches that is typical at most companies.

Principle 5. Work to establish standardized processes as the foundation for continuous improvement.

- Strive for stable, repeatable methods to maintain a steady cadence in your processes based on customer takt. It is the foundation for flow and pull.
- Capture the accumulated learning about a process up to a point in time by standardizing today's best practices.
- Allow creative and individual expression to improve upon the standardized work; then incorporate it into the new standardized work so that when a person moves on, you can hand off the learning to the next person.

Principle 6. Build a culture of stopping to identify out-of-standard conditions and build in quality.

- Quality for the customer drives your value proposition.
- Use appropriate quality assurance methods.
- Build into your equipment the capability of detecting problems and stopping itself and allow people to activate an andon to call for assistance.
- Build into your organization rapid support systems to respond to calls for help and make appropriate decisions to contain the problem and later solve the problem.
- Build into your culture brutal honesty about weaknesses in the system and use deviations from standard as data to drive improvements.

Principle 7. Use visual control to support people in decision-making and problem solving.

- Use simple visual indicators to help people determine immediately whether they are in a standard condition or deviating from it.

- When using a computer screen design simple computer displays that instantly clarify the actual and desired conditions.
- When possible, design simple visual systems built into the work process, to support flow and pull.

Principle 8. Adopt and adapt technology that supports your people and processes.

- Use technology to support people and processes. Often it is best to work out a process manually before adding technology to support the process.
- Pull technology to help address real problems rather than pushing technology because it is the latest fad.
- Conduct tests before adopting new technology in business processes, manufacturing systems, or products.
- Develop people to understand technology deeply in order to continually improve even automated processes.
- Use IoT technologies to support people in problem solving and improvement.

Part III: People—Respect, Challenge, and Grow Your People and Partners Toward a Vision of Excellence

Principle 9. Grow leaders who thoroughly understand the work, live the philosophy, and teach it to others.

- Grow leaders from within when possible, rather than buying them from outside the organization, to build and sustain the culture.
- Do not view the leader's job as simply accomplishing tasks and having good people skills. Leaders must be role models of the company's philosophy and way of doing business.
- A good leader must understand the daily work in sufficient detail so he or she can be the best teacher of your company's philosophy.
- One of the most important jobs of a leader is to develop other leaders through coaching.

Principle 10. Develop exceptional people and teams who follow your company's philosophy.

- Develop exceptional individuals and teams to work within the corporate philosophy to achieve exceptional results.
- Use cross-functional teams to improve quality and productivity and enhance flow by solving difficult technical problems. Empowerment occurs when people use the company's tools to improve the company.

- Localize control of daily operations within work groups with leaders who self-manage internal disturbances and develop their people.
- Build an environment of mutual trust with job security where possible as the foundation.

Principle 11. Respect your value chain partners by challenging them and helping them improve.

- Have respect for your value stream partners, from suppliers to dealers to services, and treat them as extensions of your business.
- Challenge your outside business partners to grow and develop. It shows that you value them. Set challenging targets and assist your partners in achieving them.

Part IV: Problem Solving—Think and Act Scientifically to Improve Toward a Desired Future

Principle 12. Observe deeply and learn iteratively (PDCA) to meet each challenge.

- Solve problems and improve processes by going to the source and personally observing and verifying data rather than theorizing on the basis of what other people or the computer screen tells you.
- Become a learning organization by developing in people the mindset to think scientifically about all problems and challenging goals.
- Learn to appropriately switch between "slow thinking" and "fast thinking."
- Develop scientific thinking, with deliberate practice based on kata and usually with a coach.

Principle 13. Focus the improvement energy of your people through aligned goals at all levels.

- Hoshin kanri (policy deployment) is Toyota's approach to jointly aligning goals and plans at all levels to lay out the challenges and targets for the year.
- Hoshin kanri uses a planning period to lay out challenges and milestones, with execution step-by-step through experimentation and learning.
- The process of working toward breakthrough objectives to achieve new standards (PDCA) is supported by daily management to identify and eliminate deviations from standard (SDCA).
- The simple A3, a sheet of paper 11 inches x 17 inches in size, is a tool for summarizing thinking about plans and actions and results so leaders can coach and develop people.

- Use hansei (reflection) at key milestones to openly identify weaknesses and prioritize areas for improvement.

Principle 14. Learn your way to the future through bold strategy, some large leaps, and many small steps.

- Organizations need a strategy (plan) to provide a distinctive product or service, coupled with effective execution.
- A strategy to deal with an uncertain future (external) should fit with the development of capabilities (internal).
- The competing values model can help conceptually identify where a firm needs to be externally and internally and how the strategy relates to execution.
- Each organization is in a unique position and needs its own strategy; copying benchmarked companies can stunt creative thinking and set you back competitively.

Glossary

A3 report: Toyota uses a tool called the A3 (named after the international paper size on which it fits) to convey information in a single page using bullet points, charts, and graphs. Toyota utilizes the tool to foster scientific thinking, to mentor, and to align individuals with the goals of the organization.

Andon: Andon is a Japanese term meaning "light" or "lamp." In lean manufacturing, an andon refers to a tool that is used to alert and inform leaders of problems within their production process in order to immediately address the issue and prevent its recurrence. At Toyota, the andon is usually a cord that production team members are encouraged to pull to alert team leaders if they spot something that threatens safety, quality, or productivity. Equipment has automatic sensing and signaling built in.

CASE: Sometimes referred to as C.A.S.E., and meaning connectivity, autonomous, shared, and electrified. CASE refers to the next generation of vehicles that will be able to connect to outside systems; will be able to drive by themselves or with minimal human direction; will be used by multiple people rather than a single owner; and will use electrified power.

Continuous flow: The ideal state of flowing value at the rate of customer demand through the supply chain, through various people and processes, and to the customer with minimal information or material buffers.

5S: In Japanese, the five Ss are seiri, seiton, seiso, seiketsu, and shitsuke. Translated into English, they are, respectively:

1. **Sort:** Sort through items and keep only what is needed while relocating or disposing of what is not.
2. **Straighten (orderliness):** "A place for everything and everything in its place."
3. **Shine (cleanliness):** The cleaning process often acts as a form of inspection that exposes abnormal and prefailure conditions that could hurt quality or cause machine failure.
4. **Standardize (create rules):** Develop systems and procedures to maintain and monitor the first three Ss.
5. **Sustain (self-discipline):** Maintaining a stabilized workplace is an ongoing process of continuous improvement as conditions change.

Gemba (genba): Gemba is one of the key principles of lean manufacturing and the Toyota Production System. Gemba is roughly translated from the Japanese as "the real place." In this sense, "real" refers to going to where the action is happening to study and understand the condition.

Genchi genbutsu: The actual place and actual thing. It's the Toyota principle of teaching by going directly to the source to find the facts of a situation, to make correct decisions, to build consensus, and to achieve goals.

Hansei: Refers to the process of reflection to recognize one's mistakes, feel sincerely concerned about them, and take appropriate steps to avoid their reoccurrence.

Heijunka: A Japanese word that roughly translates to "leveling." Heijunka levels demand by type and quantity over a fixed period of time to create a smooth flow of work, reducing unevenness and overburden. It is the foundation for flow, pull, and standardized work.

Hoshin kanri: The management system that helps an organization to remain competitive year after year by keeping the entire organization aligned and focused on achieving well-defined and shared goals. It starts with the firm's strategy and then several-year goals, and then cascades down vertically and horizontally so everyone has aligned objectives for each year. Individual improvement efforts should be aimed, not only at making the person more productive and effective, but at achieving the overall goals for the organization. The planning process and execution both provide opportunities for leaders to coach at each level and develop people.

Hourensou: A Japanese word made up of three parts: "hou" (hou koku—to report), "ren" (renroku—to give updates periodically), and "sou" (sou dan—to consult or advise). Toyota stresses the importance of sharing information at all levels of the organization as well as the importance of managers staying informed about the activities of their subordinates. As a result, Toyota managers strive to find efficient ways to get information fed to them and to give feedback and advice to help train and develop people. While there is no single methodology for accomplishing this, many Toyota executives ask their subordinates to give daily reports.

IoT (internet of things): The concept of connecting any device to the internet and to other connected devices. This includes everything from cell phones, coffeemakers, washing machines, headphones, lamps, and wearable devices, to manufacturing equipment and vehicles. Advanced systems use cameras and sensors to collect data and artificial intelligence to analyze the data and provide direction, for example, for maintenance of equipment.

Jidoka: A term that refers to a machine that has the capacity to stop itself whenever a problem is detected. By adding this intelligence to the machine, it frees up the operator to do value-added work and problem solving.

Just-in-time (JIT): A system of continuous flow that brings all materials and information in small lots to the point of use as they are needed—neither too early nor too late. This avoids waste including overproduction and creates a more efficient flow that quickly surfaces abnormalities so people can improve quality, cost, on-time delivery, and responsiveness to changes in customer demand.

Kaizen: A Japanese word meaning "change for the better" or "continuous improvement." It is both a philosophy of striving for excellence and a method of iterative improvement following PDCA. It is a passionate focus that engages the entire organization.

Kanban: A scheduling system for just-in-time production that puts the customer in control of ordering materials and information directly as needed. The kanban itself is a binary signal of some type—manual, sound, lights, or electronics—that says "I am ready for more of this."

Kata: Kata has two meanings. One is the form, or way of doing things. The second is the pattern of movements to be practiced in developing a fundamental skill. The improvement kata (IK) model (developed by Mike Rother) consists of four steps that reflect thinking scientifically about the direction, the current situation, short-term targets, and experiments. Practice routines have been developed for the coaching kata (CK) centered on a series of questions to help the coach keep the learner on track following the kata until thinking scientifically comes naturally.

Keiretsu: After World War II, the traditional structure of Japanese companies was upended. Most major companies reorganized as keiretsu, which translates to "lineage" or "grouping of enterprises," and structured themselves in integrated groups, horizontal and vertical integration. The formal keiretsu was later banned as being monopolistic, but the close-knit business dealings continued.

Key performance indicators (KPIs): A common term in business that refers to a standard set of metrics used to evaluate performance. Key performance indicators are measurements and metrics that support and facilitate achieving critical goals of an organization. Toyota visually displays KPIs on graphs and charts and sets targets, for example through hoshin kanri, to motivate improvement activities.

Lean: Authors James Womack, Daniel Jones, and Daniel Roos introduced the term "lean manufacturing" in their book *The Machine That Changed the World* to describe the Toyota Production System. The authors describe lean as a superior paradigm that combines the best of mass production and craft production with the goal of improving productivity, reducing lead times, cutting operating costs, improving product quality, and providing safety and high morale for members.

Muda: Muda refers to waste, which is Toyota's term for anything that takes time but does not add value for your customer. Seven types of common muda were identified in manufacturing: overproduction, waiting, unnecessary transport, overprocessing, excess inventory, unnecessary movement, and defects. This list has been modified by others for service and information industries.

Mura: Unevenness that results from an irregular production schedule or fluctuating production volumes due to internal problems, like downtime, missing parts, or defects. Unevenness in production levels makes it necessary to have on hand the equipment, materials, and people for the highest level of production—even if the average requirements are far less. And unevenness leads to too little work sometimes and overburden at other times.

Muri: Overburdening people or equipment. Muri is pushing a machine or person beyond natural limits. Overburdening people results in safety and quality problems. Overburdening equipment causes breakdowns and defects. In other words, muri can cause muda. And even worse, overburdening people can cause health and safety problems.

Nemawashi: An informal process of laying the foundation for a proposed change or project by talking to the people concerned and gathering support and feedback. The goal is to establish consensus and broad support for change by involving everyone impacted by the change before formally announcing the new initiative.

PDCA: The acronym for plan-do-check-act, or sometimes, plan-do-check-adjust. PDCA is a cornerstone of scientific thinking and is at the center of the process of continuous improvement.

Pull system: A pull system is designed to avoid overproduction. Under a pull system, after materials are used or purchased, a signal is sent to the preceding process step authorizing replacement or production of what is needed next. A common example of a pull system is a supermarket. When products are purchased in a grocery store, a vacant spot is created on the shelf. At a regular interval, a stockperson will check for quantities of goods removed and will replenish them. In manufacturing, the idea is the same: maintain small quantities of items that are needed and replenish only after reaching a trigger point.

Scientific thinking: Scientific thinking acknowledges our comprehension is incomplete so works to test ideas and learn from the tests. Toyota takes a fact-based, iterative learning approach to overcoming difficult challenges. Scientific thinking is at the center of the Toyota Way 4Ps: philosophy, process, people, and problem solving.

Sensei: Honored teachers who have achieved mastery in a certain area. A lean sensei has repeatedly demonstrated mastery at the gemba. Whether they are called a coach, teacher, mentor, or sensei, experts in lean have been instrumental in teaching the Toyota Production System within Toyota, particularly as it expanded among its suppliers and into other countries.

Standardized work: Standardized work allows for a repeatable process at the rate of customer demand and is integral to a smooth flow of work. By documenting the current best known way of performing the work, standardized work forms the baseline for kaizen, or continuous improvement. As the standard is improved, the new standard becomes the baseline for further improvements, and so on.

Toyota Business Practices (TBP): When Fujio Cho led the introduction of the Toyota Way in 2001, he realized that wasn't enough to help employees to develop the mindset for continuous improvement and to learn how to respect and develop people. Within a few years, he introduced Toyota Business Practices—which, on the surface, was an eight-step problem-solving process. Cho did not set out to create a rigid problem-solving method that always has to be followed, but rather to use it as the framework for developing Toyota Way thinking through practice on real-world problems. The eight steps are:

1. Clarify the problem.
2. Break down the problem.
3. Set a target.
4. Analyze the root cause.
5. Develop countermeasures.
6. See countermeasures through.
7. Evaluate both results and process.
8. Standardize successful processes.

Toyota Production System (TPS): The Toyota Production System is Toyota's unique approach to manufacturing and the basis for much of the lean production movement that has dominated manufacturing and service trends for the last 30 years or more. Led by Taiichi Ohno, TPS was constructed in a time of low demand and a high need for variety in Japan, which necessitated a manufacturing approach that allowed for quick changeovers, low inventories, and flexibility.

Based on the philosophies of jidoka and just-in-time, TPS can efficiently and quickly produce products of sound quality, one at a time, that fully satisfy customer requirements.

Value stream mapping: A method to understand the material and information flow in a sequence of work processes. The current-state map depicts how value flows to the customers and the various wastes that are obstacles to this flow. The future-state map is an aspirational vision of how material and information need to flow to achieve business objectives.

Visual management: An approach for quickly showing visually the current status of a process, procedure, or project and how that relates to the standard. Gaps are the focus of improvement.

Toyota has made an art form out of visual management. The Toyota Way recognizes that visual management complements humans because we are visually, tactilely, and audibly oriented.

Yokoten: A Japanese term that means "across everywhere" or "spread horizontally." In the parlance of lean manufacturing, yokoten refers to the transfer of lean manufacturing knowledge and practices from one operation to another or laterally across the organization. Importantly, yokoten is not about replicating a process exactly; rather, it is meant to encourage managers to become aware of good practices, observe them, reflect upon them, and creatively utilize that knowledge to improve the functions they manage.

For Further Reading

TOYOTA WAY SERIES AND OTHER LIKER BOOKS

Eduardo Lander, Jeffrey Liker, and Tom Root, *Lean in a High-Variety Business: A Graphic Novel About Lean and People at Zingerman's Mail Order* (New York: Productivity Press, 2020).

Jeffrey Liker (ed.), *Becoming Lean: Inside Stories of U.S. Manufacturers* (New York: Productivity Press, 1997).

Jeffrey Liker and Gary Convis, *The Toyota Way to Lean Leadership: Achieving and Sustaining Excellence Through Leadership Development* (New York: McGraw-Hill, 2011).

Jeffrey Liker and James Franz, *The Toyota Way to Continuous Improvement: Linking Strategy and Operational Excellence to Achieve Superior Performance* (New York: McGraw-Hill, 2011).

Jeffrey Liker and Michael Hoseus, *Toyota Culture: The Heart and Soul of the Toyota Way* (New York: McGraw-Hill, 2008).

Jeffrey Liker and David Meier, *The Toyota Way Fieldbook* (New York: McGraw-Hill, 2006).

Jeffrey Liker and David Meier, *Toyota Talent: Developing People the Toyota Way* (New York: McGraw-Hill, 2007).

Jeffrey Liker with Timothy Ogden, *Toyota Under Fire: Lessons for Turning Crisis into Opportunity* (New York: McGraw-Hill, 2011).

Jeffrey Liker and Karyn Ross, *The Toyota Way to Service Excellence: Lean Transformation in Service Organizations* (New York: McGraw-Hill, 2016).

J. K. Franz and Jeffrey Liker, *Trenches: A Lean Transformation Novel* (CreateSpace Independent Publishing Platform, 2016).

James Morgan and Jeffrey Liker, *The Toyota Product Development System: Integrating People, Process, and Technology* (New York: Productivity Press, 2006).

James Morgan and Jeffrey Liker, *Designing the Future: How Ford, Toyota, and Other World-Class Organizations Use Lean Product Development to Drive Innovation and Transform Their Business* (New York: McGraw-Hill, 2018).

TOYOTA KATA BOOKS

Mike Rother, *Toyota Kata: Managing People for Improvement, Adaptiveness, and Superior Results* (New York: McGraw-Hill, 2009).

Mike Rother, *Toyota Kata Culture: Building Organizational Capability and Mindset Through Kata Coaching* (New York: McGraw-Hill, 2017).

Mike Rother, *The Toyota Kata Practice Guide* (New York: McGraw-Hill, 2017).

SELECTED LEAN ENTERPRISE INSTITUTE BOOKS

Freddy Ballé and Michael Ballé, *The Gold Mine: A Novel of Lean Turnaround* (Boston: Lean Enterprise Institute, 2005).

Pascal Dennis, *Getting the Right Things Done: A Leader's Guide to Planning and Execution* (Boston: Lean Enterprise Institute, 2006).

Karen Gaudet, *Steady Work* (Boston: Lean Enterprise Institute, 2020).

Mike Rother and John Shook, *Learning to See: Value-Stream Mapping to Create Value and Eliminate Muda* (Boston: Lean Enterprise Institute, 2000).

John Shook, *Managing to Learn: Using the A3 Management Process to Solve Problems, Gain Agreement, Mentor, and Lead* (Boston: Lean Enterprise Institute, 2008).

Art Smalley, *Four Types of Problems: From Reactive Trouble Shooting to Creative Innovation* (Boston: Lean Enterprise Institute, 2018).

OTHER BOOKS

Jim Collins, *Good to Great: Why Some Companies Make the Leap . . . and Others Don't* (New York: HarperBusiness, 2001).

Charles Duhig, *The Power of Habit: Why We Do What We Do in Life and Business* (New York: Random House, 2012).

Carol Dweck, *Mindset: The New Psychology of Success* (New York: Ballantine Books, 2007).

Takahiro Fujimoto, *The Evolution of a Manufacturing System at Toyota* (New York: Oxford University Press, 1999).

John Medina, *Brain Rules: 12 Principles for Surviving and Thriving at Work, Home, and School* (Seattle, WA: Pear Press, 2014).

Yashuhiro Monden, *Toyota Production System: An Integrated Approach*, 4th ed. (Boca Raton, FL: CRC Press, 2012).

Taiichi Ohno, *Workplace Management* (New York: McGraw-Hill, 2012).

Taiichi Ohno, *Toyota Production System: Beyond Large-Scale Production* (New York: Productivity Press, 2019).

Richard Sheridan, *Joy, Inc.: How We Built a Workplace People Love* (New York: Portfolio, 2015).

Shigeo Shingo and Andrew P. Dillon, *A Study of the Toyota Production System: From an Industrial Engineering Viewpoint* (Boca Raton, FL: CRC Press, 2019).

Durward Sobek II and Art Smalley, *Understanding A3 Thinking: A Critical Component of Toyota's PDCA Management System* (Boca Raton, FL: CRC Press, 2008).

Steven Spear, *The High-Velocity Edge: How Market Leaders Leverage Operational Excellence to Beat the Competition* (New York: McGraw-Hill, 2010).

James Womack and Dan Jones, *Lean Thinking: Banish Waste and Create Wealth in Your Corporation* (New York: Free Press, 2003).

James Womack, Dan Jones, and Dan Roos, *The Machine That Changed the World* (New York: Free Press, 2007).

Ashlee Vance, *Elon Musk: Tesla, SpaceX, and the Quest for a Fantastic Future* (New York: Ecco, 2015).

Index